Genetic Programming
Theory and Practice III

T0134620

GENETIC PROGRAMMING SERIES

Series Editor

John Koza
Stanford University

The cover art was created by Leslie Sobel in Photoshop from an original photomicrograph of plant cells and genetic programming code. More of Sobel's artwork can be seen at www.lesliesobel.com.

Genetic Programming
Theory and Practice III

Edited by

Tina Yu
Chevron Information Technology Company

Rick Riolo
Center for the Study of Complex Systems
University of Michigan

Bill Worzel
Genetics Squared, Inc.

 Springer

Tina Yu
Chevron Information Technology Company

Rick Riolo
Center for the Study of Complex Systems
University of Michigan

Bill Worzel
Genetics Squared, Inc.

e-ISBN: 0-387-28111-8
ISBN: 978-1-4419-3921-0   e-ISBN: 978-0-387-28111-7

Printed on acid-free paper.

© 2006 by Springer Science+Business Media, Inc.
Softcover reprint of the hardcover 1st edition 2006
All rights reserved. This work may not be translated or copied in whole or in part
without the written permission of the publisher (Springer Science + Business
Media, Inc., 233 Spring Street, New York, NY 10013, USA), except for brief
excerpts in connection with reviews or scholarly analysis. Use in connection with
any form of information storage and retrieval, electronic adaptation, computer
software, or by similar or dissimilar methodology now known or hereafter
developed is forbidden.
The use in this publication of trade names, trademarks, service marks and similar
terms, even if they are not identified as such, is not to be taken as an expression
of opinion as to whether or not they are subject to proprietary rights.

springeronline.com

Contents

Contributing Authors

Arpit Arvindkumar Almal is an evolutionary engineer at Genetics Squared, Inc., a computational discovery company (aalmal@umich.edu).

Sameer H. Al-Sakran is a researcher at Genetic Programming, Inc. in Mountain View, CA (al-sakran@genetic-programming.com).

R. Muhammad Atif Azad is a Post Doctoral Researcher at the Biocomputing and Developmental Systems Group in the Department of Computer Science and Information Systems at University of Limerick, Ireland (atif.azad@ul.ie).

Wolfgang Banzhaf is Professor and Head of the Department of Computer Science at Memorial University of Newfoundland, St. John's, Canada (banzhaf@cs.mun.ca).

Ian Burleigh is a Ph.D student at the University of Calgary in the Department of Computer Science (burleigh@cpsc.ucalgary.ca).

Flor A. Castillo is a Research Specialist in the Modeling Group within the Engineering and Process Sciences R&D Organization of the Dow Chemical Company (facastillo@dow.com).

Ellery Fussell Crane is an undergraduate at the University of Minnesota, Morris (cran0117@morris.umn.edu).

Jason M. Daida is an Associate Research Scientist in the Space Physics Research Laboratory, Department of Atmospheric, Oceanic and Space Sciences, and is affiliated with the Center for the Study of Complex Systems at the University of Michigan, Ann Arbor (daida@umich.edu).

Daryl Essam is a lecturer of Computer Science at the Australian Defense Force Academy, a school of the Universiy of New South Wales (daryl@cs.adfa.edu.au).

Georges Gielen is Full Professor in the ESAT-MICAS microelectronics group at Katholieke Universiteit Leuven, Belgium (Georges.Gielen@esat.kuleuven.be).

Erik D. Goodman is Professor of Electrical and Computer Engineering and of Mechanical Engineering at Michigan State University (goodman@egr.msu.edu).

Tuan Hao Hoang is a lecturer in the School of Information Technology at Le Quy Don University (Vietnamese Military Technical Academy), 100 Hoang Quoc Viet, Hanoi, Vietnam.

Xuan Hoai Nguyen is a lecturer in the School of Information Technology at Le Quy Don University (Vietnamese Technical Academy), 100 Hoang Quoc Viet, Hanoi, Vietnam.

Gregory S. Hornby is a computer scientist with QSS Group Inc. working in the Evolvable Systems group in the Intelligent Systems Division at NASA Ames Research Center (hornby@email.arc.nasa.gov).

Jianjun Hu is a Postdoctoral Fellow of the Department of Computer Science at Purdue University (hujianju@purdue.edu).

Christian Jacob is Associate Professor of Computer Science and of Biochemistry & Molecular Biology at the University of Calgary (cjacob@ucalgary.ca).

Lee W. Jones is a researcher at Genetic Programming, Inc. in Mountain View, CA (lee@genetic-programming.com).

Elsa M. Jordaan is a Research Specialist in the Modelling Group within the Engineering and Process Sciences R&D Organization of the Dow Chemical Company (emjordaan@dow.com).

Jon Klein is a Senior Research Fellow in the School of Cognitive Science at Hampshire College in Amherst, Massachusetts, and a doctoral candidate in

Physical Resource Theory at Chalmers University of Technology and Göteborg University in Göteborg, Sweden.

Arthur K. Kordon is a Research and Development Leader in the Modelling Group within the Engineering and Process Sciences R&D Organization of the Dow Chemical Company (akordon@dow.com).

Mark E. Kotanchek is a Research and Development Leader in the Modelling Group within the Engineering and Process Sciences R&D Organization of the Dow Chemical Company (mkotanchek@dow.com).

John R. Koza is Consulting Professor at Stanford University in the Biomedical Informatics Program in the Department of Medicine and in the Department of Electrical Engineering (koza@stanford.edu).

W. B. Langdon is a Senior Research Fellow of Computer Science in Essex University, England.His research includes the fundamentals of genetic programming, whilst his applications include GP in Bioinformatics and drug discovery (http://www.cs.essex.ac.uk/staff/W.Langdon/).

Andre Leier is a Postdoctoral Researcher in the Department of Computer Science at Memorial University of Newfoundland, St. John's, Canada (leier@cs.mun.ca).

Derek Linden is the Chief Technical Officer of Linden Innovation Research LLC, a company which specializes in the automated design and optimization of antennas and electromagnetic devices (dlinden@lindenir.com).

Jason Lohn leads the Evolvable Systems group in the Exploration Systems Division at NASA Ames Research Center (jlohn@email.arc.nasa.gov).

Duncan MacLean is co-founder of Genetics Squared, Inc., a computational discovery company working in the pharmaceutical industry (dmaclean@acm.org).

Trent McConaghy is a serial entrepreneur, and a Ph.D student in the ESAT-MICAS microelectronics group at Katholieke Universiteit Leuven, Belgium. (Trent.McConaghy@esat.kuleuven.be).

Bob McKay is a Senior Visiting Research Fellow in the School of Information Technology at the University of New South Wales (Australian Defence Force Academy campus).

Nicholas Freitag McPhee is Associate Professor at the University of Minnesota, Morris in the Division of Science and Mathematics (mcphee@morris.umn.edu).

H. Van Dyke Parunak is Chief Scientist and Scientific Fellow at the Altarum Institute, and leads research in applications of complex adaptive systems in the Emerging Markets Group of Altarum's Enterprise Systems Division (van.parunak@altarum.org).

Riccardo Poli is Professor of Computer Science at the University of Essex (rpoli@essex.ac.uk).

Rick Riolo is Director of the Computer Lab and Associate Research Scientist in the Center for the Study of Complex Systems at the University of Michigan (rlriolo@umich.edu).

Ronald C. Rosenberg is Professor of Mechanical Engineering at Michigan State University (roserber@egr.msu.edu).

Conor Ryan is Senior Lecturer in the Department of Computer Science and Information Systems at University of Limerick, Ireland where he leads the Biocomputing and Developmental Systems Group (conor.ryan@ul.ie).

Guido F. Smits is a Research and Development Leader in the Modelling Group within the Engineering and Process Sciences R&D Organization of the Dow Chemical Company (gfsmits@dow.com).

Lee Spector is Dean of the School of Cognitive Science and Professor of Computer Science at Hampshire College in Amherst, Massachusetts (lspector@hampshire.edu).

Katherine Vladislavleva is a Ph.D student at the Tilburg University and the Modelling Group within the Engineering and Process Sciences R&D Organization of the Dow Chemical Company (cvladislavleva@dow.com).

Eric A. Wollesen is a gradute of the University of Michigan. He is currently employed as a software developer by Genetics Squared, Inc., a computational discovery company working in the pharmaceutical industry (ericw@genetics2.com).

Bill Worzel is the Chief Technology Officer and co–founder of Genetics Squared, Inc., a computational discovery company working in the pharmaceutical industry (billw@genetics2.com).

Tina Yu is a computer scientist in the Mathematical Modeling Team at Chevron-Texaco Information Technology Company (Tina.Yu@chevrontexaco.com).

Preface

The work described in this book was first presented at the Third Workshop on Genetic Programming, Theory and Practice, organized by the Center for the Study of Complex Systems at the University of Michigan, Ann Arbor, 12-14 May 2005. The goal of this workshop series is to promote the exchange of research results and ideas between those who focus on Genetic Programming (GP) theory and those who focus on the application of GP to various real-world problems. In order to facilitate these interactions, the number of talks and participants was small and the time for discussion was large. Further, participants were asked to review each other's chapters *before* the workshop. Those reviewer comments, as well as discussion at the workshop, are reflected in the chapters presented in this book. Additional information about the workshop, addendums to chapters, and a site for continuing discussions by participants and by others can be found at http://cscs.umich.edu:8000/GPTP-2005/.

We thank all the workshop participants for making the workshop an exciting and productive three days. In particular we thank all the authors, without whose hard work and creative talents, neither the workshop nor the book would be possible. We also thank our keynote speakers Dr. H. Van Parunak of Altarum, Ann Arbor, Professor Michael Yarus, Biology-MCD, University of Colorado, and Dr. Inman Harvey, CCNR (Centre for Computational Neuroscience and Robotics) and Evolutionary and Adaptive Systems Group Informatics University of Sussex, who delivered three thought-provoking speeches that inspired a great deal of discussion among the participants.

The workshop received support from these sources:

- The Center for the Study of Complex Systems (CSCS);

- Third Millennium Venture Capital Limited;

- State Street Global Advisors, Boston, MA;

- Biocomputing and Developmental Systems Group, Computer Science and Information Systems, University of Limerick;

- Christopher T. May, RedQueen Capital Management;

- Dow Chemical, Core R&D/Physical Sciences;

- Michael Korn; and

- Genetics Squared, Inc., Ann Arbor, Michigan.

and from Professor Scott A. Moore of the University of Michigan School of Business, for providing the Assembly Hall Board Room for the workshop. We thank all of our sponsors for their kind and generous support for the workshop and GP research in general.

A number of people made key contributions to running the workshop and assisting the attendees while they were in Ann Arbor. Foremost among them was Howard Oishi, assisted by Mike Charters. After the workshop, many people provided invaluable assistance in producing this book. Special thanks go to Sarah Cherng, who stepped in and learned a lot of LaTeXand other skills in a very short time, and who also did a wonderful job working with the authors, editors and publishers to get the book completed very quickly. In addition to thanking Bill Tozier for his extraordinary efforts reading and copy-editing chapters, we also thank Duncan MacClean and Eric Wollesen for helping with copy-editing. Melissa Fearon's editorial efforts were invaluable from the initial plans for the book through its final publication. Thanks also to Valerie Schofield and Deborah Doherty of Springer for helping with various technical publishing issues. Finally, we thank Carl Simon, Director of CSCS, for his support for this endeavor from its very inception.

TINA YU, RICK RIOLO AND BILL WORZEL

Foreword

Enabled by relentless advances in computing power and the increasing availability of distributed computing, genetic programming (GP) has become successful in solving a wide array of previously intractable industrial problems. However, as a relatively new kid on the block, this growing community of early-GP-adopter faces many obstacles, such as entrenched institutional resistance and the competition of other existing technologies (decision forests, kernel learning methods, and support vector machines). Ultimately, the technique of GP will find a home in industry if and only if it is competitive.

The Workshop of Genetic Programming Theory and Practice organized by the Center for the Study of Complex Systems and held at the University of Michigan, Ann Arbor, in May 2005, is a unique venue where applied and theoretical researchers focus on how theory and practice should interact and what they can learn from each other. Such exchange is essential in advancing GP to overcome its adversaries.

I was very excited to receive an invitation to this workshop, since the application of GP to industrial scale symbolic regression and classification problems is a timely topic in our enterprise. After attending the workshop, I was ecstatic. Many of the most respected and influential GP researchers as well as an impressive array of applied researchers from industrial sectors were in attendance. They presented focused and topical papers and participated in the discussion. With their knowledge and experiences, the discussion was deep and enormously productive. We spent our days listening to workshop presentations, asking questions, and our evenings writing programs. We left the workshop with many practical issues resolved.

I hope to attend this event next year. If we are to advance the application of GP in industry, it is critical to have a venue where applied and theoretical researchers can exchange ideas, critically review past efforts, and inspire future research directions.

Michael Korns
President and Chief Technologist,
Korns Associates Nevada, USA

Chapter 1

GENETIC PROGRAMMING: THEORY AND PRACTICE

An Introduction to Volume III

Tina Yu,[1] Rick Riolo[2] and Bill Worzel[3]

[1]*Chevron Information Technology Company,* [2]*Center for the Study of Complex Systems, University of Michigan,* [3]*Genetics Squared, Inc.*

In theory, there is no difference between theory and practice. But, in practice, there is.
—Jan L.a. Van De Snepscheut

Keywords: genetic programming, theory, practice, continuous recurrent neural networks, evolving robots, swarm agents

Close Encounter, the Third Time

To leverage theoretical and practical works in the field of genetic programming (GP), the Genetic Programming Theory and Practice (GPTP) Workshop series was conceived and launched in 2003. For the past two years, theoreticians and practitioners have come to Ann Arbor to present their works and to listen to others' (Riolo and Worzel, 2003) (O'Reilly et al., 2004). Gathered in a friendly environment, they debated with enthusiasm, pondered in silence, and laughed in between. All of these interactions have paved the way to future integration of theory and practice.

In this year's workshop, we are very pleased to see some signs of convergence:

- Papers developing techniques tested on small-scale problems include discussion of how to apply those techniques to real-world problems, while papers tackling real-world problems have employed techniques developed from theoretical work to gain insights.

- Multiple papers addressed GP open challenges, such as industry funding, new opportunities and previously overlooked issues. During the open discussion on the last day of the workshop, considerable enthusiasm was generated regarding these topics.

All those developments indicate that both theoreticians and practitioners acknowledge that their approaches complement each other. Together, they advance GP technology.

1.   Three Challenging Keynote Talks

As in the first two GPTP workshops, each day commences with a keynote talk from a distinguished researcher, one each with a strong background in the fields of evolutionary computation, biology and application of advanced technologies in real-world settings, respectively. For GPTP-2005 we were again fortunuate to have three enlightening, inspiring, challenging and sometimes controversial talks.

On the first day of the workshop, Van Parunak, Chief Scientist of Altarum Institute, delivered a keynote on evolving "Swarms" of agents in real-time. As a practitioner of population-based search techniques, one of Van's challenges is mapping a real-world problem into an appropriate representation. Sometimes, each individual in the population is the entire solution while other times, an individual is one component (an agent) of a solution. In the later case, the collection of individuals (the "Swarm") which yields the desired global behavior is the solution. The art and craft of designing problem-specific representations mentioned by Van was a challenge echoed by other presenters throughout the workshop.

One type of real-world problem that Van works on is to evolve swarms in real-time to meet a constantly changing environment. In Chapter 2, he discusses two such systems they have developed. The first one plans flight paths for uninhabited robotic vehicles (URVs). The path should lead URVs to the target while avoiding threats on the way. To detect moving threats, an URV generates many "ghost" agents which explore (in a virtual model of the world) possible paths by depositing digital pheromones. Each step in the path then is chosen based on information represented by the pheromone deposits, using a parameterized equation associated with the ghost agent. The Altarum group has explored several approaches to optimizing the parameters in real-time to guide URVs, including evolutionary algorithms and human designers. The evolved parameters produce paths that are superior to those produced by human designed parameters by an order of magnitude.

Using the ghost agent concept, they developed a second system to predict future behavior of soldiers in urban combat. A soldier's behaviors are influenced by his/her own personality, the behaviors of other soldiers and their surrounding environment. To extrapolate a soldier's possible future behavior, a stream of ghost agents are continuously generated. These ghost agents begin their lives in the past using a faster clock than the clock used by the soldier it represents. When the time reaches the present, the ghost agents whose behaviors match well with the past behaviors of the soldier it represents are assigned a high fitness. These ghost agents are allowed to bred offspring and to run past the present into the future, where their behaviors are observed to derive predictions.

Modeling complex systems in real-time, with models that run and adapt faster than real-time in order to allow for prediction, is a non-trivial task. Van showed us one way to make it work. However, he acknowledged that their efforts were aimed at solving the problems at hand, and hence so far they have not focused on generating theoretical insights. However, he asserts that although the systems they have developed doesn't give "perfect" predictions, it outperforms the current systems in use. From the practical point of view, it is a success. This evaluation standard is also used in other lines of business, such as finance, chemical and oil companies, as confirmed by the work and comments of other workshop participants.

The second day started with a keynote entitled "Evolution From Random Sequences" by Mike Yarus, Professor of Molecular Biology at University of Colorado, Boulder. This is not evolution by mutation of existing sequences with a fixed translation mechanism generating "solutions," he emphasized. Instead, it is a completely different process where both the genetic code (information) and the translation system (a "machine") are randomly generated, and evolution proceeds as selection acts upon this coupled pair.

Their studies are based on the laboratory examination of the RNA-binding sites of eight biological amino acids, which show significant evidence that cognate codons and/or anticodons are unexpectedly frequent at these binding sites. Consequently, they proposed the *Escaped triplet theory*: The coding triplets began as parts of amino acid binding sites, then escaped to become codons and anticodons. In other words, at least part of the genetic code is stereo-chemical in origin-from chemical interactions between amino acids and RNA-like polymers. The code is not just a *frozen accident* as suggested by Watson and Crick. Instead, the code's mapping is a result of selection based on affinities between an amino acids and parts of random RNA sequences.

Not only the genetic code is selected from random sequences, Yargus argued— so is the hardware for translation. He used the peptide transferase to support his argument. Their laboratory study shows that proteins are assembled by reaction of the aa-RNAs within a cradle of RNA whose octamer can be selected from random sequence. Therefore, both coding triples and the peptidyl transferase emerge when random sequences are placed under selection. Put another way, they were originally made by selection from populations of RNAs of arbitrary sequence.

The issues involved with the *invention of a genetic code* are generally not considered by the GP community, who usually assume the existence of a "code" and machinery to map from a "genome" to active agents (*e.g.*, programs). However, as a field constantly looking to biological mechanisms and processes for inspiration, GP might due well to consider these issues in the future, perhaps leading to more "open-ended" evolutionary systems.

Following a suggestion to be challenging and controversial, Inman Harvey delivered a keynote on "Evolutionary Robotics for Both Engineering and Science" with comments on some aspects of GP and the interaction of human and evolution process. He started by describing their approach to evolve dynamic systems which interact with the environment in real-time. Formally, a standard dynamic system is a set of (continuous) variables with equations that determine how each variable changes over time as a function of all current values. These equations are represented in Continuous Time Recurrent Neural Networks (CTRNN) and are evolved using a steady-state GA with tournament selection.

Inman was questioned about his decision to not use GP for the evolutionary component. He gave his reasons based on his observations of the early GP work. First, he thought GP-style evolution is *wide and short*, *i.e.* it consists of a large population evolving for just a few (*e.g.*, hundreds or fewer) generations. But biological evolution is *narrow and long*, *i.e.* the number of generations is generally far more than the size of the population. Secondly, biological evolution is always an open-ended work in progress, not just an attempt to solve a single specific problem. It seemd likely that Inman has not been in touch with the GP field for a long time and thus he did not have much familiarity with recent progress and trends. Workshop participants quickly corrected his misconceptions, claiming that those ideas have been incorporated in some of the more current GP systems. However, Inman's basic point should still be seriously considered, *i.e.*, while GP systems are run longer and are work toward more openedness than in the past, it is clear that the ratio of generations to population size is still far from that in biological systems, and that GP systems are still generally applied to solve specific problems. It then remains to be seen how important those differences are across the range of GP applications, given the different goals researchers have for GP systems,

The subject then turned to the evolutionary robotics (ER) systems Inman's group has built for scientific purposes. The first one is an artificial ant that has to find its way back to its nest or hive with minimal noisy visual cues. Biologists used the system to compare simulation behaviors with the real ant behaviors to disprove or to generalize hypothesis. For example, if the original hypothesis states that a behavior requires A and the evolved artificial ant show the behavior without A, a new hypotheses can be developed to explain this behavior. Another ER system they developed is for studying the human ability to adjust to a world turned upside-down. They incorporated some general homeostasis constraints to evolve a robot with normal eyes first. After that, they switched the eyes upside-down and ran the system again. A reasonable proportion (50%) of the evolved robots with normal eyes can adapt, after time, to visual inversion. These experiments allow generation of relatively unbiased models (*i.e.*, with minimal assumptions) to challenge existing hypotheses and to generate new ones.

For engineering purposes, Inman and his group applied their ER technique to evolve control systems for robots. Two such examples are a hexapod walker for a robot for Mars exploration that is robust to damage and a humanoid biped walker. They used an incremental approach to evolve the system. Initially, a hand-designed system for a simple task is used at population 0. Once the evolved system is able to perform the simple task reasonably well, a new task (parameters and neurons) is added and starts a new evolutionary cycle. Evolution gradually learns to perform new tasks without forgetting how to do the old task. This style of incremental learning through the interaction of human intervention and an evolutionary algorithm is a practical approach to tackle this engineering task. However, it seems to conflict with the *work in progress* evolutionary paradigm that Inman advocated previously, pointed out by a workshop participants. Inman agreed with this comment. Maybe devising an evolutionary system which can continuously learn, *i.e.* always in work-in-progress mode, without human intervention is a challenge for all who are interesting in evolutionary learning, not just those using GP.

2. Real-World Application Success Stories

Besides the successful applications of evolutionary approaches described by Van Parunak and Inman Harvey in their keynote addresses, clear-cut Genetic Programming success stories were told in four presentations. They either produced better results than the preexisting systems, made breakthroughs or opened a new frontier. These results cheered the spirits of all workshop participants.

In Chapter 3, Lee Jones, Sameer H. Al-Sakran and John Koza present their success in delivering GP human-competitive results in a new domain: optical design. In this work, the simple forms of representation, genetic operations and fitness function were elaborated to work with this non-trivial domain, where finding a solution is an art or craft rather than science. Many pathological designs were identified and the system was adjusted accordingly to avoid generating such kinds of designs. As an invention machine, GP was able to create lens designs that gives characteristics, *e.g.* spherical aberration and distortion, that are competitve with a lens design patented in 1996. Since the evolved design differs considerably from the patented design, it does not infringe the patent. Instead, it is considered as a new invention created by GP.

Chapter 4 also reports the success of a GP solution that improves over a preexisting technology. In this work, Frank Francone, Larry Deschaine, Tom Battenhouse and Jeffery Warren applied a linear GP system to discriminate unexploded Ordnance (UXO) from clutter (scrap metal that poses no danger to the public) in retired military fields. A higher quality solution allows UXO to be revealed by digging fewer holes, hence is more cost-effective. The project was conducted in two phases. The first phase used sensor data gathered from a military field where UXO and clutter locations are known. The quality of a solution is evaluated by the percentage of UXO and clutter correctly identified. They compared the GP-generated solution with solutions based on geophysics first principles and by other technologies, and showed that the GP-generated solution gives a significantly higher accuracy. In the second phase of the project, the sensor data was collected from a different field where UXO and clutter locations are unknown. In order to devise GP solutions, many more processing steps, such as anomaly identification and feature extraction for the identified targets, were conducted. Unlike the phase I study, the quality of a solution in this phase is judged by the number of holes that must be dug to uncover all UXO. They reported that their GP-generated solution improves over the preexisting technique with 62% fewer holes dug. Although the data set is noisy with only a small number of positive samples, a common dilemma in real-world applications, GP is able to overcome the difficulties and deliver good solutions.

In last year's workshop, Lohn, Hornby and Linden presented their success in evolving two human-competitive antennas for NASA's Space Technology 5 mission. While those antennas met the mission requirements at that time, new requirements were introduced as a result of an orbit change. In Chapter 5, they updated the project with two new antennas they evolved to meet the new mission requirements. Unlike the conventionally designed quadrifilar antenna which require several months to develop a new design and prototype it, their antennas were evolved (with slightly modifications of their evolutionary system) and prototyped in four weeks. These two antennas have passed the flight testing and are expected to be launched into space in 2006, a "first" for systems designed by evolutionary algorithms. This story highlights an important advantage of evolutionary design over human design: the ability to rapidly re-evolve new designs to meet changing requirements. It is an essential ingredient for successful real-world applications.

Variable selection plays an important role in industrial data modeling, particularly in chemical process domain where the number of sensor readings is normally large. To generate robust models, a small number of important variables must be identified. Unfortunately, preexisting linear variable selection methods, such as Principle Components Analysis (PCA) combined with Partial Least Squared (PLS), fail to work on non-linear problems. In Chapter 6, Guido Smits, Arthur Kordon, Katherine Vladishlavleva, Elsa Jordaan and Mark Kotanchek developed a non-linear variable selection method based on their Pareto GP system. This method assigns variable importance by evenly distributing an individual's fitness to all variables that appear in the individual. The accumulated importance of each variable in the population in the Pareto front archive is then used to rank their importance.

They have applied this method on two inferential sensors problems. The first one (emission prediction) has 8 variables and GP selected 4 of them as highly important while PCA-PLS gives a different ranking. The final deployed models, which were evolved by GP using the 4 selected variables, give very high correlation coefficient values (0.93 and 0.94). This confirms that the 4 selected variables are indeed important, which PCA-PLS fails to recognize. The second inferential sensor (propylene concentration predication) has 23 variables. Four important variables were selected by GP whereas PCA-PLS suggests 12 important variables, which included only 3 of the 4 GP selected variables. The final winning inferential model is an ensemble of 4 models, which included all 4 GP-selected variables and 1 variable recommended by an expert's model. The GP solution also was more effective than the PCA-PLS solution in this case.

In addition to providing demonstrably better performace, one prerequisite for "success" is acceptance by the people working in the problem domain. It is only when the solutions are accepted by the users in the domain that the technology will have a significant impact. Thus an important question is: Are those fields where GP has been applied inclined to accept the solutions? If not, how do we change their attitudes?

The feeling of the GPTP Workshop participants was that in general, the more successful and mature a field is, the less likely it accepts new ideas. Lens and analog circuit designs are two fields that have longer histories and are considered more mature, said Koza. In contrast, antenna design engineers and geophysicists working on UXO communities are very accepting of new concepts as there is not solid theory and they don't know systematic approaches for finding solutions themselves, according to Lohn and Francone. In terms of enticing end-users to accept GP solutions, one critical step is to invite them to participate in the project from the very beginning, said Kordon. Otherwise, people tend to not accept any work that they have no part of. In corporate environments, it also is important to show management the advantages the technology can bring to them. If the success of a technology will lead to problems for them, *e.g.* losing their jobs, they will make every effort to assure the technology fails, commented by Goodman.

3.   Techniques with Real-World Applications in Mind

Although GP theory does not progress as rapidly as practice does, techniques to enhance GP capabilities and theoretical work to analyze GP processes are continually being developed. Four such papers were presented in the workshop. These works so far have been applied to small scale problems. Nevertheless, relevance to real-world applications was discussed.

In Chapter 7, Tina Yu introduced a functional technique to evolve recursive programs. In functional programs, recursion is carried out by non-recursive application of a higher-order function. This chapter demonstrates one way to evolve this style of recursive programs by including higher-order functions in the GP function set. Two small-scale problems were studied using this approach. The first one is a challenge by Inman Harvey, STRSTR C library function, and the second one is the Fibonacci sequence. In both cases, problem-specific knowledge was used to design/select higher-order functions, and GP was able to evolve the recursive programs successfully by evaluating a small number of programs.

Programs with higher-order functions naturally give the structure of code abstraction and reuse. For these two problems studied, the structures were defined by the given higher-order functions. With an appropriate set-up, GP can be used to discover the structure, *i.e.* evolve the higher-order function. Such a GP would be particularly suitable for solving open-ended designs where no optimum is known and creativity is essential to problem solving. In this case, evolved higher-order functions might deliver interesting solutions.

Lee Spector and Jon Kleinsold present their "trivial geography" technique in Chapter 8. Trivial geography structures the GP population in a simple geographically distributed manner. The location of an individual is taken into account when selection for competition and reproduction. This concept is not new. Many existing evolutionary computation systems divide their populations into discrete or overlapping sub-populations, often called demes, as a form of geography. However, their implementation is significantly simpler; only a few lines of programming code need to be added/modified, they argued. In their implementation, a population is structured as a ring. When producing a new generation, the location into which an offspring is going to be placed in the new population decides where its parents are from; *i.e.*, only the individuals near to the location for the offspring are selected for tournament and thus are candidates to be parents. This essentially gives overlapping sub-populations where independent evolution takes place. Despite being such small change, this trivial geographic bias in parent selection significantly improves performance for the two problems they tested. Although the generality of the method has not been studied yet, they recommended broader usage of the technique. "It is easy to implement and you might be surprised what you can gain from it," said Lee.

In Chapter 9, Riccardo Poli and Bill Langdon developed a backward chaining technique to reduce GP computational efforts. This technique first reorders the typical create-select-evaluate evolutionary system cycle to construct the genealogy network for the entire evolutionary run. After that, the genetic makeup of the individuals are filled in a backward manner. This is done by tracing the genealogy of each individual in the last population back to generation 0. The "root individuals" are then initialized randomly and all their descendants are created using genetic operators subsequently. Since only individuals in the geneological network are created and evaluated, backward chaining GP is computationally more effective than the traditional GP. However, there is trade-off of memory to store the genealogy network. Mathematically, they computed the time and space complexities to show the cost and saving. Experimentally, they tested this technique on symbolic regression problems and reported that using population size 10000 with tournament size 2, backward chaining GP gives computational saving of 19.9%. Once the tournament size is increased to 3, the saving is marginal. They recommend this method to GP systems with very large populations, short runs and relatively small tournament sizes. The computational saving for large scale real-world problem using this type of GP might be significant.

Co-evolving grammar and the solutions defined by the grammar is an attractive idea since the biases induced by the grammar are not always favorable throughout the evolutionary run. Conceptually, it seems that it should be possible to learn good bias from the evolved good solutions. In Chapter 10, R. Muhammad Atif Azad and Conor Ryan test the hypothesis by using a diploid genotype: one part for the grammar rule and the other for solution mapped. This approach is very similar to the co-evolution of genetic operation rates and the solutions generated by the operation. By encoding the rate as a part of the genotype, the rate is normally reduced as evolution progresses to provide appropriate exploration and exploitation.

They added the diploid genotype to their Grammatical Evolution system and tested it on a set of small scale problems. While the results are not as good as expected—the system using static grammars finds better solutions—this talk stimulated much discussion at the workshop. Many recommendations were given to improve the system.

Chapter 11 is a contribution by Tuan Hao, Xuan Nguyen, Bob McKay and Daryl Essam. This work applies their previously developed techniques to a real-world problem, which is an important step to transfer the technology for wider applications (Bob was not able to come to present the paper in person, so there was not discussion of it at the workshop). Their work is based on Tree Adjoining Grammar (TAG) GP which they have developed and used to study two local search operators: point insertion and deletion. Local search operators are generally useful to tune final solutions. While their previous study reported that they are also effective search engines on small-scale problems, when applied to the larger scale ecological modeling problem described in Chapter 11, the results are not conclusive. On training data, GP with local search operators produces a better model than the model evolved by GP alone. However, on blind testing data, it is the other way around. This indicates that local search operators generate over-fitting solutions and reduce generality. They are continuing the study to produce more robust solutions.

4.   Visualization: A Practical Way to Understand GP Process

Unlike the work describe by Mike Yarus in Section 1, which examines biological data to study evolution, A. Almal, W. P. Worzel, E. A. Wollesen and C. D. MacLean analyze biomedical data for diagnostics and prognostics purposes. One such project is modeling medical data to predict the stage of bladder cancer. Medical data is notorious in its small sample sets and large dimensionality, which makes the modeling task very difficult. In Chapter 12, they describe a tool to visualize the content diversity (the diversity of functions and terminals) of GP populations and study its relationship to the fitness diversity of the solutions.

They used the new tool they developed to plot population contents in generation 0, 10, 20 and 38, which show how diversity decreases as evolution progress. Fitness diversity, however, does not have such a trend. The fitness variance among individuals remained high throughout the runs, although high fitness bands became dominant when the content diversity became very low, *i.e.*, the population's structures converged. This interesting relationship stimulated much discussion at the workshop. The relationship between structure, content and fitness in a population is a subject that always interests both theoreticians and practitioners.

Visualization is a powerful and practical way to study many dynamical systems, including those generated by evolutionary processes. Thus, it may not be surprising that there were three other visualization papers presented at the workshop.

The first one is by Christian Jacob and Ian Burleigh. In Chapter 13, they present an agent-based model that simulates lactose operon gene regulatory system. Although this is one of the most extensively studied biological systems, there are still many unknowns. A visual simulation can help biologists to understand the complex system better. To develop such a model, they first incorporated biological data/rules to construct the system. The simulation behaviors are then presented to biologists, whose feedbacks are used to improve the model. This interactive evolution process led to parameters which give behaviors close to the known behaviors. It appears that GP can be used to fine-tune the parameters. Furthermore, the mechanism of the gene regulatory system may serve as an inspirational platform to design GP systems suitable for complex systems modeling.

Biological systems have always been inspiration to GP. Motivated by the research of neutral networks in biological systems, Wolfgang Banzhaf and Andre Leier investigate GP search behavior in a Boolean function space with the presence of neutral networks. In Chapter 14, they enumerated the problem search space and showed that the genotype to phenotype mapping is similar to the RNA folding landscape: there are many very uncommon phenotypes and few highly common phenotypes. This suggests that the neutral evolution theory for biological systems might apply to this GP search space. They plotted the phenotype network of the search space, including neutral networks where the connected phenotypes having the same fitness. This visualization of the network provides a clear picture of phenotypes with different fitness and how they are connected.

Another work which relies heavily on visualization for analysis is by Ellery Crane and Nic McPhee. In Chapter 15, they study the effects that size and depth limits have on the dynamics of tree-based GP. Based on a simple one-than-zero problem, many GP experiments were conducted using both tree-size and depth-size limits. Visualization of the statistical results indicates that both kinds of limit have similar effects on the average tree size (number of nodes) in the population. However, depth limits effect program shapes more than size limits do. With depth limits, the program shape in the population has less diversity. They are investigating the generality of this phenomena by studying other type of problems under different selection and genetic operation conditions, and if practitioners adopt their recommendations for problem solving, we may learn even more about its generality and usefulness.

5.   Open Challenges

In addition to the deep challenges presented by the keynote addresses, several other chapters also described various kinds of open challenges that GP practitioners must overcome before GP will be easily and widely accepted in various industries and business.

For example, in Chapter 16 Arthur Kordon, Flor Castillo, Guido Smits and Mark Kotanchek of Dow Chemical discuss many challenges faced by industrial research and development groups when applying GP technology. In addition to technical issues, such as data quality and extrapolation of the solutions, non-technical issues are important to the success adoption of a new technology in corporate environment. They summarized how they address these non-technical issues: create a team to work on GP, link GP to proper corporate initiatives, secure management support, address skepticism and resistance and marketing the technology continuously. Although GP has had good track record at Dow, the technical team still has to adapt to the fast changing environment and to produce profits to survive. They described a set of "10 commandments" of industrial R&D humorously to illustrate the challenges they are facing:

- Thou shalt have no other thoughts before profit.

- Thou shalt not serve consultants.

- Thou shalt not take the research money for granted.

- Remember the budget, to keep it holy.

- Honour the cuts and the spending targets.

- Thou shalt not explore.

- Thou shalt not commit curiosity.

- Thou shalt not create.

- Thou shalt not develop anything before outsourcing it.

- Thou shalt not covet thy professors, nor their students, nor their graduate students, nor their post-docs, nor their conferences and workshops.

Open-ended problem solving has been a quintessentially human capability. Is it possible to equip GP to become the first machine capable of open-ended problem solving? In Chapter 17, Jason M. Daida argued that it would be very difficult, if not impossible, based on the MPS open-ended problem solving paradigm. In this widely used problem solving paradigm, there are 6 stages of problem solving: engage, define stated problem, create internal idea of problem, plan a solution, carry out the plan and evaluate (check) and look back. Clearly, it would be very hard for GP to undertake some of the activities, *e.g.* engage and define stated problems. In fact, until now, GP has been partnered with human to carry out these problem solving activities. This is demonstrated in typical GP application work-flow, which includes pre-GP (*e.g.* data preparation) and post-GP (*e.g.* solution interpretation) process. Nevertheless, there are opportunities to make GP a more competent partner. One such area is tools to transform/analyze GP solutions so that they can be explained and incorporated into the evaluate, check and look back process. Visualization has been recommended as one great approach to achieve the goal. There are many other opportunities to strengthen GP which remains open for the community to explore.

Jianjun Hu, Ronald Rosenberg and Erik Goodman have started exploring new application domains using their bound-graph representation GP system. Chapter 18 reports their initial study on evolving mechanical vibration absorbers.

This is an area with a history of patents and it poses a great challenge for GP human-competitive results. To evolve single, dual and bandpass vibration absorber, they designed various domain-specific functions. They also devised different fitness functions to direct GP search. The evolved absorber, however, are not practically useful and extremely difficult to implement, although their fitness are high. They concluded that exploiting domain or problem-specific knowledge to embody physically meaningful building blocks is necessary for GP to be successful in real-world problems. Otherwise, the evolved solutions may not be physically realizable. How much domain knowledge to use so that GP has room for creativity and is able to deliver human-competitive results is an open challenge for the community.

Pushing GP toward industrial success in the analog CAD domain, Trent McConaghy and Georges Gielen outline new GP applications and challenges in Chapter 19. They started by distinguishing "success" in the GP research domain, which is demonstrated by the number of publications, and in the industrial success, which is measured by the number of different chip designs that have been sent to fabrication. With great research success in analog design, they suggested using GP to pursue industrial success in three application areas: automated topological design, symbolic modeling and behavioral modeling. They showed their recent work on these problems. The results are very encouraging and accepted well by the CAD design community. Although there are many obstacles to overcome, *e.g.* computational feasibility and earning CAD designers' trust, these applications are great opportunities for GP to become industrial success in the analog CAD field.

There was a lot of interest in discussing GP challenges throughout the workshop. On the last day, a list of open challenges was created by workshop participants:

- Handling large data sets (10 millions).

- Complexity of problems (k-complexity).

- How weird can GP be and still be invited to GPTP?

- The problems associated with analysis of GP systems.

- Mapping GP to customer satisfaction.

- How do we stack GP techniques (avoid "backdrop").

- GP integration with other techniques.

- Theoretical tools for understanding large modular systems.

- How do ADFs affect the GP system?

- Systematizing our understanding of GP: a taxonomy of GP; a GP Periodic Table; mathematical formulation of GP; a GP "Pattern" book; a dictionary of pathologies of GP behavior.

- Understanding Solution Classes.

- Using tools developed in other fields to enhance our understanding and use of GP;

- How to make good use of pre- and post-processing.

- How to move beyond dumping scalars?

- Better infrastructure for visualization; probes to visualize the behavior of GP.

- More complicated fitness functions.

- Looking toward AI, aiming at "real" AI goals (but don't promise too much).

- Exploring alternative computing paradigms, beyond the microprocessor.

- How to integrate domain knowledge?

- GP as a Reinforcement Learning system.

- Scalability and Dynamics.

- Crossing the application chasm—how to make GP attractive to industry? What kind of marketing packages would be useful?

This list provides a starting point and possible directions for contributions to next year's Genetic Programming Theory and Practice Workshop. We look forward to the continued progress of theory and practice integration.

References

O'Reilly, Una-May, Yu, Tina, Riolo, Rick L., and Worzel, Bill, editors (2004). *Genetic Programming Theory and Practice II*, volume 8 of *Genetic Programming*, Ann Arbor, MI, USA. Springer.

Riolo, Rick L. and Worzel, Bill (2003). *Genetic Programming Theory and Practice*, volume 6 of *Genetic Programming*. Kluwer, Boston, MA, USA. Series Editor - John Koza.

Chapter 2

EVOLVING SWARMING AGENTS IN REAL TIME

H. Van Dyke Parunak[1]

[1]*Altarum Institute*

Abstract   An important application for population search methods (such as particle swarm optimization and the several varieties of synthetic evolution) is the engineering problem of configuring individual agents to yield useful emergent behavior. While the biological antecedents of population-based search operate in real time, most engineered versions run off-line. For some applications, it is desirable to evolve agents as they are running in the system that they support. We describe two instances of such systems that we have developed and highlight lessons learned.

Keywords: applications, real-time, emergence, agents, population-based search, evolution

1.   Introduction

Research in the Emerging Markets Group of the Altarum Institute focuses on practical applications of swarm intelligence. We[1] exploit the emergent system-level behavior exhibited by interacting populations of fairly simple agents to solve a wide range of real-world problems, including control of uninhabited air vehicles (Parunak et al., 2002; Sauter et al., 2005), sensor coordination (Parunak and Brueckner, 2003; Brueckner and Parunak, 2004), resource allocation (Savit et al., 2002), information retrieval (Weinstein et al., 2004), and prediction (Parunak et al., 2005), among others.

The central problem in engineering emergent behavior is determining the individual behaviors that will yield the required system-level behavior. The most

[1]The results described in this paper reflect the creative ideas and implementation skill of my colleagues, including Rob Bisson, Steve Brophy, Sven Brueckner, Paul Chiusano, Jorge Goic, Bob Matthews, John Sauter, Peter Weinstein, and Andrew Yinger.

promising techniques that we have identified are those drawing on techniques such as particle swarm optimization and various forms of synthetic evolution. We describe these techniques collectively as population-based search (PBS), since they use interactions among a population of searchers to solve a problem. It is philosophically reinforcing to our basic approach, and perhaps not coincidental, that these techniques themselves exemplify the emergent paradigm of deriving global results from local interactions.

This paper emphasizes two aspects of this approach: the elements of the population are individual agents rather than representations of the whole system, and the evolution takes place in real time, while the system runs. The first aspect has antecedents in the literature, but should be more widely explored. The second appears to be novel.

In Section 2, we summarize some other examples of agent-centered evolution in order to provide a context for our methods. Sections 3 and 4 discuss two examples from our work, using real-time agent-based evolution to solve a Configuration problem and a Fitting problem, respectively. Section 5 draws lessons from our experience and concludes.

2.   Background

Evolutionary and particle swarm methods take their inspiration from natural agents that adapt in the same temporal space in which they are born, live, and die. Yet applications of these techniques differ from their metaphorical roots in two ways. First, many applications have little to do with computational agents, and instead focus on optimization of structures or functions that cut across individual agents, even when the domain naturally lends itself to an agent-based model. Second, even when PBS is applied to individual agents, most applications execute in a temporal space distinct from that occupied by the agents. That is, the PBS is a planning or configuration process that determines agent parameters off-line, for later deployment.

In this section we first distinguish agent-based applications from other approaches, then describe two broad uses of agent-based PBS, and consider some previous work on real-time agent-based PBS.

Three Perspectives on PBS

It is useful to distinguish three different applications of PBS: structure optimization, function optimization, and agent optimization. While the three categories can readily be mapped into one another, each suggests a particular perspective on the problem. For many engineering problems, the agent perspective offers particular benefits.

Structure optimization includes spatial organization problems such as the traveling salesperson problem (TSP), layout of VLSI chips, or design of mechanical mechanisms. It also includes problems of temporal organization such as factory scheduling. Population-based search is typically applied to these problems by constructing a population whose members are complete candidate structures, and taking this approach encourages the practitioner to view the structure holistically. Indeed, the value of PBS for such problems is largely in overcoming the tendency to local sub-optimization that results from traditional mechanisms such as greedy search. Symbolic regression may be considered an instance of structural optimization in which the structure being manipulated is an abstract mathematical expression.

In *function optimization*, each member of the population is a vector that constitutes an argument to some mathematical function, and the objective of the search is to find a vector that yields a desired value for the function (such as an extreme or an inflection point). Effective application of PBS to such problems often requires adjustments to take advantage of the ordered nature of the domain of each allele (Corne et al., 1999). Reduction of an engineering problem to a mathematical function that needs to be optimized is the utmost in abstraction. While such abstraction can help develop general solutions that are applicable across multiple domains, it also makes it difficult to take advantage of domain-specific heuristics, which may not readily be cast as closed-form mathematical expressions.

Agent optimization is a natural way to apply PBS to domains that are effectively modeled as sets of interacting autonomous agents. These domains may be engineered or natural.

Engineered domains that lend themselves to multi-agent modeling include processing information from networks of sensors, coordinating the movement of multiple vehicles, retrieving information from large collections of documents, and managing extended communication networks. Agent architectures are particularly attractive for engineering problems when the domain consists of discrete elements that are distributed in some topology, where central control is difficult or impossible, and whose environment is changing dynamically (so that adaptiveness is more important than reaching a steady-state optimum).

Natural domains that lend themselves to multi-agent modeling include many biological systems, ranging from predator-prey ecologies and insect colonies to human communities.

In both cases, the behaviors of these systems emerge from the interactions of their parts, and a central problem in configuring them is determining the behavior of individuals that will yield the desired overall system behavior. In applying PBS from this perspective, each member of the population is a candidate for a single agent in the system. Taking an agent-centered perspective on PBS aligns well with the natural modularity of such system.

Recently, agent-based mechanisms such as ant colony optimization (ACO) have been applied to structure optimization (*e.g.*, TSP and scheduling); population search has been used to tune these mechanisms. It seems most natural to search over populations of individual agents (White et al., 1998). However, these mechanisms include some system-wide parameters (*e.g.*, the number of agents), so population members are sometimes defined at the level of the system rather than the individual agents (Botee and Bonabeau, 1998).

This latter approach violates the distinction between the individual agents and their environment (Weyns et al., 2004), a distinction that is important from the point of view of engineering effectiveness. On the one hand, it is usually appropriate to consider issues such as the number of agents and the physics of pheromone evaporation as part of the environment. Though they may emerge from interactions among the agents, no single agent can change them. On the other hand, deposit rates and sensitivity to different pheromones clearly pertain to individual agents, and it makes sense to model them in the chromosomes of each agent. If one wishes to explore the total space of both agent and environmental variables, it would be cleaner to co-evolve the agents and the environment as two different populations. (The whole area of engineering environments for agents is quite new in the agent software community, and we do not know of anyone who has explored the pros and cons of these alternative ways of applying PBS to such systems).

Varieties of the Agent Approach

We are not by any means the first to apply PBS to individual agents in order to improve their collective behavior. Two areas where this approach has been widely applied are robotics and biology.

Biologists use PBS (particularly its genetic varieties) retrospectively, in at least two distinct ways. *Ethologists* seek to discover possible processes by which various animal behaviors have evolved. The actual behavior of the agent is knownand provides the standard against which the fitness of an evolved agent is evaluated. Examples of work in this field include the development of communications (Quinn, 2001; Steels, 2000), the evolution of cooperation (Riolo et al., 2001), and the development of foraging (Panait and Luke, 2004), to name only a few. *Ecologists* are more concerned with the overall patterns of interactions among multiple agents (*e.g.*, food webs and population dynamics), rather than the individual behaviors. These examples can be viewed as attempts to fit a model to observed agent and system behaviors, respectively.

Roboticists have long used PBS prospectively, to find behaviors (equivalently, control laws) that satisfy various functional requirements. A variety of representations have been adopted for programming the behavior of these agents, including GP-like higher-order operations (Brooks, 1992), tropistic execution engines (Agah and Bekey, 1996), and neural networks (Harvey et al.,

1992). These examples can be viewed as configuration problems, seeking to configure the agent's behavioral engine to achieve desired outcomes.

Most of these instances run "off-line." That is, the timeline within which the PBS operates is disjoint from the timeline within which the system being studied or designed operates. While ubiquitous among practitioners of PBS, off-line search is at variance with the natural processes that inspired these mechanisms. Our examples illustrate the potential of on-line search (conducted while the system itself operates).

Examples of Real-Time PBS

A few examples of PBS have been published[2] in which evolution takes place as the system runs, and merit comparison with our approach.

Nordin and Banzhaf (Nordin and Banzhaf, 1997) use GP to evolve the controller for a Khepera robot to improve its ability to avoid obstacles. The evolution runs as the robot operates, but the objective is to evolve a single algorithm that can handle various inputs, not to vary the algorithm to accommodate environmental changes. While the system is learning (40-60 minutes in one version, 1.5 in another), the robot does not successfully avoid obstacles. Dadone and VanLandingham (Dadone and VanLandingham, 1999) take a similar approach in evolving a controller for a chemical plant. Each member of the population is given a chance to run the plant while its fitness is evaluated, and when every member of the population has been evaluated, a new population is generated. These systems deal only with a single entity (the robot or the controller), and are not concerned with developing appropriate emergent behavior from a system of agents.

Spector and colleagues (Spector et al., 2005) evolve the behaviors of a population of simulated mobile entities living in 3-d space, whose behavior evolves as they execute. They describe two systems. In one, the agents' behavior is a version of Reynolds' flocking behavior (Reynolds, 1987), and the genotype is a list of coefficients for the various vectors that are summed in that algorithm. In the other, it is a program that yields a flocking algorithm. This work exhibits emergent group behavior across the population of agents. However, that behavior is achieved over the course of the run. The dynamics of the environment are handled by the adaptive capabilities of the flocking algorithm that is evolved, not the ongoing adaptation of that algorithm by evolution.

These examples are robotics applications. They develop control instructions for robots, like the more common off-line applications of PBS, but do so fast enough to be deployed on the robot as it executes. They both rely on adaptive

---

[2]We are grateful to participants in GPTP2005 and other reviewers for suggesting a number of examples, of which these are illustrative.

mechanisms in the evolved behavior to handle a changing environment, rather than using evolution itself as the main adaptive mechanism.

Dynamic Flies (Boumaza and Louchet, 2001) is a vision processing algorithm for obstacle avoidance. A population of points in three-space evolve to fit their coordinates in the robot's visual field to occupy the surfaces of obstacles. The fitness function is based on the observation that the pixels in the vicinity of a fly on a surface will vary relatively little from two different vantage points, compared with the pixel neighborhoods of flies that are in free space. The flies influence one another, in that the fitness is adjusted to penalize grouping. The aggregate fitness of the flies in each cell of a square lattice that maps the robot's environment generates a repulsive field to guide the robot. This application is like ours in both dimensions. It is truly emergent, generating a system-level behavior (obstacle avoidance) from the evolution of individual flies. Also, it uses evolution as its adaptive engine. However, the individual flies, consisting only of the coordinates of a point in three-space and a fitness value, have no intrinsic behavior, and fall below the threshold of what most researchers would consider an agent. While the application as a whole is robotic, the actual adaptation of the flies to the surfaces of obstacles in the environment can be considered a retrospective or fitting application of real-time PBS, since the flies are evolving to provide a model of an exogenous feature of the environment.

The evolving entities in classifier systems (Booker et al., 1989) and artificial immune systems (Forrest et al., 1997), unlike Dynamic Flies, do have (very simple) behaviors associated with them, and could be considered minimal agents. These systems exhibit real-time PBS.

Li and colleagues (Li et al., 2000a; Li et al., 2000b) evolve the strategies of agents playing the minority game, a simple model of emergent market dynamics. The agents' fitnesses are evaluated as the game proceeds, but the population is updated all at once every 10,000 time steps, rather than permitting each agent to evolve asynchronously with respect to the others, as in nature.

3.   A Configuration Application

The most direct application of PBS to swarming systems is finding configurations of the individual agents so heir interactions yield the desired system-level behavior. We illustrate this in the context of ADAPTIV (Adaptive control of Distributed Agents through Pheromone Techniques and Interactive Visualization), a system developed for planning flight paths for uninhabited robotic vehicles (URV's). This system uses a digital analog of insect pheromone mechanisms to guide vehicles around threats and toward targets.

Our implementation of digital pheromones has four components:

1 A distributed network of *place agents* maintains the pheromone field and performs aggregation, evaporation, and diffusion. Each place agent is

responsible for a region of the physical space. In our simulation, we tile the physical space with hexagons, each represented by a place agent with six neighbors, but both regular and irregular tiling schemes can be employed. Place agents ideally are situated physically in the environment using unattended ground sensors distributed over an area and connected to their nearby neighbors through a wireless network. They may also be located in a distributed network of command and control nodes.

2 *Avatars* represent physical entities. Red avatars represent the enemy targets and threats, while blue represent friendly URVs. Blue avatars are normally located on the robot vehicle. The name "Avatar" is inspired by the incarnation of a Hindu deity, and by extension describes a temporary manifestation (a software agent) of a persistent entity (a robot vehicle).

3 Blue avatars create *Ghost agents* that wander over the place agents looking for targets, and then continually building a path from the avatar to the target. Both of these entities deposit pheromones at their current locations.

4 Different classes of agents deposit distinct *pheromone flavors*. Agents can sense pheromones in the place agent in whose sector they reside as well as the neighboring place agents. The underlying mathematics of the pheromone field, including critical stability theorems, is described in (Brueckner, 2000).

Battlefield intelligence from sensors and reconnaissance activities causes the instantiation of red avatars representing known targets and threats. These agents deposit pheromones on the places representing their location in the battlespace. The field they generate is dynamic since targets and threats can move, new ones can be identified, or old ones can disappear or be destroyed. A blue avatar representing a URV is associated with one place agent at any given time, the place agent within whose physical territory the URV is currently located. It follows the pheromone path created by its ghost agents.

Ghosts initially wander through the network of place agents, attracted to pheromones deposited by targets and repelled by threat pheromones. Once they find a target, they return over the network of place agents to the avatar, depositing pheromones that contribute to building the shortest, safest path to the target. The basic pheromone flavors are *RTarget* (deposited by a Red target avatar, such as the Red headquarters), *RThreat* (deposited by a Red threat avatar, such as an air defense installation), *GTarget* (deposited by a ghost that has encountered a target and is returning to its blue avatar, forming the path to the target), and *GNest* (deposited by a ghost that has left the blue avatar and is seeking a target).

A ghost agent chooses its next sector stochastically by spinning a roulette wheel with six weighted segments (one for each of its six neighbors). The size of each segment is a function of the strength of the pheromones and is designed to guide the ghost according to the algorithm above. We experimented with several different forms of the function that generates the segment sizes. Evolution of such a form using genetic programming would in itself be a useful exercise. In our case, manual experimentation yielded the form (for outbound ghosts):

$$F_n = \frac{\theta \cdot RTarget_n + \gamma \cdot GTarget_n + \beta}{(\rho GNest_n + \beta)(Dist_n + \varphi)^{\delta + \alpha(RThreat_n + 1)} + \beta}$$

F_n is the resultant attractive force exerted by neighbor n and $Dist$ is the distance to the target if it is known. Table 2-1 lists the tunable parameters in the equation and the effect that increasing each parameter has on the ghost's behavior. Though this table provides general guidance to the practitioner, in practice, the emergent dynamics of the interaction of ghost agents with their environment makes it impossible to predict the behavior of the ghosts. Thus tuning the parameters of this or any pheromone equation becomes a daunting task. Even if a skilled practitioner were able to tune the equation by hand, the system would still be impractical for end users who don't think of their problem in terms of α, β, and γ. This observation led us to investigate the possibility of using evolutionary methods to tune the parameters of the equation.

Table 2-1. Tunable Parameters and their Effects on Ghosts.

α	Increases threat avoidance further from the target
δ	Increases probability of ghosts moving towards a known target in the absence of RTarget pheromone
γ	Increases sensitivity to other ghosts
ρ	Increases ghost exploration (by avoiding GhostNest pheromone)
θ	Increases attraction to RTarget pheromone
β, ϕ	Avoids divison by zero

We explored several PBS algorithms on the problem of defining ghost parameters, including three varieties of evolution strategies (ES) and a genetic algorithm (GA). Details on these approaches and the scenarios on which they were tested are described in our original paper (Sauter et al., 2002). In all cases, ghosts have a fixed lifetime. Within this lifetime they first execute a search, and then breed sexually until they die. Thus ghosts that complete their search faster have longer to breed, and generate more offspring. The GA and one ES approach took account of threats that the ghost encountered during its search, and the GA also rewarded the ghost for the value of the target that it discovered. In all cases, as each ghost returns to the URV, it is evaluated and selectively participates in generating subsequent generations of ghosts. Thus the ghosts being emitted by the avatar are evolved in real time, as the system runs.

One could envision evolving the parameters for the ghosts off-line. The success of this approach would depend on the stability of the environment. In the test examples reported here, the environment was static, and we were exploring the speed with which the evolutionary process converged, and the resulting performance achieved. However, on different runs we gave the system different scenarios, to which it developed distinct parameters. In a real-world application, scenarios are not static, and a set of parameters evolved for one scenario would not function well on another. By adapting the parameters in real time, we can accommodate dynamic changes in the environment.

Figure 2-1 shows the performance of the system, measured by the strength of the GTarget pheromone adjacent to the avatar (and thus available to guide it). The left-hand plot shows two benchmarks. The "Hand Tuned" line shows the behavior of a set of parameters derived by manual experimentation. The "Random" line shows the behavior when ghosts are generated with small random excursions around the hand tuned values.

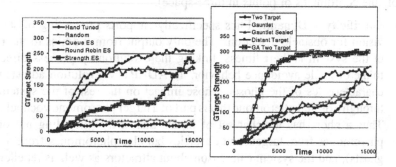

Figure 2-1. Performance of PBS on path planning. Left: comparison of ES's on Two Target scenario. Right: comparison of Strength ES on various scenarios, and GA on Two Target scenario.

The left-hand plot shows that all three versions of the ES outperformed the hand tuned and random configuration by an order of magnitude. The Strength ES takes into account the damage suffered by the ghost in simulated encounters with threats, and while it takes longer to converge, it outperforms the other ES approaches on a wider range of scenarios. The slight superiority of the random to the hand tuned configuration is an interesting illustration of the value of stochasticity in breaking symmetries among swarming agents and permitting more effective exploration of the environment.

The right-hand plot compares the Strength ES on four different scenarios with the GA on one of them.

This system has striking similarities with the Dynamic Flies system, though each was developed without knowledge of the other. In both cases, interacting entities continuously evolve under the influence of the environment, and generate a field that guides the movement of a physical vehicle. Table 2-2 makes this comparison explicit.

Table 2-2. Comparison of ADAPTIV and Dynamic Flies.

Feature	ADAPTIV	Dynamic Flies
Entities	Ghosts	Flies
Environmental Influences	Targets and Threats	Obstacles
Generated Field	GTarget pheromone	Aggregate Fly fitness
Physical Agent	URV	Robot

The systems differ in their specificity and their dynamics. Both of these differences reflect the distinction between ADAPTIV's ghosts (which are real, though simple agents with autonomous behaviors) and the flies (which are simply the coordinates of points in three-space).

- **Specificity.**—Dynamic Flies specifically supports processing of stereo vision for obstacle detection. The only output from the flies to the rest of the system is their fitness, linking the evolutionary process directly to the obstacle avoidance behavior. In ADAPTIV, evolution adjusts the characteristics of the ghosts, whose impact on the rest of the system is through a digital pheromone that is part of a larger pheromone vocabulary. Thus a ghost has a richer set of inputs than a fly (including not only pheromones from targets and obstacles but also pheromones from other ghosts), and the system can reason about attractors as well as repellers.

- **Dynamics.**—The Dynamic Flies system has no memory. A fly repels the vehicle only while it is actually at a location, and only in proportion to its current fitness. This feature is appropriate for the specific obstacle avoidance application for which the system is designed. The ADAPTIV architecture supports more general geospatial reasoning, including the need to maintain a memory of a threat or target that may not currently be visible. Because pheromones are distinct from the agents that deposit them, they can persist in a location after the agent has moved on, or they can vanish almost immediately, depending on the setting of the evaporation rate associated with a given pheromone flavor.

4.   A Behavior Fitting Application

Our second example addresses the problem of predicting the future behavior of soldiers in urban combat, based solely on their observed past behavior. We assume that an individual soldier's behavior is a function of his[3] individual personality as well as his interactions with other soldiers and with the urban environment. Prediction in this highly nonlinear system merits comparison with prediction in nonlinear systems without the social and psychological aspects of combat (Kantz and Schreiber, 1997). The general approach in such systems is to extrapolate future behavior using functions fitted to the recent past. While the nonlinear nature of the systems may lead to divergence of trajectories over time, continuously refreshing the fit and limiting the distance of the projection into the future can yield useful predictions (Figure 2-2).

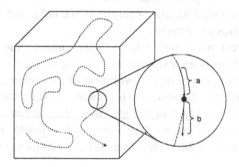

Figure 2-2. By constantly updating a fit of the system's trajectory through state space on the basis of the recent past (a), one can generate useful predictions a short distnce into the future (b).

Historically, this approach has been applied to systems that can be described analytically, permitting a functional form to be fit to recent behavior. We have extended this approach to entities, such as soldiers, whose behavior cannot readily be fit using analytical techniques. The basic approach is to represent the entity by a software agent whose behavioral parameters are fit using PBS. We call this approach "Behavioral Emulation and Extrapolation," or BEE.

BEE must operate very rapidly, in order to keep pace with the ongoing evolution of the battle. Thus we use simple agents coordinated using pheromone mechanisms similar to those described in our configuration example.

Figure 2-3 explains BEE further. Each active entity in the battlespace has an avatar that continuously generates a stream of ghost agents representing itself. The ghosts' behavioral parameters are selected from distributions to explore possible intentions of the entity they represent. Thus BEE mimics at the agent level the nonlinear track analysis outlined in Figure 2-2.

Ghosts live on a timeline indexed by τ that begins in the past at the insertion horizon and runs into the future to the prediction horizon. The avatar inserts

---

[3] We use the masculine gender generically.

the ghosts at the insertion horizon. The ghosts representing different entities interact with one another and with the terrain. These interactions mean that their fitness depends not just on their own actions, but also on the behaviors of the rest of the population, which is also evolving. Because τ advances faster than real time, eventually $\tau = t$ (actual time). At this point, the ghosts are evaluated based on their locations compared with the entity represented by their avatar.

The fittest ghosts have two functions. First, they are bred and their offspring are reintroduced at the insertion horizon to continue the fitting process. Second, they are allowed to run past the avatar's present into the future. Each ghost that is allowed to run into the future explores a different possible future of the battle, analogous to how some people plan ahead by mentally simulating different ways that a situation might unfold. Analysis of the behaviors of these different possible futures yields predictions.

This entire process runs continuously, in real time, as the system monitors the environment. Ghosts are evolving against the world as its state changes. As in the Dynamic Flies system, the evolution of the swarming agents is what enables them to track a dynamic environment. Unlike the Dynamic Flies, but like ADAPTIV, the output of the ghosts in BEE is not an immediate by-product of the evolutionary process (the fitness of the agents), but a second-order phenomenon produced by the agents (their behavior as they run into the future).

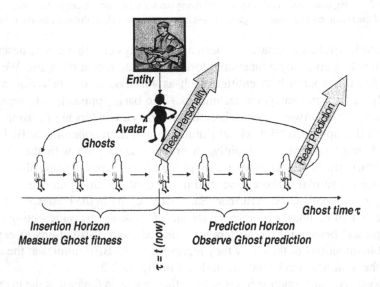

Figure 2-3. Behavioral Emulation and Extrapolation. Each avatar generates a stream of ghosts that sample the personality space of the entity it represents. They are evolved against the observed behavior of the entity in the recent past, and the fittest ghosts then run into the future to generate predictions.

The personality of each ghost includes four categories of information, all represented as scalars (Parunak et al., 2005):

1 *Desires* are anticipated future state of the world toward which the agent is positively disposed. We have defined a basic set of desires relevant to the combat scenario. An agent's goals are considered to be stable over the time horizon that we are considering. They may be mutually exclusive, since they have no effect on an agent's actions until they are instantiated as goals in the face of environmental information. A desire might be "occupy key sites."

2 *Goals* are selected by the agent from among its desires based on its current state and recent history, and it chooses its actions in an effort to accomplish the goals. Unlike desires, the set of goals held by an agent at a given time are believed by the agent to be consistent with one another, and may change over the time horizon of the battle. A goal instantiated from the "key sites" desire might be "occupy building 34 by time = 1520." The agent continually reviews its goals to ensure their consistency with the current state of the world. If it discovers that two goals are inconsistent with one another, it will drop at least one of them.

3 *Emotions* are defined following the OCC model (Ortony et al., 1988) as "valenced reactions to events, agents, or objects." Emotions vary based on the events, agents, or objects that the agent experiences, and modulate its analysis of which goals to instantiate over time. For example, an event of being attacked will raise the level of an agent's fear emotion.

4 *Dispositions* reflect an agent's tendency to adapt a given emotion. For example, an agent with a high level of the "cowardice" disposition will experience a faster rate of increase of fear in the presence of an attack than an agent with a low level of this disposition. Dispositions are assumed to be constant over the time horizon in question.

Figure 2-4 shows how these four personality elements interact with one another and with environmental stimuli to generate the agent's behavior.

This system has been tested in a series of realistic wargaming experiments in which the actions of the red and blue fighters were directed by experienced military commanders. While the results of these experiments have not yet been released for publication, BEE was successful in detecting which units were being played to exhibit specified dispositions.

5. Discussion and Conclusion

These applications are both instances of agent-centered PBS. The configuration problem is directly comparable to the many applications of PBS to robotic

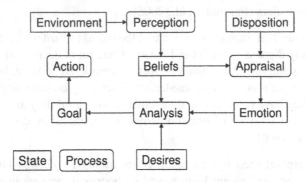

Figure 2-4. Desires, beliefs, dispositions, and emotions generate an agent's basic behaviors in response to environmental stimuli.

configuration, while the fitting problem can be compared to biological studies that seek to understand existing behavior in the natural world.

What sets these applications apart from most others is their real-time nature. In many instances of PBS, the entire population is synchronized. Even when the focus of search is the single agent rather than the system as a whole, it is common to update all agents at the same time, replacing the entire population at each generation. In our approach, breeding occurs in parallel with the evaluation of the ghosts. In the configuration example, only 1% of the population is replaced in each generation. Since the evaluation of an individual can take 100 - 300 time steps (the round trip distance with room for wandering), forcing a complete evaluation cycle before breeding would have slowed down the algorithm considerably. Similarly, in the fitting example, ghosts are continually compared with the behavior of the entities they represent as the battle unfolds, and breeding affects only a small fraction (about 3%) of the ghosts at each time step. By changing only a fraction of the population at each time step, we leave the bulk of the agents to carry on the work that the system is intended to do and avoid catastrophic shifts due to maladaptive individuals. At the same time, we limit the ability of the system to respond rapidly to catastrophic exogenous events, a weakness to which natural real-time evolution is not immune.

It is common in agent-centered PBS to evaluate the fitness of an individual in isolation, or in a tournament where individuals from separate populations compete with each other. In our examples, the ghosts are part of a mixed population. Each of them is depositing pheromones and reacting to pheromones in a common environment. Thus, unfit individuals are depositing pheromones in the same environment being sensed by fit individuals, potentially causing the fit individuals to score lower than they would otherwise. This fact initially concerned us. We weren't sure whether PBS would even work under those circumstances. However, this particular problem appears to have a number of reasonable solutions, so the effect of having a mixed population did not prevent the algorithms from identifying and rewarding the better individuals.

Three details of our approach make it possible to apply PBS in real time:

1 Real-time PBS is facilitated by an agent-centric approach so that some components of the system can be modified while others carry on the system's work.

2 This approach is realistic only with populous systems, so that the effect of a change in a single agent do not discontinuously change the dynamics of the whole system. We know empirically that the systems described in this paper can function with populations on the order of 100 and more, but we have not systematically explored the lower bound.

3 Agents should be light-weight , so that multiple copies can be executed fast enough to keep up with the real world. We have found that the digital pheromone model, using simple functions to combine the pheromones sensed by the agent in its environment, is efficient enough to support tens of thousands of agents concurrently, thus providing both the population sizes and repeated cycles needed for effective evolution while keeping pace with real time.

Our experiments show that it is feasible to evolve a complex system in real time, element by element, rather than in a planning step that is temporally discontinuous with the system's operation. This approach opens new opportunities for applying PBS to dynamically changing systems that do not lend themselves to lengthy planning cycles.

References

Agah, A. and Bekey, G.A. (1996). A genetic algorithm-based controller for decentralized multi-agent robotic systems. In *The 1996 IEEE International Conf. on Evolutionary Computation*, pages 431–436, Nagoya, Japan. IEEE.

Booker, L. B., Goldberg, D. E., and Holland, J. H. (1989). Classifier systems and genetic algorithms. *Artificial Intelligence*, 40:235–282.

Botee, Hozefa M. and Bonabeau, Eric (1998). Evolving ant colony optimization. *Adv. Complex Systems*, 1:149–159.

Boumaza, Amine M. and Louchet, Jean (2001). Dynamic flies: Using real-time parisian evolution in robotics. In Boers, Egbert J. W., Cagnoni, Stefano, Gottlieb, Jens, Hart, Emma, Lanzi, Pier Luca, Raidl, Gunther R., Smith, Robert E., and Tijink, Harald, editors, *Applications of Evolutionary Computing*, volume 2037 of *LNCS*, pages 288–297, Lake Como, Italy. Springer-Verlag.

Brooks, Rodney A. (1992). Artificial life and real robots. In Varela, Francisco J. and Bourgine, Paul, editors, *The First European Conference on Artificial Life*, pages 3–10.

Brueckner, Sven (2000). *Return from the Ant: Synthetic Ecosystems for Manufacturing Control*. Dr.rer.nat., Humboldt University Berlin.

Brueckner, Sven A. and Parunak, H. Van Dyke (2004). Swarming distributed pattern detection and classification. In Weyns, Danny, Parunak, H. Van Dyke, and Michel, Fabien, editors, *Workshop on Environments for Multi-Agent Systems (E4MAS 2004)*, volume LNAI 3374, New York, NY. Springer.

Corne, D., Dorigo, M., and Glover, F., editors (1999). *New Ideas in Optimisation*. McGraw-Hill, New York.

Dadone, P. and VanLandingham, H.F. (1999). Adaptive online parameter tuning using genetic algorithms. In *Proceedings of WSC4: 4th Online World Conference on Soft Computing in Industrial Applications*.

Forrest, S., Hofmeyr, S., and Somayaji, A. (1997). Computer immunology. *Communications of the ACM*, 40:88–96.

Harvey, I., Husbands, P., and Cliff, D. (1992). Issues in evolutionary robotics. In Meyer, J-A, Roitblat, H, and Wilson, S, editors, *The Second International Conference on Simulation of Adaptive Behaviour (SAB92)*, pages 364–373.

Kantz, Holger and Schreiber, Thomas (1997). *Nonlinear Time Series Analysis*. Cambridge Nonlinear Science Series. Cambridge University Press, Cambridge, UK.

Li, Yi, Riolo, Rick, and Savit, Robert (2000a). Evolution in minority games. i. games with a fixed strategy space. *Physica A*, 2000(276):234 – 264.

Li, Yi, Riolo, Rick, and Savit, Robert (2000b). Evolution in minority games ii. games with variable strategy spaces. *Physica A*, 2000(276):265 – 283.

Nordin, P. and Banzhaf, W. (1997). Real time control of a khepera robot using genetic programming. *Cybernetics and Control*, 26(3):533–561.

Ortony, A., Clore, G.L., and Collins, A. (1988). *The cognitive structure of emotions*. Cambridge University Press, Cambridge, UK.

Panait, Liviu A. and Luke, Sean (2004). Learning ant foraging behaviours. In Pollack, Jordan, Bedau, Mark, Husbands, Phil, Ikegami, Takashi, and Watson, Richard A., editors, *Artificial Life XI Ninth International Conference on the Simulation and Synthesis of Living Systems*, pages 575–580, Boston, Massachusetts. The MIT Press.

Parunak, H. Van Dyke, Bisson, Robert, Brueckner, Sven, Matthews, Robert, and Sauter, John (2005). Representing dispositions and emotions in simulated combat. In Thompson, Simon, Ghanea-Hercock, Robert, Greaves, Mark, Meyer, Andre, and Jennings, Nick, editors, *Workshop on Defence Applications of Multi-Agent Systems (DAMAS05, at AAMAS05)*, page (forthcoming), Utrecht, Netherlands.

Parunak, H. Van Dyke and Brueckner, Sven (2003). Swarming coordination of multiple UAV's for collaborative sensing. In *Second AIAA "Unmanned Unlimited" Systems, Technologies, and Operations Conference*, San Diego, CA. AIAA.

Parunak, H. Van Dyke, Purcell, Michael, and O'Connell, Robert (2002). Digital pheromones for autonomous coordination of swarming UAV's. In *First AIAA Unmanned Aerospace Vehicles, Systems, Technologies, and Operations Conference*, Norfolk, VA. AIAA.

Quinn, M. (2001). Evolving communication without dedicated communication channels. In Kelemen, J. and Sosik, P., editors, *Advances in Artificial Life: Sixth European Conference on Artificial Life: ECAL2001*, pages 357–366, Prague, Czech Republic. Springer.

Reynolds, Craig W. (1987). Flocks, herds, and schools: A distributed behavioral model. *Computer Graphics*, 21(4):25–34.

Riolo, Rick L, Axelrod, Robert, and Cohen, Michael D. (2001). Evolution of cooperation without reciprocity. *Nature*, 414(22 Nov):441–443.

Sauter, John A., Matthews, Robert, Parunak, H. Van Dyke, and Brueckner, Sven (2002). Evolving adaptive pheromone path planning mechanisms. In *Autonomous Agents and Multi-Agent Systems (AAMAS02)*, pages 434–440, Bologna, Italy.

Sauter, John A., Matthews, Robert, Parunak, H. Van Dyke, and Brueckner, Sven A. (2005). Performance of digital pheromones for swarming vehicle control. In *Fourth International Joint Conference on Autonomous Agents and Multi-Agent Systems*, page (forthcoming), Utrecht, Netherlands.

Savit, Robert, Brueckner, Sven A., Parunak, H.Van Dyke, and Sauter, John (2002). Phase structure of resource allocation games. *Physics Letters A*, 311:359–364.

Spector, Lee, Klein, Jon, Perry, Chris, and Feinstein, Mark (2005). Emergence of collective behavior in evolving populations of flying agents. *Genetic Programming and Evolvable Machines*, 6. Prepublication Date: 6 August 2004.

Steels, L. (2000). The puzzle of language evolution. *Kognitionswissenschaft*, 8(4):143–150.

Weinstein, Peter, Parunak, H. Van Dyke, Chiusano, Paul, and Brueckner, Sven (2004). Agents swarming in semantic spaces to corroborate hypotheses. In *AAMAS 2004*, pages 1488–1489, New York, NY.

Weyns, Danny, Parunak, H. Van Dyke, Michel, Fabien, Holvoet, Tom, and Ferber, Jacques (2004). Multiagent systems, state-of-the-art and research challenges. In Weyns, Danny, Parunak, H. Van Dyke, and Michel, Fabien, editors, *Workshop on Environments for Multi-Agent Systems (E4MAS 2004)*, volume LNAI 3374, New York, NY. Springer.

White, Tony, Pagurek, Bernard, and Oppacher, Franz (1998). ASGA: Improving the ant system by integration with genetic algorithms. In Koza, John R.,

Banzhaf, Wolfgang, Chellapilla, Kumar, Deb, Kalyanmoy, Dorigo, Marco, Fogel, David B., Garzon, Max H., Goldberg, David E., Iba, Hitoshi, and Riolo, Rick, editors, *Genetic Programming 1998: Proceedings of the Third Annual Conference*, pages 610–617, University of Wisconsin, Madison, Wisconsin, USA. Morgan Kaufmann.

Chapter 3

AUTOMATED DESIGN OF A PREVIOUSLY PATENTED ASPHERICAL OPTICAL LENS SYSTEM BY MEANS OF GENETIC PROGRAMMING

Lee W. Jones[1], Sameer H. Al-Sakran[1] and John R. Koza[2]

[1]*Genetic Programming Inc., Mountain View, California;* [2]*Stanford University, Stanford, California*

Abstract   This chapter describes how genetic programming was used as an invention machine to automatically synthesize a complete design for an aspherical optical lens system (a type of lens system that is especially difficult to design and that offers advantages in terms of cost, weight, size, and performance over traditional spherical systems). The genetically evolved aspherical lens system duplicated the functionality of a recently patented aspherical system. The automatic synthesis was open-ended — that is, the process did not start from a pre-existing good design and did not pre-specify the number of lenses, which lenses (if any) should be spherical or aspherical, the topological arrangement of the lenses, the numerical parameters of the lenses, or the non-numerical parameters of the lenses. The genetically evolved design is an instance of human-competitive results produced by genetic programming in the field of optical design.

Keywords: automated design, optical lens system, aspherical lenses, developmental process, genetic programming, replication of previously patented invention, human-competitive result

1.   Introduction

An optical lens system is an arrangement of refractive or reflective materials that manipulate light (Smith, 1992; Smith, 2000). Their design is more of an art than a science. As Warren J. Smith states in Modern Optical Engineering (Smith, 2000):

> "There is no 'direct' method of optical design for original systems; that is, there is no sure procedure that will lead (without foreknowledge) from a set of performance specifications to a suitable design."

Lens systems have historically been composed of lenses with spherical surfaces. Recently, it has been economically feasible to manufacture lenses with aspherical surfaces. The use of aspherical lenses can potentially reduce the total number of lenses, thereby reducing the costs of manufacturing and assembling the optical system. Moreover, an aspherical lens is often thinner than the replaced spherical lens, thereby further reducing the system's weight and cost.

A complete design for an optical lens system encompasses numerous decisions, including the choice of the system's topology (that is, the number of lenses and their topological arrangement), choices for numerical parameters, and choices for non-numerical parameters.

The topological decisions required to define a lens system include the sequential arrangement of lenses between the object and the image, decisions as to whether consecutive lenses touch or are separated by air, the nature of the mathematical expressions defining the curvature of each lens surface (traditionally spherical, but nowadays often aspherical), and the locations and sizes of the field and aperture stops that determine the field of view and the maximum illumination of the image, respectively.

The numerical choices include the thickness of each lens and the separation (if any) between lens surfaces, the numerical coefficients for the mathematical expressions defining the curvature of each surface (which, in turn, implies whether each is concave, convex, flat, or aspheric), and the aperture (semi-diameter) of each surface.

The non-numerical choices include the type of material (*e.g.* glass, polymer) for each lens. Each type of material has various properties of interest to optical designers, notably including the index of refraction, n (which varies by wavelength); the Abbe number, V; and the cost. Choices of material are typically drawn from a standard catalog.

This paper describes how genetic programming (Koza, 1990; Koza, 1992; Koza, 1993; Koza, 1994; Koza et al., 1999; Koza et al., 2003; Banzhaf et al., 1998; Langdon and Poli, 2002) was used to create a complete design for an optical lens system that satisfies the inventors' requirements specified in U.S. Patent 5,568,319 (Kaneko and Ueno, 1996). The automatic synthesis is open-ended–that is, the process did not start from a pre-existing good design and did not pre-specify the number of lenses, which lenses should be spherical or aspherical, the topological arrangement of the lenses, the numerical parameters of the lenses, or the non-numerical parameters of the lenses.

Section 2 provides background on the design of optical lens systems. Section 3 discusses the developmental representation used to apply genetic programming to optical systems. Section 4 discusses five domain-specific adjustments to standard genetic programming that we use in problems of optical design. Section 5 presents the results. Section 6 is the conclusion.

2. Design of Optical Lens Systems

A classical lens system is conventionally specified by a table called a *prescription* (or, if the system is being analyzed by modern-day optical simulation software, a lens file). In 1996, Masanobu Kaneko and Yasunori Ueno received U.S. Patent 5,568,319 entitled "Aspherical Eyepiece." Figure 3-1 shows the patented Kaneko-Ueno lens system. This system has three groups of lenses containing a total of four lenses.

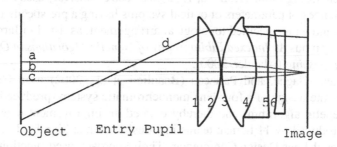

Figure 3-1. Kaneko-Ueno patent.

Table 3-1 shows a prescription for the patented Kaneko-Ueno lens system of Figure 3-1. Because of space limitations here, the reader is referred to a general textbook on optics (Smith, 2000; Fischer and Tadic-Galeb, 2000) for a detailed explanation of this widely used representation. Surface 6 in the patented system is aspherical. The value in column 6 represents the coefficient C_4 of the y^4 term in the general aspherical expression:

$$X = \frac{Cy^2}{1 + \sqrt{1 - (k+1)C^2y^2}} + \sum_{i=2}^{\infty} C_{2i}y^{2i}$$

In this expression, y is the height from the system's main axis (line b in figure 1), C is the curvature of the underlying spherical surface, the C_{2i} are coefficients of the even-numbered polynomial terms, and k is the conic constant. If the conic constant $k = 0$, the system is spherical; if $-1 < k < 0$, the system is ellipsoid; if $k < -1$, the system is hyperboloid; and if $k = 1$, the system is paraboloid). In the expression, x is the distance between the Y-axis to the three-dimensional surface (of which we only see the projection lying on the plane of the paper).

Table 3-1. Lens file for the Kaneko-Ueno patent.

Surface	Distance	Radius	Material	Aperture	C_4
Object	10^{10}	Flat	Air		
Entry pupil	1.091668	Flat	Air	0.125	
1	0.333334	40.07506	SK55	0.634053	0.0
2	0.016667	−1.01667	Air	0.727958	0.0
3	0.500001	1.083335	SK5	0.728162	0.0
4	0.166667	−1.08334	SFL6	0.607429	0.0
5	0.125	11.66668	Air	0.583186	0.0
6	0.125	Flat	K10	0.555395	−0.3715184
7	0.317441	Flat	Air	0.536884	0.0
Image		Flat		0.466308	

The genetic algorithm (Holland, 1992) has been extensively used for optimizing the choices of parameters of optical systems having a pre-specified number of lenses and a pre-specified topological arrangement, as listed in Jarmo Alander's voluminous *An Indexed Bibliography of Genetic Algorithms in Optics and Image Processing* (Alander, 2000).

Beaulieu, Gagné, and Parizeau (Beaulieu et al., 2002) used GP to "re-engineer" the design of a four-lens monochromatic system (produced by a run of the genetic algorithm) and thereby created an improvement over the best design produced by 11 human teams in a design competition held at the 1990 International Lens Design Conference. Their approach used functions that incrementally adjusted (additively or multiplicatively) the distance between lens surfaces, radius of curvature of lens surfaces, and stop location values.

It has been demonstrated that genetic programming can be used to automatically synthesize a complete design for spherical optical lens systems (Al-Sakran et al., 2005), including six previously patented systems (Koza et al., 2005).

3.   Developmental Representation Used for Optical Design

Pioneering work on developmental representations for use with genetic algorithms and genetic programming was done by Wilson (Wilson, 1987), Kitano (Kitano, 1990), and Gruau (Gruau, 1992). In 1993, Koza (Koza, 1993) used genetic programming to evolve developmental rewrite rules (Lindenmayer system rules) using a turtle to create shapes such as the quadratic Koch island. In 1996, Koza, Bennett, Andre, and Keane (Koza et al., 1996a) used developmental genetic programming to automatically synthesize a variety of analog electrical circuits, including several previously patented circuits and human-competitive results and provided for reuse of portions of circuits (by means of subroutines and iterations), parameterized reuse, and hierarchical reuse of substructures in evolving circuits (Koza et al., 1996b). In 1996, Brave (Brave, 1996) used developmental genetic programming to evolve finite automata. In 1996, Spector and Stoffel (Spector and Stoffel, 1996) extended the notion of development to genetic programming.

The widely-used and well-established format for optical prescriptions (and lens files for optical analysis software) suggests a developmental process suitable for representing optical lens systems. This developmental representation employs a turtle similar to that used in the Lindenmayer systems (Lindenmayer, 1968), (Prusinkiewicz and Lindenmayer, 1990), in our previous work in synthesizing geometric patterns (such as the Koch island) where we used developmental genetic programming and a turtle (Koza, 1993). These two techniques were also used in our other works in synthesizing antennas (Comisky et al., 2000), (Koza et al., 2003).

The function set, F, contains two functions:

$$F = \{AS4, PROGN2\}$$

The two-argument PROGN2 function is a connective function that first executes its first argument and then executes its second argument.

The four-argument AS4 ("aspherical surface") function causes the turtle to do three things at its starting point (and each subsequent point to which the turtle moves). First, it inserts an aspherical surface with a specified radius of curvature (second argument of the AS4 function) and specified coefficient C_4 (fourth argument) at the turtle's present location. Second, the AS4 function moves the turtle to the right by a specified distance (first argument) along the system's main axis. Third, the AS4 function fills the space to the right of the just-added surface with a specified type of material (third argument).

Values for radius of curvature (second argument of the AS4 function), distance (first argument), and the coefficient C_4 (fourth argument) are each established by a value-setting subtree of the AS4 function consisting of a single perturbable numerical value. The material (third argument of the AS4 function) is established by a value-setting subtree of the AS4 function consisting of a single terminal identifying the type of material.

The following LISP S-expression represents the optical lens system of Figure 3-1 and Table 3-1:

```
(PROGN2 (PROGN2 (PROGN2 (AS4 0.333334 40.07506 SK55 0.0)
                        (AS4 0.016667 -1.01667 Air 0.0))
                (PROGN2 (AS4 0.500001 1.083335 SK5 0.0)
                        (AS4 0.166667 -1.08334 SFL6 0.0)))
        (PROGN2 (PROGN2 (AS4 0.125 11.66668 Air 0.0)
                        (AS4 0.125 1E10 K10 -0.3715184))
                (AS4 0.317441 1E10 Air 0.0)))
```

In the previous expression, a radius of curvature of 1E10 corresponds to a flat surface.

Figures 3-2, 3-3, 3-4, 3-5, and 3-6 show selected steps in the developmental process for the Kaneko-Ueno lens system of Figure 3-1 and Table 3-1.

In our developmental representation, the turtle starts at point g of Figure 3-2. For the Kaneko-Ueno lens system, point g is at a distance of 1.09 mm from point e (where the entry pupil surface intersects the system's main axis b). This distance comes from the row labeled "entry pupil" in Table 3-1 and defines the eye relief of the Kaneko-Ueno system.

Figure 3-3 shows the result of the insertion of surface 1 with a radius of curvature of 40.07506 and a coefficient C_4 of 0 (as shown in the row labeled "1" in Table 3-1). A coefficient C_4 of 0 indicates that this surface is spherical. After inserting this (nearly flat) surface, the turtle moves 0.333334 mm from its starting point g to point h along axis line b. Glass of type "SK55" will fill the space between g and the surface that will be subsequently inserted at h (by the turtle's next step).

Figure 3-4 shows the result of the insertion by the turtle of surface 2 with a radius of curvature of −1.01667 and a coefficient C_4 of 0 (as shown in the row labeled "2" in Table 3-1). After inserting this surface, the turtle moves 0.016667 mm from point h to i. Surfaces 1 and 2 together define a lens of thickness 0.333334 of SK55 glass. Because air fills the space between h and the surface that will be subsequently inserted at i (by the turtle's next step), this lens is a singlet (stand-alone) lens.

Figure 3-5 shows the lens of SK5 glass resulting from the insertion of surfaces 3 and 4 corresponding to the rows labeled "3" and "4" in Table 3-1.

Figure 3-6 shows the result of the insertion by the turtle of surface 5 with a radius of curvature of 11.66668 and a coefficient C_4 of 0 (as shown in the row labeled "5" in Table 3-1). Because SFL6 glass fills the space to the right of surface 4, a doublet is formed by the insertion of surface 5. The doublet consists of a lens of SK5 glass and a lens of SFL6 glass.

Finally, surfaces 6 and 7 are inserted (corresponding to the rows labeled "6" and "7" in Table 3-1). Surfaces 6 and 7 together define a lens of thickness 0.125 of K10 glass. This final lens is shown at the right end of Figure 3-1. Surfaces 6 and 7 both have an infinite radius of curvature. Surface 7 is totally flat because its aspherical coefficient C_4 is 0. However, surface 6 has a non-zero aspherical adjustment (a coefficient C_4 of −0.3715184). Thus, in the patented Kaneko-Ueno lens systems, the first three lenses shape the image and the final lens serves as an aspherical correction plate.

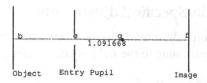

Figure 3-2. Turtle starts at point g along main axis b.

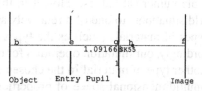

Figure 3-3. Turtle inserts surface 1.

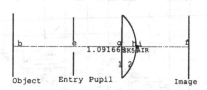

Figure 3-4. Turtle inserts surface 2 thereby completing the first singlet lens.

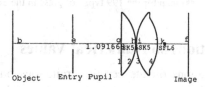

Figure 3-5. Turtle inserts surfaces 3 and 4 thereby completing the second singlet lens.

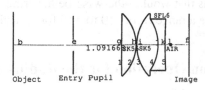

Figure 3-6. Turtle inserts surfaces 5 thereby completing the doublet.

4.   Five Domain-Specific Adjustments

Five domain-specific adjustments are necessary (or advantageous) in order to apply genetic programming to the field of optical design.

Glass Mutation Operation

In the field of optical design, the numerical parameter values for distance and the radius of curvature of a lens can each be established using the standard technique of perturbable numerical values. However, the choice of materials is limited, in real-world situations, to one of a relatively small number of commercially available types of materials (such as the types of glass found in the Schott catalog). Accordingly, our mutation operation for materials changes one type of material to another type of material in the chosen catalog (the offspring being nearby in the multidimensional space of properties for the materials as shown in Figure 3-7).

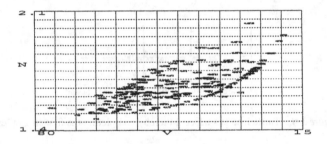

Figure 3-7. Glass map for the 199 types of glass in the Schott catalog.

Practical Limitations on Numerical Values

Practical considerations dictate certain limitations on the numeric values that are allowed for distance and radius of curvature. The minimum radius of curvature is −15 and the maximum is +15. The maximum thickness (for glass or air) is 1.0. The minimum thickness for air is 0.01 and the minimum thickness for glass is 0.1. The minimum aperture is 0.1 (where an opaque mounting is added to cradle a lens that would otherwise be hovering in air). The aspheric coefficient terms have a range from −10 to +10 for optical systems normalized to a focal length of 1.

Toroidal Mutation Operation for the Radius of Curvature

However, a slight modification of the standard method for numerical parameter mutation is advantageous when perturbing the radius of curvature. The reason is that a flat surface can be viewed as a spherical surface with a very large positive or negative radius of curvature. That is, a very large positive or negative radius represents the same thing. Accordingly, our numerical parameter mutation operation for curvatures operates in a toroidal way (wrapping +15 to –15) when it is applied to a terminal representing the radius of curvature.

Lens Splitting Operation

A lens-splitting operation appears to be useful for the field of optical design. The lens-splitting operation is performed on a single parent selected probabilistically from the population based on its fitness. The lens-splitting operation replaces one randomly picked lens with two new lenses. Figure 3-8 shows an illustrative lens system and Figure 3-9 shows the result of applying the lens-splitting operation.

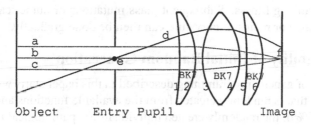

Figure 3-8. Lens system before lens-splitting operation.

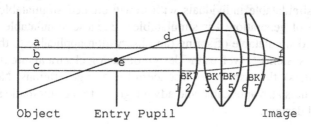

Figure 3-9. Lens system after lens-splitting operation.

The thickness of each of the two new lenses is half of the thickness of the original lens. The radius of curvature of the first surface of the first new lens is set equal to the radius of curvature of the first surface of the original lens. The radius of curvature of the second surface of the second new lens is set equal to the radius of curvature of the second surface of the original lens. The new second surface of the first lens also serves as the new first surface of the second lens. This new common surface is flat. When the original lens is a single lens (as is the case in Figure 3-8), the result of the lens splitting operation is a doublet lens (as shown in Figure 3-9). The lens-splitting operation is intended to be optically neutral (*i.e.*, it ordinarily does not change the fitness of the lens system involved). The only exception is that if half of the thickness of the original lens is less than the minimum permissible lens thickness, the thickness of each new lens is set to the minimum lens thickness (and the overall length of the lens system is slightly increased accordingly). Note that because of the toroidal behavior of the numerical parameter mutation operation, the newly created flat surface has an equal probability of being perturbed to a negative or positive radius of curvature when it is first mutated.

The motivation for the lens-splitting operation is that the insertion of additional surfaces or lenses by means of crossover rarely yields an improved individual. This operation creates a child that almost always has the same (reasonably good) fitness as its parent. It thus introduces topological diversity without changing fitness. Subsequent glass mutations or numerical mutations of the distance or radius of curvature can then be done gradually.

Simulatability of Initial Random Generation

The run of genetic programming described in this paper starts with an initial population that is randomly created from the available functions and terminals. About 94.6% of the randomly created individuals are pathological in some way and cannot be simulated. If we retained these individuals in the population for generation 0 (say, penalizing them heavily because of their unsimulatability), the genetic material generally available for crossovers would be only about 1/20 of what it otherwise might be. Thus, in creating generation 0, we replace unsimulatable individuals with newly created simulatable individual until 100% of generation 0 is simulatable. Because simulatable individuals tend to breed simulatable offspring (an observation applicable to the design of optical lens systems as well as the design of analog electrical circuits, antenna, and controllers), this issue is not a concern for later generations. Note that this improvement is also applicable and advantageous to the automatic synthesis of non-optical designs.

5.   Fitness

Once a classical optical system is specified by means of its prescription (lens file), its optical properties can be calculated by tracing the path of light rays of various wavelengths through the system. Ray-tracing analysis by hand is extremely time-consuming. Ray tracing is typically performed nowadays by optical simulation software (*e.g.*, OSLO, Zemax, Code V, KOJAC). The ray tracing analysis yields a set of characteristics of interest to optical designers, including distortion, astigmatism, and chromatic aberration. In addition to ray tracing for the ascertainment of aberrations, an optical lens systems is also evaluated in terms of the system's image-forming quality. To do this, a 17×17 grid is overlaid on the entry pupil and a ray is shot through the corner defining each grid position contained inside the entry pupil. A three-color spot diagram is then formed and evaluated. Several other system metrics are derived from this ddata, including modulation transfer functions and point spread functions.

A multiobjective fitness measure involving numerous elements is required for optical design. The fitness measure and other preparatory steps are substantially the same as those used in our recent work on the automatic synthesis of optical lens systems by means of genetic programming (Al-Sakran et al., 2005; Koza et al., 2005).

6.   Results

This run of genetic programming starts with an initial population (generation 0) that is randomly created from the available functions and terminals. In generation 0, we continued to replace unsimulatable individuals with new randomly created individuals until the entire initial population consisted of simulatable individuals. For non-trivial problems, even the simulatable individuals in the population at generation 0 of a run of genetic programming are invariably poor in terms of satisfying the problem's requirements. This was the case here. The best-of-generation individual from the initial random population (generation 0) consisted of a lens system with one lens (Figure 3-10).

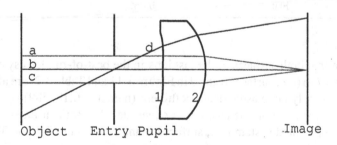

Figure 3-10. Best of generation 0 for the Kaneko-Ueno problem

Although the best-of-generation individual from generation 0 is poor in terms of satisfying the problem's requirements, the single lens provides a toehold that enables the evolutionary process to proceed. Figure 3-11 shows the best-of-run lens system from generation 746. This lens system has five lenses (arranged in four groups).

Table 3-2 shows the prescription (lens file) for the best-of-run individual.

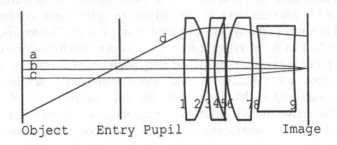

Figure 3-11. Best-of-run lens system from generation 746 for the Kaneko-Ueno problem.

Table 3-2. Lens file for best-of-run lens system from generation 746.

Surface	Distance	Radius	Material	Aperture	C_4
Object	10^{10}	Flat	Air		
Entry pupil	1.091668	Flat	Air	0.123873	
1	0.352192	10.35241	LAKN12	0.632926	0.0271156
2	0.01	−1.38146	Air	0.722105	0.0271156
3	0.100694	6.911665	SF59	0.72281	0.0271156
4	0.170295	1.693854	LAFN28	0.721309	0.0271156
5	0.01	−8.47601	Air	0.725851	0.0271156
6	0.39326	1.776476	LAK10	0.725661	0.0271156
7	0.125374	−7.75645	Air	0.654089	0.0271156
8	0.517407	−7.50353	SFL4A	0.607231	−0.180589
9	0.206743	6.893007	Air	0.515071	0.0271156
Image	Flat		0.462102		

Notice that both surfaces of the last lens in the best-of-run lens system from generation 746 (*i.e.*, surfaces 8 and 9 in Figure 3-11 and Table 3-2) are almost flat and that the only large aspherical coefficient (namely −0.180589) is associated with the left surface of this last lens (*i.e.*, surface 8). Both surfaces of the last lens of the patented system (*i.e.*, surfaces 6 and 7 of Figure 3-1 and Table 3-1) are flat and the only non-zero aspherical coefficient (namely −0.3715184) is associated with the left surface of the last lens (*i.e.*, surface 6).

Table 3-3 compares characteristics of the best-of-run individual from generation 746 with those of the patented lens system for the Kaneko-Ueno problem. In this table, lower values are better, with the exception of the except for the last three entries. As seen in the table, the evolved individual is superior to the lens system in the Kaneko-Ueno patent for each characteristic in the table (except for slight differences in two characteristics, coma and astigmatism, that are not listed among the inventors' design goals, as stated in the patent). Note that there is an order of magnitude reduction in distortion (the inventors' major goal as stated in the patent).

Table 3-3. Comparison of the Kaneko-Ueno systems and the genetically evolved system

	Kaneko-Ueno	Evolved
Coma	−0.001933	−0.002084
Astigmatism	0.003879	0.004130
Petzval	−0.008434	−0.007911
Distortion	−0.012582	−0.000239
Distortion Percentage	0.82	0.074
Max Distortion Percentage	0.82	0.083
Axial Chromatic	−0.000695	0.000067269
Lateral Chromatic	−0.003290	−0.002854
Spot RMS Axial Error	0.0	0.0
Spot RMS 70% FOV Error	0.308779	0.308562
Spot RMS Full Field Error	0.462908	0.456778
MTF Axial Tangential	0	0
MTF Axial Sagittal	0	0
MTF 70% Tangential	0	0
MTF 70% Sagittal	0	0
MTF Full Tangential	0	0
MTF Full Sagittal	0	0
Peak-Valley OPD Axial	0.07581	0.06772
RMS OPD Axial	0.02322	0.02075
Peak-Valley OPD 70%	0.484	0.398
RMS OPD 70%	0.09556	0.07959
Peak-Valley OPD Full	0.8392	0.5497
RMS OPD Full	0.1664	0.1197 0
Peak PSF Axial	0.956	0.9830
Peak PSF 70% Field	0.5975	0.6150
Peak PSF Full Field	0.29875	0.369
Spherical Aberration	−0.001403	−0.001268

Note that the last nine lines of Table 3-3 are measured quantities that are not part of the fitness measure. The best-of-run individual from generation 746 for the Kaneko-Ueno problem differs considerably from Kaneko-Ueno's patented invention (Kaneko and Ueno, 1996) and therefore does not infringe the patent. However, as shown in Table 3-4, the inventors' design goals, as stated in the patent, are achieved.

Thus, the best-of-run lens individual from generation 746 has performance superior to that of the lens system in the Kaneko-Ueno patent and accomplishes the inventors' major design goals. Therefore, the best-of-run lens individual is a non-infringing novel design that duplicates (and indeed improves upon) the performance specifications for the invention-that is, the evolved lens system can be considered as a new invention.

Table 3-4.   Design goals of the Kaneko-Ueno patent.

Kaneko-Ueno Patent	Genetically evolved
Wide field of view (50 degrees)	Wide field of view (50 degrees)
Reduced distortion across the field	Lens system has an order of magnitude reduction in distortion versus the patented system
Reduced lens count and size usable for binoculars (4 lenses)	Evolved solution has 5 lenses has a 22% larger footprint
Utilizes aspherical members	Utilizes aspherical members

One of the eight criteria presented in (Koza et al., 2003) for saying that an automatically created result is "human-competitive" is that:

> "The result was patented as an invention in the past, is an improvement over a patented invention, or would qualify today as a patentable new invention."

Based on our results and this definition, we claim that the genetically evolved design in this paper is an instance of a "human-competitive" result produced by genetic programming in the field of optical design.

7.   Conclusions

This chapter describes how genetic programming was used as an invention machine to automatically synthesize a complete design for an aspherical optical lens system (a type of lens system that is especially difficult to design and that offers advantages in terms of cost, weight, size, and performance over traditional spherical systems). The genetically evolved aspherical lens system duplicated the functionality of a recently patented aspherical system. The automatic synthesis was open-ended-that is, the process did not start from a pre-existing good design and did not pre-specify the number of lenses, which lenses (if any) should be spherical or aspherical, the topological arrangement of the lenses, the numerical parameters of the lenses, or the non-numerical parameters of the lenses. The genetically evolved design is an instance of human-competitive results produced by genetic programming in the field of optical design.

References

Al-Sakran, Sameer H., Koza, John R., and Jones, Lee W. (2005). Automated re-invention of a previously patented optical lens system using genetic programming. In Keijzer, Maarten, Tettamanzi, Andrea, Collet, Pierre, van Hemert, Jano I., and Tomassini, Marco, editors, *Proceedings of the 8th European Conference on Genetic Programming*, volume 3447 of *Lecture Notes in Computer Science*, pages 25–37, Heidelberg. Springer-Verlag, Heidelberg.

Alander, Jarmo T. (2000). An indexed bibliography of genetic algorithms in optics and image processing. Technical Report 94-1-OPTICS, Department of Information Technology and Production Economics, University of Vaasa; Vaasa, Finland.

Banzhaf, Wolfgang, Nordin, Peter, Keller, Robert E., and Francone, Frank D. (1998). *Genetic Programming – An Introduction; On the Automatic Evolution of Computer Programs and its Applications.* Morgan Kaufmann Publishers, Inc.

Beaulieu, Julie, Gagné, Christian, and Parizeau, Marc (2002). Lens system design and re-engineering with evolutionary algorithms. In Langdon, W. B., Cantú-Paz, E., Mathias, K., Roy, R., Davis, D., Poli, R., Balakrishnan, K., Honavar, V., Rudolph, G., Wegener, J., Bull, L., Potter, M. A., Schultz, A. C., Miller, J. F., Burke, E., and Jonoska, N., editors, *GECCO 2002: Proceedings of the Genetic and Evolutionary Computation Conference*, pages 155–162, New York. Morgan Kaufmann Publishers.

Brave, Scott (1996). Evolving deterministic finite automata using cellular encoding.

Comisky, William, Yu, Jessen, and Koza, John R. (2000). Automatic synthesis of a wire antenna using genetic programming. In Whitley, Darrell, editor, *Late Breaking Papers at the 2000 Genetic and Evolutionary Computation Conference*, pages 179–186, Las Vegas, Nevada.

Fischer, Robert E. and Tadic-Galeb, Biljana (2000). *Optical System Design.* McGraw-Hill, New York, NY.

Gruau, F. (1992). Cellular encoding of genetic neural networks. Technical report 92-21, Laboratoire de l'Informatique du Parallilisme. Ecole Normale Supirieure de Lyon, France.

Holland, John H. (1992). *Adaptation in Natural and Artificial Systems: An Introductory Analysis with Applications to Biology, Control, and Artificial Intelligence.* Complex Adaptive Systems. A Bradford book, The MIT Press, Cambridge MA, first MIT Press edition.

Kaneko, Masanobu and Ueno, Yasunori (1996). Aspherical eyepiece. Issued October 22, 1996.

Kitano, Hiroaki (1990). Designing neural networks using genetic algorithms with graph generation system. *Complex Systems*, 4(4):461–476.

Koza, John R. (1990). Genetic programming: A paradigm for genetically breeding populations of computer programs to solve problems. Technical Report STAN-CS-90-1314, Dept. of Computer Science, Stanford University.

Koza, John R. (1992). *Genetic Programming: On the Programming of Computers by Means of Natural Selection.* MIT Press, Cambridge, MA, USA.

Koza, John R. (1993). Discovery of rewrite rules in lindenmayer systems and state transition rules in cellular automata via genetic programming. In *Symposium on Pattern Formation (SPF-93), Claremont, California, USA.*

Koza, John R. (1994). *Genetic Programming II: Automatic Discovery of Reusable Programs*. MIT Press, Cambridge Massachusetts.

Koza, John R., Al-Sakran, Sameer H., and Jones, Lee W. (2005). Automated re-invention of six patented optical lens systems using genetic programming. In *To appear in GECCO-2005 Proceedings*.

Koza, John R., Andre, David, Bennett III, Forrest H, and Keane, Martin (1999). *Genetic Programming 3: Darwinian Invention and Problem Solving*. Morgan Kaufman.

Koza, John R., Bennett III, Forrest H, Andre, David, and Keane, Martin A (1996a). Automated design of both the topology and sizing of analog electrical circuits using genetic programming. In Gero, John S. and Sudweeks, Fay, editors, *Artificial Intelligence in Design '96*, pages 151–170, Dordrecht. Kluwer Academic.

Koza, John R., Bennett III, Forrest H, Andre, David, and Keane, Martin A (1996b). Reuse, parameterized reuse, and hierarchical reuse of substructures in evolving electrical circuits using genetic programming. In Higuchi, Tetsuya, Masaya, Iwata, and Liu, Weixin, editors, *Proceedings of International Conference on Evolvable Systems: From Biology to Hardware (ICES-96)*, volume 1259 of *Lecture Notes in Computer Science*, Tsukuba, Japan. Springer-Verlag.

Koza, John R., Keane, Martin A., Streeter, Matthew J., Mydlowec, William, Yu, Jessen, and Lanza, Guido (2003). *Genetic Programming IV: Routine Human-Competitive Machine Intelligence*. Kluwer Academic Publishers.

Langdon, W. B. and Poli, Riccardo (2002). *Foundations of Genetic Programming*. Springer-Verlag.

Lindenmayer, A. (1968). Mathematic models for cellular interactions in development. *Journal of Theoretical Biology*, 18:280–315.

Prusinkiewicz, P. and Lindenmayer, A. (1990). *The Algorithmic Beauty of Plants*. Springer-Verlag, New York.

Smith, Warren J. (1992). *Modern Lens Design: A Resource Manual*. McGraw-Hill, Boston, MA.

Smith, Warren J. (2000). *Modern Optical Engineering*. McGraw-Hill, New York, third edition.

Spector, Lee and Stoffel, Kilian (1996). Ontogenetic programming. In Koza, John R., Goldberg, David E., Fogel, David B., and Riolo, Rick L., editors, *Genetic Programming 1996: Proceedings of the First Annual Conference*, pages 394–399, Stanford University, CA, USA. MIT Press.

Wilson, Stewart W. (1987). The genetic algorithm and biological development. In Grefenstette, John J., editor, *Proceedings of the 2nd International Conference on Genetic Algorithms and their Applications*, pages 247–251, Cambridge, MA. Lawrence Erlbaum Associates.

Chapter 4

DISCRIMINATION OF UNEXPLODED ORDNANCE FROM CLUTTER USING LINEAR GENETIC PROGRAMMING

Frank D. Francone[1], Larry M. Deschaine[2], Tom Battenhouse[2] and Jeffrey J. Warren[3]

[1]RML Technologies, Inc and Chalmers University of Technology, 7606 S. Newland St., Littleton CO USA 80128; [2]Science Applications International Corp. and Chalmers University of Technology, 360 Bay St., Augusta GA USA 30901; [3]Science Applications International Corp., 6310 Allentown Boulevard., Harrisburg, PA USA 17112.

Abstract   We used Linear Genetic Programming (LGP) to study the extent to which automated learning techniques may be used to improve Unexploded Ordinance (UXO) discrimination from Protem-47 and Geonics EM61 non-invasive electromagnetic sensors. We conclude that: (1) Even after geophysicists have analyzed the EM61 signals and ranked anomalies in order of the likelihood that each comprises UXO, our LGP tool was able to substantially improve the discrimination of UXO from scrap—preexisting techniques require digging 62% more holes to locate all UXO on a range than do LGP derived models; (2) LGP can improve discrimination even though trained on a very small number of examples of UXO; and (3) LGP can improve UXO discrimination on data sets that contain a high-level of noise and little preprocessing.

Keywords: genetic programming, unexploded ordnance, UXO discrimination.

1.   Introduction

The Department of Defense (DoD) recently stated: "The UXO cleanup problem is a very large-scale undertaking involving 10 million acres of land at some 1400 sites (Report 2003)." One of the key problems is, according to DoD, ". . . instruments that can detect the buried UXO's also detect numerous scrap metal objects and other artifacts, which leads to an enormous amount of expensive digging. Typically 100 holes may be dug before a real

UXO is unearthed (Report 2003)!" Buried UXO poses a hazard to life-and-limb and further prevents huge tracts of land—frequently urban—from being returned to civilian use.

Digital Geophysical Mapping

Geophysicists have recently begun gathering magnetic and electromagnetic data about potential UXO sites using non-invasive, above-ground sensors. They gather UXO data by pulling various active and passive sensors across a UXO site and record the sensor readings. This process is called Digital Geophysical Mapping ('DGM'). Unfortunately, the digital signal for UXO frequently resembles the signal from clutter (scrap metal that poses no danger to the public) and OE fragments (pieces of UXO that have sheared-off during impact). Figure 4-1 illustrates the difficulty of distinguishing UXO from clutter. Currently, most UXO discrimination from DGM is made by human experts analyzing the DGM signal.

The UXO Discrimination Process

This paper reports the successful application of a process we refer to as UXO/MineFinder™ service to the problem of UXO discrimination on two data-sets acquired from DoD UXO test-beds. This is a multi-step process that includes five high-level tasks:

1. **Acquisition** of DGM data by geophysicists; We studied DGM data from the Jefferson Proving Grounds IV (Advanced 2000) and V (Cespedes 2001) test-plots (JPG-IV and JGP-V, respectively) for the two different phases of this study. For this study, DGM data acquisition (Step 1) was performed by third-party contractors engaged by the DoD. In particular, we used data acquired by NAVEA on a Protem-47 from JPG-IV (Geonics 2004) and by the National Research Laboratory (NRL) on an EM61 for JPG-V (Geonics 2004).

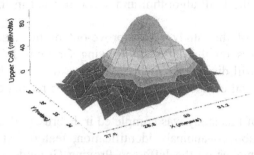

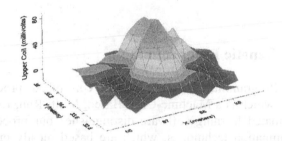

Figure 4-1. Signature of buried UXO (top) versus clutter (bottom)

2. **Anomaly Identification** by geophysicists of physical locations where the DGM indicates there may be potential UXO;

3. **Extraction** of relevant features pertaining to each anomaly by geophysicists;

4. **Ranking** of anomalies by the likelihood that the anomalies are UXO using the Linear Genetic Programming (Banzhaf 2003; Francone 2004) software, Discipulus™ (Francone 2002), and;

5. **Characterization** of UXO (such as ordnance type, depth, and orientation).

Paper Organization

This paper focuses on Step 4 of the UXO discrimination process, and is organized as follows.

First, Linear Genetic Programming is at the heart of our process. We will briefly describe the LGP algorithm and software used in this study in Section 2 below.

Second, Phase I of this study was a prove-out of the discrimination portion of our process on the Jefferson Proving Grounds IV data from NAVEA. Section 3 will discuss the methodology we used for this Phase I, the results obtained, and compare those results with the results obtained by other contractors.

Third, Phase II of this study was completed in February of 2004. Phase II tested Steps 2-4 above—anomaly identification, feature extraction and LGP ranking of anomalies on the Jefferson Proving Grounds V data from the NRL. Section 4, below, discusses the methodology we used for Phase II, our results, and compares them with the best-known results from other contractors.

2.   Linear Genetic Programming

Linear Genetic Programming ('LGP') is at the core of our process. We used Discipulus™, which is a Machine-Code-Based, Multi-Run, Linear GP system. This automated learning software distinguishes our process from other UXO discrimination techniques, which are based mostly on human engineering expertise.

Genetic Programming

Genetic Programming (GP) is the automatic, computerized creation of computer programs to perform a selected task using Darwinian natural selection. GP developers give their computers examples of how they want the computer to perform a task. Here, the 'examples' would be paired inputs and outputs—the inputs being features of the DGM and the output representing ground-truth: that is, Is the anomaly a UXO? From these examples, GP software then writes a computer program that performs the task described by the examples. Good overall treatments of Genetic Programming may be found in (Banzhaf 1998) and (Koza 1999).

LGP represents the evolving population of programs as linear genomes—that is, a linear string of executable instructions to the computer (Nordin 1998). The LGP algorithm is surprisingly simple. A detailed description of it is available in (Francone 2002) and (Francone 2004).

Machine-code-based, LGP is the direct evolution of binary machine code through GP techniques (Nordi 1998; Nordin 1994). Here, an evolved LGP program is a sequence of binary machine instructions. While LGP programs are apparently very simple, it is actually possible to evolve functions of great complexity using only simple arithmetic functions on a register machine (Nordin 1998; Nordin 1995; Fukunaga 1998). The machine-code approach to GP has been documented to be between 60 and 200 times faster than comparable interpreting systems (Nordin 1998; Nordin 1994; Fukunaga 1998).

Multi-Run LGP is based on our observation that, if one performs many runs with the same parameters, varying only the random seed, a histogram of best performance found in many different runs will tend to describe a normal-like distribution, with a long tail of good solutions (Fukunaga 1998; Francone 1996). To know that the full extent of the distribution of runs has been discovered, it is necessary to perform multiple LGP runs until a stable distribution is achieved. The LGP software we used performs this process automatically (Francone 2002).

After completing a multi-run LGP project, the LGP software decompiles the best evolved models from machine code into Java, ANSI C, or Intel Assembler programs (Francone 2002). The resulting decompiled code may be linked to other code and compiled or it may be compiled into a DLL or COM object.

Having now described the LGP software used, we will now turn to describing, in order, the two phases of this applied LGP project.

3.   Phase I: Proof-Of-Concept Study of JPG-IV, PROTEM-47 UXO DGM Signatures

Phase I of this investigation was a proof-of-concept phase that applied LGP to the JPG-IV test-bed data. JPG-IV is a research quality test-bed. UXO and clutter were buried at known locations and depths. Contractors with sensors were invited to measure the geophysical signatures at these known locations (Advanced 2000). Altogether, sensor readings for 50 UXO and 110 clutter items were available from the JPG-IV site.

This technique of gathering data is significantly different than is typical on an actual UXO site. On an actual UXO site, there is no preexisting knowledge of where to look for UXO. Accordingly, DGM must often be conducted for the entire site. Thus, the JPG-IV data is very high-quality data gathered from known anomalies and using sensors in a stationary mode, rather than being pulled across the site.

From the DGM, contractors attempted to discriminate between UXO and clutter (Advanced 2000). The DGM acquired by the various sensors at the JPG-IV locations were then made available to other contractors to test their ability to discriminate between UXO and clutter and it is these data that were used in Phase 1. Data was collected by NAEVA on the JPG-IV site using a Protem-47 transmitter and receiver, configured with 20 time-gates (Geonics 2004). The data from all twenty time-gates were made available as inputs to the LGP algorithm.

The data were randomly split into training and validation sets, which were used, respectively to train the LGP algorithm and to select the best programs for testing on unseen data. A portion of the data was held back from the training and validation sets. LGP was run until a stable distribution of results was produced. At that point, the best program produced by LGP on the training and validation data sets was selected as the best program from the project.

Once a best-program was produced by LGP, it was tested on the held out data. All results reported here are on the unseen, held-out data.

The LGP software produced excellent results on the NAEVA data (Deschaine 2002). As noted above, out of ten contractors, only one produced results that were better than random guessing (Advanced 200). Their results are shown as small black points on Figure 4-2. Our results are shown as a large black point in the upper right-hand-corner of Figure 4-2. The arrow represents the amount by which our approach improved the discrimination results obtained by NAEVA using the same data we used. The difference between our results and those of the next best contractor, Geophex, Ltd., were statistically significant at the 95% level.

This test established that using LGP as a classifier tool for UXO discrimination was very promising. Accordingly, further testing was required to prove-out our process as an integrated production service. The next section details our findings in that regard.

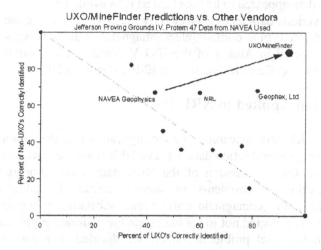

Figure 4-2. Comparison of UXO/MineFinder UXO Discrimination Results and Other Vendor's Discrimination Results on JPG-IV Test-Bed Data

4. Phase II: Production Prove-Out on The JPG-V, EM61 UXO DGM Signatures

Our Phase II prove-out was performed to test our process on production-grade data where it was necessary to integrate data-cleansing, anomaly-identification, feature-extraction and selection and UXO-discrimination into a single package. This section reports our methodology and results for that prove-out.

Data Used in Production Prove-Out

We selected the NRL data from Jefferson Proving Grounds V, Area 3 (Cespedes 2001) as being most suitable to the goals of this project because:

- The JPG-V project was designed to mimic an actual impact area. The DoD's JPG IV project failed to do so in several regards (Advanced 2000);
- The JPG-V data was from production-quality instruments and collection techniques, rather than research-quality;
- The JPG-V data was gathered by contractors in a manner consistent with data acquisition in the field—trailers bearing sensors were pulled across the JPG-V site.

- The NRL data appeared to be the cleanest data available.

From the various data feeds collected by the NRL, we chose the NRL's single time-channel time-domain electromagnetic induction sensor data (MTADS), collected in Area 3 of the JPG V demonstration survey. The instrument used to collect the data was an EM61 (Geonics 2004).

Preprocessing Applied to NRL Data

While the NRL data appeared to be the highest-quality data amongst the three contractors, no calibration data was available from the NRL to iron out inconsistencies. On examination of the NRL data, there appeared to be substantial calibration problems as among tracks. In addition, the background level of geomagnetic noise varies substantially within single tracks of data. We elected not to try to correct the calibration problems and background noise level problems; rather, we decided to allow the LGP classifier to model the calibration and background noise along with the target signals.

Our preprocessing was, therefore, limited to gridding the data using standard procedures recommended by the Geosoft Oasis-Montaj geophysical software (an industry standard for geophysical surveying) for target identification using the default parameters.

Anomaly Identification

Anomaly selection represents the first critical UXO screening step. Advanced geophysical data processing attempts to balance target area selection of UXO with weak observed signals (because background clutter or nearby UXO create a complex signal) with the selection of a disproportionate number of target areas containing no UXO.

We used Geosoft Oasis-Montaj to select potential targets in the JPG-V, Area 3 field. The procedure was straightforward. We set a threshold of six millivolts as the smallest anomaly that should be identified as a target. Given that threshold, Geosoft located three-hundred forty-two anomalies that we thereafter treated as our targets for classification.

Feature Extraction for the Identified Targets

The JPG-V Area 3 data from NRL was transformed into a set of 1D (point statistics) and 2D (spatial statistics) features. Only physically meaningful features were generated so that the physical interpretation of evolved prediction algorithms was not prohibitively difficult.

The 1D features used were the Geosoft created values for Upper and Lower Coil readings for each identified target.

Generation of 2D features included analysis of both the gridded data and the raw data. 2D analyses of gridded data utilized standard image processing algorithms. Techniques, such as subsampling, morphological processing, and 2D filtering, were used to preprocess the gridded data. An example of extracted 2D features are the major and minor axes of an anomaly at a point 50% of the way up the anomaly and at a point located 95% of the way toward the bottom of the anomaly from the top.

Methodology for Creating LGP Target Rankings

In UXO cleanup, the primary tool used to guide engineers is called a 'dig-list.' It identifies each anomaly and its coordinates. A dig-list is often prioritized. That is, it includes instructions where to dig first, where to dig next and so forth.

This project was posed to create an efficient prioritization for the JPG-V site dig list. Efficiency is tested by how many holes must be dug (starting with the highest ranked hole and proceeding down the list) until all UXO have been located. The fewer holes dug before all UXO are located, the lower the cost of the project (Francone 2004). This measure of performance is preferred over a more classic machine learning classification confusion matrix approach because this methodology was used by the DoD in assessing contractor's performance on the JGP-V test bed (Cespedes 2001).

Our principal concern about the JPG-V, Area 3 data we used was that Geosoft located only nineteen UXO and thirty-three OE fragments.[1] This is a very small number of positive examples of UXO. Many of our decisions in configuring LGP for this project were intended to minimize overfitting arising from such a small data set.

There were several sub-tasks performed in deriving anomaly rankings using LGP. They were: (1) Feature selection; (2) LGP Configuration; (3) Creating multiple data sets; (4) Setting LGP parameters; and (6) Converting LGP outputs into Rankings. Each of these steps is discussed below.

---

[1] Altogether, there were twenty UXOs on site. But Geosoft failed to identify one of them as a target. So information about that UXO was never presented to the LGP algorithm.

Feature Selection

We started with thirty-six features for each anomaly. Given the small number of UXO and fragment signatures, we were confident that we would not be successful with LGP using all of these features as inputs because of overfitting problems. Thus, we went through a three-step winnowing process to select the most promising features.

The first step of the winnowing process involved statistical analysis of the various features to select those features with the most significant relationship with the classification task and with the lowest cross-correlation amongst the inputs themselves[16]. We used primarily correlation analysis and ANOVA for this step.

The second step involved using the feature set in traditional modeling tools such as logistic regression and classification trees, for two purposes: (1) To determine which features provided the most UXO discrimination ability, and (2) to determine whether either of these traditional tools produced satisfactory discrimination results. There were no surprises from this process in terms of feature selection—it merely confirmed our earlier statistical analysis. This step also made clear that these traditional modeling tools did not perform particularly well in discriminating UXO from clutter. Accordingly, we determined that a more powerful modeling tool, such as LGP, was required.

The third step involved further narrowing the number of features used by conducting multiple LGP runs and examining the "Input Impacts" report generated by the LGP software. That report tells which inputs to LGP were actually used by LGP in a significant way to solve the problem[4]. For example, this "Input Impacts" report shows how frequently each input appears in the thirty best programs of a Discipulus™ project and the effect on fitness of those thirty best programs of replacing each input with a series containing only the average value of that input. From this information, it is quite simple to determine which inputs are contributing least to solving the problem and to eliminate those inputs in subsequent projects. We iterated thru this process three times, each time removing some inputs from the project until removal of further inputs began to effect the quality of the solutions.

When these three winnowing steps were concluded, we selected eight inputs to use in LGP for the remainder of our runs.

LGP Configuration

Based on an input-by-input statistical analysis, we determined that it might be possible to use the OE Fragment data points as "quasi-positive" examples of UXO. ANOVA for many of the extracted features revealed that the mean of their values for OE Fragments was between the mean values for UXO and Clutter. Furthermore, the mean value of those features for fragments was considerably closer to the mean UXO value than the mean clutter value. This raised the possibility that the OE Fragment anomalies contained useful information about what UXO looked like. Because of the small data set size, this possibility was very attractive because it increased the amount of information available to the LGP algorithm about the characteristics of a UXO as opposed to clutter.

Of course, to use OE Fragments in this manner required that we configure LGP for regression and assign different, but sensible, target values for UXO, OE Fragments and clutter.

Based on these observations, we configured LGP for regression and assigned the following values to as the target output to be approximated: For clutter, we assigned a regression target output value of 0. For OE Fragments, we assigned a regression target output of 0.75. Finally for UXO, we assigned a regression target output of 1.0. These values reflected the reality that OE Fragment feature values tended to fall between UXO values and clutter feature values but were closer to the UXO feature value than to the clutter value.

We interpreted the LGP output as a ranking. That is, higher output values were ranked higher than lower output values. Thus, the highest output was ranked as the most likely to be UXO.

Multiple Data Sets

Because there were a total of fifty-two UXO and OE Fragment items, we created fifty-two separate data-sets. Each of those data-sets held out as unseen data only one of the UXO or Fragment items together with 145 clutter points for model validation. The clutter points were chosen randomly for each of the 52 data sets. After creating the held-out data set, the remaining data points were used for model creation.

Thus, we performed in effect 55-fold cross-validation, with the stipulation that each cross-validation data set contained one—and only one—example of a UXO or fragment. Because of our scheme, the clutter points appeared in multiple cross-validation data sets. To obtain a single prediction for a particular data point, we averaged the rankings across all 55 cross-validation sets.

LGP Parameter Settings

Several runs were performed on several of the data sets to come up with a parameterization of LGP that provided enough robustness and generalization to solve the problem, but not so much as to overfit the data. Based on this, we started all runs using the default parameters of Discipulus™ except for the setting for run termination, which we reduced to 10 generations without improvement. This decision was made based on preliminary runs which indicated that seldom was more time needed to derive a good quality model from the data, and that additional time in the run sometimes lead to overfitting.

LGP was then run separately on all 52 data sets using the base parameter settings derived above. Each run was observed while in progress for overfitting—sampling noise makes it unlikely that the same parameters will be optimal for reducing overfitting for all data sets. In checking for overfitting, we watched for situations in which the fitness of the targets for training LGP was negatively correlated with the fitness on the held-out targets.

Fewer than half of the runs showed signs of overfitting. For those runs, we progressively changed the LGP parameters so as to reduce the computational power available to the LGP algorithm until observed overfitting was minimized. At that point, we inserted a new random seed into the LGP algorithm and ran it at those parameters. The resulting run was then accepted as the production run.

Converting LGP Outputs into Anomaly Rankings

We converted LGP outputs on unseen data points into anomaly rankings as follows: for each of the fifty-two data sets, the anomalies held out as unseen data were ranked so that the anomaly with the highest LGP output was ranked number 1, the next highest ranked as number 2, and so forth. Then those rankings were averaged for each anomaly over each of the data sets in which the anomaly appeared as an unseen data point. That average ranking was the ranking assigned to a particular anomaly for our simulated prioritized dig list.

Evaluation of LGP Prioritized Dig-List

The LGP produced rankings of the 342 anomalies in JPG-V, Area 3 were evaluated against UXO predictions on these same data derived from best-known conventional methods. Those best-known results are reported in the DoD's JPG-V final report for Area 3 (Cespedes 2001). The results of the comparison may be stated simply: The previous best UXO discrimination results on these data were reported by the geophysicists at NRL. NRL's rankings of anomalies required that ninety-six holes be dug before the last UXO was located. The LGP prioritized dig list required that only sixty-four holes be dug before the last UXO was located. Thus, the NRL ranking required digging 62% more holes than did the LGP based ranking. Figure 4-3 shows the results of our rankings in a pseudo-ROC format.

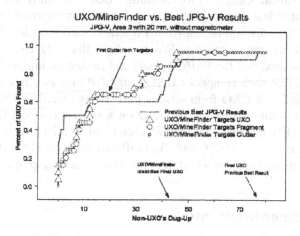

Figure 4-3. Ranked Anomalies for JPG-V, Area 3. Comparison of LGP Based Rankings and Rankings by Previous Best Results for JPG-V, Area 3.

Thus, if the order of digging were determined entirely by prioritization, and digging ceased when the last UXO was uncovered, the LGP based rankings would have required digging forty-five empty holes (that is, holes not containing a UXO) and the NRL rankings would have dug seventy-seven empty holes.

Digging up OE fragments is a secondary goal in UXO cleanup. Forty-five of the top sixty-four targets identified by our process contained OE fragments. In a field project, those fragments would be recovered in the process of digging up the UXOs. In fact, only nineteen truly empty anomalies were prioritized by LGP above the lowest priority UXO.

5.   Future Work

In Francone (Francone 2004), we described an information theoretic optimal method to apply machine learning techniques to UXO discrimination across an entire site, even though no ground-truth is available at the start of the site cleanup. This technique permits *site-specific* discrimination that takes into account factors such as soil conditions and peculiarities of UXO distribution, munition type and depth on a particular site. Our next step will be to apply LGP in the site-specific manner outlined in that work.

6.   Conclusion

We used Linear Genetic Programming (LGP) to study the extent to which automated learning techniques may be used to improve Unexploded Ordinance (UXO) discrimination from Protem-47 and Geonics EM61 non-invasive electromagnetic sensors. We conclude that: (1) Even after geophysicists have analyzed the EM61 signals and ranked anomalies in order of the likelihood that each comprises UXO, our LGP tool was able to improve the discrimination of UXO from scrap—preexisting techniques require digging 62% more holes to locate all UXO on a range than do LGP derived models; (2) LGP can improve discrimination even if trained on a very small number of examples of UXO; and (3) LGP can improve UXO discrimination on data sets that contain a high-level of noise and little preprocessing.

7.   Acknowledgments

The researchers would like to extend their thanks to Dr. Clinton W. Kelly III, manager of SAIC's Internal Research and Development division, who supported this research with management and technical analysis, and by providing corporate funding to get the concept off the drawing board and into productive research.

References

Report of the Defense Science Board Task Force on Unexploded Ordnance. Department of Defense. December (2003).

Francone, F. D., and Deschaine, L.M.: Extending the Boundaries of Design Optimization by Integrating Fast Optimization Techniques with Machine-Code-Based Linear Genetic Programming. In: Information Sciences Journal, Elsevier Press, In-press: Amsterdam, The Netherlands (2004).

Francone, F. D., Discipulus Owner's Manual. RML Technologies, Inc. (2002). Available at www.aimlearning.com.

Advanced UXO Detection/Discrimination Technology Demonstration, U.S. Army Jefferson Proving Ground, Madison, Indiana,. Technology Demonstration Plan, Washington, DC. Naval Explosive Ordnance Disposal Technology Division (NAVEOD-TECHDIV). (2000).

Cespedes, E.: Advanced UXO Detection/Discrimination Technology Demonstration—U.S. Army Jefferson Proving Ground, Madison, Indiana. US Army Corps of Engineers, Engineer Research and Development Center, ERDC/EL TR-01-20 (2001).

Geonics, Ltd., http://www.geonics.com/tdem.html (2004)

Geonics, Ltd., http://www.geonics.com/em61.html (2004).

J. Koza, J., Bennet, F., Andre, D., Keane, M.: Genetic Programming III, Morgan Kaufman, San Francisco, CA, (1999).

Nordin, P., Francone, F. Banzhaf, W.: Efficient Evolution of Machine Code for CISC Architectures Using Blocks And Homologous Crossover. In: Advances in Genetic Programming 3, MIT Press, Cambridge, MA (1998).

Nordin, P.: A Compiling Genetic Programming System that Directly Manipulates the Machine Code. In: K. Kinnear Jr. (Ed.), Advances in Genetic Programming, MIT Press, Cambridge, MA, 1994.

Nordin, P, Banzhaf, W.: Evolving Turing Complete Programs for a Register Machine with Self Modifying Code. In: Proceedings of Sixth International Conference of Genetic Algorithms, Morgan Kaufmann Publishers, Inc., 1995.

Fukunaga, A. Stechert, D. Mutz, A: A Genome Compiler for High Performance Genetic Programming. In: Proceedings of the Third Annual Genetic Programming Conference, Jet Propulsion Laboratories, California Institute of Technology Pasadena, CA, Morgan Kaufman Publishers (1998), pp. 86–94.

Francone, F., Nordin, P., Banzhaf, W.: Benchmarking the Generalization Capabilities of a Compiling Genetic Programming System using Sparse Data Sets. In: Koza et al. (Eds.), Proceedings of the First Annual Conference on Genetic Programming, Stanford, CA, (1996).

Deschaine, L. M., Hoover, R. A., Skibinski, J. N., Patel, J. J., Francone, F. D., Nordin, P. and Ades, M. J.: Using Machine Learning to Compliment and Extend the Accuracy of UXO Discrimination Beyond the Best Reported Results of the Jefferson Proving Ground Technology Demonstration. In: Proceedings of the Society for Modeling and Simulation International's Advanced Technology Simulation Conference, April 2002. San Diego, CA, USA (2002).

Hall, M.: Correlation-based Feature Selection for Machine Learning. PhD Dissertation. The University of Waikato, Hamilton New Zealand (1999).

Francone, F. D. and Deschaine L.M: Getting It Right at the Very Start - Building Project Models where Data is Expensive by Combining Human Expertise, Machine Learning and Information Theory. In: Proceedings of the Business and Industry Symposium, 2004 Advanced Simulation Technologies Conference (Arlington, Virginia, April 18 - 22, 2004), The Society for Modeling and Simulation International, 162-168

Chapter 5

RAPID RE-EVOLUTION OF AN X-BAND ANTENNA FOR NASA'S SPACE TECHNOLOGY 5 MISSION

Jason D. Lohn[1], Gregory S. Hornby[2] and Derek S. Linden[3]

[1]*NASA Ames Research Center;* [2]*QSS Group Inc.;* [3]*JEM Engineering*

Abstract   One of the challenges in engineering design is adapting a set of created designs to a change in requirements. Previously we presented two four-arm, symmetric, evolved antennas for NASA's Space Technology 5 mission. However, the mission's orbital vehicle was changed, putting it into a much lower earth orbit, changing the specifications for the mission. With minimal changes to our evolutionary system, mostly in the fitness function, we were able to evolve antennas for the new mission requirements and, within one month of this change, two new antennas were designed and prototyped. Both antennas were tested and both had acceptable performance compared with the new specifications. This rapid response shows that evolutionary design processes are able to accommodate new requirements quickly and with minimal human effort.

Keywords: design, computational design, evolutionary design, antenna, spacecraft

1.   Introduction

One of the challenges in engineering design is adapting a set of created designs to a change in requirements. Previously we presented our work in using evolutionary algorithms to automatically design an X-band antenna for NASA's Space Technology 5 (ST5) spacecraft (Lohn et al., 2004). Since our original evolutionary runs and the fabrication and testing of antennas ST5-3-10 and ST5-4W-03, the launch vehicle for the ST5 spacecraft has changed resulting in a lower orbit and different antenna requirements. With traditional engineering design, such a change in requirements would necessitate redoing much of the design work with a near doubling of design costs. In contrast,

Table 5-1. Key ST5 Antenna Requirements

Property	Specification
Transmit Frequency	8470 MHz
Receive Frequency	7209.125 MHz
VSWR	$< 1.2 : 1$ at Transmit Freq
	$< 1.5 : 1$ at Receive Freq
Original Gain Pattern	≥ 0 dBic, $40° \leq \theta \leq 80°, 0° \leq \phi \leq 360°$
Additional Gain Pattern Requirement	≥ -5 dBic, $0° \leq \theta \leq 40°, 0° \leq \phi \leq 360°$
Input Impedance	$50\ \Omega$
Diameter	< 15.24 cm
Height	< 15.24 cm
Antenna Mass	< 165 g

with an evolutionary design system for automatically creating antennas, once the software has been developed, modifying it to produce antennas for a similar design problem requires only a minimal amount of human effort to implement the change with minimal additional cost.

The ST5 mission consists of three spacecrafts which will orbit at close separations in a highly elliptical geosynchronous transfer orbit, and will communicate with a 34 meter ground-based dish antenna.[1] Initially, the spacecrafts were to fly approximately 35,000 km above Earth and the requirements for the communications antenna were for a gain pattern of ≥ 0 dBic from 40° - 80° from zenith, a voltage standing wave ratio (VSWR) of under 1.2 at the transmit frequency (8470 MHz) and under 1.5 at the receive frequency (7209.125 MHz), and fit inside a 6" cylinder.[2]

With the change in launch vehicle and the new lower orbit, this necessitated the addition of a new requirement on the gain pattern of ≥ -5 dBic from 0° - 40° from zenith. The complete set of requirements for the antennas on the ST5 Mission are summarized in Table 5-1.

In the rest of this chapter we describe the two evolutionary design systems we used for evolving the initial antennas for this mission and the changes we made to them to address the change in mission requirements. We then present the results of new antenna designs, both from simulation and from fabricated units. Finally we close with an overview of the challenges we experienced in taking our basic research in evolutionary antenna design all the way to fabricating and testing flight units that have successfully passed flight testing and will be launched in 2006.

---

[1]Space Technology 5 Mission: http://nmp.jpl.nasa.gov/st5/
[2]VSWR is a way to quantify reflected-wave interference, and thus the amount of impedance mismatch at the junction.

2.   Evolutionary Antenna Design Systems

The new mission requirements required us to change both the type of antenna we were evolving and the fitness function. The original antennas we evolved for the ST5 mission were constrained to a monopole wire antenna consisting of four identical arms, with each arm rotated 90° from its neighbors. There, the EA evolved genotypes that specified the geometry for one arm and the phenotype consisted of four copies of the evolved arm. Because of symmetry, the previous four-arm design has a null at zenith that is built into the design and is unacceptable for the revised mission. To achieve an antenna that meets the new mission requirements, designs were configured to produce a single arm. In addition, because of the difficulties we experienced in fabricating branching antennas to the required precision, we constrained our antenna designs to non-branching antennas. Finally, because the satellite is spinning at about 40 RPM, it is important that the antennas have a uniform gain pattern in azimuth. This is difficult to meet with a single-arm antenna, because it is inherently asymmetric.

In the remainder of this section, we describe the two evolutionary algorithms we used to evolve antennas for the ST5 mission and how we changed them to address the new requirements. The first algorithm was used in our previous work in evolutionary antenna design (Linden and Altshuler, 1996) and it is a standard genetic algorithm (GA) that evolves non-branching wire forms using a vector of real-valued parameters as its representation. The second algorithm is based on our previous work evolving rod-structured, robot morphologies (Hornby et al., 2003) and uses an open-ended representation which contains operations for constructing an antenna. In addition, the two evolutionary algorithms (EAs) use different fitness functions.

Parameterized EA

With the Parameterized EA, the design space consisted of a vector of real-valued triplets that specify the X, Y and Z locations of segment end-points. The fitness function for this EA used pattern quality scores at 7.2 GHz and 8.47 GHz. Unlike the second EA, VSWR was not explicitly used in this fitness calculation, rather it was included implicitly by how it affects the gain pattern. To quantify the pattern quality at a single frequency, PQ_f, the following formula was used:

$$PQ_f = \sum_{\substack{0° \le \phi < 360° \\ 0° \le \theta \le 80°}} (gain_{\phi,\theta} - T)^2, \quad \text{if } gain_{\phi,\theta} < T$$

where $gain_{\phi,\theta}$ is the gain of the antenna in dBic (right-hand polarization) at a particular angle, T is the target gain (3 dBic was used in this case), ϕ is the azimuth, and θ is the elevation. To compute the overall fitness of an antenna design, the pattern quality measures at the transmit and receive frequencies were summed, lower values corresponding to better antennas:

$$F = PQ_{7.2} + PQ_{8.47}$$

Modifying this evolutionary design system to produce antennas for the new orbit consisted of changing the fitness function to check angles $0° \leq \theta < 40°$ as well the original range of $40° \leq \theta \leq 80°$.

Open-Ended, Constructive EA

The second EA uses an open-ended representation in which the nodes of the genotype specify how to construct the antenna. Each node in the open-ended representation is an antenna-construction operator and an antenna is created by executing the operators at each node in the representation, starting with the root node. In constructing an antenna the current state (location and orientation) is maintained and operators add wires or change the current state. The operators are as follows:

- forward(length, radius) - add a wire with the given length and radius extending from the current location and then change the current state location to the end of the new wire.

- rotate-x(angle) - change the orientation by rotating it by the specified amount (in radians) about the x-axis.

- rotate-y(angle) - change the orientation by rotating it by the specified amount (in radians) about the y-axis.

- rotate-z(angle) - change the orientation by rotating it by the specified amount (in radians) about the z-axis.

Since we constrained antennas to a single bent wire with no branching, each node in the genotype has at most one child. This open-ended representation for encoding antennas is an extension of our previous work in using a linear-representation for encoding rod-based robots (Hornby et al., 2003).

Aside from restricting antennas to not having branches, the only other change made to this evolutionary design system to address the new mission requirements was the fitness function. The fitness function used to evaluate antennas is a function of the VSWR and gain values on the transmit and receive frequencies. The VSWR component of the fitness function is intended to put strong pressure to evolving antennas with receive and transmit VSWR values below the required amounts of 1.2 and 1.5, reduced pressure at a value below these requirements (1.15 and 1.25) and then no pressure to go below 1.1:

$$v_r = \text{VSWR at receive frequency}$$

$$v_r' = \begin{cases} v_r + 2.0(v_r - 1.25) & \text{if } v_r > 1.25 \\ v_r & \text{if } 1.25 > v_r > 1.1 \\ 1.1 & \text{if } v_r < 1.1 \end{cases}$$

$$v_t = \text{VSWR at transmit frequency}$$

$$v_t' = \begin{cases} v_t + 2.0(v_t - 1.15) & \text{if } v_t > 1.15 \\ v_t & \text{if } 1.15 > v_t > 1.1 \\ 1.1 & \text{if } v_t < 1.1 \end{cases}$$

$$vswr = v_r'v_t'$$

The gain-penalty component of the fitness function uses the gain (in dBic) in 5° increments about the angles of interest: from $0° \leq \theta \leq 90°$ and $0° \leq \phi \leq 360°$. For each angle, the calculated gain score from simulation is compared against the target gain for that elevation and the outlier gain, which is the minimum gain value beyond which lower gain values receive a greater penalty. Gain penalty values are further adjusted based on the importance of the elevation:

    gain penalty (**i, j**):
       gain = calculated gain at $\theta = 5° i$, $\phi = 5° j$;
       if (**gain** $\geq$ target[i]) {
         penalty := 0.0;
       } *else if* ((target[i] > **gain**) and (**gain** $\geq$ outlier[i])) {
         penalty := (target[i] - **gain**);
       } *else* {   /* outlier[i] > **gain** */
         penalty := (target[i]-outlier[i]) + 3.0 * (outlier[i] - **gain**));
       }
       return **penalty** * weight[i];

Target gain values at a given elevation are stored in the array `target[]` and are 2.0 dBic for i equal from 0 to 16 and are -3.0 dBic for i equal to 17 and 18. Outlier gain values for each elevation are stored in the array `outlier[]` and are 0.0 dBic for i equal from 0 to 16 and are -5.0 dBic for i equal to 17 and 18. Each gain penalty is scaled by values scored in the array `weight[]`. For the low band the values of `weight[]` are 0.1 for i equal to 0 through 7; values 1.0 for i equal to 8 through 16; and 0.05 for i equal to 17 and 18. For the high band the values of `weight[]` are 0.4 for i equal to 0 through 7; values 3.0 for i equal to 8 through 12; 3.5 for i equal to 13; 4.0 for i equal to 14; 3.5 for i equal to 15; 3.0 for i equal to 16; and 0.2 for i equal to 17 and 18. The final gain component of the fitness score of an antenna is the sum of gain penalties for all angles.

To put evolutionary pressure on producing antennas with smooth gain patterns around each elevation, the third component in scoring an antenna is based on the standard deviation of gain values. This score is a weighted sum of the standard deviation of the gain values for each elevation θ. The weight value used for a given elevation is the same as is used in calculating the gain penalty.

These three components are multiplied together to produce the overall fitness score of an antenna design:

$$F \; = \; vswr \times gain \times standard\,deviation$$

The objective of the EA is to produce antenna designs that minimize F.

This fitness function differs from the one we used previously (Lohn et al., 2004) in the fidelity to which the desired gain pattern can be specified and in explicitly rewarding for a smooth pattern. Our previous fitness function with the constructive EA had one target gain value for all elevations and weighted all elevations equally. With the new fitness function, different target gain values can be set for different elevation angles and also the importance of achieving the desired gain at a given angle is specified through setting the weight value for a given elevation. The other difference with this fitness function is that previously there was a separate penalty for "outlier" gain values whereas in the new fitness function, this is included in the gain component of the fitness score and a new component that measures pattern smoothness is also present. As described in the following section, these changes resulted in the evolution of antennas that had noticeably smoother patterns and acceptable gain.

3.   Evolved Antennas

To re-evolve antennas for the new ST5 mission requirements, we used the same EA setup as in our initial set of evolutionary runs. For the parameterized EA, a population of fifty individuals was used, 50% of which are kept from generation to generation. The mutation rate was 1%, with the Gaussian mutation standard deviation of 10% of the value range. The parameterized EA was halted after one hundred generations had been completed, the EA's best score was stagnant for forty generations, or the EA's average score was stagnant for ten generations. For the open-ended EA, a population size of two hundred individuals was evolved using generational evolution. Parents were selected with remainder stochastic sampling based on rank, using exponential scaling (Michalewicz, 1992). New individuals were created with an equal probability of using mutation or recombination.

The Numerical Electromagnetics Code, Version 4 (NEC4) (Burke and Poggio, 1981) was used to evaluate all antenna designs. Antennas were simulated on an infinite ground plane to reduce simulation time: for these runs a single antenna evaluation took a few seconds of wall-clock time to simulate and an entire run took approximately six to ten hours. In contrast, evaluating a single antenna using a wire mesh of the 6" ground plane on the spacecraft requires two to three minutes to simulate.

The best antennas evolved by the two EAs were then evaluated on a second antenna simulation package, WIPL-D, with the addition of a 6" ground plane to determine which designs to fabricate and test on the ST5 mock-up. Based on these simulations the best antenna design from each EA was selected for fabrication and these are shown in Figure 5-1. A sequence of evolved antennas that produced antenna ST5-33.142.7 is shown in Figure 5-2.

Simulated Results

Both antenna designs have excellent simulated RHCP patterns, as shown in Figure 5-3 for the transmit frequency. The antennas also have good circular polarization purity across a wide range of angles, as shown in Figure 5-4 for ST5-104.33. To the best of our knowledge, this quality has never been seen before in this form of antenna.

Measured Results

The antennas were measured on the ST5 mock-up (Figure 5-5), and the results are shown in Figure 5-6. The evolved antennas were arrayed with a Quadrafilar Helix Antenna (QHA) developed by New Mexico State University's Physical Science Laboratory (the original antenna for this mission). This figure shows plots of two QHA antennas together, a QHA, and an ST5-104.33 antenna. Results are similar for ST5-33.142.7. Compared to using two QHAs together, the evolved antennas have much greater gain across the angles of interest.

4. Discussion: From a Proof-of-Concept to Flight Hardware

Perhaps, just as interesting and useful as the science that went on in producing an evolutionary design system capable of evolving human-competitive antennas for a NASA space mission, are the steps taken in going from a simple proof-of-concept study to producing deployable flight hardware. Here we touch briefly on the highlights of this process.

Our work began as a series of proof-of-concept studies, using deployed antennas on NASA missions, for example, the quadrifilar UHF antenna on Mars Odyssey (Lohn et al., 2002). The results of that study were encouraging and lent us some credibility within the space communications community. Through a series of meetings, we learned of the ST5 mission. Our intent was to do another proof-of-concept study, mainly because we did not feel we were ready to build prototypes and we were entering the mission development so late, or so we thought at the time, that there was no chance to produce hardware for ST5.

We later learned that there were a series of delays in the ST5 schedule, which gave us enough time to fabricate our designs and field test them. Around

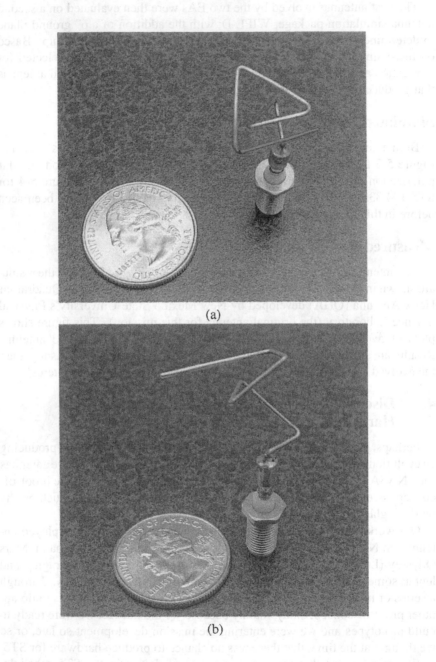

(a)

(b)

Figure 5-1. Evolved antenna designs: (a) evolved using a vector of parameters, named ST5-104.33; and (b) evolved using the open-ended, constructive representation, named ST5-33.142.7.

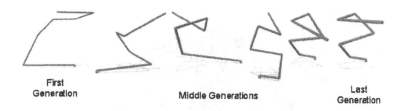

First
Generation

Middle Generations

Last
Generation

Figure 5-2. Sequence of evolved antennas leading up to antenna ST5-33.142.7.

this time, the conventionally designed quadrifilar antenna was going through prototype testing. We met the quadrifilar design team and they were intrigued with our approach and were receptive to working with us. Surprisingly, the only two designs that we prototyped in hardware worked on the test range as well as in simulation. Consequently, we stuck with these two designs for the baseline antennas that we later intended to fly on the ST5 mission (Lohn et al., 2004). When the ST5 mission managers saw the field patterns for the evolved antennas they informed us that they met the mission requirements and encouraged us to build space-qualified hardware.

Over the next year, we experienced a rollercoaster ride of hope and despair as we worked through space-hardware development and qualification. As we neared the end of this tumultuous twelve months, we were disheartened to learn of the change in orbit of the ST5 mission. This came with the resultant change in antenna requirements since our original pair of antennas did not meet the new mission requirements.

This change in requirements turned out to be a blessing in disguise because it showed the advantages of the evolutionary design process. Whereas the quadrifilar design team would likely have needed several months to develop a new antenna design and prototype it, we were able to re-evolve and prototype new antennas in four weeks. As we described in this paper, this was done by simply changing the fitness function to match the new antenna requirements and constraining designs to non-branching antennas.

The first set of ST5 evolved antenna flight units were delivered to Goddard Space Flight Center (GSFC) on February 25, 2005 (Figure 5-7) to undergo environmental tests. On April 8, 2005 the last test was completed. This process consisted of a thermal vacuum testing in which the antenna performed the above requirements during one survival cycle (-80°C to +80°C) and through each of eight qualification cycles (-70°C to +50°C). Having passed all tests, the current baseline plan is to fly at least three evolved antennas when the mission launches in 2006.

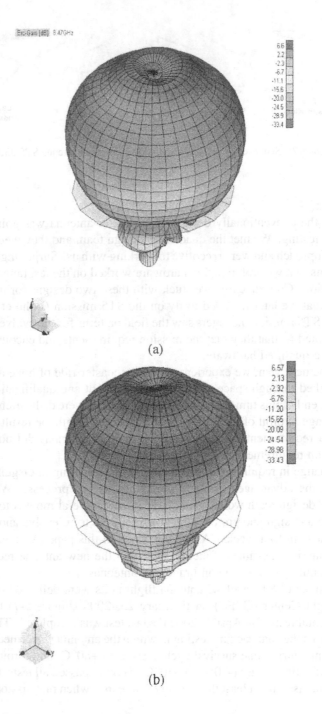

(a)

(b)

Figure 5-3. Simulated 3D patterns for ST5-104.33 and ST5-33.142.7 on 6" ground plane at 8470 MHz for RHCP polarization. Simulation performed by WIPL-D. Patterns are similar for 7209 MHz.

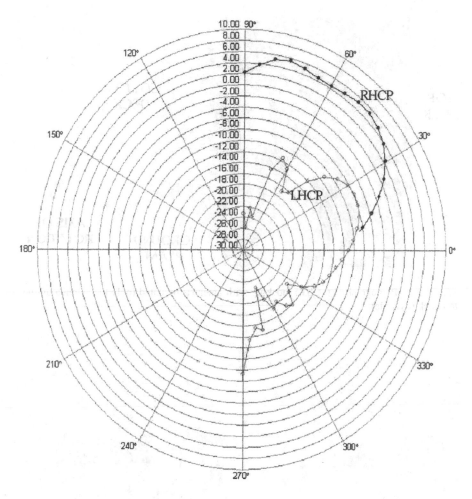

Figure 5-4. RHCP vs LHCP performance of ST5-104.33. Plot has 2 dB/division.

5. Conclusion

Previously, we reported our work on evolving two X-band antennas for potential use on NASA's upcoming ST5 mission to study the magnetosphere. While those antennas were mission compliant, a change in launch vehicle resulted in a change in orbit for the ST5 spacecraft and a change in requirements for their communication antennas. In response to this change in requirements, we reconfigured our evolutionary design systems and in under four weeks, we were able to evolve new antenna designs that were acceptable to ST5 mission planners. One of the evolved antennas, ST5-33.142.7, has passed all of the

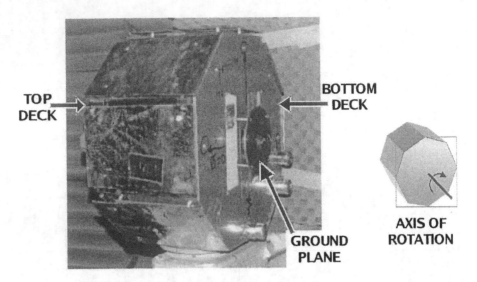

Figure 5-5. Photograph of the ST5 mock-up with antennas mounted (only the antenna on the top deck is visible).

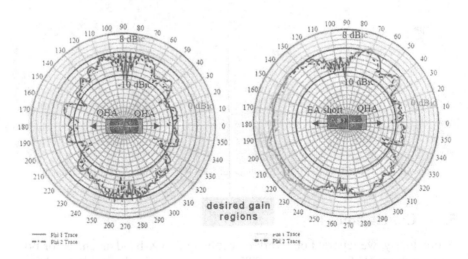

Figure 5-6. Measured patterns on ST-5 mock-up of QHA antenna and ST5-104.33 plus QHA antenna. Phi 1 = 0 deg., Phi 2 = 90 deg.

flight tests and the current plan is to fly at least three evolved antennas when these spacecraft are launched in 2006. Our ability to rapidly re-evolve new antenna designs shows that the evolutionary design process lends itself to rapid

Figure 5-7. Three images of a flight antenna; the evolved wire configuration for the radiator sits on top of a 6" diameter ground plane and is encased inside a radome

response to changing requirements, not only for automated antenna design but for automated design in general.

Acknowledgements

The work described in this paper was supported by Mission and Science Measurement Technology, NASA Headquarters, under its Computing, Information, and Communications Technology Program. The work was performed at the Computational Sciences Division, NASA Ames Research Center, Linden Innovation Research and JEM Engineering, and NASA Goddard Space Flight Center. The support of Ken Perko of Microwave Systems Branch at NASA Goddard and Bruce Blevins of the Physical Science Laboratory at New Mexico State University is gratefully acknowledged.

Appendix: Genotype of ST5-33.142.7

Listed below is the evolved genotype of antenna ST5-33.142.7. The format for this tree-structured genotype consists of the operator followed by a number stating how many children this operator has, followed by square brackets which start '[' and end ']' the list of the node's children. For example the format for a node which is operator 1 and has two subtrees is written: operator1 2 [subtree-1 subtree-2]. For the ST5 mission, antennas were constrained to be non-branching so each node in this genotype has at most one child, the only exception is the leaf node. The different operators in the antenna-constructing language are given in section 2.0.

```
rotate-z(0.723536) 1 [ rotate-x(2.628787) 1 [ rotate-z(1.145415) 1 [
rotate-x(1.930810) 1 [ rotate-z(2.069497) 1 [ rotate-x(1.822537) 1 [
forward(0.007343,0.000406) 1 [ rotate-z(1.901507) 1 [
forward(0.013581,0.000406) 1 [ rotate-x(1.909851) 1 [ rotate-y(2.345316)
1 [ rotate-y(0.308043) 1 [ rotate-y(2.890265) 1 [ rotate-x(0.409742) 1
[ rotate-y(2.397507) 1 [ forward(0.011671,0.000406) 1 [
rotate-x(2.187298) 1 [ rotate-y(2.497974) 1 [ rotate-y(0.235619) 1 [
rotate-x(0.611508) 1 [ rotate-y(2.713447) 1 [ rotate-y(2.631141) 1 [
forward(0.011597,0.000406) 1 [ rotate-y(1.573367) 1 [
```

```
forward(0.007000,0.000406) 1 [ rotate-x(-0.974118) 1 [
rotate-y(2.890265) 1 [ rotate-z(1.482916) 1 [ forward(0.019955,0.000406)
] ] ] ] ] ] ] ] ] ] ] ] ] ] ] ] ] ] ] ] ] ] ] ] ]
```

References

Burke, G. J. and Poggio, A. J. (1981). Numerical electromagnetics code (nec)-method of moments. Technical Report UCID18834, Lawrence Livermore Lab.

Hornby, Gregory S., Lipson, Hod, and Pollack, Jordan B. (2003). Generative representations for the automated design of modular physical robots. *IEEE transactions on Robotics and Automation*, 19(4):709–713.

Linden, D. S. and Altshuler, E. E. (1996). Automating wire antenna design using genetic algorithms. *Microwave Journal*, 39(3):74–86.

Lohn, J. D., Kraus, W. F., and Linden, D. S. (2002). Evolutionary optimization of a quadrifilar helical antenna. In *IEEE Antenna & Propagation Society Mtg.*, volume 3, pages 814–817.

Lohn, Jason, Hornby, Gregory, and Linden, Derek (2004). Evolutionary antenna design for a NASA spacecraft. In O'Reilly, Una-May, Yu, Tina, Riolo, Rick L., and Worzel, Bill, editors, *Genetic Programming Theory and Practice II*, chapter 18. Kluwer, Ann Arbor.

Michalewicz, Z. (1992). *Genetic Algorithms + Data Structures = Evolution Programs*. Springer-Verlag, New York.

Chapter 6

VARIABLE SELECTION IN INDUSTRIAL DATASETS USING PARETO GENETIC PROGRAMMING

Guido Smits[1], Arthur Kordon[2], Katherine Vladislavleva[1], Elsa Jordaan[1] and Mark Kotanchek[3]

[1]Dow Benelux, Terneuzen, The Netherlands; [2]The Dow Chemical Company, Freeport, TX; [3]The Dow Chemical Company, Midland, MI

Abstract   This chapter gives an overview, based on the experience from the Dow Chemical Company, of the importance of variable selection to build robust models from industrial datasets. A quick review of variable selection schemes based on linear techniques is given. A relatively simple fitness inheritance scheme is proposed to do nonlinear sensitivity analysis that is especially effective when combined with Pareto GP. The method is applied to two industrial datasets with good results.

Key words: Genetic programming, symbolic regression, variable selection, pareto GP

1.   Introduction

Many industrial applications are based on high-dimensional multivariate data. The dominant approach for data analysis in this case is dimensionality reduction by Principal Component Analysis (PCA) and building linear models with projections to latent structures by means of Partial Least Squares (PLS) (Eriksonn *et al*, 2001). This approach, however, has two key issues: (1) the model interpretation is difficult and (2) it is limited to linear systems. One approach to extend this to nonlinear systems is to use neural networks. The variable selection algorithm in this case is based on gradually reducing the number of inputs until an optimal structure is obtained (Saltelli *et al*,

2001). However, this process is coupled with the hidden layer structure selection and requires high quality data sets. One of the unique features of Genetic Programming (GP) is its built-in mechanism to select the variables that are related to the problem during the simulated evolution and to gradually ignore variables that are not. In this way, a different type of nonlinear variable selection can be used for dimensionality reduction that could be appropriate for industrial data analysis. This idea was explored in (Gilbert *et al*, 1998) for variable selection from a spectral data set with 150 variables. Only between 6 and 9 variables were selected in the GP-derived predictive rules. Other applications can be found in (Francone *et al*, 2004, RML Technologies, 2002 and Johnson *et al*, 2000)

An approach for GP-based variable selection with emphasis on multi-objective Pareto-front GP will be described in the chapter. The organization is as follows. The generic issue of dealing with high-dimensional spaces is addressed in Section 2. Section 3 gives a short overview of the linear techniques for variable selection. The proposed method for variable selection using Pareto GP is discussed and illustrated with synthesized data for re-discovering of Newton's Law of gravity in Section 4. The method is demonstrated with two successful industrial applications, described in Section 5.

2.　　　The Curse of Dimensionality

In modeling projects, the assumption is implicitly made that we know the "true" inputs to a given problem and that the reference data set feature vectors are defined in the space of these "true" inputs. In practice, many times one has to select the relevant inputs from a possibly large set of candidate inputs: input selection is an integral part of the modeling problem. All too often, people don't worry enough about this input selection problem. They build models using all the available inputs thinking that, in a magical way, the modeling system will figure out which inputs are relevant and which are not. To build robust models it is essential to limit the number of inputs to an absolute minimum for a number of reasons, all of which all have to do with the so-called "curse of dimensionality".

The goal of a data-driven modeling problem is to estimate an unknown function based on a finite number of samples. Because we only have a finite number of samples available, there will always be an infinite number of possible functions that can be selected and that will interpolate the data equally well. To come up with a unique solution it is necessary to impose some kind of constraints on possible solutions. In the absence of first-principle constraints that can be obtained from a understanding of the physics behind the problem, these constraints are often defined in terms of the smoothness of the function in a given neighborhood around a data point. The accuracy of the function estimation obviously depends on having enough samples within that neighborhood. If the dimensionality of the problem is increased, there are basically two routes to obtain sufficient data points within such a local neighborhood. First, one can try to collect sufficient samples to get this high density, something which is very often not possible. Second, one can increase the size of this "local" neighborhood, but this is at the expense of imposing stronger (possible incorrect) constraints on the problem solution. This is the essence of the "curse of dimensionality."

The properties of high-dimensional spaces often appear counter-intuitive because our experience is limited to low-dimensional spaces (Cherkassky, 1998). For example, objects like a hypercube have an increasing ratio of surface area to volume with increasing dimensionality. Following are four properties of high-dimensional spaces that contribute to the problem:

- *Samples sizes with the same data density increase exponentially with dimensionality.* If ρ is the reference data density in one dimension ρ^d is the equivalent density in d dimensions.

- *An increasingly large radius is needed to enclose a given fraction of data points in higher dimensional space.* For example, the edge length of a hypercube which encloses a given fraction of samples p is given by:

$$el_d(p) = p^{1/d}$$

Figure 6-1 shows the corresponding graph for up to dimensionality 20 for fractions of 5, 10 and 20 %. Notice that high edge lengths (>0.75) are needed very quickly. An edge length of 1 would result in a hypercube that covers the entire space.

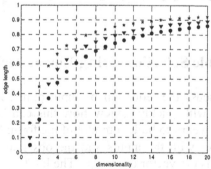

Figure 6-1. Edge length needed for a hypercube to include 5%, 10% and 20% of the data.

- *In higher dimensional spaces, almost every point is closer to an edge than to another point.* Or, in other words, in higher dimensional spaces extrapolation is the norm rather than the exception. For a sample size n, the expected distance between data points sampled from a uniform distribution in the unit hypercube is given by:

$$D(d,n) = \frac{1}{2}\left(\frac{1}{n}\right)^{y_d}$$

- *Almost every point is an outlier in its own projection on the line defined by the prediction point and the origin.* The expected location of this prediction point is $\sqrt{d-1/2}$. The remaining points will follow a standard normal distribution with mean zero and standard deviation one since the other points are unrelated to the direction of the projection. For example when d=10, the expected value of the prediction point is 3.1 standard deviations away from the center of the training data. In this sense this point can be considered to be an outlier of the training data.

These properties of high-dimensional spaces have serious consequences for building models based on a limited number of samples. The higher the dimensionality of the space the more likely it is that we will not have the data points we need to make a local estimate. Also, the higher the dimensionality, the more we have to resort to extrapolation instead of interpolation to make predictions. For these reasons, it is essential to limit the number of inputs to a data driven model to an absolute minimum. In the next sections we will describe how this can be done using linear techniques but also how this can be done effectively using genetic programming.

3.   Variable Selection Using Linear Techniques

Before we discuss the reduction of input dimensionality using genetic programming we will quickly review how this can be achieved for linear models. Suppose we try to build a model of the form: $Y = X.b + \varepsilon$ where X and Y are matrices with the inputs and the observations, b is a vector of parameters and e is the vector of errors. The least squares solution of b that minimizes $\varepsilon'. \varepsilon$ is obtained from $b = (X'X)^{-1} X'Y$ irrespective of any distribution properties of the errors. A large number of statistical procedures are available to select the best subset of inputs to use in the linear regression equation (Draper and Smith, 1981). Examples of these procedures are: (1)

all possible regressions, (2) best subset regressions, (3) backward elimination, (4) stepwise regression, (5) ridge regression, (6) principal components regression, (7) latent root regression, (8) stagewise regression *etc.* Some of these procedures, like principal components and latent root regression, are specific to linear methods and do not have an immediate analogue to apply in non-linear modelling. Most of the other procedures rely on some sort of significance test (*e.g.* the partial F-test) to decide which variable to keep or to discard depending on the specific procedure. The use of these significance tests automatically implies an assumption about the underlying distribution of the errors. Frequently these are assumed to be normally distributed. The preferred procedures are either or a combination of the backward elimination and stepwise regression procedures. Although theoretically the all possible regression procedure would be the best, in practice this is only feasible for a limited number of possible inputs.

The backward elimination method starts from a regression equation containing all variables. At each iteration the variable with the lowest partial F-test value is compared to a preselected significance level and is eliminated whenever the significance is lower than the preselected value. The procedure stops when no more variables can be found that meet this criterion. The stepwise regression method attempts to achieve the same result by working in the other direction, *i.e.* to insert variables into the equation as long as they meet certain significance criteria; see (Draper and Smith, 1981) for more details on these procedures. These procedures usually work fine within a linear framework but one has to realize that there are many possibilities for any variable selection scheme to go wrong whenever the data set being used is not balanced (in the sense that not all input dimensions are properly represented), or some of the variables are related to other unmeasured latent variables.

4.   Variable Selection Using Pareto Genetic Programming

Fitness Inheritance in the Total Population

As mentioned earlier, one of the potential applications of symbolic regression via genetic programming is sensitivity analysis of nonlinear problems with a potentially large set of candidate input variables. These kinds of problems are frequently encountered in the chemical processing industry. Sensitivity analysis is also called the "problem of feature selection" in machine learning terminology. Many problems in the chemical industry are of this type. There usually are a large number of measurements available at a plant, many of which are redundant or not relevant to the problem that one tries to solve.

Engineering knowledge about the problem is usually the first step to try and narrow down the number of inputs. Sensitivity analysis generates a ranking of all the input variables in terms of how important they are in modeling a certain unknown process. In linear problems the sensitivity of an input variable is related to the derivative of the output with respect to that variable. In nonlinear problems, however, the derivative becomes a local property and has to be integrated over the entire input domain to qualify as a sensitivity. Since this approach is not really practical in a genetic programming context, we've opted to relate the sensitivity of a given input variable to its fitness in the population of equations. The reasoning is that important input variables will be used in equations that have a relatively high fitness. So the fitness of input variables is related to the fitness of the equations they are used in. There is, however, a question with respect to credit assignment, *i.e.* what portion of the fitness goes to what variable in the equation. The easiest approach is to distribute the credit (the fitness of the equation) equally over all variables present. A complicating factor is that probably not every variable is equally important in a given equation. In addition, most equations in a genetic programming population are not parsimonious and possess chunks of inactive code (a good description of the problem of 'bloat' can be found in Banzhaf *et al*, 1998).

Variables that are present in these chunks of inactive code do not contribute to the final fitness of the equation but still obtain some credit for being part of that equation. There is no direct solution for this problem on the individual equation level but still reliable answers can be obtained provided we evaluate a large number of equations. Again the reasoning is simple, if a given input variable is absolutely essential to solve the problem, it must be present in the high fitness equations. Other nonessential variables will be present in both low-fitness and high-fitness equations so their fitness will be closer to the average fitness over all equations. More important variables will obtain more credit and will have a fitness that exceeds this average value. So provided the population size is large enough, we can take the fitness of each equation in the population, distribute this fitness in equal amounts over the input variables present in that equation and sum all these contributions for each input variable over the entire population. An improved version of this, at the expense of a little bit of extra computation, is doing the same but instead of just using the equations in the population also include every sub-equation in each of these equations. The extra computational step will considerably improve the statistics of the input variable fitnesses since now the number of equations is equal to the *total number of nodes in every equation-tree in the population* rather than the population size itself.

A Simple Example

As a simple example we'll try to rediscover Newton's Law of gravitation. This states that any two objects attract one another gravitationally. The attractive force depends linearly on the mass of each object (doubling the mass doubles the force) and inversely on the square of the distance between the two objects:

$$F = -g \cdot \frac{m_1 \cdot m_2}{r^2}$$

g is the gravitational constant which is just a number to match up the results of the equation with our system of measurement. The minus sign ($-$) indicates that the force is attractive. A synthetic dataset with 50 patterns was generated where the two masses are random numbers in the range [0,1] and the radius is a real number in the range [1,2]. An additional 50 inputs with random numbers in the range [0,1] were added. These extra inputs are just "noise" variables and make the task of discovering Newton's law progressively harder since part of the problem now is to discover the "true" variables x_1, x_2 and x_3 in the total set.

From Figure 6-2, which shows the correlation coefficient from each of the input variables to the force, the output variable that needs to be predicted, we see that the masses (variables 1 and 2) have a relatively high absolute correlation to the force but the others (the distance and the random variables) cannot be easily distinguished from each other.

Next we'll apply genetic programming to do a nonlinear sensitivity analysis. The particular version of Genetic Programming we use is called Pareto GP and is described in (Smits and Kotanchek, 2004). In Pareto GP an archive is used to store equations that are at or near the Pareto border of fitness versus some equation complexity measure. This archive is maintained during a run. All the equations in the next generation are obtained either by mutation of existing equations in the archive or by crossover between members of the archive and the previous population. A typical run consists of a number of different cascades. At the start of a new cascade a new population is generated from scratch but, since the archive is maintained, good solutions appear very quickly again in the population. A cascade usually has a fixed number of generations. The final result is the set of the equations in the archive, which represents the Pareto front of fitness versus complexity. When we apply genetic programming to do a nonlinear sensitivity analysis to the augmented Newton dataset as described earlier, the picture shown in Figure

6-3 emerges. The important variables are identified very quickly and then stabilize in sensitivity. The unimportant variables die out relatively fast after an initial period and final fitness values become very small.

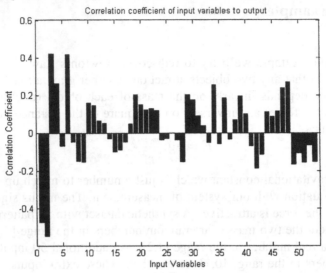

Figure 6-2. Correlation coefficients of inputs relative to the output for Newton's problem

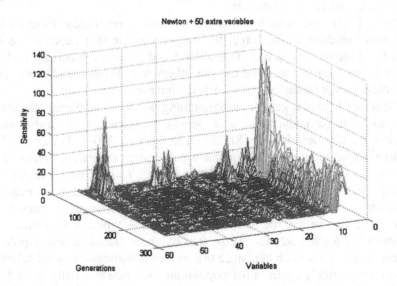

Figure 6-3. Evolution of fitness for all variables in the Newton problem. Notice that the important variables on the right-hand side are identified very quickly

Fitness Inheritance in the Pareto Front Only

We already mentioned that when variables accumulate fitness from the entire population there is a chance that we get somewhat of a distorted picture because unimportant variables that happen to be part of equations with a relatively high fitness will also pick up fitness from those. To compensate for this we introduced a modification where variables only accumulate fitness from equations that reside in the archive. Since the archive contains the Pareto front of all of the high fitness equations relative to their complexity this modifications is expected to make the variable selection more robust. In the next section with two industrial applications we will show that this is indeed the case.

5.   Applications

Variable selection and dimensionality reduction are critical for developing parsimonious empirical models from industrial data sets. One of the key application areas for symbolic regression models generated by GP is inferential sensors (Kordon *at al*, 2003). This type of empirical model predicts difficult-to-measure process variables (outputs), such as NOx emissions, polymer properties, biomass, *etc.*, with easy-to-measure sensors such as temperatures, flows, and pressures (inputs). Usually model development begins with the broadest possible selection of input sensors that process engineers think may influence the output.

The proposed method for variable selection will be illustrated in two applications of inferential sensors development on (1) a data set with middle-sized dimensionality (8 inputs and 251 data points) and on (2) a high-dimensional data set of 23 inputs and 7000 data points.

Variable Selection on Middle-Sized Industrial Data

The inferential sensor in this application predicts emissions from process variables. The correlation coefficients of the eight potential inputs relative to the emissions (the output) are shown in Figure 4. For this problem it is difficult to satisfy the regulatory requirements of 7.5% error with a linear model and so a nonlinear solution is needed.

Pareto GP was used for variable selection and nonlinear model generation. The results from the variable selection are shown in Figures 6-5 — 6-8. The results are based on 5 independent runs of 10 cascades with 50 generations. The average sensitivities with their standard deviations for each input, as defined in the previous section, for two population sizes of 100 and 1000 are shown in each figure. The sensitivities in Figures 5 and 6 are based on all models in the population at the last generation and the sensitivities in Figures 7 and 8 are based on the models in the archive at the last generation of the Pareto GP evolution.

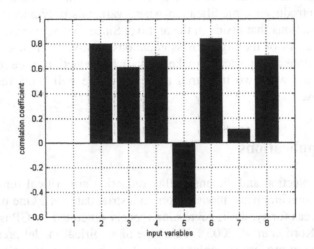

Figure 6-4. Correlation coefficients of process inputs relative to emissions

The last sensitivity analysis is a better demonstration for variable selection because it is based on the high-quality potential models which are the breeding source for the Pareto front. In principle, the most sensitive inputs (x2, x5, x6, and x8) have been consistently selected in all cases, but the difference is clearer with the archive selection in Figures 7 and 8. For comparison, a linear variable selection, based on PCA-PLS model with two principal components, is shown in Figure 9. The inputs ranking is represented by a Variable Importance in the Projection (VIP, described in Eriksonn *et al.*, 2001). Variables with VIP > 1 are treated as important.

One of the differences between the linear and the GP-based variable selection is that input x5 is insignificant from the linear point of view (which is supported by the low correlation coefficient of -0.5 in Figure 4). However, it is one of the most significant inputs, according to the nonlinear sensitivity analysis and process experts. The experts also selected two models for the final implementation, which included the four most influential inputs from the GP variable selection – x2, x5, x6, and x8. The correlation coefficient of the selected models is 0.93 and 0.94, much higher than the linear option and within the regulatory limits. The application details are given in (Kordon *at al*, 2003).

Table 6-1. Sensitivity analysis of models in the population at the last generation (mean and standard deviation over five independent runs)

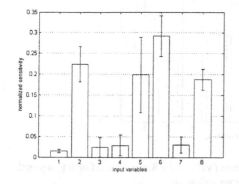 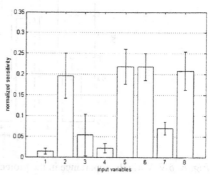

Figure 6-5. Population size 100   *Figure 6-6.* Population size 1000

Table 6-2. Sensitivity analysis of models in the archive at the last generation (mean and standard deviation over five independent runs)

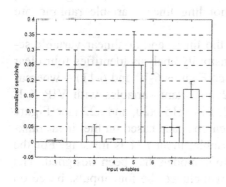 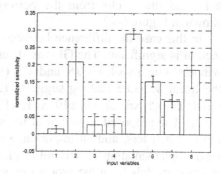

Figure 6-7. Population size 100   *Figure 6-8.* Population size 1000

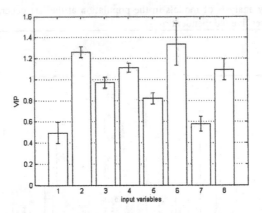

Figure 6-9. Variable importance in the projection (VIP) of the 8 inputs based on a two principal components PCA-PLS model of the emissions soft sensor

Variable Selection on High-Dimensional Industrial Data

The inferential sensor in the high-dimensional application predicts propylene concentration. This application illustrates the scale-up performance of the proposed method on an industrial problem with a much larger search space. The results from the GP sensitivity analysis are shown in Figure 6-10, 6-11 and the results from the corresponding linear variable ranking are shown in Figure 6-12.

In this case the difference between the linear and nonlinear variable selection is significant. The GP-based sensitivity analysis identifies four clear winners – inputs $x4$, $x6$, $x8$, and $x21$ (see Figures 6-10 and 6-11) – whereas the linear variable ranking suggests 12 important variables with VIP > 1: inputs $x4$, $x5$, $x6$, $x8$, $x9$, $x19$, $x11$, $x12$, $x14$, $x15$, $x20$, and $x22$ (see Figure 6-12). The proposed reduction of the search space based on the linear ranking is much less, and an important variable, input $x21$ is missing. For the final implementation an ensemble of four models has been designed. The selected models from the process expert included the four inputs, based on the GP sensitivity analysis, i.e., inputs $x4$, $x6$, $x8$, and $x21$, and input $x11$, recommended in a backup model from the experts. The application details are given in (Jordaan *et al*, 2004).

Table 6-3. Sensitivity analysis of models in the archive at the last generation (mean and standard deviation over five independent runs)

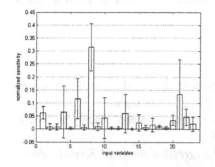

| *Figure 6-10.* Population size 100 | *Figure 6-11.* Population size 1000 |

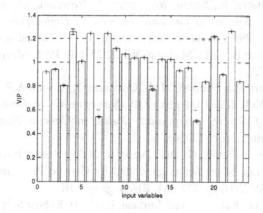

Figure 6-12. Variable importance in the projection (VIP) of the 23 inputs based on a four principal components PCA-PLS model of the propylene soft sensor

6. Summary

Sensitivity analysis using Genetic Programming and more specifically Pareto GP has been used successfully in many industrial applications to do nonlinear variable selection. It has been observed that the results are quite consistent and often allow for a considerable reduction in the feature space before final models are built. This, in general, leads to more robust models. The variable sensitivity is accomplished through a relatively simple fitness inheritance scheme that imposes little additional overhead in terms of computational effort.

References

Banzhaf, W., Nordin, P., Keller, R., and Francone, F. (1998). *Genetic Programming: An Introduction*, San Francisco, CA: Morgan Kaufmann.

Cherkassky V, Mulier, F., 1998, "Learning from data, Concepts, Theory and Methods", Wiley Interscience, ISBN 0-471-15493-8.

Draper, N. R. and Smith, H. (1981) *Applied Regression Analysis, Second Edition*, New York, NY: Wiley.

Eriksson, L., Johansson, E., Wold, N., and Wold, S. (2001). *Multi and Megavariate Data Analysis: Principles and Applications*, Umea, Sweden, Umetrics Academy.

Francone, F. *et al* (2004). *Discrimination of Unexploded Ordnance from Clutter Using Linear Genetic Programming*, Genetic and Evolutionary Computation Conference, Late Breaking Papers.

Gilbert, R.J., Goodacre, R., Shann, B., Taylor, J., Rowland, J.J. and Kell, D.B., *Genetic Programming-Based Variable Selection for High-Dimensional Data*, in J.R.Koza et al., editors, Genetic Programming 1998: Proceedings of the Third Annual Conference (GP-98), Madison, WI 22-25 July 1998, Morgan Kaufmann, San Fransisco, CA.

Ohnson, H.E, Gilbert, R.J., Winson, M.K., Goodacre, R., Smith, A.R., Rowand, J.J., Hall, M.A. and Kell, D.B. *Explanatory Analysis of he Metabolome Using Genetic Programming of Simple, Interpretable Rules*, in Genetic Programming and Evolvable Machines, Vol 1 (2000)

Jordaan, E., Kordon, A., Smits, G., and Chiang L. (2004). Robust Inferential Sensors based on Ensemble of predictors generated by Genetic Programming, In *Proceedings of PPSN 2004*, pp. 522-531, Birmingham, UK.

Kordon, A., Smits, G., Kalos, A., and Jordaan, E.(2003). Robust Soft Sensor Development Using Genetic Programming, In *Nature-Inspired Methods in Chemometrics*, (R. Leardi-Editor), Amsterdam: Elsevier

Kotanchek, M, Smits, G. and Kordon, A. (2003). Industrial Strength Genetic Programming, In *Genetic Programming Theory and Practice,pp 239-258,* R. Riolo and B. Worzel (Eds), Boston, MA:Kluwer.

Koza, J. (1992). Genetic Programming: On the Programming of Computers by Means of Natural Selection, Cambridge, MA: MIT Press.

RML Technologies, Inc. (2002) *Discipulus Owner's Manual*.

Saltelli A., Chan K., and Scott E. (2001). Sensitivity Analysis, Baffins Lane, Chichester, UK: Wiley.

Smits, G. and Kotanchek. (2004), Pareto -Front Exploitation in Symbolic Regression, *Genetic Programming Theory and Practice, pp 283-300,* R. Riolo and B. Worzel (Eds), Boston, MA:Kluwer.

Chapter 7

A HIGHER-ORDER FUNCTION APPROACH TO EVOLVE RECURSIVE PROGRAMS

Tina Yu[1]

[1] *Chevron Information Technology Company*

Abstract   We demonstrate a functional style recursion implementation to evolve recursive programs. This approach re-expresses a recursive program using a non-recursive application of a higher-order function. It divides a program recursion pattern into two parts: the recursion code and the application of the code. With the higher-order functions handling recursion code application, GP effort becomes focused on the generation of recursion code. We employed this method to evolve two recursive programs: a STRSTR C library function, and programs that produce the Fibonacci sequence. In both cases, the program space defined by higher-order functions are much easier for GP to search and to find a solution. We have learned about higher-order function selection and fitness assignment through this study. The next step will be to test the approach on applications with open-ended solutions, such as evolutionary design.

Keywords: recursion, Fibonacci sequence, strstr, PolyGP, type systems, higher-order functions, recursion patterns, filter, foldr, scanr, λ abstraction, functional programming languages, Haskell

1.   Introduction

In August of 2000, I met Inman Harvey at the Seventh International Conference on Artificial Life in Portland, Oregon. "I just finished my Ph.D in genetic programming last year," I told Inman at the dinner table. "Great, I have a challenge for you. Can you evolve (faster than random search) the STRSTR program?"

He was referring to the C library function which scans the first appearance of one character string in another character string. If the first string does not exist in the second string, STRSTR returns an empty string. For example [1]

```
strstr (''example'',''test example'') = ''example''
strstr (''example'',''example test'') = ''example test''
strstr (''example'',''test'') = '' ''
```

This program clearly needs recursion or iteration, a subject which I spent half of my Ph.D to investigate. Although I was eager to undertake the challenge, many other projects had higher priorities at that time. It was not until early this year when I got the chance to work on this problem.

In this chapter, I present my results of using a higher-order function approach to evolve the STRSTR program. Additionally, I will show that programs generating the Fibonacci sequence can be evolved using higher-order functions.

This chapter is organized as follows: Section 2 explains higher-order functions and reviews previous work on using higher-order functions to evolve computer programs. In Section 3, the PolyGP system is described. Section 4 presents Genetic Programming (GP) (Koza, 1992) experiments to evolve STRSTR. The experiments to generate programs producing the Fibonacci sequence are given in Section 5. In Section 6, we discuss our results and review other approaches to evolve recursive programs. Finally, section 7 concludes the chapter.

2.   Higher-Order Functions and Program Evolution

Higher-order functions are functions which take other functions as inputs or return functions as outputs. This ability to pass functions around as inputs and outputs can be used to express patterns of recursion. A recursion pattern has two components: operations (recursion code) and application of the operations. By extracting the operations into a function and passing it to a higher-order function, the operations can be carried out by the higher-order function.

For example, if the pattern of recursion is performing a series of operations on every element of a list, the operation can be extracted as a function f which is then passed as an argument to the higher-order function *map*, which applies it to every element of the list:

```
map f [] = []
map f list = cons (f (head list)) (map f (tail list))
map (+1) [1,2,3,4,5] = [2,3,4,5,6]
```

---

[1]In this study, STRSTR returns a character string itself instead of the pointer to the character string.

Consequently, a recursive function can be re-expressed using a non-recursive application of a higher-order function (Field and Harrison, 1988).

In a previous work, we have adapted this programming style to evolve recursive EVEN-PARITY programs (Yu, 1999). Semantically, EVEN-PARITY takes a list of Boolean inputs and returns True if an even number of inputs are True and False otherwise. Experienced circuit design engineers might be able to identify one or two familiar methods to obtain recursion. One example is applying XOR to each pair of the Boolean inputs and then negating the result as the final output.

When combined with the higher-order function *foldr* (with polymorphic types), the PolyGP system (described in Section 3) discovered 8 different recursion patterns; each of which operates differently by applying different Boolean function (XOR, NOR, NAND) to the Boolean input pairs (Yu,1999, Chapter 6). This work not only shows that higher-order functions provide a feasible way to evolve recursive programs, but also demonstrates the power of GP for discovering solutions that are beyond human capability.

Higher-order functions are not restricted to express recursion patterns for *list* data structures. Other data types, such as *tree* and *integer*, can have higher-order functions defined over them to carry out the recursive operations. In Section 5, we will show such an example. In that case, a higher-order function is defined over an integer value. A set of operations are performed repeatedly until the integer value reaches zero. We have applied this higher-order function to evolve programs generating the Fibonacci sequence successfully.

Higher-order functions are not expressly limited to programs with recursion patterns. Non-recursive programs can also incorporate higher-order functions to create modular programs. As an argument to a higher-order function, a function becomes a self-contained module (a λ abstraction) in a program. This module has its own identity and can only exchange materials with the same kind of modules in another program during evolution. Consequently, higher-order functions provide the ability to explore the regularity in a given problem during GP evolution. This module mechanism has been incorporated with GP to evolve financial technical trading rules based on S&P500 index (Yu et al., 2004). Those results demonstrated that modular GP rules give higher returns than the returns of non-modular GP rules.

3.   The PolyGP System

PolyGP (Yu, 1999) is a GP system which is able to evolve programs containing higher-order functions. The programs have the following syntax:

$$
\begin{array}{ll}
exp :: c & \text{constant} \\
\mid x & \text{identifier} \\
\mid f & \text{built-in function} \\
\mid exp1\ exp2 & \text{application of one expression to another} \\
\mid \lambda x.exp & \text{lambda abstraction}
\end{array}
$$

Constants and identifiers are given in the terminal set while built-in functions are provided in the function set. Application of expressions and λ abstractions are constructed by the system.

Each program expression has an associated type. The types of constants and identifiers are specified with known types or type variables. For example, the input variable *str1* has type [char] and constant *True* has Boolean type.

```
str1::[char]
True::Bool
```

Each function in the function set is also specified with its argument and return types. For example, the function *and* takes two Boolean type inputs, and returns a Boolean type output.

```
and::Bool→Bool→Bool
```

Higher-order functions have brackets around their function arguments. For example, *filter* takes two arguments: one is a function and the other is a [char] type value. The function argument has type (char→Bool), which indicates that it is a function which takes one input of char type and return a Boolean value. The output of *filter* is a [char] value.

```
filter::(char→Bool)→[char]→[char]
```

Using the specified type information, a type system selects type-matching functions and terminals to construct type-correct program trees. A program tree is grown from the top node downwards. There is a required type for the top node of the tree. The type system selects a function whose return type matches the required type. The selected function will require arguments to be created at the next (lower) level in the tree; there will be type requirements for each of those arguments. If the argument has a function type, a λ abstraction tree will be created. Otherwise, the type system will randomly select a function (or a terminal) whose return type matches the new required type to construct the argument node. This process is repeated many times until the permitted tree depth is reached.

Lambda Abstraction and Higher-order Functions

λ abstractions are local function definitions, similar to function definitions in a conventional language such as C. The following is an example λ abstraction together with an equivalent C function:

```
(λ x (+ x 1))                (λ abstraction)
Inc (int x){return (x+1)} (C function)
```

However, λ abstractions are anonymous and can not be invoked by name. The application of λ abstractions is done by passing them as arguments to a higher-order function. The following shows the above defined λ abstraction is applied by the higher-order function *twice*:

```
twice f x = f (f x)
twice (λ x (+ x 1)) 2
= (λ x (+ x 1))((λ x (+ x 1)) 2)
= + ((λ x (+ x 1)) 2) 1
= + (+ 2 1) 1
= + 3 1
= 4
```

The procedure to create λ abstraction trees is similar to that used to create the main program tree. The only difference is that their terminal set consists not only of the terminal set used to create the main program, but also the input variables to the λ abstraction. Input variable naming in λ abstractions follows a simple rule: each input variable is uniquely named with a hash symbol followed by an unique integer, *e.g.* #1, #2. This consistent naming style allows crossover to be easily performed between λ abstraction trees with the same number and the same type of inputs and outputs. Figure 7-1 gives the program tree with higher-order function *twice* and λ abstraction described in the above example.

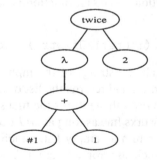

Figure 7-1. The program tree with higher-order function *twice and* λ *abstraction.*

4.   Evolving STRSTR Programs

To evolve STRSTR program, the first step is to select higher-order functions that facilitate the evolution of recursion patterns. Functional programming languages, such as Haskell , have a rich set of higher-order functions in their libraries. From the Haskell library (Jones, 2002), we selected two higher-order functions: *filter* and *scanr*.

The function *filter* applies a predicate to a list and returns the list of those elements that satisfy the predicate.

```
filter::(a→Bool)→[a]→[a]
filter (/= 'p') ['a','p','p','l','e']=['a','l','e']
```

The function *scanr* first applies its function argument (*f*) to the last item of the list argument and the second argument (*q0*). Next , it applies *f* to the penultimate item from the end of the list argument and the result from the previous application. This operation continues until all elements in the list argument is processed. It then returns the list of all intermediate and final results.

```
scanr::(a→b→b)→b→[a]→[b]
scanr f q0 []      = [q0]
scanr f q0 (x:xs) = f x q:qs
          where qs@(q_)= scanr f q0 xs
scanr cons [] [''apple'']=
          [''apple'',''pple'',''ple'',''le'',''e''].
```

In addition, the library function *isPrefixOf* is handy for implementing STRSTR. It checks if the first argument is a prefix of the second argument.

```
isPrefixOf::[a]→[a]→Bool
isPrefixOf [''app''] [''apple'']= True
```

With the 3 library functions, STRSTR function is defined as:

```
strstr str1 str2 =
        head (filter (isPrefixOf str1) (scanr cons [] str2))
```

Here, *scanr* produces all sub-strings of the input *str2*. The function *filter* checks each of the sub-strings and returns the list of the sub-strings where *str1* is the prefix. The function *head* then returns the first sub-string in the list. This STRSTR implementation works fine as long as *str1* occurs in *str2*. When this is not the case, *filter* would return an empty list, which will cause *head* return a run-time error. To avoid such an error, a function *headORnil* is defined:

```
headORnil [] = []
headORnil list = head list
```

The recursive STRSTR defined using higher-order functions is therefore:

```
strstr str1 str2=
  headORnil (filter (isPrefixOf str1) (scanr cons [] str2)
```

Figure 7-2a is the defined STRSTR program tree. As explained, the role of higher-order functions in a recursive program is to apply the recursion code to data inputs. The recursion code, however, is defined by programmers. In the case where GP is the programmer, we have to provide terminals and functions for GP to evolve the code. Figure 7-2b shows the areas of the code which are generated by GP. In particular, the triangle with a λ root is the recursion code for *filter* to apply. The recursion code for *scanr* is inside the other triangle which is also evolved by GP.

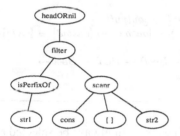

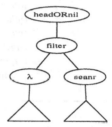

Figure 7-2a The defined recursive STRSTR program tree.

Figure 7-2b. The STRSTR program tree structure; the code inside the two triangles will be evolved by GP.

Experimental Setup

Table 7-1 gives the function set for GP to evolve STRSTR. Among them, three are higher-order functions: *filter* and *scanr* are selected from the Haskell library while *fold2lists* is defined for GP to evolve a function operating like *isPrefixOf*. *fold2lists* is an extension of *foldr*. Instead of applying recursion code on single list, *fold2lists* applies recursion code over two lists. When an empty list is encountered, *fold2lists* returns different default value, depending on which one of the two lists is empty.

```
fold2lists f default1 default2 [] list2 = default1
fold2lists f default1 default2 list1 [] = default2
fold2lists f default1 default2 (front1:rest1)(front2:rest2) =
f front1 front2 (fold2lists f default1 default2 rest1 rest2)
```

The second column of Table 7-1 specifies the type of each function. We used special types such as input and output to constrain the functions on certain tree nodes, so that the top two layers of the program trees have the same structure as that shown in Figure 7-2b.

For example, we specify the return type of STRSTR to be [output]. The only function which returns this type is *headORnil*, which will always be selected as the program tree root. The single argument of *headORnil* has type [[output]] and the only function that returns this type is *filter*, which will always be selected as the argument node below *headORnil*. Although there are other ways to constrain tree structures, typing is convenient since the PolyGP system has a powerful type system to perform type checking for the program trees.

Table 7-1. Function Set

function	type
headORnil	$[output] \rightarrow [output]$
filter	$([char] \rightarrow Bool) \rightarrow [char] \rightarrow [output]$
scanr	$(char \rightarrow [char] \rightarrow [char]) \rightarrow [output] \rightarrow [output] \rightarrow [char]$
cons	$char \rightarrow [char] \rightarrow [char]$
fold2lists	$(char \rightarrow char \rightarrow Bool \rightarrow Bool) \rightarrow Bool \rightarrow Bool \rightarrow$
	$[input] \rightarrow [char] \rightarrow Bool$
and	$Bool \rightarrow Bool \rightarrow Bool$

Table 7-2 gives the terminal set. The variable *str1* will always be selected as the fourth argument to *fold2lists*. Similarly, *str2* and [] will always be selected as either the second or the third argument to *scanr*. At a first look, it seems that the program trees are so constrained that the generation of STRSTR programs would be very easy. However, after careful examination, you will find that all that have been specified are the skeleton of STRSTR program: the higher-order functions and the inputs list which the recursion code will apply. The core of a recursive program, the recursion code must be discovered by GP.

Table 7-2. Terminal Set

terminal	type	terminal	type
str1	$[input]$	str2	$[output]$
true	$Bool$	false	$Bool$
[]	$[output]$		

The GP parameters are given in Table 7-3 while the three test cases used to evaluate GP programs are listed in Table 7-4. For this problem, three test cases are sufficient as they include all possible scenarios: the first string appears at the beginning of the second string; the first string appears in the middle of the second string and the first string does not exist in the second string.

Table 7-3. GP Parameters

population size	500	max generation	100
maximum tree depth	5	crossover rate	50%
mutation rate	40%	copy rate	10%
selection method	tournament of size 2	number of runs	100

The fitness function is defined as follows:

$$f = \sum_{i=1}^{3} \text{diff}(R_i, Ei) + \begin{cases} \text{length}(R_i) - \text{length}(E_i), & \text{length}(R_i) \geq \text{length}(E_i) \\ 5 * (\text{length}(E_i) - \text{length}(R_i)), & \text{otherwise} \end{cases}$$

R is the output returned by a GP program and E is the expected output; *diff* computes the number of different characters between the two outputs. If the two outputs have different length, *diff* stops computing when the shorter output ends. The length difference then becomes a penalty in the fitness calculation. Note that a program which returns an output shorter than the expected length is given a penalty five times higher than a program which returns an output longer than the expected length. This is based on my observation that the most frequently produced shorter output is an empty list. Such programs obtain a reasonably good fitness by satisfying the easiest test case: case number 3. However, they are very poor in handling the other two test cases. Once the population converges toward that kind of program, some important terminal nodes (*e.g.* False) become distinct and crossover or mutation are not able to correct them. To avoid such premature convergence, programs which generate shorter outputs than the expected outputs are penalized severely. A program which satisfies all 3 test cases successfully has fitness 0.

Table 7-4. Three Test Cases

case no.	*str1*	*str2*	*expected output*
1	"sample"	"sample test"	"sample test"
2	"sample"	"test sample"	"sample"
3	"sample"	"test"	""

Results

The program space turns out to be very easy for GP to search: all 100 runs find a solution before generation 31. The "computation effort" required to find a solution is given in Figure 7-3a. The minimum number of programs GP has to process in order to find a solution is 20,000.

The computational effort was calculated using the method described in (Koza, 1992). First, the cumulative probability of success by generation i using a population size M ($P(M,i)$) is computes. This is the total number of of runs that succeeded on or before the ith generation, divided by the total number runs conducted. Next, the number of individuals that must be processed to produce a solution by generation i with probability greater than z (by convention, z=99%) is computed using the following equation:

$$I(M, i, z) = M * (i + 1) * \lceil \tfrac{log(1-z)}{log(1-P(M,i))} \rceil$$

The hardware CPU time used on a Pentium 4 machine to complete the 100 runs is 40 minutes, which is longer than our other GP experimental runs. This is because each program has 3 recursions. In particular, *fold2lists* is inside of *filter*. This nested recursion takes machines a long time to evaluate.

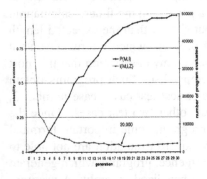

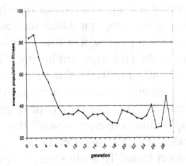

Figure 7-3a. Computation effort required to generate a STRSTR programs.

Figure 7-3b. The average population fitness during program evolution.

After editing, all evolved STRSTR programs look the same (see Figure 7-4). The *scanr* function generates a list of sub-strings from input *str2*. The *filter* function then removes the sub-strings whose initial characters do not match the input *str1*. The *headORnil* function then returns the first item in the resulting list. If the resulting list is empty, *headORnil* returns an empty list.

To investigate if a random search can do as well a job as GP does for this problem, we made 100 random search runs, each of which generated 20,000 programs randomly. None of them found a solution. We also evaluated the average population fitness of the 100 GP runs (see Figure 7-3b). They show the average population fitness improves as the evolution progress (the data after generation 18 are insignificant as they are based on a very small number of

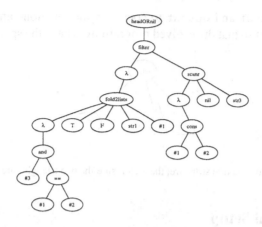

Figure 7-4. The shortest STRSTR program generated by GP.

runs); the improvement is particularly evident during the first 8 generations. In other words, GP search leads the population converge toward fitter solutions and finds an optimal at the end. All the evidences indicate that fitness and selection have positive impact on the search. GP is a better search algorithm than random search to find STRSTR programs in this program search space.

5.   Fibonacci Sequence

Fibonacci sequence is defined as the following:

$$f(n) = \begin{cases} 1 & \text{, if n=0 or n=1} \\ n_{i-1} + n_{i-2} & \text{, otherwise} \end{cases}$$

To generate the first *n* values of the sequence, a program has to compute the two previous sequence values recursively for *n* time. The recursion, recursion pattern in this case is therefore applying some operations over an integer value. A higher-order function *foldn* is designed for this pattern of recursion:

```
foldn::([int]→[int])→int→input→[output]→[output]
foldn f default 0 list = cons default list
foldn f default 1 list = cons default (foldn f default 0 list)
foldn f default n list = f (foldn f default n-1 list)
```

Here, *list* is an accumulator to store the sequence values generated so far. The recursion code (*f*) is applied on the accumulator to compute the next sequence value. As mentioned previously, the role of higher-order functions in a recursive program is to apply the recursion code, which are generated by GP. In Figure 7-5, the left triangle is the recursion code area. The right triangle is the default value. Both of them are generated by GP . Similar to the previous experiment, we use special types input and output to constrain the functions and terminals on certain tree nodes so that the evolved program trees have the specified structure.

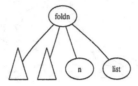

Figure 7-5. The program tree structure; the area inside the two triangles are generated by GP.

Experimental Setup

The function and terminal sets are given in Table 7-5 and Table 7-6 respectively. We specify [output] as the program return type, hence enforce *foldn*, the only function that returns this type, to be the program tree root . This function has four arguments; the third one will always be the variable *n* and the fourth one will always be the variable *list*. Initially, accumulator *list* is an empty list. It grows as the sequence values are generated. *RandomInt* is a random number generator which returns a random integer value in the range of 0 and 3. The GP parameters are listed in Table 7-3.

Table 7-5. Function Set

function	type
foldn	$([int] \rightarrow [int]) \rightarrow int \rightarrow input \rightarrow [output] \rightarrow [output]$
plus	$int \rightarrow int \rightarrow int$
minus	$int \rightarrow int \rightarrow int$
head	$[int] \rightarrow int$
tail	$[int] \rightarrow int$
cons	$int \rightarrow [int] \rightarrow [int]$

Table 7-6. Terminal Set

terminal	type	terminal	type	terminal	type
n	*input*	list	*[output]*	randomInt	*int*

Each evolved GP program is tested on *n* value of 8. The expected return list is therefore [34,21,13,8,5,3,2,1,1]. The fitness function is basically the same as the one in the previous experiments. One exception is that there is a run-time error penalty of 10 for programs applying *head* or *tail* to an empty list. The fitness function is therefore:

$$f = \text{diff}(R,E) + 10*\text{rtError} + \begin{cases} \text{length(R)-length(E)} & \text{,length(R)} \geq \text{length(E)} \\ 5*(\text{length(E)-length(R)}) & \text{,otherwise} \end{cases}$$

where R is the return list while E is the expected list. The run-time error flag *rtError* is 1 if a run time error is encountered during program fitness evaluation. Otherwise, it is 0.

Results

This program space is slightly harder than the STRSTR program space for GP. Among 100 runs, 97 found a solution; all of them are general solutions work for any value of n. The computation effort required to find a solution is given in Figure 7-6a. The minimum number of programs evaluated by GP to find a solution is 33,000. The hardware CPU time on a Pentium 4 machine to complete the 100 runs is 7 minutes. After editing, all programs become the same as that shown in Figure 7-7.

The left most branch in the program tree is the recursion code that the higher-order function *foldn* applies to a list. It is a function, specified by λ, with one argument (#1). The argument is an accumulator containing the Fibonacci sequence values generated so far. The function adds the first two elements of the list together and then concatenates the result to the accumulator. This operation is repeated until the input n becomes 0, when the default value 1 is returned. It is a general solution that produces the first n values of the Fibonacci sequence.

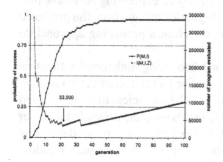 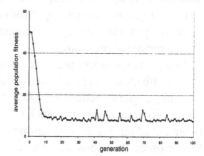

Figure 7-6a. Computation effort required to evolve a program generating Fibonacci sequence.

Figure 7-6b. The average population fitness during program evolution.

We also made 100 random search runs, each generates 33,000 programs randomly. Similar to the results of the STRSTR experiments, none of them found a program capable of producing the Fibonacci sequence. The average

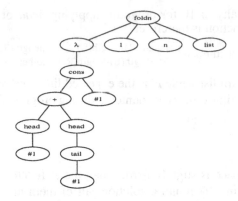

Figure 7-7. The shortest program generated by GP.

population fitness of the 100 GP runs in Figure 7-6b indicates that GP search guided by fitness and selection has led the population converging toward fitter programs and found an optimal at the end. This supports the case that GP is a better search algorithm for this program space.

6.   Discussion

Recursion is a powerful programming technique that not only reduces program size through reuse but also improves program scalability. Evolving recursive programs, however, has not been easy due to issues such as non-termination and fitness assignment (Yu, 1999, Chapter 3). By re-expressing recursive programs using non-recursive application of a higher-order function, the produced recursive programs always terminate. It is therefore a promising approach to evolve recursive programs.

In a previous work, we have shown that when using higher-order function *foldr* (with monomorphic types) to define recursive EVEN-PARITY, the problem difficulty is greatly reduced. In fact, random search is sufficient to find a solution in this program space (Yu, 1999, Chapter 7). In this chapter, we study two other recursive programs using a similar approach. Both program spaces defined by higher-order functions are not difficult for GP to find a solution. Random search, however, could not find a solution. Further analysis of population average fitness confirms that GP search is indeed superior than random search in these two problem spaces.

One important characteristic of this approach is that GP effort is mostly on evolving the recursion code (λ abstractions). The application of the code is handled by higher-order functions. It is important to note that GP has no knowledge about how the recursion code is applied. The relationship between the code and its application is learned through the iterative process of programs evaluation, correction and selection. Our experimental results indicate that GP is able to acquire such knowledge to evolve recursion code that work with the higher-order function to produce correct outputs.

Although incorporating designed/selected higher-order functions is an effective way to evolve recursive programs, it has its shortcoming: domain knowledge are not always available to design/select the appropriate higher-order functions. A more general approach would be to let GP evolve the higher-order functions suitable for a given problem. In this way, problems with poorly-defined scope can also benefit this technique.

Koza and his colleagues proposed Automatic Defined Recursion (ADR) as a way for GP to evolve recursive programs (Koza et al., 1999). An ADR tree has 4 branches: condition, body, update and ground. Since an ADR can call itself inside its body and the update branch may be ill-defined during program evolution, an ADR may never terminate. It is therefore necessary to set an ADR execution limit when evolving recursive programs. They have employed ADR with architecture-alternating operations to successfully evolve programs generating the Fibonacci sequence. However, the solution is not general and does not work for input *n* beyond 12.

Through incremental program transformation, Olsson showed that recursive programs can be developed by his ADATE system (Olsson, 1995). Instead of relying on fitness-based selection and genetic operation, his system applies four transformation operations to induce recursive programs. He gave some example programs, such as a sorting algorithm, which were successfully generated using this approach.

7.   Conclusions

Functional implementation of recursive programs is not well understood nor utilized in the GP community. The implementation does not make explicit recursive calls. Instead, recursion is carried out by non-recursive application of a higher-order function. This chapter explains this style of recursion implementation and demonstrates one way to incorporate it in a GP system to evolve recursive programs.

In this GP system, higher-order functions are included in the function set. Recursion occurs when a higher-order function appears in a program tree node. We applied this GP system to evolve two recursive programs. In the first case, a challenge by Inman Harvey, multiple recursions are involved. We selected two Haskell library functions and designed one higher-order function for these recursion patterns. In the second case, a higher-order function operating over an integer value is designed. In both cases, the GP system is able to evolve the recursive programs successfully by evaluating a small number of programs. Random search, however, is not able to find a solution.

These results clearly endorse GP ability to evolve recursive programs that random search can not. Yet, the success is linked to the problem-specific higher-order functions. When domain knowledge is available, like the two problems we studied, identify such higher-order functions is not hard. However, when this is not the case, it becomes unclear if GP is able to compose the recursive code to work with a general purpose higher-order function. An alternative approach is to have GP evolve the problem-specific higher-order functions. In this way, the GP system is more general and can be applied to problems that do not have a well-defined scope. This is the area of our future research.

Are we ready to tackle real-world problems using this approach? Maybe. We have learned quite a deal about higher-order functions selection and fitness assignment. However, both problems we studied have known solutions, which help the selection of higher-order functions. Most real-world problems are open-ended in the sense that there is no known optimum. However, this does not preclude the possibility of applying the method. In particular, in the area of evolutionary design where creativity is essential to problem solving, an imperfect higher-order function might still be able to deliver good solutions.

8.   Acknowledgements

I thank Lee Spector and Inman Harvey for their comments and suggestions.

References

Field, Anthony J. and Harrison, Peter G. (1988). *Functional Programming*. Addison-Wesley Publishing Company.

Jones, Simon Peyton (2002). Haskell 98 language and libraries, the revised report. Technical report, Haskell Org.

Koza, John R. (1992). *Genetic Programming: On the Programming of Computers by Means of Natural Selection*. MIT Press, Cambridge, MA, USA.

Koza, John R., Andre, David, Bennett III, Forrest H, and Keane, Martin (1999). *Genetic Programming 3: Darwinian Invention and Problem Solving*. Morgan Kaufman.

Olsson, Roland (1995). Inductive functional programming using incremental program transformation. *Artificial Intelligence*, 74(1):55–81.

Yu, Gwoing Tina (1999). *An Analysis of the Impact of Functional Programming Techniques on Genetic Programming*. PhD thesis, University College, London, Gower Street, London, WC1E 6BT.

Yu, Tina, Chen, Shu-Heng, and Kuo, Tzu-Wen (2004). Discovering financial technical trading rules using genetic programming with lambda abstraction. In U-M O'Reilly, T. Yu, R. Riolo and Worzel, B., editors, *Genetic Programming Theory and Practice II*, pages 11–30.

Chapter 8

TRIVIAL GEOGRAPHY
IN GENETIC PROGRAMMING

Lee Spector[1] and Jon Klein[1,2]

[1]Cognitive Science, Hampshire College, Amherst, MA, 01002-3359 USA; [2]Physical Resource
Theory, Chalmers University of Technology & Göteborg University, Göteborg, Sweden.

Abstract   Geographical distribution is widely held to be a major determinant of evolutionary dynamics. Correspondingly, genetic programming theorists and practitioners
have long developed, used, and studied systems in which populations are structured in quasi-geographical ways. Here we show that a remarkably simple version
of this idea produces surprisingly dramatic improvements in problem-solving
performance on a suite of test problems. The scheme is trivial to implement, in
some cases involving little more than the addition of a modulus operation in the
population access function, and yet it provides significant benefits on all of our
test problems (ten symbolic regression problems and a quantum computing problem). We recommend the broader adoption of this form of "trivial geography" in
genetic programming systems.

Keywords: geography, locality, demes, symbolic regression, quantum computing

1.   Geography

   All biological populations are distributed in space, with the result that some
organisms are close neighbors while others live at great distances from one
another. It has long been recognized that such geographical distribution, even
in uniform environments, can influence evolutionary dynamics in significant and
complex ways (Mayr, 1942; Wright, 1945; Avise, 2000; Lieberman et al., 2005).
In particular, positive influences of geographical distribution on the evolution of
individuals with certain desirable features (*e.g.* altruistic behavior) have been
demonstrated in both analytical models and simulations (Eshel, 1972; Nowak
and May, 1992; Axelrod et al., 2004; Spector and Klein, 2005a).

It is therefore not surprising that many evolutionary computation systems also model some form of geography, locating their evolving individuals within grid-based or continuous virtual spaces. This is a particularly natural move for systems that are designed to model aspects of natural ecosystems (Ray, 1991; Holland, 1995; Ofria and Wilke, 2004). But it is also a popular move in problem-solving evolutionary computation systems, in the context of which geography is often justified by the ways in which it can be used to maintain population diversity.

Standard genetic algorithms and genetic programming techniques are non-spatial in their most common formulations (Holland, 1992; Koza, 1992; Banzhaf et al., 1998). However, many researchers and practitioners routinely divide their populations in to discrete or overlapping sub-populations, often called *demes*, that provide a form of geography (Collins and Jefferson, 1991). In these systems selection and competition takes place locally but selected individuals occasionally mate or migrate across demes. Because the computations taking place in different demes are generally independent—particularly when the demes are non-overlapping, in which case they are sometimes called "islands"—one can often run them on independent processors and reap benefits both of parallelism and of the diversity maintenance supported by geographical distribution (Maruyama et al., 1993; Nowostawski and Poll, 1999; Andre and Koza, 1996).

Demes have been demonstrated, in certain cases, to improve problem solving performance (see *e.g.* (Collins and Jefferson, 1991; Fernandez et al., 2003)). A wide range of connectivity patterns and migration regimes has been discussed in the literature, and there are initial results linking specific connectivity patterns to expected performance on specific problems (Bryden et al., 2005).

In this chapter we present a form of geography that is considerably simpler than those generally used in genetic programming. Our *trivial geography* model is a 1-dimensional "overlapping neighborhoods" model that implements a concept of geography similar to that used in many artificial life simulations (Ray, 1991; Ofria and Wilke, 2004; Axelrod et al., 2004). It is also similar in many respects to the "local selection" genetic algorithm of Collins and Jefferson (1991); although their work is often cited as inspiration for the use of isolated demes with migration, the individuals in their model were actually distributed across 1-dimensional or 2-dimensional grids, with one individual per grid location, and selection and mating were performed in local areas of the grid. For example, short random walks through the grid were used to pair mates. A more recent genetic programming model, known as "cellular" or "diffusion" genetic programming, locates individuals on a 2-dimensional grid and allows interactions only between immediate neighbors (Pettey, 1997; Folino et al., 1999; Folino et al., 2003). Several other models involving related notions of locality have been used in other genetic programming work, often in the context of additional innovations (*e.g.* co-evolution or autoconstructive evolution) (D'haeseleer and Bluming, 1994; Spector, 2001).

Trivial geography requires no explicit representation of demes, connectivity patterns, or migration rates. It requires only minimal changes to a standard genetic programming system and a single new parameter. The question we set out to investigate was whether such a minimal form of geography could make much of a difference with respect to problem-solving performance, and if so what that difference might be. Our data show that trivial geography does indeed appear to make a substantial positive difference, improving problem-solving performance.

In the next section we describe our concept of trivial geography and its simple implementation. This is followed by two sections demonstrating the utility of trivial geography, first on a suite of ten symbolic regression problems and then on a difficult problem in quantum computing. We follow these demonstrations with a general discussion and a recommendation that trivial geography be incorporated into genetic programming systems more broadly.

2. Trivial Geography

In our trivial geography scheme the population is viewed as having a 1-dimensional spatial structure—actually a circle, as we consider the first and last locations to be adjacent. The production of an individual for location i is permitted to involve only parents from i's local neighborhood, where the neighborhood is defined as all individuals within distance R (the neighborhood radius) of i. Aside from this restriction no changes are made to the genetic programming system.

This scheme can be applied to most standard genetic programming systems with very little effort. Since most systems store their populations in 1-dimensional data structures (arrays or lists) anyway, all that is required is that one restrict the selection of parents relative to the index of a child.

To avoid conflation of geography and genetic operators we assume that genetic operators are chosen independently of location. Presumably the operators are chosen randomly, with biases incorporated into the random choice to achieve desired operator ratios. This is indeed a common implementation strategy (used, for example, in ECJ[1]), although in some implementations (*e.g.* that described in (Koza, 1992)) a particular genetic operator is applied to produce the first segment of the population, another operator is applied to produce the next segment, and so on. Under such an implementation operators would be restricted to certain geographic areas and one can imagine that strange dynamics

---

[1]http://cs.gmu.edu/~eclab/projects/ecj/

Table 8-1. Symbolic regression problems used for tests of trivial geography.

#	Problem
1	$y = 8x^3 + 3x^2 + x$
2	$y = 7x^3 - 3x^2 + 17x$
3	$y = 5x^3 + 12x^2 - 3x$
4	$y = x^3 + x^2 + x$
5	$y = x^3 - 2x^2 - x$
6	$y = 8x^5 + 3x^3 + x^2 + 6$
7	$y = 7x^4 - 6x^3 + 3x^2 + 17x - 3$
8	$y = 5x^6 - 2x^5 - 5x^3 + 3x^2 + 5$
9	$y = x^4 + x^3 + x^2 + x - 8$
10	$y = x^6 - 2x^4 + x^2 - 2$

would result; one would probably want to convert first to location-independent operator selection, which is itself usually a simple modification.

While trivial geography can be used with various selection schemes it is particularly simple to describe in terms of tournament selection. In this context it can be implemented simply by changing the function that chooses a random individual to participate in a tournament. Whereas the standard scheme chooses each such individual randomly from the entire population, in trivial geography we choose each such individual from the neighborhood of the location for which we are creating a new individual. In particular we choose only from individuals with indices in the range $(i - R, i + R)$, where i is the index of the location for which we are creating an individual, R is a *radius* parameter, and we "wrap around" from the bottom to the top of the range and vice versa.[2] The modification to restrict the range of choices is indeed often trivial, involving only one or a few lines of code.

3.   Trivial Geography Applied to Symbolic Regression

We tested trivial geography on the ten arbitrarily chosen symbolic regression problems listed in Table 8-1. We used the PushGP genetic programming system, which evolves programs in the Push language (Spector, 2001; Spector and Robinson, 2002; Spector et al., 2005).[3] Push is a multi-type, stack-based programming language that supports the evolution of novel control structures

---

[2]In some programming languages this "wrapping around" can be accomplished with a single call to the modulus function.
[3]http://hampshire.edu/lspector/push.html

Table 8-2. Parameters for symbolic regression tests of trivial geography. The instruction set is limited to simple integer manipulation and integer stack manipulation. The INPUT instruction pushes the current input (x) value onto the integer stack.

Problems	Symbolic regression problems listed in Table 8-1.
Input (x) values	0–9
Fitness	Sum of absolute values of errors for all inputs.
Runs per problem	115 with trivial geography,
	115 without trivial geography.
Radius (R)	10
Population size	2000
Crossover rate	40%
Mutation rate	40%, fair mutation
	(Crawford-Marks and Spector, 2002)
Duplication rate	20%
Tournament size	7
Maximum generations	200
Initial program size limit	100
Child program size limit	100
Program evaluation limit	100
Ephemeral random constants	integer $(-10, 10)$
Instructions	INTEGER.+, INTEGER.-, INTEGER.*,
	INTEGER./, INTEGER.POP, INTEGER.DUP,
	INTEGER.SWAP, INTEGER.SHOVE,
	INTEGER.YANK, INTEGER.YANKDUP, INPUT

through explicit code and control manipulation, but none of these novel features were used in the present study. For the experiments reported here we used only a minimal integer-oriented instruction set, so that PushGP was acting here much like any standard genetic programming system.[4] We have no reason to believe that the remaining differences between PushGP and other genetic programming systems contributed to our results in any significant way. The full set of parameters used for our runs is presented in Table 8-2.

We examined the results in two ways, looking both at the "computational effort" required to find a solution (Koza, 1994) and the mean best fitness across all runs on a particular problem. Computational effort was computed as described by Koza (pp. 99–103), first calculating $P(M, i)$, the cumulative probability of success by generation i using a population of size M (this is just the total number of runs that succeeded on or before the ith generation, divided by the total number of runs conducted). $I(M, i, z)$, the number of individuals that must be

---

[4]We used the version of PushGP distributed with the Breve simulation environment (Klein, 2002). Breve is available from http://www.spiderland.org/breve.

Table 8-3. Successes/runs and computational efforts for the symbolic regression problems with and without trivial geography.

#	Successes/runs without trivial geography	Effort without trivial geography	Successes/runs with trivial geography	Effort with trivial geography
1	67/115	600, 000	113/115	316, 000
2	24/115	3, 024, 000	64/115	2, 176, 000
3	8/114	12, 566, 000	50/115	3, 160, 000
4	115/115	36, 000	115/115	30, 000
5	106/115	132, 000	115/115	66, 000
6	17/115	5, 928, 000	76/113	1, 840, 000
7	2/114	54, 810, 000	6/114	38, 406, 000
8	0/113	∞	1/113	144, 282, 000
9	73/113	848, 000	113/113	276, 000
10	101/113	280, 000	113/113	164, 000

processed to produce a solution by generation i with probability greater than z (by convention, $z = 99\%$) is then calculated as:

$$I(M, i, z) = M * (i + 1) * \left\lceil \frac{\log(1 - z)}{\log(1 - P(M, i))} \right\rceil$$

The minimum of $I(M, i, z)$ over all values of i is defined to be the "computational effort" required to solve the problem.

The computational efforts calculated from our 2, 283 runs (115 runs for each of the 2 conditions for each of the 10 problems, with 17 runs lost to miscellaneous system problems) are shown in Table 8-3. Lower efforts are, of course, better, so this data demonstrates that trivial geography provides a considerable benefit on all of the symbolic regression problems.

Because the problems vary widely in difficulty we also show, in Figure 8-1, a graph of these results normalized independently for each problem, with the effort for the standard configuration (without trivial geography) set to 100; the values for the runs with trivial geography therefore indicate the computational effort as a percentage of that in the standard configuration. From this graph it is clear that the benefits provided by trivial geography are indeed substantial.

The mean best fitness values from our runs are shown in Table 8-4. Lower fitness values are better, so this data also demonstrates that trivial geography provides a considerable benefit for all of the symbolic regression problems. We also show, in Figure 8-2, a graph of these results normalized for each problem, with the mean best fitness for the standard configuration (without trivial geography) set to 100; the values for the runs with trivial geography therefore indicate the mean best fitness as a percentage of that in the standard configuration. For problems #5, #9 and #10 trivial geography achieved a 100%

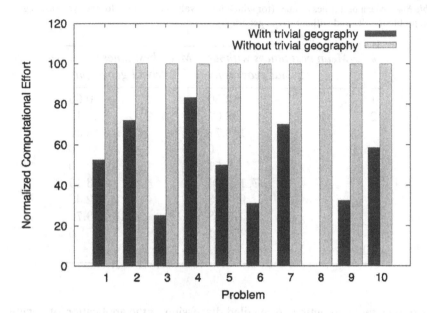

Figure 8-1. Computational efforts calculated for the symbolic regression problems with and without trivial geography. This plot is normalized independently for each problem, with the values for runs in the standard configuration (without trivial geography) shown as 100%. Problem #8 is anomalous because no solutions were found without trivial geography, producing an infinite computational effort.

solution rate (best fitness = 0 for all runs). Problem #4 was exceptionally easy, leading to 100% solution rates in both configurations; both are therefore plotted as 100%. From the mean best fitness values it is also clear that the benefits provided by trivial geography are indeed substantial.

For the mean best fitness values we conducted T tests to assess the statistical significance of the differences between the configurations with and without trivial geography. Aside from problem #4 (in which both configurations achieved 100% solution rates) all differences are significant with $p < 0.01$.

4. Trivial Geography Applied to a Quantum Computing Problem

Quantum information technology is expected to provide revolutionary benefits for computing, but quantum computers are counter-intuitive and difficult to program. Genetic programming can be used to automatically develop quantum computing algorithms, and the resulting algorithms may be useful both for solving practical problems and for answering open questions in the the-

Table 8-4. Mean best fitness values (for which lower values are better) for the symbolic regression problems with and without trivial geography.

#	Mean best fitness without trivial geography	Mean best fitness with trivial geography
1	52.50	0.65
2	98.67	19.13
3	148.77	48.39
4	0	0
5	5.51	0
6	7, 149.94	63.19
7	957.43	332.48
8	27, 475.48	16, 859.71
9	22.41	0
10	1.81	0

ory of quantum computing. A detailed discussion of the application of genetic programming to quantum computing problems can be found in (Spector, 2004).

The problem we set out to solve, like many quantum computation problems, involves determining how a "black box" computational gate called an *oracle* transforms the qubits to which it is applied.[5] In particular, we were interested in determining whether a given 2-input, 1-output Boolean oracle flips its output qubit under the conditions illustrated in Figure 8-3. That is, we are asked to determine if the cases for which the oracle flips its output qubit satisfy the logical formula $(I_{00} \vee I_{01}) \wedge (I_{10} \vee I_{11})$, where I_{ab} indicates whether or not the output is flipped for the input (a, b).

This problem, which is called the "AND/OR" oracle problem, has been the subject of several of our previous investigations (Spector et al., 1999; Barnum et al., 2000; Spector, 2004). We previously used genetic programming to find quantum algorithms that perform better than any possible classical algorithm (that is, they have lower probability of error) when restricted to a single oracle call. We have recently been investigating the two-oracle-call version of this problem. The lowest error probability obtainable by a probabilistic classical algorithm on the two-oracle-call version of this problem is $\frac{1}{6} = 0.1666...$, but in our recent work we have found, using genetic programming, quantum algorithms with an error probability of less than 0.11 (Spector and Klein, 2005b).

---

[5] A qubit is the quantum analog of a classical "bit"; see (Spector, 2004) for a detailed description of qubits and the ways in which they are manipulated by quantum gates.

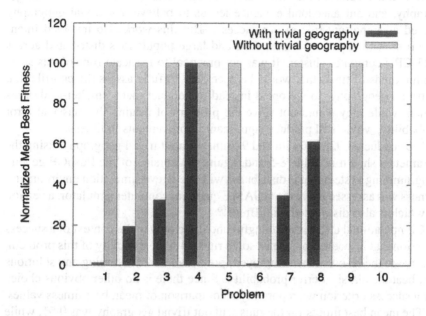

Figure 8-2. Mean best fitness values (for which lower values are better) for the symbolic regression problems with and without trivial geography. This plot is normalized independently for each problem, with the values for runs in the standard configuration (without trivial geography) shown as 100%. For problems #5, #9 and #10 trivial geography achieved a 100% solution rate (fitness = 0 for all runs). For problem #4 both configurations achieved a 100% solution rate.

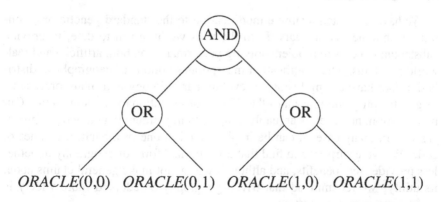

Figure 8-3. An "AND/OR" tree describing the property of interest in the AND/OR oracle problem (see text).

Our new results on the two-oracle-call AND/OR problem used trivial geography, and our anecdotal evidence led us to believe that trivial geography played an important role in our success. But this work also involved intensive runs with expensive fitness tests and large populations distributed across a 23-CPU computer cluster. It was not practical to replicate runs of this scale the hundreds of times that would be necessary to fully assess the contribution of trivial geography, so we opted instead to conduct many smaller-scale runs which, while they would not solve the problem of beating the classical error probability, would still produce significant improvements in fitness.

We conducted 92 runs with and 92 runs without trivial geography, using the parameters shown in Table 8-5 and, again, the version of the PushGP genetic programming system that is distributed with the Breve simulation environment. Fitness was assessed using the QGAME quantum computer simulator, a version of which is also distributed with Breve.[6]

Computational effort is meaningful and finite only in the context of a success criterion that is reached in at least some runs. But the difficulty of this problem, relative to the resources we employed, prevented us from finding any solutions that beat the classical error probability. Since there is no other obvious choice for a success criterion we reportonly a comparison of mean best fitness values.

The mean best fitness for the runs without trivial geography was 0.51, while the mean best fitness for the runs with trivial geography was better, at 0.32. A T test shows this difference to be statistically significant with $p < 0.005$. Again, we see a substantial improvement in problem-solving performance provided by trivial geography.

5.   Discussion

We have presented a simple modification to the standard genetic programming technique that appears, from the tests we have run to date, to provide substantial benefits to problem-solving performance on both artificial and real-world problems. The modification incorporates notions of geographical distribution that have a long history in evolutionary biology and many precedents in genetic programming and other forms of evolutionary computation. Our modification, however, is arguably simpler to implement than any of its predecessors; in many cases it can be implemented in one or a handful of lines of code. We were surprised to find that this "trivial" form of geography nonetheless provides real benefits, and although we cannot make general claims about its utility[7] we recommend that trivial geography be adopted more widely in genetic programming systems.

---

[6]QGAME documentation and code is available from http://hampshire.edu/lspector/qgame.html.
[7]Such claims would require analysis and discussion of the results in the context of the No Free Lunch theorem (Wolpert and Macready, 1997; Droste et al., 1999).

Table 8-5. Parameters for quantum computing tests of trivial geography. For this problem a developmental approach was used in which certain instructions add quantum gates to a developing "embryo"; see (Spector, 2004) for details.

Problem	AND/OR oracle problem (Spector, 2004), with two calls to the oracle permitted.
Embryo	Three-qubit quantum circuit with a final measurement on one qubit (index 2 of (0–2)).
Fitness cases	All possible two-input, one-output Boolean oracles, specifically $(I_{00}I_{01}I_{10}I_{11} : answer)$: 0000:0, 0001:0, 0010:0, 0011:0, 0100:0, 0101:1, 0110:1, 0111:1, 1000:0, 1001:1, 1010:1, 1011:1, 1100:0, 1101:1, 1110:1, 1111:1
Fitness function	$Misses + MaxError$ where $Misses$ is the number of cases for which the probability of error is greater than 0.48 and $MaxError$ is the maximum probability of error of any case.
Runs	92 with trivial geography, 92 without trivial geography.
Radius (R)	15
Population size	2500
Crossover rate	40%
Mutation rate	40%, fair mutation (Crawford-Marks and Spector, 2002)
Duplication rate	20%
Tournament size	7
Maximum generations	500
Initial program size limit	100
Child program size limit	250
Program evaluation limit	250
Ephemeral random constants	integer $(-10, 10)$, float $(-10.0, 10.0)$
Instructions	FLOAT.%, FLOAT.*, FLOAT.+, FLOAT.-, FLOAT./, FLOAT.DUP, FLOAT.POP, FLOAT.SWAP, FLOAT.FROMINTEGER, LIMITED-ORACLE, HADAMARD, U-THETA, MEASURE, SRN, CNOT, U2, CPHASE, SWAP, END

For researchers and practitioners using genetic programming systems that already involve geographical distribution (*e.g.* in isolated demes with migration) an obvious practical question, not addressed here, is that of how trivial geography compares to their presumably more complex techniques. One might also be interested in the effects of combining several forms of geography, for example by using an island model in which trivial geography is used within each island. Although comparisons of these techniques are simple to make in principle, one would have to conduct large numbers of tests using each of many geographical schemes to make definitive recommendations. Our contention here is not that trivial geography necessarily outperforms other forms of geography, but only that it appears to provide benefits over non-geographical models in many cases for nearly no cost.

The mechanism by which trivial geography improves problem-solving performance is presumably a form of diversity maintenance. An obvious follow-up study would apply diversity measures to runs like those conducted here and investigate the relations between problems, performance, and diversity. Many diversity measures for genetic programming have been developed, as have methodologies for correlating various diversity measures and aspects of system performance (Burke et al., 2004).

The values of R, the neighborhood radius, that we used in the experiments reported here (10 and 15) were chosen somewhat arbitrarily. We conducted preliminary runs with several values of R and many appeared to perform well; we chose the values that we did because they appeared to give good results, but did not investigate other values of R systematically.

## 6.	Summary

An extremely simple modification to the genetic programming algorithm, incorporating "trivial geography," appears to improve problem-solving performance for nearly no cost. This modification has many precedents in genetic programming and evolutionary computation, but it is surprising that so simple a form of the idea can have such substantial effects. We recommend that trivial geography be adopted more broadly in genetic programming.

Acknowledgements

This material is based upon work supported by the National Science Foundation under Grant No. 0308540 and Grant No. 0216344. Any opinions, findings, and conclusions or recommendations expressed in this publication are those of the authors and do not necessarily reflect the views of the National Science Foundation. We thank Nic McPhee, Ellery Crane, Christian Jacob, and the other participants in the Genetic Programming Theory and Practice Workshop for many helpful comments that led to substantial improvements in this chapter.

References

Andre, David and Koza, John R. (1996). A parallel implementation of genetic programming that achieves super-linear performance. In Arabnia, Hamid R., editor, *Proceedings of the International Conference on Parallel and Distributed Processing Techniques and Applications*, volume III, pages 1163–1174, Sunnyvale. CSREA.

Avise, J. C. (2000). *Phylogeography: The History and Formation of Species*. Harvard University Press.

Axelrod, R., Hammond, R. A., and Grafen, A. (2004). Altruism via kin-selection strategies that rely on arbitrary tags with which they coevolve. *Evolution*, 58(8):1833–1838.

Banzhaf, Wolfgang, Nordin, Peter, Keller, Robert E., and Francone, Frank D. (1998). *Genetic Programming – An Introduction; On the Automatic Evolution of Computer Programs and its Applications*. Morgan Kaufmann.

Barnum, Howard, Bernstein, Herbert J, and Spector, Lee (2000). Quantum circuits for OR and AND of ORs. *Journal of Physics A: Mathematical and General*, 33(45):8047–8057.

Bryden, Kenneth M., Ashlock, Daniel A., Corns, Steven, and Willson, Stephen J. (2005). Graph based evolutionary algorithms. *IEEE Transactions on Evolutionary Computation*, forthcoming.

Burke, Edmund K., Gustafson, Steven, and Kendall, Graham (2004). Diversity in genetic programming: An analysis of measures and correlation with fitness. *IEEE Transactions on Evolutionary Computation*, 8(1):47–62.

Collins, Robert J. and Jefferson, David R. (1991). Selection in massively parallel genetic algorithms. In Belew, Rick and Booker, Lashon, editors, *Proceedings of the Fourth International Conference on Genetic Algorithms*, pages 249–256, San Mateo, CA. Morgan Kaufman.

Crawford-Marks, Raphael and Spector, Lee (2002). Size control via size fair genetic operators in the PushGP genetic programming system. In Langdon, W. B., Cantú-Paz, E., Mathias, K., Roy, R., Davis, D., Poli, R., Balakrishnan, K., Honavar, V., Rudolph, G., Wegener, J., Bull, L., Potter, M. A., Schultz, A. C., Miller, J. F., Burke, E., and Jonoska, N., editors, *GECCO 2002: Proceedings of the Genetic and Evolutionary Computation Conference*, pages 733–739, New York. Morgan Kaufmann Publishers.

D'haeseleer, Patrik and Bluming, Jason (1994). Effects of locality in individual and population evolution. In Kinnear, Jr., Kenneth E., editor, *Advances in Genetic Programming*, chapter 8, pages 177–198. MIT Press.

Droste, Stefan, Jansen, Thomas, and Wegener, Ingo (1999). Perhaps not a free lunch but at least a free appetizer. In Banzhaf, Wolfgang, Daida, Jason, Eiben, Agoston E., Garzon, Max H., Honavar, Vasant, Jakiela, Mark, and Smith, Robert E., editors, *Proceedings of the Genetic and Evolutionary Computation Conference*, volume 1, pages 833–839, Orlando, Florida, USA. Morgan Kaufmann.

Eshel, I. (1972). On the neighbor effect and the evolution of altruistic traits. *Theoretical Population Biology*, 3:258–277.

Fernandez, Francisco, Tomassini, Marco, and Vanneschi, Leonardo (2003). An empirical study of multipopulation genetic programming. *Genetic Programming and Evolvable Machines*, 4(1):21–51.

Folino, G., Pizzuti, C., Spezzano, G., Vanneschi, L., and Tomassini, M. (2003). Diversity analysis in cellular and multipopulation genetic programming. In

Sarker, Ruhul, Reynolds, Robert, Abbass, Hussein, Tan, Kay Chen, McKay, Bob, Essam, Daryl, and Gedeon, Tom, editors, *Proceedings of the 2003 Congress on Evolutionary Computation CEC2003*, pages 305–311, Canberra. IEEE Press.

Folino, Gianluigi, Pizzuti, Clara, and Spezzano, Giandomenico (1999). A cellular genetic programming approach to classification. In Banzhaf, Wolfgang, Daida, Jason, Eiben, Agoston E., Garzon, Max H., Honavar, Vasant, Jakiela, Mark, and Smith, Robert E., editors, *Proceedings of the Genetic and Evolutionary Computation Conference*, volume 2, pages 1015–1020, Orlando, Florida, USA. Morgan Kaufmann.

Holland, J. H. (1992). *Adaptation in Natural and Artificial Systems*. MIT Press.

Holland, J. H. (1995). *Hidden Order: How Adaptation Builds Complexity*. Perseus Books.

Klein, Jon (2002). BREVE: a 3d environment for the simulation of decentralized systems and artificial life. In Standish, R. K., Bedau, M. A., and Abbass, H. A., editors, *Proceedings of Artificial Life VIII, the 8th International Conference on the Simulation and Synthesis of Living Systems*, pages 329–334. The MIT Press.

http://www.spiderland.org/breve/breve-klein-alife2002.pdf.

Koza, John R. (1992). *Genetic Programming: On the Programming of Computers by Means of Natural Selection*. MIT Press, Cambridge, MA, USA.

Koza, John R. (1994). *Genetic Programming II: Automatic Discovery of Reusable Programs*. MIT Press, Cambridge Massachusetts.

Lieberman, E., Hauert, C., and Nowak, M. A. (2005). Evolutionary dynamics on graphs. *Nature*, 433:312–316.

Maruyama, Tsutomu, Hirose, Tetsuya, and Konagaya, Akihiko (1993). A fine-grained parallel genetic algorithm for distributed parallel systems. In Forrest, Stephanie, editor, *Proc. of the Fifth Int. Conf. on Genetic Algorithms*, pages 184–190, San Mateo, CA. Morgan Kaufmann.

Mayr, Ernst (1942). *Systematics and the origin of species from the viewpoint of a zoologist*. Columbia University Press.

Nowak, M. A. and May, R. M. (1992). Evolutionary games and spatial chaos. *Nature*, 359:826–829.

Nowostawski, M. and Poll, R. (1999). Parallel genetic algorithm taxonomy.

Ofria, Charles and Wilke, Claus O. (2004). Avida: A software platform for research in computational evolutionary biology. *Artificial Life*, 10(2):191–229.

Pettey, Chrisila C. (1997). Diffusion (cellular) models. In Bäck, Thomas, Fogel, David B., and Michalewicz, Zbigniew, editors, *Handbook of Evolutionary Computation*, pages C6.4:1–6. Institute of Physics Publishing and Oxford University Press, Bristol, New York.

Ray, Thomas S. (1991). Is it alive or is it GA. In Belew, Richard K. and Booker, Lashon B., editors, *Proceedings of the Fourth International Conference on Genetic Algorithms*, pages 527–534, University of California - San Diego, La Jolla, CA, USA. Morgan Kaufmann.

Spector, Lee (2001). Autoconstructive evolution: Push, pushGP, and pushpop. In Spector, Lee, Goodman, Erik D., Wu, Annie, Langdon, W. B., Voigt, Hans-Michael, Gen, Mitsuo, Sen, Sandip, Dorigo, Marco, Pezeshk, Shahram, Garzon, Max H., and Burke, Edmund, editors, *Proceedings of the Genetic and Evolutionary Computation Conference (GECCO-2001)*, pages 137–146, San Francisco, California, USA. Morgan Kaufmann.

Spector, Lee (2004). *Automatic Quantum Computer Programming: A Genetic Programming Approach*, volume 7 of *Genetic Programming*. Kluwer Academic Publishers, Boston/Dordrecht/New York/London. in press.

Spector, Lee, Barnum, Howard, Bernstein, Herbert J., and Swamy, Nikhil (1999). Finding a better-than-classical quantum AND/OR algorithm using genetic programming. In Angeline, Peter J., Michalewicz, Zbyszek, Schoenauer, Marc, Yao, Xin, and Zalzala, Ali, editors, *Proceedings of the Congress on Evolutionary Computation*, volume 3, pages 2239–2246, Mayflower Hotel, Washington D.C., USA. IEEE Press.

Spector, Lee and Klein, Jon (2005a). Genetic stability and territorial structure facilitate the evolution of tag-mediated altruism. *Artificial Life*. Forthcoming.

Spector, Lee and Klein, Jon (2005b). Machine invention of quantum computing circuits by means of genetic programming. In preparation.

Spector, Lee, Klein, Jon, and Keijzer, Maarten (2005). The push3 execution stack and the evolution of control. In *Proc. of the Genetic and Evolutionary Computation Conference*. Springer-Verlag.

Spector, Lee and Robinson, Alan (2002). Genetic programming and autoconstructive evolution with the push programming language. *Genetic Programming and Evolvable Machines*, 3(1):7–40.

Wolpert, David H. and Macready, William G. (1997). No free lunch theorems for optimization. *IEEE Transactions on Evolutionary Computation*, 1(1):67–82.

Wright, Sewall (1945). Tempo and mode in evolution: a critical review. *Ecology*, 26:415–419.

Chapter 9

RUNNING GENETIC PROGRAMMING BACKWARDS

Riccardo Poli[1] and William B. Langdon[1]

[1]*Department of Computer Science, University of Essex, UK*

Abstract   Backward chaining evolutionary algorithms (BC-EA) offer the prospect of run-time efficiency savings by reducing the number of fitness evaluations without significantly changing the course of genetic algorithm or genetic programming runs. "Tournament selection, iterated coupon-collection problem, and backward-chaining evolutionary algorithm," Poli, *FOGA*, 2005 describes how BC-EA does this by avoiding the generation and evaluation of individuals which never appear in selection tournaments. It suggests the largest savings occur in very large populations, short runs, small tournament sizes and shows actual savings in fixed-length binary GAs. Here, we provide a generational GP implementation, including mutation and two offspring crossover of BC-EA and empirically investigate its efficiency in terms of both fitness evaluations and effectiveness.

Keywords: Backward-Chaining, genetic programming, tournament selection, efficient algorithms

1.   Introduction

Due to its simplicity and efficiency, particularly for large populations, tournament selection is currently the most popular form of fitness selection in Genetic Programming (GP). The average number of tournaments per generation depends upon whether crossover generates one or two children. With non-overlapping populations of size M and if crossover produces one child from two parents the expected number of tournaments needed to form a new generation is $M(1 + p_c)$ (p_c is the crossover probability). However, if each crossover produces two offspring then only (and exactly) M tournaments are needed.

Here we focus on genetic programming with two-offspring crossover.[1] So, if n is the tournament size, creating a new generation requires drawing exactly nM individuals uniformly at random (with resampling) from the current population. As we highlighted in (Poli, 2005), an interesting side effect of this process is that not all individuals in a particular generation are necessarily sampled. This is particularly true where tournament groups are small. For example, $n = 2$.

Except in special cases (such as elitism), the individuals that do not get sampled by the selection process have no influence whatsoever on future generations. However, these individuals use up resources, especially CPU time. So one might wonder whether it is possible to avoid generating such individuals and what sort of saving one could obtain.

In (Poli, 2005) we provided a theoretical analysis based on Markov chains of the sampling behaviour of tournament selection that started to show the savings. In addition it described a general scheme, *Backward-Chaining, Evolutionary Algorithms* (BC-EA), which exploits the sampling deficiencies of tournament selection to reduce (or make better use of) the fitness evaluations in an EA. (Poli, 2005) suggests the greatest benefits of backward chaining EAs come with very large populations, short runs and relatively small tournament sizes. These are the settings used frequently in genetic programming, particularly when attacking large real-world problems, so a backward-chaining GP system would appear to have a great potential.

The next section provides a review of previous relevant work, including the main findings of (Poli, 2005). The third section describes the implementation and time and space complexity of our backward chaining GP system. Section 4 experimentally compares its performance and behaviour with standard GP. We conclude with Section 5.

2.   Background

One of the main lines of research on selection in EAs has been into *loss of diversity*, *i.e.* the proportion of individuals of a population that are not selected. In (Blickle and Thiele, 1997; Motoki, 2002) different selection methods, including tournament selection, were analysed in depth mathematically.

It is important to understand the difference between *not selecting* and *not sampling* an individual in a particular generation. *Not selecting* refers to an individual that did not win any tournaments. This is exactly what research on the loss of diversity has concentrated on. *Not sampling*, instead, refers to an individual that did not participate in any tournament at all, simply because it was not sampled during the creation of the required tournament sets. (Poli, 2005) and this paper focus on individuals that are not sampled.

---

[1] We have considered the one-offspring case in (Poli, 2005; Poli and Langdon, 2005).

(Sastry and Goldberg, 2001) show cases where the performance of a GA using a particular version of tournament selection (which guarantees that all individuals in a run are sampled) is better than a GA with standard tournament selection. Similar results have been recently reported in (Sokolov and Whitley, 2005), which proposes a different tournament strategy that also guarantees that all individuals are sampled. While these two lines of work concentrate on modifying tournament selection, we focus on understanding and exploiting the sampling behaviour of standard tournament selection.

Tournament Selection and the Coupon Collector

In (Poli, 2005), a connection between tournament selection and the coupon collection problem was proposed and analysed. In the coupon collection problem (Feller, 1971), every time a collector buys a certain product, a coupon is given to him. The coupon is equally likely to be any one of N types. In order to win a prize, the collector must have at least one coupon of each type.

How is the process of tournament selection related to the coupon collection problem? We can imagine that the individuals in the current population are distinct coupons and that tournament selection will draw (with replacement) nM times from this pool of coupons. Results on the coupon collector problem tell us that if $n < \log M$, there may be a substantial number of individuals that selection did not sample. That is, for small tournament sizes or large populations, many individuals will not be sampled.

In (Poli, 2005), we found that the expected number of distinct individuals sampled by tournament selection in one generation is approximately $M(1 - e^{-n})$. So for $n = 2$, we should expect about 13.5% of the population not to be sampled. For $n = 3$ this drops to 5%, and becomes quickly negligible for larger tournament sizes. This suggests that saving computational resources by avoiding the creation and evaluation of individuals that will not be sampled by the tournament selection process may be possible only for small tournament sizes. However, low selection pressures are quite common in GP practice, particularly when attacking hard, multi-modal problems which require extensive exploration of the search space before zooming in on any particular region. Also, much greater savings in computation are possible if we exploit the transient behaviour of tournament selection *over multiple generations*.

To understand what happens over multiple generations, let us imagine we are interested in knowing the genetic makeup and fitness of m_0 individuals in a particular generation, G. Clearly, in order to create such individuals, we will need to know who their parent(s) were. On average, this will require running m_0 tournaments to select such parents. In each tournament we pick n individuals randomly from generation $G - 1$. After nm_0 such trials, we will be in a position to determine which individuals in generation $G - 1$ will have an influence on generation G.[2] Let m_1 be the number of individuals sampled. We can now perform nm_1 trials to determine which individuals in generation $G - 2$ (the new coupon set) will have an influence on future generations. Let m_2 be their number. The process continues until we reach the initial random generation.

The quantities m_t for $t = 0, 1, \ldots$ are stochastic variables. Their probability distributions are necessary in order to evaluate the sampling behaviour of tournament selection over multiple generations. In (Poli, 2005) we analysed this process by defining and studying a new and more complex form of coupon collection problem: the iterated coupon collection problem. We modelled the iterated effects of tournament selection as a Markov chain and we showed that under very mild conditions the transition matrix for the chain is ergodic. Therefore, the probability distributions of m_t converge (roughly exponentially) towards a limit distribution that is independent from the initial conditions and so, the expected value of m_t converges to a constant value.

In other words, for long runs (*i.e.* large G) the number of individuals required in the final generation, m_0, makes almost no difference to the total number of individuals sampled by tournament selection. However for short runs, the transient of the Markov chain is what one needs to focus on. Both are given by the Markov chain theory, but one needs to be able to numerically compute the eigenvalues and eigenvectors of the transition matrix.

Efficient Tournament Selection and Backward Chaining EAs

From a practical perspective, the question is: how can we modify an EA to achieve a computational saving from not evaluating and creating individuals not sampled by selection? The idea proposed in (Poli, 2005) is to reorder the different phases of an EA. These are: a) the choice of genetic operator to use to create a new individual, b) the formation of a random pool of individuals for the application of tournament selection, c) the identification of the winner of the tournament (parent) based on fitness, d) the execution of the chosen genetic operator, and e) the evaluation of the fitness of the resulting offspring.[3]

The genetic makeup of the individuals is required only in phases (c), (d) and (e), but not (a) and (b). So, it is possible to change the order in which we perform these phases without affecting the behaviour of our algorithm. For example, we can first iterate phases (a) and (b) as many times as needed to create a full new generation (of course, memorising all the decisions taken), and then iterate phases (c)–(e).[4]

---

[2] The other individuals in generation $G - 1$ have not been sampled and so cannot contribute. Of course only the winners of tournaments pass their genetic material to generation G.

[3] Phases (b) and (c) are repeated once for mutation and twice for crossover. That is as many times as the arity of the genetic operator chosen in phase (a).

[4] (Teller and Andre, 1997) used a similar idea to speed up (but not reduce!) GP fitness evaluations.

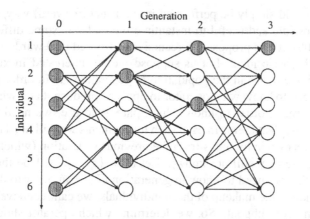

Figure 9-1. Example of graph structure induced by tournament selection in a population of $M = 6$ individuals, run for $G = 3$ generations, using binary tournaments ($n = 2$) and crossover rate $p_c = 1/3$. Nodes with four incoming links were created by crossover. The remaining nodes were created by either mutation or reproduction. Shaded nodes are the potential "ancestors" involved in the creation of the first individual in last generation.

In fact, one can even go further. If we fix in advance the maximum number of generations G we are prepared to run our EA, then phases (a) and (b) (random choices of genetic operations and who will be in which tournament) can be done, not just for one generation, but for a whole run. Then we iterate phases (c)–(e) as required.

We can view the selection of genetic operations and tournament members (phases (a) and (b)) during the whole run, as producing a graph structure containing $(G + 1)M$ nodes. The nodes represent the individuals to be created during the run and the edges connect each individual to the individuals that were involved in the tournaments necessary to select its parents (see Figure 9-1). Nodes without outgoing nodes are not sampled by tournament selection.

If we are interested in calculating and evaluating m_0 individuals in the population at generation G, maximum efficiency can be achieved by considering (flagging for evaluation) only the individuals that are directly or indirectly connected with those m_0 individuals. For example, if in Figure 9-1 we were interested only in the first individual in the last generation, we would need to create and evaluate only that individual and its potential ancestors (shown with shaded nodes). The possible ancestors of our m_0 individuals can be found with a trivial connected-component graph algorithm. Once the relevant sub-graph is known, we evaluate the individuals in it from generation 0 to generation G.

The graph induced by tournament selection can be created without the need to know either what each individual (node) represents or its fitness. So one might ask whether the construction and the evaluation of the individuals in the sub-graph should simply be performed in the usual (forward) way, or whether it may be possible and useful to instantiate the nodes in some different order. In (Poli, 2005), it was proposed to recursively proceed backwards.

Here is the basic idea. Let us suppose we are interested in knowing the makeup of individual i in the population at generation G. In order to generate i, we only need to know what operator to apply to produce it and which parents to use. In turn, in order to know which parents to use, we need to perform tournaments to select them. In each such tournaments we will need to know the relative fitness of n individuals from the previous generation (which of course, at this stage we may still not know). Let $S = \{s_1, s_2, \dots\}$ be the set of the individuals that we need to know in generation $G - 1$ in order to determine i. If we don't know the makeup of these individuals, we can recursively consider each of them as a subgoal. So, we determine which operator should be used to compute s_1, we determine which set of individuals at generation $G - 2$ is needed to do so, and we continue with the recursion. When we emerge from it, we repeat the process for s_2, etc. The recursion can terminate in one of two ways: a) we reach generation 0, in which case we can directly instantiate the individual in question by invoking the initialisation procedure, or b) the individual for which we need to know the genetic makeup has already been evaluated before. Once we have finished with i, we repeat the same process for any other individuals of interest at generation G, one by one.

This algorithm is effectively a recursive depth-first traversal of the graph induced by tournament selection (*c.f.* Figure 9-1). While we traverse the graph, as soon as we are in a position to know the genetic makeup of a node encountered we invoke the fitness evaluation procedure. An EA running in this mode is a *Backward-Chaining, Evolutionary Algorithms (BC-EA)*.

Irrespectively of the problem being solved and the parameter settings used, because the decisions as to which operator to adopt to create a new individual and which elements of the population to use for a tournament are random, this version of the algorithm is almost statistically identical to a standard EA (see (Poli, 2005)). However, there is an important difference: the *order* in which individuals in the population are evaluated. For example, let us consider the population depicted in Figure 9-1 and suppose we are interested in knowing the first individual in the last generation, *i.e.* individual $(3, 1)$. In a standard EA, we evaluate individuals column by column from the left to the right in the following sequence: $(1, 0)$, $(2, 0)$, $(3, 0)$, $(4, 0)$, $(5, 0)$, $(6, 0)$, $(1, 1)$, $(2, 1)$, ... until, finally, we reach node $(1, 3)$. A BC-EA would instead evaluate nodes in a different order, for example, according to the sequence: $(1, 0)$, $(3, 0)$, $(4, 0)$, $(1, 1)$, $(2, 0)$, $(2, 1)$, $(1, 2)$, $(6, 0)$, $(4, 1)$, $(5, 1)$, $(3, 2)$, and finally $(1, 3)$. So, the algorithm would move back and forth evaluating nodes at different generations.

Why is this important? Typically in an EA, the average fitness of the population and the maximum fitness in each generation grow as the generation number grows. In the standard EA, the first 3 individuals evaluated have an expected average fitness equal to the average fitness of the individuals at generation 0, and the same is true for the BC-EA. However, unlike for the standard EA, the fourth individual created and evaluated by BC-EA belongs to generation 1, so its fitness is expected to be higher than that of the previous individuals. Individual 5 has same expected fitness in the two algorithms. However, the 6th individual drawn by BC-EA is a generation 1 individual again, while the forward EA draws a generation 0 individual. So again, the BC-EA is expected to produce a higher fitness sample than the other EA. This applies also to the 7th individual drawn. Of course, this process cannot continue indefinitely, and at some point the individuals evaluated by BC-EA start being on average inferior.

This behaviour is typical: a BC-EA will find fitter individuals faster than an ordinary EA in the first part of a run and slower in the second part. So if one restricts oneself to that first phase, the BC-EA is not just faster than an ordinary EA because it avoids evaluating individuals neglected by tournament selection, it is also a faster search algorithm!

3.   Backward-Chaining GP

Based on these ideas, we have designed and implemented a *Backward-Chaining, Genetic Programming* (BC-GP) system in Java. The objective is to evaluate whether the BC-EA approach indeed brings significant efficiency gains in the case of large populations and short runs, and whether a BC-GP compares well with an equivalent standard (forward) version of GP in terms of ability to solve problems.

Backward-Chaining GP Implementation

Figure 9-2 provides a pseudo-code description of the key components of our system. The main thing to notice is that we use a "lazy-evaluation" approach. We do not create the full graph structure induced by tournament selection: we statically create the nodes in the graph (and store them using two-dimensional arrays). However, the edges are dynamically generated only when needed and stored in the stack as we do recursion. This is achieved by choosing genetic operator and invoking the tournament selection procedure only when needed in order to construct an individual, rather than at the beginning of a run and for all individuals and generations. Also note that our implementation is rather simplistic, in that it requires the pre-allocation of three $G \times M$ arrays:

Population is an array of pointers to the programs in the population at each generation. Programs are stored as strings of bytes, where each byte represents a primitive.

Fitness is an array of single precision floating point numbers. This is used to store the fitness of the programs in Population.

Known is an array of bits. A bit set to 1 indicates that the corresponding individual in Population has been computed and evaluated.

Pre-allocating these arrays is wasteful since only the entries corresponding to individuals sampled by tournament selection are actually used. By using more efficient data structures, one could save some memory. BC-GP also uses an expandable array sibling_pool to temporarily store the second offspring generated in each crossover.

Space and Time Complexity of BC-GP

Let us evaluate the space complexity of BC-GP and compare it to the space complexity of standard GP. We divide the calculation into two parts:

$$C = C_{\text{fixed}} + C_{\text{variable}},$$

where C_{fixed} represents the amount of memory (in bytes) required to store the data structures necessary to run GP excluding the GP programs themselves, while C_{variable} represents the memory used by the programs. This can vary as a function of the random seed used, the generation number and other parameters and details of a run.[5] As far as the fixed complexity is concerned, in a forward generational GP system

$$C_{\text{fixed}}^F = 2 \times M \times (4 + 4) = 16M$$

The factor of 2 arises since, in our generational approach, we store both the current and the new generation. This requires 2 vectors of pointers (4 byte each) to the population members and two vectors of fitness values (floats, 4 byte each), where the vectors are of size M. In BC-GP, instead, we need

$$C_{\text{fixed}}^B = G \times M \times (4 + 4 + \frac{1}{8}) \approx 8GM$$

since we need to store one array of pointers, one of floats, and one bit array, all of size $G \times M$.

Variable complexity is harder to compute. In a standard GP system this is

$$C_{\text{variable}}^F \approx 2 \times M \times S_{\text{max}}^F,$$

where S_{max}^F is the maximum value taken by the average program size during each generation of a run. In a BC-GP

$$C_{\text{variable}}^B = E^B \times S_{\text{avg}}^B,$$

---

[5]The array *sibling_pool* typically includes only very few individuals and so we ignore it in our calculations.

```
run(G,M):
begin
  Create G x M tables Known, Population and Fitness
  For each individual I of interest in generation G
    evolve_back(I,G)
  return all I of interest
end
```

```
evolve_back(indiv,gen):
begin
  if Known[indiv][gen] then
    return
  if gen == 0 then
    Population[gen][indiv] = random program
  else
    myrand = random_float()
    if myrand < crossover_rate then
      if myrand < crossover_rate/2 or sibling_pool[gen] = empty then
        parent1 = tournament(gen-1)
        parent2 = tournament(gen-1)
        offsprings = crossover(parent1,parent2)
        Population[gen][indiv] = offspring[1]
        sibling_pool[gen].add(offspring[2])
      else
        Population[gen][indiv] = sibling_pool[gen].remove_random_indiv();
      endif
    else
      parent = tournament(gen-1)
      Population[gen][indiv] = mutation(parent)
    endif
  endif
  Fitness[gen][indiv] = fit_func(Population[gen][indiv])
  Known[gen][indiv] = true
end
```

```
tournament(gen)
begin
  fbest = 0; best = -1
  repeat tournament_size times
    candidate = random integer 1...M
    evolve_back( gen, candidate )
    if Fitness[gen][candidate] > fbest then
      fbest = Fitness[gen][candidate]
      best = candidate
    endif
  endrepeat
  return( Population[gen][best] )
end
```

Figure 9-2. Pseudo-code for backward-chaining GP. Note use of sibling_pool for second child produced by crossover.

where S_{avg}^B is the average program size during a BC-GP run (*i.e.*, it is the program size averaged over all individuals created *in a run*) and E^B is the number of programs actually created and evaluated during the run ($E^B \leq E^F = GM$). So, the difference in memory required by the two algorithms is

$$\Delta C = C^B - C^F = M(8G - 16) + E^B \times S_{\text{avg}}^B - 2 \times M \times S_{\text{max}}^F,$$

which indicates that in most conditions the use of BC-GP carries a significant memory overhead. However, this does not prevent the use of BC-GP.[6]

The memory overhead of BC-GP, ΔC, is a function of the average average-program-size S_{avg}^B and the maximum average-program-size S_{max}^F. We know that statistically BC-GP and GP behave the same, so we expect $S_{\text{max}}^F = S_{\text{max}}^B$ and so $S_{\text{avg}}^B < S_{\text{max}}^F$. An additional complicating factor is that the size of programs often evolves. If *bloat* (Langdon et al., 1999) happens in a particular problem, then programs in both GP and BC-GP will increase in size towards the end of the run. However, since with BC-GP, in certain conditions ($m_0 \ll M$), we evaluate few individuals in the last generations of a run, where bloat is typically most marked, S_{avg}^B can be be a lot smaller than S_{avg}^F. That is, with bloat the programs created in a BC-GP may be on average smaller than those created by forward GP. So, we may have $S_{\text{avg}}^B \ll S_{\text{max}}^F$.

These effects partly mitigate the memory overhead, ΔC, of BC-GP. Also, because BC-GP tends to evaluates smaller programs than GP, it has an impact on run time too. To see this we need to assess the computational complexity T required to run GP and BC-GP. T is effectively dominated by the cost of running the fitness function. The cost of fitness evaluation depends on various factors, but it is typically approximately proportional to the number of primitives in the program to be evaluated (*i.e.*, executed) and the number of fitness cases N. So if we express T in number of primitives executed, we have

$$T^F = G \times M \times N \times S_{\text{avg}}^F$$

for standard GP, and

$$T^B = E^B \times N \times S_{\text{avg}}^B$$

for BC-GP. So, the saving provided by BC-GP is

$$\Delta T = T^F - T^B = N \times (G \times M \times S_{\text{avg}}^F - E^B \times S_{\text{avg}}^B).$$

That is, for a bloating population, the parsimony of BC-GP in terms of fitness evaluations is compounded with its parsimony in terms of program sizes. In some cases (Poli and Langdon, 2005) this leads to considerable savings.

---

[6]For example, in the worst possible case (where all programs are constructed and evaluated) a BC-GP with a population of 100,000 individuals run for 50 generations and with an average program size (throughout a run) of 100 nodes would require around 540MB of memory.

4.   Experimental Results

Test problems and setup

We used BC-GP in a variety of experiments on three continuous symbolic regression problems where the objective was to induce a target function from examples. The target functions were an univariate quartic polynomial, a four variable quadratic polynomial and a ten variable cubic polynomial. The quartic polynomial is $f(x) = x^4 + x^2 + x^3 + x$. For this problem we used 20 fitness cases of the form $(x, f(x))$ obtained by choosing x uniformly at random in the interval $[-1, +1]$. The first multivariate polynomial, Poly-4, is $f(x_1, x_2, x_3, x_4) = x_1 x_2 + x_3 x_4 + x_1 x_4$. For Poly-4, 50 fitness cases of the form $(x_1, x_2, x_3, x_4, f(x_1, \cdots, x_4))$ were used. They were generated by randomly setting $x_i \in [-1, +1]$. The second multivariate polynomial, Poly-10, is $f(x_1, \cdots, x_{10}) = x_1 x_2 + x_3 x_4 + x_5 x_6 + x_1 x_7 x_9 + x_3 x_6 x_{10}$. For Poly-10 we also used 50 fitness cases of the form $(x_1, \cdots, x_{10}, f(x_1, \cdots, x_{10}))$; again, each of the ten variables is chosen at random from the range $[-1, +1]$. The function set for GP included the functions $+, -, \times$ and the protected division DIV (if $|y| <= 0.001$ DIV$(x, y) = x$ else DIV$(x, y) = x/y$). The terminal set included the independent variables in the problem (x for Quartic, x_1, x_2, x_3, x_4 for Poly-4 and x_1, x_2, ... x_{10} for Poly-10).

Fitness was calculated as the negation of the sum of the absolute errors between the output produced by a program and the desired output on each of the fitness cases. A problem was considered to be solved if a program with an error of less than 10^{-5} summed across all fitness cases was found. We used binary tournaments ($n = 2$) for parent selection. The initial population was created using the "grow" method with max depth of 6 levels (the root node being at level 0). We used 80% two-offspring sub-tree crossover (with uniform random selection of crossover points) and 20% point mutation with a 2% chance of mutation per tree node. The population size M was 100, 1,000, 10,000 and 100,000. The maximum number of fitness evaluations was $30M$ (shorter runs were explored in (Poli and Langdon, 2005)). For different experiments, depending on statistical requirements, we performed 100, 1,000 or even 5,000 independent runs of both backward and forward GP.

In symbolic regression problems, the fitness of programs in the population even after a prolonged period of evolution, can be extremely variable. Since the mean is a linear function, the mean population fitness can be seriously changed by individuals with outstandingly poor fitness. So while both algorithms draw, at each generation, individuals from the same distribution the measured means can be different. While observed means are similar in most generations, even averaging over many runs, the mean of means is still sometimes affected by noise injected by poor individuals. In contrast other statistics, *e.g.* the median

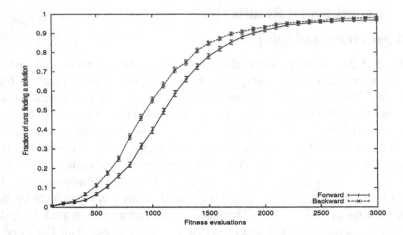

Figure 9-3. Quartic polynomial regression problem. Normal GP contrasted with chance of success with BC-GP (population size 100, average over 1000 runs).

and best, are non-linear and much less effected by the worst in the population. Therefore, we chose to plot the best and the proportion of successful runs.

To make a comparison between the algorithms possible, we computed statistics every M fitness evaluations for BC-GP. We treated this interval as a generation even though the fitness evaluations may be spread over several generations. In the BC-GP we computed 80% of the final generation (*i.e.* $m_0 = 0.8M$).[7]

Effectiveness and efficiency comparison

Figures 9-3 and 9-4 compare the success probabilities of BC-GP and GP for the quartic polynomial for population sizes 100 and 1,000. The error bars indicate standard error (based on the binomial distribution). As expected BC-GP does better and the difference is statistically significant except for the final generations. With a population of 1,000 (Figure 9-4) or bigger (data not reported), BC-GP is also always statistically better than or equal to standard GP. Naturally, with big populations both forward and backward GP almost always solve the quartic polynomial. Nevertheless BC-GP reaches 100% faster.

The four-variate polynomial, Poly-4, is much harder than Quartic. This is an interesting test case since it requires large populations to be solvable in most runs. Figure 9-5 shows the fraction of successful runs with a population of 1,000. Figure 9-6 plots similar data but for a population of 10,000. The

---

[7] (Poli and Langdon, 2005) reports experiments where we calculated only one individual in the last generation (*i.e.* $m_0 = 1$).

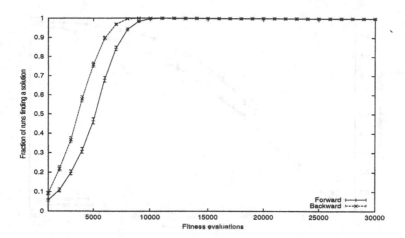

Figure 9-4. Quartic polynomial regression problem. As Figure 9-3 but with population of 1000.

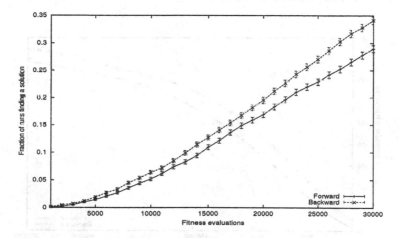

Figure 9-5. Fraction of successful runs (out of 5,000 runs) on the Poly-4 problem for forward GP and BC-GP (30 generations) with populations of 1,000.

difference between BC-GP and forward GP is statistically significant for all population sizes used.

Symbolic regression of Poly-10 is very hard. We tried 1,000 runs with populations of 100, 1,000 and 10,000, and 100 runs with 100,000 individuals. Neither standard GP nor BC-GP found a solution in any of their runs. As illustrated in Figure 9-7 for the case $M = 10,000$, BC-GP on average finds better programs for the same number of fitness evaluations.

So far we have compared forward GP and BC-GP when both algorithms are given the same number of fitness evaluations. In Table 9-1, we show a

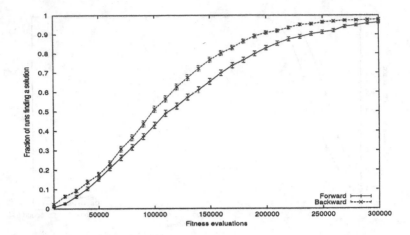

Figure 9-6. Fraction of successful runs (out of 1000 runs) on the Poly-4 problem for forward GP and BC-GP with populations of 10000.

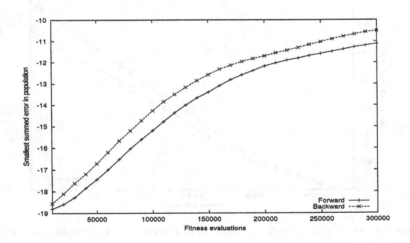

Figure 9-7. Error summed over 50 test cases for Poly-10 regression problem (means of 1,000 runs, with populations of 10,000).

comparison when they are run for the same number of generations ($G = 30$). Thanks to the savings obtained by avoiding to create and evaluate individuals not sampled by selection (and any of their unnecessary ancestors), by the end of the runs, BC-GP evolved solutions of similar fitness but took around 20% fewer fitness evaluations. Similar savings are obtained at all population sizes.

The tests mentioned above have been performed also for the case of tournament size $n = 3$. In all cases BC-GP was superior, but by a smaller margin.

Table 9-1. Normal GP v. Backward chaining on Quartic, Poly 4 and Poly 10. Population 10,000.
Generations 30. Means of 1 000 runs.

Problem	Forward			Backward			Saving
	Best Fit	Evals	Succ Prob	Best Fit	Evals	Succ Prob	
Quartic	0.00	300,000	100.0%	0.00	240,321	100.0%	19.9%
Poly-4	0.12	300,000	96.3%	0.16	240,315	96.0%	19.9%
Poly-10	11.12	300,000	0.0%	11.29	240,299	0.0 %	19.9%

5.   Conclusions

We exploited a recent theoretical analysis (Poli, 2005) of the sampling behaviour of tournament selection over multiple generations to build a new, highly
efficient realisation of GP: backward chaining genetic programming (BC-GP).
Thanks to its special way of recursively computing programs and fitnesses
backward from the last generation to the first, BC-GP offers a combination of
simplicity, fast convergence, increased efficiency in terms of fitness evaluations
and primitive evaluations, statistical equivalence to a standard GP, reduced bloat
and broad applicability. This comes at the cost of an increased memory use.

The BC-GP algorithm is not hard to implement (see pseudo-code in Figure 9-2). Also, BC-GP tends to find better individuals faster irrespective of
the value of the tournament sizes n. However, if one wants use tournaments
with more than three individuals and to compute a large proportion of the final
generation, the computational saving provided by BC-GP may be too limited to
be worth the implementation effort and the memory overhead. In applications
which require computing only a small number of individuals in a given generation of interest and where a very large population is used, then BC-GP can be
fruitfully applied even for large tournament size. For example, with BC-GP,
tournament size 7 and a population of a million individuals, one could calculate
1 individual at generation 7, 7 individuals at generation 6, 49 individuals at
generation 5, /emphetc. Note that this costs less than initialising the population
in a forward GP. The information gained by BG-GP in this way could prove
very important, for example, in deciding whether to continue a run or not.

In future research we intend to test the new algorithm on other problems and
explore possible ways of further improving the allocation of trials and decision
making in BC-GP and GP.

Acknowledgements

The authors would like to thank Chris Stephens, Darrell Whitley, Kumara
Sastry and Bob McKay for their useful comments.

References

Blickle, Tobias and Thiele, Lothar (1997). A comparison of selection schemes used in evolutionary algorithms. *Evolutionary Computation*, 4(4):361–394.

Feller, William (1971). *An Introduction to Probability Theory and Its Applications*, volume 2. John Wiley.

Langdon, William B., Soule, Terry, Poli, Riccardo, and Foster, James A. (1999). The evolution of size and shape. In Spector, Lee, Langdon, William B., O'Reilly, Una-May, and Angeline, Peter J., editors, *Advances in Genetic Programming 3*, chapter 8, pages 163–190. MIT Press, Cambridge, MA, USA.

Motoki, Tatsuya (2002). Calculating the expected loss of diversity of selection schemes. *Evolutionary Computation*, 10(4):397–422.

Poli, Riccardo (2005). Tournament selection, iterated coupon-collection problem, and backward-chaining evolutionary algorithms. In *Proceedings of the Foundations of Genetic Algorithms Workshop (FOGA 8)*.

Poli, Riccardo and Langdon, William B. (2005). Backward-chaining genetic programming. Technical Report CSM 425, Department of Computer Science, University of Essex.

Sastry, K. and Goldberg, D. E. (2001). Modeling tournament selection with replacement using apparent added noise. In *Proceedings of ANNIE 2001*, volume 11, pages 129–134.

Sokolov, Artem and Whitley, Darrell (2005). Unbiased tournament selection. In *Proceedings of the Genetic and Evolutionary Computation Conference (GECCO 2005)*. ACM.

Teller, Astro and Andre, David (1997). Automatically choosing the number of fitness cases: The rational allocation of trials. In Koza, John R., Deb, Kalyanmoy, Dorigo, Marco, Fogel, David B., Garzon, Max, Iba, Hitoshi, and Riolo, Rick L., editors, *Genetic Programming 1997: Proceedings of the Second Annual Conference*, pages 321–328, Stanford University, CA, USA. Morgan Kaufmann.

Chapter 10

AN EXAMINATION OF SIMULTANEOUS EVOLUTION OF GRAMMARS AND SOLUTIONS

R. Muhammad Atif Azad [1] and Conor Ryan [1]

[1] *CSIS Department, University of Limerick. Limerick, Ireland.*

Abstract   This chapter examines the notion of co-evolving grammars with a population of individuals. This idea has great promise because it is possible to dynamically reshape the solution space while evolving individuals. We compare such a system with a more standard system with fixed grammars and demonstrate that, on a selection of benchmark problems, the standard approach appears to be better. Several different context free grammars, including one inspired by Koza's GPPS system are examined, and a number of surprising results appear, which indicate that several representative GP benchmark problems are best tackled by a standard GP approach.

Keywords: grammatical evolution, evolving grammars, grammatical ADFs, generative representations

1.   Introduction

Work such as (Whigham, 1995; Keller and Banzhaf, 1999; O'Neill and Ryan, 2004; Piaseczny et al., 2004) has demonstrated that context free grammar based GP systems are capable of evolving both the grammar (which specifies and constrains the solution space) and a population of individuals. Intuitively, this is an attractive idea, especially given that something similar had to have happened in nature; that is, the genetic code had to evolve either before or in parallel with the species that use it.

Although the above examples all demonstrated that this is possible, it was not clear under what circumstances one would want to use these methods. In particular, as each of these papers were a *proof of concept*, most of them were not focused at a comparative analysis against a system with fixed grammars.

The promise of these systems is that they would be able to tune the system towards solving a particular problem, but the question this chapter is concerned with is what is the cost of this tuning?

This chapter investigates a number of different ways of treating the grammars or function sets made available to a system, varying from a simple, closure obeying system like GP, up to a multiple type evolving system. We start by introducing Grammatical Evolution (GE), the evolutionary system used to conduct these experiments, and describe the effects that different kinds of grammars can have. The chapter then looks at the various ways in which these grammars can be modified on the fly - including no modification, as in standard GP, before applying them to five benchmark problems.

We show that, in general, the simpler the grammar, the more successful the search is, and on occasions the results demonstrate that a GPPS inspired grammar that provides more functionality than is necessary can be competitive.

2.   Grammatical Evolution

Grammatical Evolution (Ryan et al., 1998) (O'Neill and Ryan, 2001) (O'Neill and Ryan, 2003) is a Genetic Programming system that uses a Genetic Algorithm to search the space of structures specified by a grammar such as a Context Free Grammar or an Attribute Grammar.

The key difference between GE and GP is the use of linear chromosomes by GE. Rather than evolving programs directly, GE employs a separation of the search and solution spaces, by performing a mapping from the linear structure to a program (or whatever structure is being evolved).

This mapping is made possible by the use of a grammar, which specifies what structures are syntactically valid. The mapping involves the generation of a derivation tree, using genes from the chromosome to resolve choices.

One of the main advantages of using a grammar in this way is that one avoids the closure problem; that is, it is trivial to have multiple types in the grammar. Another potential advantage is the ability to tune a grammar. The grammar not only specifies what structures are syntactically valid, it can also be used to bias the search, by making the system more likely to produce certain types of structures, or structures that are more likely to have certain characteristics.

Grammars

A grammar can be described using Backus Naur Form (BNF) which consists of a four tuple $< N, T, P, S >$ where T is the set of *terminals* (symbols that can appear in programs produced by the grammar) .N is a set of *non-terminals*, intermediate symbols used by the grammar, S is a *start symbol* from which all programs are developed, and P is a set of production rules that map from the start symbol to the terminals.

Consider the following grammar, which produces expressions similar to those generated by GP for standard symbolic regression problems.

```
<expr> ::= (<op> <expr> <expr>) | (<sop> <expr>) | <var>
<op>   ::= + | - | % | *
<sop>  ::= sin | cos | log
<var>  ::= X | 1.0
```

In this case, the start symbol is <expr>.

Grammars are useful in an evolutionary setting because, by their very nature, they express a set of syntactic constraints. However, it is possible to have some more explicit constraints than shown above. For example, one could force every individual to start with (* <expr> <expr>), or to ensure that only certain variables can appear in conditional tests.

Example

To use a grammar in a generative way, one creates a derivation tree, which records each choice made in the derivation sequence. GE operates by evolving sequences of choices which, when interpreted with a particular grammar produce syntactically valid structures.

Individuals in GE are binary strings, which are interpreted as a sequence of eight bit *codons*, each of which is used to make a single choice in the derivation sequence.

Consider an example individual 222, 31, 74, 122, 67, 201, 14, 26, 22, already divided into eight bit codons and expressed in decimal for clarity. The codons are in the range 0..255, so, when being used to make a choice, have a modulus operation applied to them with the number of choices available.

Recall the start symbol is <expr>. There are three choices available for this, so we have $222 \mod 3 = 0$, which corresponds to the first choice. The start symbol is then replaced with (<op> <expr> <expr>).

The process continues with the left most non-terminal until there are either no non-terminals left (the individual is completely mapped) or all of the codons have been used. In the latter case, the individual is considered non-viable and given a zero fitness.

In this case, all but the last two codons are consumed, resulting in:
(* X (sin X)).

Biasing of Grammars

All grammars contain inherent bias. In the example grammar above, if random initialisation of the population was employed, one would expect a third of all individuals to consist of just a single point of either X or 1.0.

An alternative approach is to use a *closed grammar*, which is analogous to a GP system that has the closure property. In this case, there is just one non-terminal, so the grammar from above would be rewritten as :

```
<expr> ::= (+ <expr> <expr>)  |  (- <expr> <expr>)
        |  (% <expr> <expr>)  |  (* <expr> <expr>)
        |  (sin <expr>)  |  (cos <expr>)
        |  (log <expr>)  |  X  |  1.0
```

Although this grammar represents the same set of legal individuals, it contains a different bias to the original one, and this can have implications for the success or otherwise of a GE run. In this new grammar, it is now twice as likely that a randomly generated individual will contain something of the form $(< op >< expr >< expr >)$ as it is to contain an X or 1.0.

This shows that the hierarchical nature of grammars using BNF can contain hidden biases, and some work (Nicolau, 2004) has looked at identifying how much bias. The following section examines work which has tried to take advantage of the fact that changing the bias of a grammar can effect the performance of the system.

3.   Simultaneously evolving Grammars and the Solutions

One of the first investigations into grammar bias was carried out by Whigham (Whigham, 1995). He discussed that depending upon the structure of the grammar, it can have a relatively higher number of paths through it to generate certain sentences or forms of the sentences. For example, if a certain symbol appears in most of the production rules it has a high chance of being represented in a randomly generated set of sentences. With the use of different hand crafted grammars he showed that if the grammar design is guided by the problem specific knowledge it can boost the performance. He went on to propose an *inductive biasing* mechanism where the grammar is modified every generation by looking at the best individual found thus far. The terminal symbol found at the deepest location in the derivation tree is propagated up one level to create a new rule. For example the derivation sequence

```
<IF> -> if <T> <NT1> <NT2>
     -> if a0 <NT1> <NT2>
```

can be collapsed into a single production `<IF> -> if a0 <NT1> <NT2>`, so the grammar can be modified to incorporate the new rule. The same modification may be suggested more than once during the course of evolutionary run, thus increasing its likelihood to be used in the generation of new individuals or in the case of a mutation event.

Keller and Banzhaf (Keller and Banzhaf, 1999) argued that the structure of the grammar has implications towards the problem landscape as certain areas of the solution space can become more accessible than others. In the absence of domain knowledge, a poorly designed grammar can hamper the progress of the algorithm. They made a case for the evolution of the mapping from the genotype to the phenotype *i.e.* the structure of the grammar. However, instead of having one *global* grammar, they proposed that every individual should have its own set of rules. This paves the way for the evolution of grammar along with the phenotypes they encode, in this case using diploid chromosomes. The purpose of this study was to demonstrate that co-evolution of genetic code and problem solution can work. However, no performance comparisons were made with a normal GP system.

Working on a similar idea O'Neill and Ryan (O'Neill and Ryan, 2004) used GE to simultaneously evolve the grammar and the problem solution. As in the Keller-Banzhaf approach, a diploid chromosome is used to encode the two evolving entities. Each individual uses a pre-specified *grammar's grammar* or a meta grammar to produce a *local* grammar. The meta grammar has production rules to specify a context free grammar. One strand of the chromosome is used to pick rules from the meta grammar to produce a local grammar. The second strand uses this grammar to produce a sentence or a phenotype. The prosperity of a grammar in future generations depends upon the fitness obtained by the corresponding phenotype. A dynamically changing symbolic regression problem was used where the target function changed after a fixed number of generations. The exercise agreed with Keller and Banzhaf in demonstrating that such a co-evolutionary setup worked as the system was able to adapt to the changing behaviour of the problem, acquiring high frequencies of the symbols that constitute the target function every time.

Chemical Genetic Programming (Piaseczny et al., 2004) is a recent addition to the list of grammar evolving systems. As the setup discussed in the current study is very similar to Chemical GP, we discuss it in relative detail in the following subsection.

Chemical GP

As with GE, Chemical GP is based on linear strings and makes use of the context free grammar. The name of the system derives its basis from the metabolic chemical reactions going on in a cell. These reactions enable the amino acids to produce proteins, which in turn are used to produce amino acids, thus constituting a *feedback loop*. Assuming that this extra degree of freedom has helped nature in evolving complex entities, Chemical GP claims a coarse analogy with this process to reformulate the structure of the grammar specified at the start of the run. Starting with a non-terminal from the pre-specified grammar, a subtree is generated. The subtree is then collapsed to form a single production rule or *translation* such that the frontier (the set of the leaves of the subtree) becomes the right hand side of the rule. Consider the following derivation sequence:

```
<expr> -> <pre-op> ( <expr> ) <op> <expr>
       -> tanh ( <expr> ) <op> <expr>
       -> tanh ( <var> )  <op> <expr>
       -> tanh ( x )  <op> <expr>
```

Considering that the same can be represented by a derivation tree, collapsing the tree can produce a translation like this:
```
<expr> -> tanh ( x ) <op> <expr>
```
which is a more compact way of arriving at the same result. This is similar to the concept of ADFs in canonical GP where a piece of code can be encapsulated into an ADF and repeatedly used through a function call. Likewise, a number of derivation steps can be replaced by a single production rule that produces the same effect as the derivation sequence. This effect is absent in most of the grammar evolving approaches discussed earlier.

Chemical GP considers the production rules analogous to the amino acids that produce proteins (the frontier of the subtree). After the subtree collapse, these proteins themselves act as amino acids during the derivation process and can combine with other amino acids, the production rules in this case. Part of the grammar or the amino acid pool for a particular individual comes from a pre-specified grammar while the rest is formed from the derived rules. The proportion coming from the pre-specified grammar is determined by a parameter to the system.

An individual comprises of three parts. The first part, termed DNA, is used to pick the rules from the grammar available to the individual, and the last part is used to encode new amino acids in the manner described before. The middle part encodes a *tRNA* sequence that produces a local grammar by incorporating the synthesized rules into the pre-specified grammar.

Every rule in the local grammar has an associated integer value that is not necessarily unique. The DNA is any sequence of these integer values. Starting from a start symbol, the DNA is read and the corresponding rule is applied to continue the derivation sequence. If more than one rule has the same identifier, the one that can be applied to the left most non-terminal in the derivation sequence is chosen. If multiple rules are applicable, a random choice is made. This can lead to difficulties in analysing the individuals. Therefore, further work is awaited that demonstrates the motivation behind such a mapping function as against a deterministic scheme. Another consequence of the mapping process is possibility of introns arising *within* the chromosome length used for mapping. This happens if an integer value is read from the DNA that is not associated with any applicable rule, as it is ignored, thus producing introns. This is additional to the introns appearing towards the end of the chromosome if mapping terminates earlier on.

In the wake of this discussion we now describe our grammar evolving setup in conjunction with GE.

Our Approach

The first design choice is how to represent the grammar encoding and the solution encoding parts of a GE individual. GE uses variable length one point crossover. It is not known a priori, what length an individual will require to map to a valid sentence of arbitrary size. Moreover, the grammar should be clearly defined before the mapping process starts. This means that a portion of the individual should be clearly marked to encode the grammar. For this purpose, a variable length GA with diploid chromosomes is employed. One chromosome is used to evolve new rules from a pre-specified grammar and the other chromosome is used to produce a sentence of the grammar that includes the new rules, possibly replacing some from the original grammar.

GE uses the grammar encoding chromosome to derive new rules. First, we decode a codon to pick a non-terminal from the grammar using the modulo operation. Then, we grow a derivation tree rooted at this non-terminal as the normal GE mapping ensues. Once the tree growth stops, a new production is formed that has the root of the tree as its left hand side and the frontier constitutes the right hand side (RHS). In haploid GE, the mapping stops when either the entire chromosome is consumed or all the non-terminals have been resolved into terminal symbols. The objective is to have a valid solution that can be evaluated. The mapping of grammar encoding chromosome, on the other hand, is only meant for producing new production rules where it is allowed to have non-terminals on the RHS. Moreover, waiting for a terminal-only frontier can exhaust the entire grammatical chromosome, whereas we want to take a flexible approach by letting the evolution decide whether or not it should be the case. Even if the tree growth stops leaving a few non-terminals left in the frontier, a production is formed as mentioned before. If some part of the chromosome is still unread, it can be used to produce more rule(s) in a similar fashion.

To decide when to stop growing a tree, we make use of a *stopCodon*. After picking a non-terminal and before starting to grow the tree, we read a codon and save it as a stopCodon. Then, when we start the tree growth, at each step we read a codon (let's call it newCodon) to pick a rule from the set of available choices in the following manner:

$$stopChances = stopCodon \bmod (|applicableRuleSet| + 1)$$
$$chosenIndex = newCodon \bmod (|applicableRuleSet| + stopChances)$$

If $chosenIndex > |applicableRuleSet|$, tree growth is stopped, otherwise it is continued with the selected rule marked by the $chosenIndex$. Thus, depending upon the value of the $stopCodon$ the chances of stopping a tree growth can be as much as the number of rules available for selection. This is an adaptable measure and was preferred over keeping a system parameter. The derivation tree growth can also stop if it maps completely to terminal symbols or the end of the chromosome is reached. Except in the latter case, another derivation tree growth ensues to encode for a new rule.

When a rule is encoded, it can either just add to or replace a rule from the corresponding rule set. This Boolean decision is made by reading another codon before growing the tree. If $codon \bmod 2 == 1$ a rule is replaced. The index of the replaced rule is determined by decoding another codon. Thus a rule encoding comprises of four control codons (the first picking a non-terminal to grow) and the codon sequence that encodes the tree.

If some rules are omitted from the grammar, it makes it impossible to generate legal sentences from the grammar. Such rules are therefore marked and are not allowed to be removed in our setup. Consider the following example:

```
<expr> ::= <expr> + <expr> | Sin ( <expr> ) | <var>
<var>  ::= x | y | z
```

In this case `<expr> -> <var>` is the only link to the terminal symbols. Thus it is marked for non-removal.

Instead of having an unconstrained one point crossover, we employ a *sensible crossover* for the rule encoding chromosome. It is a two point crossover with the restriction being that it can only swap entire rule encodings. This is hoped to be less disruptive than the normal one point crossover.

4.   Experimental Setup

In this study we compare different grammatical setups along with the afore-mentioned grammar evolving system. As mentioned before that structure of the grammar is a major design issue for grammar based evolutionary algorithms and it is no different with GE. For the current study we use a single non-terminal grammar, (*closed grammar*, as described in section 2.0) a multiple non-terminal grammar, grammar evolving setup seeded with each of the aforementioned grammars, a domain specific hand crafted grammar and a unified grammar that has the functions used by all the problems available in it. This gives us a diverse set of designs to test.

We are interested in seeing how the extra degree of freedom available with evolvable grammars compares with the other setups on standard GP problems. In particular, whether they can exploit or overcome the inherent peculiarities of the pre-specified grammars to produce a comparable or superior performance. It is also interesting to see how a structurally simple closed grammar fares against the other setups. The use of grammars makes it possible for GE to incorporate domain specific knowledge without any programming overhead. When such information is available, it is informative to investigate if it can lead to performance enhancements in any or all the cases. We also examine a *unified* grammar, which is inspired by Koza's (Koza et al., 1999) GPPS. This is a function rich system which makes as many functions as possible available, thus removing the onus from the user to choose a function set. Koza estimated that this system was two orders of magnitude slower than standard GP, but argued that, as hardware continues to improve, this will become less of an issue. We are interested in GPPS in this context because evolvable grammars could have a similar use, that is, they are concerned with the identification of useful function.

We use five benchmark problems from the GP literature. These include symbolic regression of the quartic polynomial, the discovery of a 6 bit multiplexer (Koza, 1992), the even 6 parity problem (Koza, 1994), the regression of a sextic polynomial (Piaseczny et al., 2004) and a 28 dimensional regression problem (Keller and Banzhaf, 2001). The quartic polynomial problem involves the discovery of a target function of $x^4 + x^3 + x^2 + x$ with 20 training points drawn from the interval$[-1, 1]$. The sum of squared error is normalized between 0 and 1.0 with an aim to maximize the fitness. The Sextic polynomial was used to demonstrate the efficacy of Chemical GP and entails the target function $2x^6 + 3x^4 + 3x^2 + 100$. We use the same fitness measure as used in (Piaseczny et al., 2004). When d represents the sum of squared errors, the raw fitness is calculated as follows:

$$e^{8e^{-d/50000000}}$$

When $d = 0$ (the ideal case), the expression produces the best fitness *i.e.* e^8. Hence this value is used to normalize the raw fitness values. 50 uniformly distributed points from the domain $[-5, 5]$ constitute the training cases. Keller's problem is defined as follows: $f(A, B, a, b, \cdots, y, z) = j + x + d + j*o + e* r - t - a + h - k*u + a - k - s*o*i - h*v - i - i - s + l - u*n + l + r - j*j*o* v - j + i + f*c + x - v + n - n*v - a - q*i*h + d - i - t + s + l*a - j*g*v - i - p*q*u - x + e + m - k*r + k - l*u*x*d*r - a + t - e*x - v - p - c - o - o*u* c*h + x + e - a*u + c*l*r - x*t - n*d + p*x*w*v - j*n - a - e*b + a$. Four of the inputs A, B, y, z are not used in the objective function and add noise. 100 randomly selected training cases are used all coming from the domain $[0, 1]$. Normalized sum of the squared errors represents the fitness of an individual.

For both the boolean problems, the maximum fitness value is the correct categorization of all the 64 training cases.

The grammars used in this study are listed in the appendix. The hand tuned grammars for the two polynomials encourage the use of the multiplication and addition operators. For the sextic polynomial, the *pow* function is also a preferred function. For this problem it is not possible to write a single non-terminal grammar for the corresponding multiple non-terminal grammar. Therefore we have tried to minimize the number of the non-terminals to have an approximate effect of a closed grammar. For the multiplexer problem, the hand crafted grammar forces that the condition part of an if-statement should only work on the address bits whereas the action part should only be concerned with the data bits. This approach has also been used elsewhere with success to improve performance (Janikow, 2004). For the even parity problem hand tuning the grammar was not so obvious. Therefore, no such grammar is used for this problem.

All the experiments involve 100 independent runs with a population size of 500[1]. The runs execute for 200 generations. Crossover probability of 0.9 and bit mutation probability of 0.01 is used. The initialisation involves random generation of linear strings with an average length of 20 integers and a standard deviation of 5. Roulette wheel selection is used with steady state replacement. At every generation 500 parents are selected that probabilistically undergo genetic operators. If any of the offspring are better than the worst member of the existing population, the former replaces the latter.

Crossover in Effective Lengths

For the solution encoding or the sentence mapping chromosomes of the individuals a variable length one point crossover is employed. However, the nature of the mapping process in GE is such that it may finish well before exhausting the entire length of the chromosome. This can also lead to the emergence of *tails* in the haploid GE chromosomes (O'Neill and Ryan, 2003). The tails are helpful in mapping the individual to a valid sentence due to the ripple effect in GE (O'Neill et al., 2003) the crossed over segment may require to encode for a different set of non-terminals. For such a context shift large tails can be suitable as they provide a greater chance of mapping the individuals completely. However, if the tails grow too large comparatively, the crossover point is more likely to be chosen from the tails. Thus, after the crossover the two offsprings will have the mapping parts intact with the variation only being in the tails. Such individuals with large tails can be attractive for selection because crossover involving them is unlikely to produce invalid or incompletely mapped individuals that are chastised by assigning the worst possible fitness in a typical GE setup. As the individuals grow large tails, the normal one point crossover becomes increasingly ineffective because it merely swaps the segments that can not express themselves in the phenotype as the mapping terminates earlier

---

[1]The population size of 500 is fairly small for the even 6 parity problem in comparison with Koza's setup where it is of the order of many thousands. However, we keep a uniform setup for all the problems.

on. This causes the loss of phenotypic diversity. Therefore, we restrict the crossover point to be selected within the length that is *effective* in the mapping process. We term such a crossover as *effective crossover*.

Results

Figure 10-1 shows the mean best fitness plots for the two boolean problems. For this section we refer to the grammar evolving GE as GEGE.

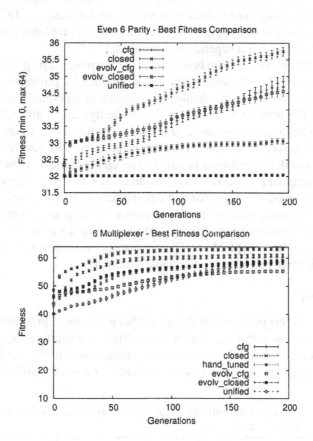

Figure 10-1. Depicted is the mean best fitness for the two Boolean problems. It was not obvious to design a hand tuned grammar for the even 6 parity problem. 'evolv-cfg' and 'evolv-closed' represent the grammar evolving setups with an initial multiple and single nonterminal grammars respectively.

The results show that for the two Boolean problems, GEGE with an initial multiple non-terminal grammar (CFG) is among the worst performers. GE with a closed grammar does better than all the other setups except for the hand tuned grammar in the case of multiplexer problem.The ideal individual count for the hand tuned grammar is 91% while the closed grammar yeilded a 51% success for the multiplexer problem. These numbers are far higher than the rest of the setups which could only achieve at best 20% success. The relatively small population size probably hampered the progress in the case of the parity problem where no ideal individual was found for any setup. This shows that the grammars represent a convenient mechanism for incorporating domain specific knowledge when available with no algorithmic modifications. However, it is also interesting to see that the closed grammar with its simple structure and no domain knowledge does better than the rest of the setups. GEGE with the closed grammar also does reasonably well in both the problems but we do not witness any instance of a superior performance.

Figure 10-2 shows the mean best fitness for the problems from the real-value problem domain. For the quartic and sextic polynomial problems, the end of the run results are indistinguishable. The quartic polynomial problem seems too easy for GE with all of the setups. From the figure it is difficult to see but numerical data reflects that closed grammar again had a faster convergence to better fitness values. The use of hand tuned grammar did not have any clear advantage in both the problems in terms of mean best fitness. However, it was able to find a higher number of ideal individuals 41% for the quartic polynomial compared to the other setups that had a maximum of 10% to show. GE shows the best performance whether employed with a closed grammar or a CFG.

The unified grammar is the slowest to pick up in the even 6 parity, sextic polynomial and Keller's problem. The performance is somewhere in the middle of the multiplexer and quartic polynomial problems.

Discussion

Overall, the best performer is the set up that used closed grammar. The only case that it was outperformed was in the multiplexer experiments, and then by the hand-tuned grammar. However, our experiences with producing hand-tuned grammars suggestin the case of the multiplexer) or it is very difficult.

Table 10-1. Percentage of the individuals that fail to map all the non-terminals to terminal symbols in the final generation.

Problem	cfg	closed	evol-cfg	evol-closed	unified	hand-tuned
6 Parity	13.5±0.9	4.2±0.29	13.3±0.67	6.9±0.5	22.1±0.41	not-used
Multiplxr	30.4±1.1	2.0±0.21	29.7±1.46	3.71±0.4	36.47±1.1	28.9±1.13
Sextic	15.4±1.0	20.5±2.1	27.0±1.13	29.6±1.23	21.7±0.72	22.7±1.61
Quartic	8.5±0.6	8.5±0.73	13.6±1.41	18.5±1.46	25.6±1.64	29.5±1.1
Keller	3.45±0.5	0.0±0.0	7.1±1.03	0.00±0.01	32.0±1.2	46.3±1.0

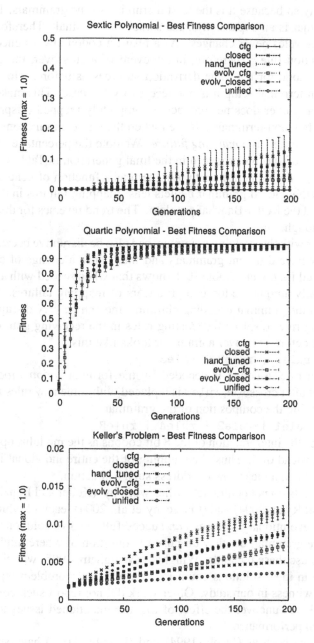

Figure 10-2. Depicted is the mean best fitness for the problems of regressing mathematical functions. 'evolv-cfg' and 'evolv-closed' represent the grammar evolving setups with an initial multiple and single nonterminal grammars respectively.

Why then, does the closed grammar perform so well? We believe that it may be partly so because it is the least disruptive of the grammars. Every rule in the grammar is an expansion of the same non-terminal. Therefore, the set of *applicable* rules never changes. As a result a codon always encodes for a fixed production rule. Therefore, in the event of a crossover, the exchanged fragments encode for the same derivation subtrees as before. However, in a multiple non-terminal setup it is not necessarily the case. This makes it more likely that crossover does not produce a completely mapped offspring *i.e.* it may have a few non-terminals left even when the entire chromosome has been read. This is termed as a *mapping failure*. We note the percentage of mapping failures in the offsprings produced in the final generation in Table 10-1. Space considerations do not permit us to plot them as a function of generation. The table shows that closed grammar depicts least mapping failures in the boolean problems and the Keller-Banzhaf problem. The trend reverses for the other two problems though.

Crossover with the evolving grammars can also be disruptive because the two parents may have different grammars and thus cause a change of context for the exchanged fragments. Table 10-1 shows that when seeded with a CFG they were generally among the top two producers of mapping failures. Moreover, crossover in the grammar encoding chromosome can be very disruptive when the incoming rules displace the existing rules in the receiving grammar. Let's assume that before crossover a grammar looks like this:

`<nt> ::= rule1 | rule2 | rule3`

To choose a rule, a codon is decoded by the formula *codon mod* 3. Let's suppose that after crossover, `rule3` is replaced with some new rules `ruleA` and `ruleB` changing the composition of the grammar.

`<nt> ::= rule1 | rule2 | ruleA | ruleB`

This changes the interpretation of the 8 bit codons as the modulus operator will now use 4 instead of 3. Thus, the mapping of the entire individual is affected. At present, it is not clear how to address such a situation.

These results do not contradict earlier work by (Keller and Banzhaf, 1999), (O'Neill and Ryan, 2004) and (Piaseczny et al., 2004), each of which demonstrated that evolutionary systems *can* successfully evolve solutions while co-evolving the grammar, but they do pose the question of where might it be appropriate to use these methods. Whigham (Whigham, 1995) was able to show an increase in ideal solutions count in the multiplexer problem that we were not able to witness in our study. Other work did not report such comparisons. Future work can uncover the effect of the aforementioned issues towards the difference in performance.

Researchers such as (Jacob, 1994) and (Hornby, 2003) have successfully evolved Lindenmayer systems (L-systems). However, L-systems have deterministic paths through the grammars. In the case of simultaneous evolution of parameters and the grammar with parametric L-systems, the number of parameters can be low and pre-determined. This is not the case in the present study where the solution mapping chromosome(that can be seen as an instance of a parameter set to the grammar) is typically of large and unspecified size. Therefore, while L-system based evolution is a successful instance of grammar evolution, it is fundamentally different from the avenues tackled in this chapter.

The study also leads us to think that adding this extra degree of freedom can increase problem difficulty due to a larger search space.

5. Summary

This chapter has confirmed that it is possible to evolve the grammars in parallel with the solutions, but it has also shown on a selection of standard problems that the subsequent increase in the size of the search space, not to mention the additional code to support this co-evolution, can outweigh the benefits. There are almost certainly problems that will benefit from co-evolving the grammar, but these remain to be identified.

It has also been shown that, where the knowledge is available (*e.g.* the Multiplexer problem) a tuned grammar can perform very well. However, this finding has the caveat that it is also possible to adversely effect the search capability of a system by using a less than ideal hand tuned grammar.

The most consistent performer was the closed grammar, but it is not always possible to use one of these. Given the current state of research, we recommend using a reasonable, *i.e.* not particularly tuned, CFG.

We also revisited Koza's idea of GPPS, and examined unified grammars, which err on the side of caution when including functions, usually providing more than are necessary. We discovered that these grammars gave surprisingly good performance on occasions despite having to deal with much larger search spaces. This is an encouraging result for any future research aiming at genetic programming black box type problem solvers.

Appendix

Listed are the grammars used in the experiments. Except for the even parity problem which had no hand crafted grammar, the others are ordered as follows: closed grammar, multiple non-terminal grammar and the hand crafted grammar.

6 Multiplexer.

```
S ::= <expr>
<expr> ::=  ( <expr> AND <expr> ) | ( <expr> OR <expr> ) | NOT ( <expr> )
  | IF ( ( <expr> ) ( <expr> ) ( <expr> ) ) | A0 | A1 | D0 | D1 | D2 | D3

S ::= <expr>
<expr> ::=  ( <expr> <op> <expr> ) | <pre-operation> | <var>
<op> ::= AND | OR
<pre-operation> ::=  NOT ( <expr> ) | IF ( ( <expr> ) ( <expr> ) ( <expr> ) )
<var>  ::= A0 | A1 | D0 | D1 | D2 | D3
```

```
S ::= <expr>
<expr>    ::=  IF ( ( <condition> ) ( <action> ) ( <action> ) )
<condition> ::= ( <condition> <op> <condition> ) | NOT ( <condition> ) | <addr-bits>
<action> ::= ( <action> <op> <action> ) | NOT ( <action> ) | <data-bits>
 | IF ( <condition>  ( <action> ) ( <action> ) )
<op> ::=  AND | OR
<addr-bits> ::= A0 | A1
<data-bits> ::= D0 | D1 | D2 | D3
```

Even 6 Parity.

```
S ::= <expr>
<expr> ::=  ( <expr> AND <expr> ) | ( <expr> OR <expr> ) | ( <expr> NAND <expr> )
 | ( <expr> NOR <expr> ) | D0 | D1 | D2 | D3 | D4 | D5

S ::= <expr>
<expr> ::=  ( <expr> <op> <expr> ) | <var>
<op> ::=  AND | OR | NAND | NOR
<var>  ::= D0 | D1 | D2 | D3 | D4 | D5
```

Quartic Polynomial.

```
S ::= <expr>
<expr> ::= ( <expr> + <expr> ) | ( <expr> - <expr> ) | ( <expr> * <expr> )
 | ( <expr> / <expr> ) | Sin ( <expr> ) | Cos ( <expr> ) | Exp ( <expr> )
 | Log ( <expr> ) | 1.0 | X

S ::= <expr>
<expr> ::= ( <expr> <op> <expr> ) | <pre-op> ( <expr> ) | <var>
<op> ::=  + | - | / | *
<pre-op> ::=  Sin | Cos | Exp | Log
<var>  ::= 1.0 | X

S ::= <expr>
<expr> ::= ( <expr> <op> <expr> ) | ( <expr> + <expr> ) | ( <expr> * <expr> )
 | <pre-op> ( <expr> ) | <var>
<op> ::=  - | /
<pre-op> ::= Sin | Cos | Exp | Log
<var>  ::= 1.0 | X
```

Sextic Polynomial.

```
S ::= <expr>
<expr> ::= ( <expr> + <expr> ) | ( <expr> - <expr> ) | ( <expr> * <expr> )
 | ( <expr> / <expr> ) | ( <expr> pow <expr> ) | X | <num>
<num> ::= <Z> . <Z> | <Z>
<Z> ::= <Z> <Z>
 | 0 | 1 | 2 | 3 | 4 | 5 | 6 | 7 | 8 | 9

S ::= <expr>
<expr> ::= ( <expr> <op> <expr> ) | <R> | <Z>
<R> ::= X | <Z> | <Z> . <Z> | ( <expr> pow <expr> )
<Z> ::= <D> | <Z> <Z>
<op> ::= + | - | * | /
<D> ::= 0 | 1 | 2 | 3 | 4 | 5 | 6 | 7 | 8 | 9

S ::= <expr>
<expr> ::= ( <expr> + <expr> ) | ( <expr> * <expr> )
 | ( <expr> <op> <expr> ) | ( <expr> pow <expr> ) | <R> | <Z>
<R> ::= X | <Z> | <Z> . <Z>
<Z> ::= <D> | <Z> <Z>
<op> ::= - | /
<D> ::= 0 | 1 | 2 | 3 | 4 | 5 | 6 | 7 | 8 | 9
```

Keller's Problem.   The grammar for this problem was very similar to the Quartic Polynomial Problem, except that it had 28 inputs and did not involve transcendental functions. It is avoided to be described here for the space

reasons. The hand tuned grammar kept the unrequired inputs i.e. A, B, y, z and the division function under separate non-terminals.

The Unified grammar.   The non-terminals `<B-var>` and `<R-var>` deal with the real and the boolean input variables. Depending upon the problem domain, the corresponding variables are specified for one of the non-terminals leaving the other non-terminals without any rules. As a result, the individuals attempting to map by taking the wrong path always fail to do so and are discarded.

```
S ::= <decide>
<decide> ::= <B-expr> | <R-expr>
<B-expr> ::= ( <B-expr> AND <B-expr> ) | ( <B-expr> OR <B-expr> ) | NOT ( <B-expr> )
   | ( <B-expr> NAND <B-expr> ) | ( <B-expr> NOR <B-expr> )
   | IF ( ( <B-expr> ) ( <B-expr> ) ( <B-expr> ) ) | <B-var>
<R-expr> ::= ( <R-expr> + <R-expr> ) | ( <R-expr> - <R-expr> ) | ( <R-expr> * <R-expr> )
   | ( <R-expr> / <R-expr> ) | ( <R-expr> pow <R-expr> ) | Sin ( <R-expr> ) | Cos ( <R-expr> )
   | Exp ( <R-expr> ) | <R-var>
```

References

Hornby, Gregory Scott (2003). *Generative Representations for Evolutionary Design Automation.* PhD thesis, Brandeis University, Dept. of Computer Science, Boston, MA, USA.

Jacob, Christian (1994). Genetic L-system programming. In Davidor, Yuval, Schwefel, Hans-Paul, and Männer, Reinhard, editors, *Parallel Problem Solving from Nature III*, volume 866 of *LNCS*, pages 334–343, Jerusalem. Springer-Verlag.

Janikow, Cezary Z. (2004). Adapting representation in genetic programming. In Deb, Kalyanmoy, Poli, Riccardo, Banzhaf, Wolfgang, Beyer, Hans-Georg, Burke, Edmund, Darwen, Paul, Dasgupta, Dipankar, Floreano, Dario, Foster, James, Harman, Mark, Holland, Owen, Lanzi, Pier Luca, Spector, Lee, Tettamanzi, Andrea, Thierens, Dirk, and Tyrrell, Andy, editors, *Genetic and Evolutionary Computation – GECCO-2004, Part II*, volume 3103 of *Lecture Notes in Computer Science*, pages 507–518, Seattle, WA, USA. Springer-Verlag.

Keller, Robert E. and Banzhaf, Wolfgang (1999). The evolution of genetic code in genetic programming. In Banzhaf, Wolfgang, Daida, Jason, Eiben, Agoston E., Garzon, Max H., Honavar, Vasant, Jakiela, Mark, and Smith, Robert E., editors, *Proceedings of the Genetic and Evolutionary Computation Conference*, volume 2, pages 1077–1082, Orlando, Florida, USA. Morgan Kaufmann.

Keller, Robert E. and Banzhaf, Wolfgang (2001). Evolution of genetic code on a hard problem. In Spector, Lee, Goodman, Erik D., Wu, Annie, Langdon, W. B., Voigt, Hans-Michael, Gen, Mitsuo, Sen, Sandip, Dorigo, Marco, Pezeshk, Shahram, Garzon, Max H., and Burke, Edmund, editors, *Proceedings of the Genetic and Evolutionary Computation Conference (GECCO-2001)*, pages 50–56, San Francisco, California, USA. Morgan Kaufmann.

Koza, John R. (1992). *Genetic Programming: On the Programming of Computers by Means of Natural Selection.* MIT Press, Cambridge, MA, USA.

Koza, John R. (1994). *Genetic Programming II: Automatic Discovery of Reusable Programs*. MIT Press, Cambridge Massachusetts.

Koza, John R., Andre, David, Bennett III, Forrest H, and Keane, Martin (1999). *Genetic Programming 3: Darwinian Invention and Problem Solving*. Morgan Kaufman.

Nicolau, Miguel (2004). Automatic grammar complexity reduction in grammatical evolution. In Poli, R., Cagnoni, S., Keijzer, M., Costa, E., Pereira, F., Raidl, G., Upton, S. C., Goldberg, D., Lipson, H., de Jong, E., Koza, J., Suzuki, H., Sawai, H., Parmee, I., Pelikan, M., Sastry, K., Thierens, D., Stolzmann, W., Lanzi, P. L., Wilson, S. W., O'Neill, M., Ryan, C., Yu, T., Miller, J. F., Garibay, I., Holifield, G., Wu, A. S., Riopka, T., Meysenburg, M. M., Wright, A. W., Richter, N., Moore, J. H., Ritchie, M. D., Davis, L., Roy, R., and Jakiela, M., editors, *GECCO 2004 Workshop Proceedings*, Seattle, Washington, USA.

O'Neill, Michael and Ryan, Conor (2001). Grammatical evolution. *IEEE Transactions on Evolutionary Computation*, 5(4):349–358.

O'Neill, Michael and Ryan, Conor (2003). *Grammatical Evolution: Evolutionary Automatic Programming in a Arbitrary Language*, volume 4 of *Genetic programming*. Kluwer Academic Publishers.

O'Neill, Michael and Ryan, Conor (2004). Grammatical evolution by grammatical evolution: The evolution of grammar and genetic code. In Keijzer, Maarten, O'Reilly, Una-May, Lucas, Simon M., Costa, Ernesto, and Soule, Terence, editors, *Genetic Programming 7th European Conference, EuroGP 2004, Proceedings*, volume 3003 of *LNCS*, pages 138–149, Coimbra, Portugal. Springer-Verlag.

O'Neill, Michael, Ryan, Conor, Keijzer, Maarten, and Cattolico, Mike (2003). Crossover in grammatical evolution. *Genetic Programming and Evolvable Machines*, 4(1):67–93.

Piaseczny, Wojciech, Suzuki, Hideaki, and Sawai, Hidefumi (2004). Chemical genetic programming - evolution of amino acid rewriting rules used for genotype-phenotype translation. In *Proceedings of the 2004 IEEE Congress on Evolutionary Computation*, pages 1639–1646, Portland, Oregon. IEEE Press.

Ryan, Conor, Collins, J. J., and O'Neill, Michael (1998). Grammatical evolution: Evolving programs for an arbitrary language. In Banzhaf, Wolfgang, Poli, Riccardo, Schoenauer, Marc, and Fogarty, Terence C., editors, *Proceedings of the First European Workshop on Genetic Programming*, volume 1391 of *LNCS*, pages 83–95, Paris. Springer-Verlag.

Whigham, P. A. (1995). Inductive bias and genetic programming. In Zalzala, A. M. S., editor, *First International Conference on Genetic Algorithms in Engineering Systems: Innovations and Applications, GALESIA*, volume 414, pages 461–466, Sheffield, UK. IEE.

Chapter 11

THE IMPORTANCE OF LOCAL SEARCH

A Grammar Based Approach to Environmental Time Series Modelling

Tuan Hao Hoang[1], Xuan Nguyen[1], RI (Bob) McKay[2] and Daryl Essam[2]

[1]*Department of Information Technology, Military Technical Academy, Hanoi, Vietnam;*
[2]*School of Information Technology and Electrical Engineering, University of New South Wales at the Australian Defence Force Academy, Canberra 2600, Australia*

Abstract   Standard Genetic Programming operators are highly disruptive, with the concomitant risk that it may be difficult to converge to an optimal structure. The Tree Adjoining Grammar (TAG) formalism provides a more flexible Genetic Programming tree representation which supports a wide range of operators while retaining the advantages of tree-based representation. In particular, minimal-change point insertion and deletion operators may be defined. Previous work has shown that point insertion and deletion, used as local search operators, can dramatically reduce search effort in a range of standard problems. Here, we evaluate the effect of local search with these operators on a real-World ecological time series modelling problem. For the same search effort, TAG-based GP with the local search operators generates solutions with significantly lower training set error. The results are equivocal on test set error, local search generating larger individuals which generalise only a little better than the less accurate solutions given by the original algorithm.

Keywords: local search, insertion, deletion, grammar guided, tree adjoining grammar, ecological modelling, time series

1.   Introduction

It has long been recognised (Nordin and Banzhaf, 1995; Nordin et al., 1995) that subtree crossover and mutation in Genetic Programming (GP) (Cramer, 1985; Koza, 1992) are highly disruptive. In the standard GP tree representations, altering a node high in the tree with subtree operators entails the likelihood of major disruption of the subtree below it. This is in strong contrast with the other main forms of artificial evolutionary algorithms, which generally support a range of operators with varying levels of disruption, and also with natural evolutionary systems (Ridley, 1996), in which mutations are often small-scale. In (O'Reilly, 1997), editing operators for making changes on a small scale were defined, namely insertion, deletion, and point mutation. However, these operators on standard GP representation (expression trees) were merely used to compute the distance metric between two GP individuals. It is not known how they can be implemented as genetic operators since the applications of insertion and deletion on GP expression trees generally results in invalid expression trees. In (Vanneschi et al., 2003), two structural mutation operators called inflation and deflation mutations were defined. These operators were proven to cause small changes in the structure of GP expression trees; however, since the definition is based on incrementing and decrementing arity, these operators become meaningless if all functions in the GP function set have the same arity. Moreover, it is difficult to extend this arity-based definition to syntactically-constrained domains, which are the primary focus of grammar guided genetic programming (GGGP).

We have previously shown (Nguyen and McKay, 2004b) that the point insertion and deletion operators supported by the Tree Adjoining Grammar (TAG) representation presented in (Nguyen et al., 2003) are effective in solving a number of standard GP test problems, and in particular, can make major inroads into Daida's (Daida et al., 2003) structural difficulty problem (Nguyen and McKay, 2004a). However these operators have not been applied to significant real-world problems. Here, we present an example of their application to an ecological time-series modelling problem. They are able to generate solutions which better fit the training data, without the concomitant risk of overfitting.

The remainder of this paper is arranged as follows: Section 2 briefly introduces TAGs and the TAG-guided GP system (TAG3P), and giving details on the point insertion and deletion operators based on them. Section 3 describes the Lake Kasumigaura modelling problem which is the focus of this application. In section 4, we describe the experimental setup used, while presenting the results and discussing their implications in section 5. Section 6 presents our general conclusions and discusses future work in this area.

2.   Grammars, Tree Adjunction and Genetic Programming

Grammar-Guided Genetic Programming (GGGP) has been an important strand in GP since its near-simultaneous introduction by three separate groups of researchers (Wong and Leung, 1995; Whigham, 1995; Geyer-Schulz, 1995) in 1995. Since the differences between the three variants are not relevant to this paper, we base our discussion on Whigham's version. GGGP offers a number of advantages, providing declarative search space restriction and homologous operators, and supporting human-guided incremental learning. However most subsequent work in GGGP has relied on the Chomsky grammar formalisms from the 1950s (string-rewriting systems), which hinder the design of search operators acting directly on their derivation trees.

Tree Adjoining Grammars

Tree Adjoining Grammars (TAGs) have become increasingly important in Natural Language Processing (NLP) since their introduction in the 1970s by Joshi et al (Joshi et al., 1975). The aim of TAG representation is to more directly represent the structure of natural languages than is possible in Chomsky languages, and in particular, to represent the process by which natural language sentences can be built up from a relatively small set of basic linguistic units by inclusion of insertable sub-structures. Thus "The cat sat on the mat" becomes "The big cat sat on the mat" by insertion of the element 'big.' Further insertions throughout the sentence can give us more complex sentences such as "The big black cat sat lazily on the comfortable mat which it had commandeered" by insertion of the elements 'black,' 'lazily,' 'comfortable,' 'which it had commandeered.' In context-free grammars (CFG - Chomsky's formalisms of type 2), the relationship between the first and last sentences can only be discerned by detailed analysis of their derivation trees; in TAG representation, the derivation tree of the latter simply extends the frontier of the former. To put it another way, the edit distance between the derivation trees of these closely related sentences is much smaller in TAG representation than in CFG representation. This will be formalised in the next example.

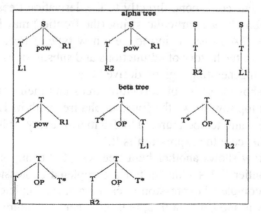

Figure 11-1. Tree Adjoining Grammar for Kasumigaura Model

In more detail, a TAG grammar is specified by providing two sets of trees, the initial or α trees, corresponding to the basic building blocks of the language, and the auxiliary or β trees, corresponding to the insertable elements of the language. Together, these trees are known as elementary trees. The trees for the primary grammar used in this paper are shown in Figure 11-1.

As in Chomsky grammars, the nodes of the trees are labelled by terminal and non-terminal symbols; internal nodes must be labelled by non-terminals, while leaf nodes may be labelled by either terminals or non-terminals. Trees whose root is labelled by a non-terminal X are known as X-type trees. β trees satisfy one additional constraint, namely that an X-type β tree must have a distinguished node on its frontier, known as the foot node, labelled by X (in diagrams, we will mark the foot node with an asterisk '*').

Consider again the trees in Figure 11-1. L1 may be any of the attributes listed in Table 1 (e.g. p for level of ortho phosphate). R1 and R2 are random epheremal constant in the ranges of [0 .. 1] and [-50 .. 50] respectively. OP may be any of '+,' '-,' '*' or '/.' L1, R1 and R2 may be altered by the process of substitution as described below.

The key operations used with tree-adjoining grammars are the adjunction and substitution of trees. Adjunction builds a new (derived) tree γ from an auxiliary tree β and a tree τ (which may be an initial tree, or an already-derived tree). If tree τ has an interior node labeled A, and β is an A-type tree, the adjunction of β into τ to produce γ is as follows: Firstly, the sub-tree σ rooted at A is temporarily disconnected from τ. Next, β is attached to τ to replace the sub-tree. Finally, σ is attached back to the foot node of τ. γ is the final derived tree generated by this process.

In substitution, a non-terminal node X on the frontier of an elementary or derived tree is substituted by an X-type initial tree.

The completed derived trees of TAG (i.e., derived trees with no non-terminals on the frontier) thus correspond directly to the derivation trees of a Chomsky grammar, recording how a particular string (the frontier) may be derived from the start symbol. TAG systems introduce a new type of tree, TAG derivation trees, which record the history of adjunctions and substitutions (including their locations) used in generating a given derived tree.

Figure 11-2 shows a series of derivation trees and their corresponding derived trees. The top row shows the fourth alpha tree with its L1 defined as 't,' representing the water temperature. The frontier of every alpha tree is a valid expression, in this case the expression is 't.'

The second row shows another beta tree with OP being '+' and L1 being 'chla.' The frontier 'T* + chla' is not a completed expression, but may be adjoined into a completed expression to create a new completed expression.

The third row is another beta tree, presented here for future reference.

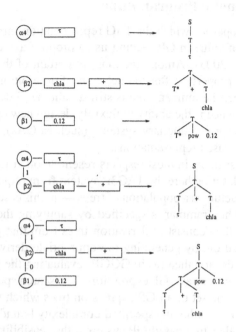

Figure 11-2. Example Derivation and Derived trees

The fourth row shows the result of adjoining the tree of the second row into the tree of the first row. The derivation tree on the left indicates that the β2 tree is adjoined into the first available adjuction point of the α4 tree. The derived tree on the right shows the result of this adjunction. The derived tree is created by first disconnecting the 'T-t' subtree of α4. The β2 tree is then reconnected at the same point where the subtree had been disconnected. Finally, that subtree is then rejoined at the adjunction point of β2.

The fifth row shows the result of adjoining the tree of the third row into the tree of the fourth row. This shows that the adjunction will occur at the first available adjunction point of β2 - this is its top node. Starting with the derived tree of row four, this proceeds by first disconnecting the subtree directly below 'S'. The tree β1 is then connected at that point, and the disconnected subtree is then re-joined at the foot node of β1.

The substitution operation can change any of the substituatable terms in the trees shown. For example, '+' can change to '*,' '0.12' to '0.78,' or 'chla' to 'p.'

TAG-based Genetic Programming

The valuable properties which the TAG representation introduces into NLP are arguably also of value in GP, leading us to propose a TAG-based GP system (Nguyen et al., 2003). Among the most important of these properties for GP is a feasibility property: after the deletion of an arbitrary subtree from a TAG derivation tree, the remnant tree is still a valid TAG derivation tree. An immediate consequence is the ability to flexibly design new operators, with the same ease as in linear evolutionary systems (such as GAs), while preserving the benefits of tree-based representations.

TAG-based GP systems in most respects resemble other tree-based GP systems closely. We describe here the TAG3P system from (Nguyen et al., 2003). The underlying structure is a population of trees — in this case, completed TAG derivation trees. The grammar is specified by supplying the sets of α and β trees. Populations then consist of derivation trees from that grammar. Fitness evaluation is carried out by generating the appropriate derived trees from the TAG derivation trees, and then (as in GGGP) evaluating the expression on the frontier of the derived tree as a GP expression. The search space is thus defined by the grammar — the set of all GP expression trees which may be generated by the given grammar, within the specified complexity bound. However unlike GGGP and most other tree-based GP systems, the feasibility property means that it is easy to control tree size so that tree size, rather than depth, is used as the complexity bound.

As in GGGP, any reasonable selection operator may be used; current versions of TAG3P use tournament selection. As with GGGP, care must be taken to ensure that crossover and mutation operators do not violate the closure requirement. In TAG3P, sub-tree mutation generates a new sub-derivation tree whose root is the non-terminal labelling the mutation point, while crossover is restricted to locations bearing the same non-terminal.

TAG3P is simply a variant GGGP system, using TAG derivation trees, in place of Context Free Grammar (CFG) derivation trees. In this form, the primary benefits of TAG representation lie in the transformation of the distance metric of the search space, as in the 'cat' example previous described, and in the ability to directly apply size rather than depth as a complexity metric.

We have shown in a number of papers (Nguyen et al., 2003; Nguyen et al., 2004) that these benefits can be important for a wide range of problems. Our working hypothesis, for which we have some preliminary evidence, is that the distance transformation implicit in the TAG representation, by allowing previously long-distance dependencies to become local, may better support the construction and preservation of appropriate building blocks for some problems.

However the representation effects are not the primary focus of this paper. Here, rather, we focus on the TAG representation's ability to support new GP tree operators. Because of the feasibility property, it is possible to design a wide range of new operators, which is otherwise difficult to achieve with standard GP representation using expression trees and in GGGP using CFG derivation trees. Moreover, many of the new operators are biologically motivated, including relocation and duplication (Nguyen et al., 2005), but also including point insertion and deletion operators motivated mainly by their local effects.

Point Insertion and Deletion Operators in TAG3P

The insertion and deletion operators in TAG3P can be viewed as extremely local mutation operators.

The deletion operator is simple to describe: it uses a uniform distribution to select one of the leaf nodes of the derivation tree, and deletes it from the tree. Because of the feasibility property, this always results in a valid derivation tree.

Conversely, the insertion operator selects uniformly randomly among the open adjunction locations within the derivation tree (*i.e.* non-terminal locations which do not already have an adjoined subtree), choosing a location with some label X. It then selects uniformly randomly amongst the X-type auxiliary trees, and adjoins the selected auxiliary tree in the chosen location.

While insertion and deletion can be treated as local mutation operators, our previous experiments have obtained significantly better results when they are used as local search operators, with sub-tree crossover and mutation remaining as the genetic operators. Hence in this application, the subtree operators are used as genetic operators only, while insertion and deletion are used as local search operators. The local search strategy used in this work is the most simple form of local search, namely, greedy-hill climbing. In more detail, for each generation, the system performs the initial stages of selection and then crossover and mutation as usual. However after that step, each new individual is then subjected to a fixed number of steps of local search.

For each step of local search, one of the two local search operators (insertion and deletion) is chosen with equal probability, the chosen operator being applied to the current individual to obtain a new one. The fitness of the new individual is assessed, and if the new individual is better than the old, it replaces the old, otherwise it is discarded.

The overall result is that the system tests a sequence of small changes in order to fine tune the individual. Note that this is feasible only because the flexibility of the TAG representation allows small changes throughout the derivation tree.

3.   The Lake Kasumigaura Modelling Problem

Phytoplankton in Lake Kasumigaura

Phytoplankton are microscopic photosynthesising organisms, primarily from several groups of algae and bacteria. A number of species (*e.g. Microcystis, Oscillatoria*) can occasionally exhibit periods of superabundance (blooms) with harmful ecological and economic effects (Reynolds, 1984), so prediction of their abundance, and especially of blooms, is of considerable importance.

Phytoplankton population dynamics are affected by a wide range of endogenous variables, including physical factors such as light and temperature, chemical factors such as pH and the levels of nitrogen and phosphorus, and biological factors such as the level of grazing by zooplankton. While there has been considerable previous work on developing predictive models (for example, see (Recknagel, 2001)), there is still room for improvement in the quality and reliability of the models.

Lake Kasumigaura is a large shallow lake in South-Eastern Japan, about 70km NE of Tokyo. At the time of dataset collection, in the 1980s and 1990s, there was high nutrient runoff into the lake, and hence high nutrient loadings. Consequently, there was also a high phytoplankton abundance, with periodic blooms. There is considerable seasonal fluctuation in temperature and light loadings, resulting in a large seasonal component to the phytoplankton levels. This is measured by chlorophyll A readings, which are presented in Figure 11-3, the blooms corresponding to the peaks in the graph.

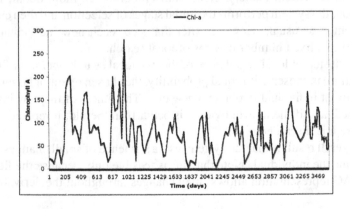

Figure 11-3. Lake Kasumigaura Chlorophyll A Readings

The Lake Kasumigaura dataset contains an extensive range of ecological variables sampled over the ten-year period 1984–1993 (Recknagel et al., 1998).

The data availability varies over the attributes, so in our work we have restricted our attention to the eight variables shown in Table 11-1.

Table 11-1. Lake Kasumigaura Data Variables

Variable	Mean ± Standard Deviation	Units
Ortho Phosphate (p)	15.46±32.11	mg/l
Nitrate (n)	517.17±525.10	$\mu g/l$
Secchi Depth (s)	84.72±47.15	cm
Water Temperature (t)	16.50±7.82	deg C
Light (l)	1199.16±695.55	MJ/m^2
Dissolved Oxygen (o)	11.13±2.41	-
Copepoda (co)	160.36±96.73	$Individuals/l$
Chlorophyll-A ($chla$)	74.35±46.60	$\mu g/l$

Modelling Approach

A wide variety of error measures are available for assessing the quality of models (and hence, to guide the computerised search for good models). For scenario modelling, Root Mean Square Error (RMSE) is the most widely accepted, and that is what we use in this paper. There is some question whether RMSE is the most suitable error measure for the use of time series models for future prediction. It is, for example, time-symmetric whereas it is arguable that error measures for time-series prediction should not be. For example, a model which anticipates an algal bloom too early may be more valuable than one which predicts its occurrence too late. Nevertheless, RMSE is widely used in predictive use of time-series models, and we follow standard practice in this area, for comparability with previous work.

In describing a model-inference system, we need to describe two components, the class of models explored, and the algorithm used to search amongst them. Here, we follow the lead of (Whigham and Recknagel, 2001) in using GP to generate difference equation models.

Since our primary purpose is to investigate the performance of local search, we compare the original TAG3P (*i.e.* with sub-tree crossover and mutation operators only) with two versions incorporating different amounts of local search with the insertion and deletion operators. For comparison with earlier works, we use CFG-based GGGP in a form close to that of Whigham and Recknagel's.

Model Space. Whigham and Recknagel discuss a number of representations in the context of equal time differences, the most general being a simple first-order difference equation,

$$y_{t+1} = f(x_t, y_t) \qquad (11.1)$$

However for irregularly-sampled data, it is essential to incorporate the time difference into the equation, the simplest approach being to incorporate it in differential form, *i.e.*:

$$\delta y / \delta t = f(x_t, y_t) \qquad (11.2)$$

which may be re-written as

$$y_{t+1} = y_t + (t * f(x_t, y_t)) \qquad (11.3)$$

The function to be learnt is $f()$.

4.   Experimental Method

Data Preparation

Data Cleaning.   We first extracted the original underlying data from the dataset (assuming linear interpolation). It was clear that the data had been sampled on an approximately monthly basis, but that there were additional observations for one variable (light level) throughout the data, and additional observations for all variables in the more recent period. We discarded these additional observations to obtain a dataset with irregular but approximately equal sampling (29.96 ± 3.65 days).

Data Categorisation.   The dataset was divided into two equal portions, for training and testing the models. The first portion, covering the years 1984–1988, was used for training, while the second portion, covering the years 1989–1993, was used to test the generalisation ability of the evolved models. As is evident from Figure 11-3, pollution control methods over the period have reduced the impact of algal blooms, so that the two periods are not fully comparable. Thus the learning technique will need to over-generalise to compensate (a better approach to evaluation would use m-fold cross-validation, but this is not well-accepted in the ecological modelling field).

Genetic Programming Setup

In these experiments, four treatments were used, incorporating four different learning methods: a fairly standard form of Context-Free Grammar Guided Genetic Programming, the original TAG3P algorithm, and two variants incorporating varying degrees of local search (TAG3P20 and TAG3P50, with 20 and 50 local search steps respectively), the population size being reduced correspondingly, so as to give the same overall number of evaluations. GP parameters for the runs are given in Table 11-2.

Table 11-2. Genetic Programming Parameters for Kasumigaura Modelling

Parameter	Value
General	
Runs per treatment	30
Generations per run	51
Probability of crossover	0.9
Probability of mutation	0.1
Selection Tournament Size	3
Parameters for GGGP	
Population size	1000
Local search steps	0
Max depth (initial generation)	6
Max depth (later generations)	10
Parameters for TAG3P/TAG3P20/TAG3P50	
Population size	1000/50/20
Local search steps	0/20/50
Max size (initial generation)	6
Max size (later generations)	40

GGGP Setup. As is usual in GGGP, the acceptable form for f in our equation 11.3 is defined by a context-free grammar, shown in Table 11-3. The variables $p, n, s, t, l, o, co, chla$ are the corresponding attributes from Table 11-1, while r_1 and r_2 are random ephemeral constants with ranges $[0.0 \ldots 1.0]$ and $[-50.0 \ldots 50.0]$ as in (Whigham and Recknagel, 2001). In this example, the independent variables p, n, s, t, l, o, co form the vector x_t, while y_t is the dependent variable $chla$. The function set consists of the arithmetic operators $(+, -, *, /)$ together with the exponential function (pow, with exponents in the range $[0..1]$), permitting the learning of very general forms for the models.

Table 11-3. Context Free Grammar for Kasumigaura Model

$S \rightarrow T$
$T \rightarrow T\_OP\_T$
$T \rightarrow T\_pow\_r1$
$T \rightarrow p|n|s|t|l|o|co|chla|r2$
$OP \rightarrow +|-|*|/$

TAG3P Setup. The TAG3P runs used the TAG shown in Figure 11-1, derived from the CFG using Schabes' transformation (Schabes and Waters, 1995)

Filtering of Results

An important complication with the function search space used in these experiments is the potential to generate invalid numeric values, either out-of-range or undefined. Out-of-range and NaN (not a number) values can be generated by arithmetic operations such as division by zero or exponentiation. Out-of-range values cause little problem for evolutionary methods, since infinite values will simply be treated as very unfit, but NaN values are more troublesome. In these experiments, we handled NaN fitness values by resetting them to a very large (*i.e.* unfit) value, namely exp(700). This is potentially disruptive to the evolutionary process, if too many NaN values occur. As a precaution, we recorded the number of NaN substitutions in each run; typical values were around 5,000 (around 1%) of the total number of fitness evaluations, suggesting that NaN substitutions did not substantially affect the evolutionary process.

In reporting results, these exp(700) values can dominate means even when relatively rare. To avoid this phenomenon, values exceeding exp(300) were filtered from the results before computing mean results or graphing. The number of such filtered values are reported along with the results. For the same reason, only best-of-generation results are reported, since population averages tended to be dominated by these misleading values.

5.   Results and Discussion

Results

Figure 11-4 shows the evolution of reduced RMSE on the training data for each of the four treatments used. Each point in the plot represents the mean, over all 30 runs for that treatment, of the Root Mean Square Error (RMSE) of the best individual in each population at the given generation.

Table 11-4 shows the mean error, over all runs for a given treatment, of the best individual in the final generation of each run. The table also shows the p-values from Student's T-test for all pairs of treatments. The null hypothesis is that there was no difference between means of the treatment pair, requiring a two-tailed unequal-variance test. Table 11-5 shows the corresponding values for the test data. In this case, a single run from the 30 for each of TAG3P20 and TAG3P50 was filtered out; no runs were filtered from the results for GGGP or TAG3P. Finally, Table 11-6 shows the mean sizes of these 'best' individuals.

Discussion

It is clear, both from Figure 11-4 and from Table 11-4, that local search does improve the training accuracy on this dataset - that is, that TAG3P with local search operators is better able to fit the data than either TAG3P alone, or a more standard GGGP system, the probabilities of the null hypotheses in these

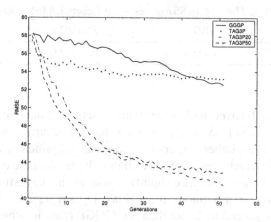

Figure 11-4. Mean of Training RMSE of Best-in-generation Individual

Table 11-4. Mean and SD of Training RMSE of Best Final-Generation Individual

	GGGP	TAG3P	TAG3P20	TAG3P50
	52.85 ± 3.33	53.23 ± 2.13	41.23 ± 3.43	42.69 ± 3.06
T test p values				
TAG3P50	9.88E-18	4.76E-21	0.89	
TAG3P20	2.98E-19	2.83E-21		
TAG3P	0.60			

Table 11-5. Mean and SD of Test of Best Final-Generation Individual

	GGGP	TAG3P	TAG3P20	TAG3P50
	136.1 ± 214.16	54.0 ± 35.8	48.9 ± 19.5	60.6 ± 40.7
T test p values				
TAG3P50	0.07	0.52	0.17	
TAG3P20	0.03	0.49		
TAG3P	0.05			

cases being very small. There may be a hint from the figure that TAG3P50's more eager search results in better early behaviour but poorer later results than TAG3P20 (*i.e.* that 50 steps of local search may be too many), and similarly, that GGGP is less eager than TAG3P, but given the T-test results, this requires more confirmation before a definite conclusion can be reached.

From Table 11-6, we see that the local search runs result in far larger individuals than TAG3P on its own; there is a concomitant risk that the results of

Table 11-6. Mean Size of Best Final-Generation Individual

GGGP	TAG3P	TAG3P20	TAG3P50
100.6 ± 47.5	5.4 ± 0.7	38.4 ± 2.6	39.0 ± 1.5

local search may be overfitted to the training data, and may generalise poorly to unseen data. Table 11-5 suggests that this has not occurred: while the differences in the table are either not, or only marginally significant, we can say that the 20 step local search runs generalise slightly better than the original version, while the 50 step runs generalise slightly worse, again suggesting that 50 steps may be too many. Furthermore, there is weakly suggestive evidence that all three TAG runs generalise better than the GGGP runs, in which a significant proportion appear to be significantly overfitted to the data, giving rise to very inaccurate predictions on the test data.

One further caution is required with Table 11-6. The table records the genotype size in each case. However GGGP genotype sizes are not strictly comparable with TAG genotype sizes - one TAG elementary tree typically subsumes a number of CFG productions (in this case, typically 2-3 as may be seen by comparing Table 11-3 and Figure 11-1, so that a TAG genotype typically corresponds to a GP genotype 2-3 times larger). Thus the best we may conclude regarding evolved GGGP sizes is that the GGGP individuals are roughly comparable in complexity with those from the TAG local search runs, and certainly much larger than those from the pure TAG3P runs.

6.   Conclusions and Further Work

The results presented here confirm the ability of local search in TAG3P, using the point insertion and deletion operators, to significantly improve the search performance of the TAG3P evolutionary system – in this case, in a real-world ecological modelling problem. The test set error obtained from TAG3P with local search is far lower than that obtainable either by TAG3P alone, or by a more standard GGGP system.

However for a learning problem such as this, in which generalisation is actually more important than test set accuracy, it is perhaps fortuitous that the large increase in individual size generated by the local search runs (*i.e.* search appeared to favour insertion over deletion) did not result in overfitting and poor generalisation. When the search method is too effective at fitting the training set data, mechanisms are required to avoid over-fitting which may lead to poor generalisation.

We plan to extend recent work on Minimum Measurement Length (MML) techniques for CFG-based GP (Shan et al., 2004) to the TAG representation, enabling us to use an MML-based metric, rather than raw accuracy, as the fitness metric for TAG3P with local search in learning problems, and thus avoid the potential generalisation problems.

References

Cramer, Nichael Lynn (1985). A representation for the adaptive generation of simple sequential programs. In Grefenstette, John J., editor, *Proceedings of an International Conference on Genetic Algorithms and the Applications*, pages 183–187, Carnegie-Mellon University, Pittsburgh, PA, USA.

Daida, Jason M., Li, Hsiaolei, Tang, Ricky, and Hilss, Adam M. (2003). What makes a problem GP-hard? validating a hypothesis of structural causes. In Cantú-Paz, E., Foster, J. A., Deb, K., Davis, D., Roy, R., O'Reilly, U.-M., Beyer, H.-G., Standish, R., Kendall, G., Wilson, S., Harman, M., Wegener, J., Dasgupta, D., Potter, M. A., Schultz, A. C., Dowsland, K., Jonoska, N., and Miller, J., editors, *Genetic and Evolutionary Computation – GECCO-2003*, volume 2724 of *LNCS*, pages 1665–1677, Chicago. Springer-Verlag.

Geyer-Schulz, Andreas (1995). *Fuzzy Rule-Based Expert Systems and Genetic Machine Learning*, volume 3 of *Studies in Fuzziness*. Physica-Verlag, Heidelberg.

Joshi, A.K., Levy, L. S., and Takahashi, M. (1975). Tree adjunct grammars. *Journal of Computer and System Sciences*, 21(2):136–163.

Koza, John R. (1992). *Genetic Programming: On the Programming of Computers by Means of Natural Selection*. MIT Press, Cambridge, MA, USA.

Nguyen, Xuan, McKay, Bob, Essam, Daryl, and Abbass, Hussein (2004). Toward an alternative comparison between different genetic programming systems. In Keijzer, Maarten, O'Reilly, Una-May, Lucas, Simon M., Costa, Ernesto, and Soule, Terence, editors, *Genetic Programming 7th European Conference, EuroGP 2004, Proceedings*, volume 3003 of *LNCS*, pages 67–77, Coimbra, Portugal. Springer-Verlag.

Nguyen, Xuan Hoai and McKay, R. I. (2004a). Softening the structural difficulty in genetic programming with TAG-based representation and insertion/deletion operators. In Deb, Kalyanmoy, Poli, Riccardo, Banzhaf, Wolfgang, Beyer, Hans-Georg, Burke, Edmund, Darwen, Paul, Dasgupta, Dipankar, Floreano, Dario, Foster, James, Harman, Mark, Holland, Owen, Lanzi, Pier Luca, Spector, Lee, Tettamanzi, Andrea, Thierens, Dirk, and Tyrrell, Andy, editors, *Genetic and Evolutionary Computation – GECCO-2004, Part II*, volume 3103 of *Lecture Notes in Computer Science*, pages 605–616, Seattle, WA, USA. Springer-Verlag.

Nguyen, Xuan Hoai, McKay, R. I., and Abbass, H. A. (2003). Tree adjoining grammars, language bias, and genetic programming. In Ryan, Conor, Soule, Terence, Keijzer, Maarten, Tsang, Edward, Poli, Riccardo, and Costa,

Ernesto, editors, *Genetic Programming, Proceedings of EuroGP'2003*, volume 2610 of *LNCS*, pages 340–349, Essex. Springer-Verlag.

Nguyen, Xuan Hoai and McKay, R I (Bob) (2004b). An investigation on the roles of insertion and deletion operators in tree adjoining grammar guided genetic programming. In *Proceedings of the 2004 Congress on Evolutionary Computation CEC2004*, Portland. IEEE Press.

Nguyen, Xuan Hoai, McKay, R I (Bob), and Essam, D L (2005). Genetic transposition in tree-adjoining grammar guided genetic programming: the duplication operator. In *Proceedings of the 8th European Conference on Genetic Programming (EuroGP2005)*, Lausanne, Switzerland.

Nordin, Peter and Banzhaf, Wolfgang (1995). Complexity compression and evolution. In Eshelman, L., editor, *Genetic Algorithms: Proceedings of the Sixth International Conference (ICGA95)*, pages 310–317, Pittsburgh, PA, USA. Morgan Kaufmann.

Nordin, Peter, Francone, Frank, and Banzhaf, Wolfgang (1995). Explicitly defined introns and destructive crossover in genetic programming. In Rosca, Justinian P., editor, *Proceedings of the Workshop on Genetic Programming: From Theory to Real-World Applications*, pages 6–22, Tahoe City, California, USA.

O'Reilly, U.M. (1997). Using a distance metric on genetic programs to undertand genetic operators. In *Late Breaking Papers at the 1997 Genetic Programming Conference*.

Recknagel, F. (2001). *Ecological Informatics*. Springer Verlag.

Recknagel, F., Fukushima, T., Hanazato, T., Takamura, N., and Wilson, H. (1998). Modelling and prediction of phyto- and zooplankton dynamics in lake kasumigaura by artificial neural networks. *Lakes and Reservoirs: Research and Management*, 3:123 – 133.

Reynolds, C. (1984). *The Ecology of Freshwater Plankton*. Cambridge University Press.

Ridley, M. (1996). *Evolution*. Blackwell Science.

Schabes, Y. and Waters, R.C. (1995). Tree insertion grammar: A cubic-time parsable formalism that lexicalizes context-free grammar without changing the trees produced. *Computational Linguistics*, 20(1):479–513.

Shan, Yin, McKay, Robert I., Baxter, Rohan, Abbass, Hussein, Essam, Daryl, and Nguyen, Hoai (2004). Grammar model-based program evolution. In *Proceedings of the 2004 IEEE Congress on Evolutionary Computation*, pages 478–485, Portland, Oregon. IEEE Press.

Vanneschi, L., Tomassini, M., Collard, P., and Clergue, M. (2003). Fitness distance correlation in structural mutation genetic programming. In *Proceedings of EuroGP*, Essex, England.

Whigham, P. A. (1995). Grammatically-based genetic programming. In Rosca, Justinian P., editor, *Proceedings of the Workshop on Genetic Programming:*

From Theory to Real-World Applications, pages 33–41, Tahoe City, California, USA.

Whigham, Peter A. and Recknagel, Friedrich (2001). An inductive approach to ecological time series modelling by evolutionary computation. *Ecological Modelling*, 146(1-3):275–287.

Wong, M. L. and Leung, K. S. (1995). Genetic logic programming and applications. *IEEE Expert*, 10(5):68–76.

Chapter 12

CONTENT DIVERSITY IN GENETIC PROGRAMMING AND ITS CORRELATION WITH FITNESS

A. Almal, W. P. Worzel[1], E. A. Wollesen[1] and C. D. MacLean[1]

[1]*Genetics Squared Inc., 210 S. Fifth Ave, Suite A, Ann Arbor, MI 48104*

Abstract   A technique used to visualize DNA sequences is adapted to visualize large numbers of individuals in a genetic programming population. This is used to examine how the content diversity of a population changes during evolution and how this correlates with changes in fitness.

Keywords: genetic programming, diversity, chaos game, fitness correlation.

1. Introduction

Genetic Programming (GP) has borrowed theory extensively from Genetic Algorithms (GAs). It is widely accepted that the building-block hypothesis (Holland, 1975) holds true for GP and Poli has proven a Schema Theorem (Holland, 1975) for GP (Poli and McPhee, 2001).

At the same time, there have been voices of dissent. Angeline (Angeline, 1997) has described crossover as "macro mutation" that is as likely to be destructive of existing building blocks as it is to create new building blocks. Daida *et al.* (Daida et al., 2003) has suggested that GP is dominated by structural considerations that significantly constrain the possible search space, thus limiting the importance of the Schema Theorem. McPhee and Hopper (McPhee and Hopper, 1999) and Daida *et al.* (Daida, 2004) both showed that the genetic material in the final generation of evolution could be traced to a very limited subset of the initial generation. Daida *et al.* (Daida, 2004) also suggests that tournament selection is better than fitness proportional selection at reaching a solution precisely because diversity is reduced quickly to a limited set of building blocks that are then shuffled to find their best combination. This is contrary to accepted wisdom that it is desirable to maintain diversity as long as possible in order to search for the best building blocks available. Instead Daida *et al.* (Daida, 2004) argues that for reasons of computational efficiency, it is better to allow fast convergence on a small number of building blocks that are selected from the initial populations. Without early convergence, a GP system will be forced to spend an inordinate amount of time evaluating inferior individuals.

This paper introduces a means for visualizing Genetic Programming content and structure so that aspects such as diversity and structure within a population may be examined during evolution and related to the progression of fitness. This may be used to test some of the theories described above as well as giving GP users some insight into the appropriateness of GP parameter settings for the problem being solved.

2.   Content Mapping

Chaos Game

Genetic programming systems, as with other evolutionary systems, are generally not in equilibrium. The dynamics of the system are usually non- linear in behavior and genetic programming systems tend to be very sensitive to initial conditions. Due to these properties, a genetic programming system may be described as a chaotic dynamical system. By applying chaos theory to the dynamics of evolution in GP, it may be possible to better understand the emergence of non-random patterns during the evolutionary process.

The Chaos Game is an interactive approach to teaching students about fractals and, indirectly, about chaotic dynamical systems. From a starting point within a simple geometric figure such as a triangle or a square, a point is plotted some fraction of a distance toward one of the figure's vertices. This is repeated, varying the targeted vertex until a figure emerges. For example, if a triangle is used and a point is plotted half way from the current position to the targeted vertex and the vertex is randomly selected, a Sierpinski triangle is created. This may be turned into a game by providing a target for the line to reach and requiring the student to pick the vertex toward which he or she moves (Voolich and Devaney, 2005).

If a square is used instead of a triangle and each corner is labeled with one of the bases in DNA (*i.e.*, A, T, C and G), then each sequence of DNA will create a different graph. By plotting multiple sequences in this way, the Chaos Game can be used for a variety of things such as identifying recurring sequences, and identifying functional regions of DNA (Jeffrey, 1990) (V. Solovyev, 1993). This method is now widely used for sequence analysis and in particular for the discovery of particular sequences of interest for further analysis.

The Circle Game

By moving from a polygon to a circle, a more flexible system is created with the values being mapped distributed evenly around the circle. This is equivalent to a polygon inset within a circle with the vertices touching the edge of the circle. By using this to plot individuals in genetic programming populations, the emergence of structure and content "motifs" during evolution may be tracked.

In this approach, to represent the content of a GP expression the tokens being tracked (*i.e.*, terminals and operators) are evenly spaced around a circle. By rendering a GP derived function as a linear string, the sequence of tokens may be plotted. As in the Chaos Game, beginning at the center of the circle, a point is plotted from the current location to a point halfway to the location of the point on the circle where the next token in the function lies. This is repeated until the function has been fully graphed in the circle and then repeated for all members of the population. (Koelle,) An alternative version plots a line from the current location to a point half way to the appropriate vertex rather than a single point. This has the virtue of showing ordered patterns that repeat within the population but at the cost of creating a more tangled plot.

It can be seen that the chaos game can capture the content diversity and show the emergence of patterns, however if we want to identify the 'motifs,' it requires us to represent the structure of the expression as well since $a \times b + c$ is quite different from $a \times (b + c)$ but their content plots would be identical. In order to do this we propose a modified approach that represents both the structure and the content.

The equation shown in Equation 12.1 can be easily mapped into a binary tree structure as shown in Figure 12-1.

$$[h!](Op3 \ (Op2 \ T1 \ T2) \ T4) \tag{12.1}$$

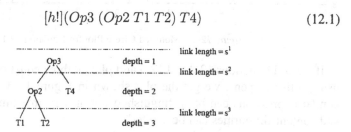

Figure 12-1. Binary Tree Representation of Equation 12.1

In the modified algorithm, the nodes are plotted using the rules for the circle game. However, the length of the links for these nodes are given by s^d, where s is a scaling factor arbitrarily chosen between 0 and 1, and d is the depth of the node the link is leading to in the binary tree. Also the link for a node in the plots should originate from the location of its parent. For example, the sequence of plotting for Equation 1, will be: plot a line from origin half the distance ($s = 0.5$) towards $Op3$, move a quarter distance towards $Op2$, move one-eighth of the distance towards $T1$, come back to the starting point for $Op2$, move one-eighth of the distance towards $T2$, come back to $Op3$ and move a quarter distance towards $T4$. The scaling parameter s can be chosen to be any arbitrary value, keeping in mind that it controls the visual divergence in the plot. Figure 12-2 shows an example of this for the expression shown in Equation 12.1.

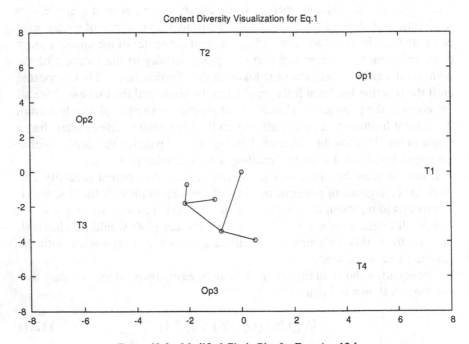

Figure 12-2. Modified Circle Plot for Equation 12.1

If we add Equations 12.2 and 12.3 and plot all three equations together using using different pens, we get the plot shown in Figure 12-3. This shows that similar expressions can be distinguished but at the same time their structural and content similarities can be spotted.

$$(Op3 \; (Op2 \; T1 \; T3) \; T4) \qquad\qquad (12.2)$$

$$(Op2 \; (Op1 \; T1 \; T2) \; T2) \qquad\qquad (12.3)$$

Showing Content Diversity During Evolution.   By looking at the structural content plots for an entire population during evolution we can gain a glimpse of the dynamic changes in structure and content. There are two different types

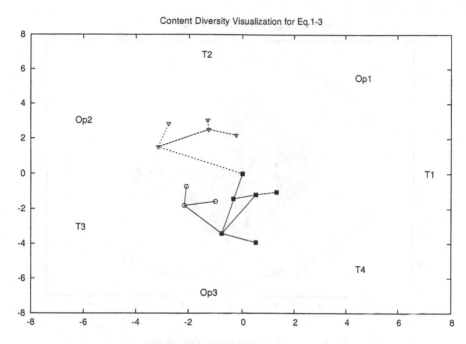

Figure 12-3. Circle Plot or Equations 12.1-12.3

of plots we use to study evolution. In one we plot the entire graph and in the other we plot the nodes and the links are omitted. Both of these methods have unique qualities, the former tells us about the connectivity of the nodes(an essential feature for finding the motifs) and the latter approach gives a nice visual representation of the diversity during evolution. Especially interesting are the emergence of the circular fractals in these plots. These suggest that the GP system is searching for the appropriate combination of elements in a structure.

Figure 12-4 shows a population of individuals at generation 0 of a run while Figure 12-5 shows the population at generation 10. Figure 12-6 shows it at generation 20 and 12-7 at the final generation, generation 40. By comparing these images we can see the appearance of shared content and structure within the population emerging from the random "ball of string" in generation 0. By the final generation shown in Figure 12-7, we can see how the content diversity has been reduced to a comparatively small number of variables and the structure is fairly similar across the individuals in the population.

The plots of only the nodes for the same problem follow in Figures 12-8 through 12-11.

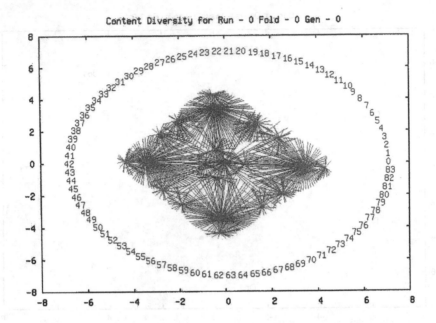

Figure 12-4. Generation 0 Content Plot

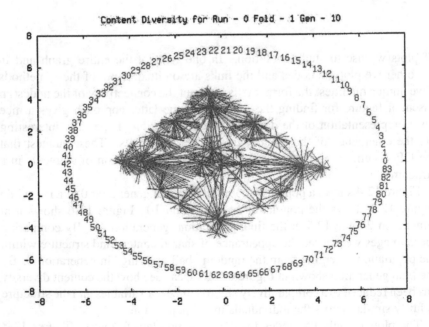

Figure 12-5. Generation 10 Content Plot

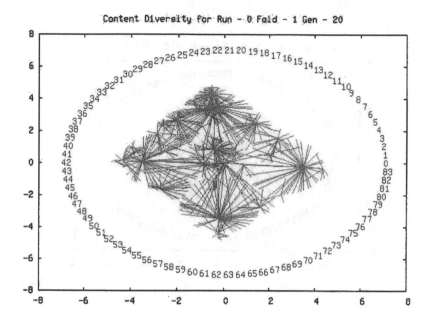

Figure 12-6. Generation 20 Content Plot

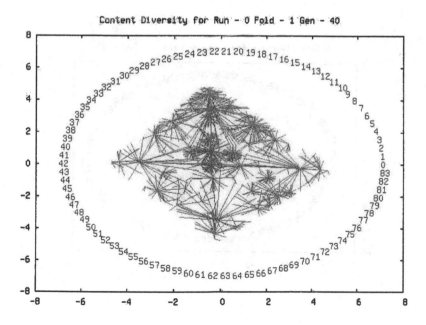

Figure 12-7. Generation 40 Content Plot

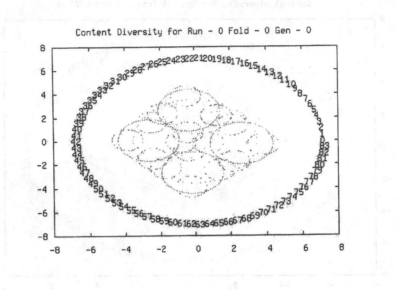

Figure 12-8. Generation 0 Content Plot - Endpoints

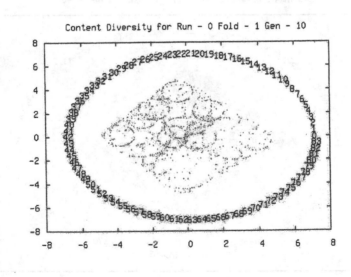

Figure 12-9. Generation 10 Content Plot - Endpoints

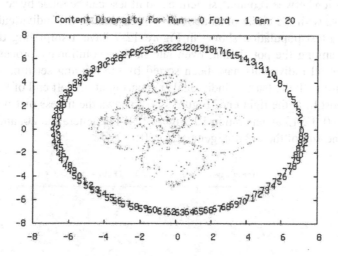

Figure 12-10. Generation 20 Content Plot - Endpoints

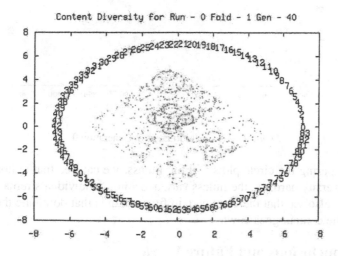

Figure 12-11. Generation 40 Content Plot - Endpoints

3.   Fitness Plots

Correlation between content, structure and fitness can be made by comparing fitness plots with the circle plots above. Scatter plots of the individual fitness values in a test population shown in Figure 12-7 have a surprising diversity of fitness among the population, even late in the evolutionary process. The fitnesses of all individuals have been sorted by the training set fitnesses (not shown here) with the least fit individuals appearing at the left end of the graph and the most fit at the right end. Figure 12-12 shows the fitness distribution in generation 0, 12-13 at generation 10, Figure 12-14 at generation 20, and Figure 12-15 at the end of the GP run, generation 40.

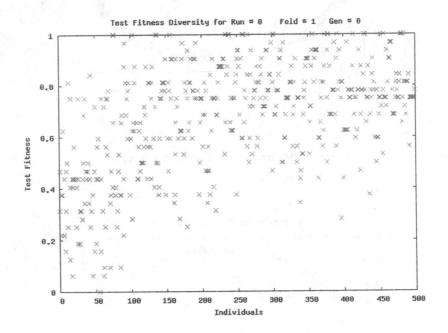

Figure 12-12.   Test Fitnesses at Generation 0

By comparing the circle plots and the fitness, we can see that although the content diversity narrows, the fitness variance among individuals remains high but we can also see that there are certain fitness bands that dominate the population as the content goes down.

4.   Conclusions and Future Work

The examples shown above were developed in a multi-deme system using generational evolution on a classification problem with a particular fitness measure suited for the type of classification problem we were working on. Any

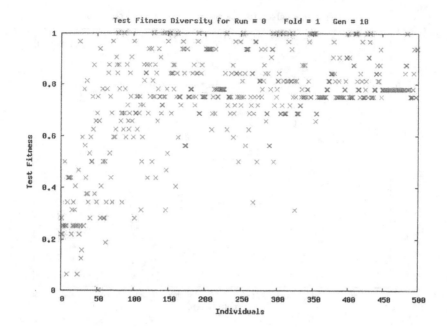

Figure 12-13. Test Fitnesses at Generation 10

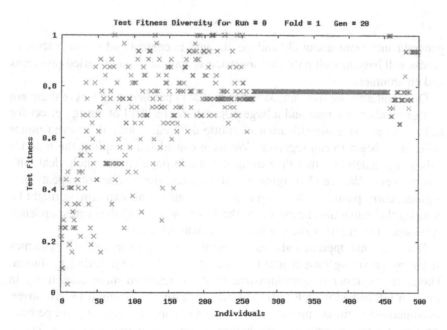

Figure 12-14. Test Fitnesses at Generation 20

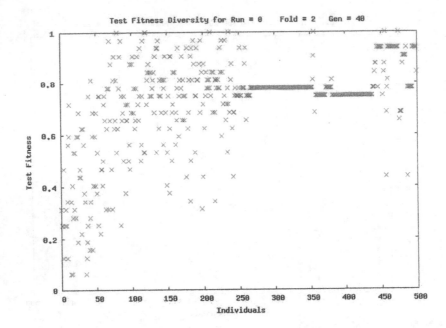

Figure 12-15. Test Fitnesses at Generation 40

general conclusions about GP and the changes in content and its correlation to fitness will have to wait until this approach is applied to more varied problems and environments.

One limitation we have encountered is that in problem sets where there are a large number of inputs and a large population, the "ball of string" effect for full plots can make identification of subtle difference difficult as even minor differences begin to run together. We have considered sampling the individuals in a population rather than using the whole population to help deal with this problem. We are also trying 3D plots where the number of repeats of a segment corresponds to plot height. Another interesting experiment might be coloring the individuals according to the fitness and seeing the correspondence in between the fitness, structure and the content diversity.

However, this approach shows potential as a way to model the dynamics of GP by providing insight into both structure and content during evolution. There are a number of questions that could be resolved more completely in terms of GP behavior such as the difference in diversity caused by crossover, a comparison of fitness proportional versus tournament selection, and perhaps most interesting, comparing populations in separate demes and the effect of different rates of transfer between the demes.

Similarly, running with varying probabilities of crossover and mutation and comparing the content distribution and its relationship to fitness will give an indication of how much GP is influenced by the building block hypothesis and the schema theory as opposed to structural limitations.

Also, by comparing the circle plots described here with Daida *et al.*'s structure plots (Daida et al., 2003), we will be able to see how much of the structure is captured in the circle plot compared to their approach. If the structure shown in the circle plots does not correspond to the structure relationships shown by Daida *et al.* (Daida et al., 2003), then adding structure plots to circle plots and correlating with fitness should show the interplay between structure, content and fitness, testing many of the current theories in Genetic Programming.

References

Angeline, Peter J. (1997). Subtree crossover: Building block engine or macro-mutation? In Koza, John R., Deb, Kalyanmoy, Dorigo, Marco, Fogel, David B., Garzon, Max, Iba, Hitoshi, and Riolo, Rick L., editors, *Genetic Programming 1997: Proceedings of the Second Annual Conference*, pages 9–17, Stanford University, CA, USA. Morgan Kaufmann.

Daida, Jason (2004). Considering the roles of structure in problem solving by a computer. In O'Reilly, Una-May, Yu, Tina, Riolo, Rick L., and Worzel, Bill, editors, *Genetic Programming Theory and Practice II*, chapter 5. Kluwer, Ann Arbor.

Daida, Jason M., Hilss, Adam M., Ward, David J., and Long, Stephen L. (2003). Visualizing tree structures in genetic programming. In Cantú-Paz, E., Foster, J. A., Deb, K., Davis, D., Roy, R., O'Reilly, U.-M., Beyer, H.-G., Standish, R., Kendall, G., Wilson, S., Harman, M., Wegener, J., Dasgupta, D., Potter, M. A., Schultz, A. C., Dowsland, K., Jonoska, N., and Miller, J., editors, *Genetic and Evolutionary Computation – GECCO-2003*, volume 2724 of *LNCS*, pages 1652–1664, Chicago. Springer-Verlag.

Holland, John H. (1975). *Adaptation in Natural and Artificial Systems: An Introductory Analysis with Applications to Biology, Control, and Artificial Intelligence*. University of Michigan Press, Ann Arbor, Michigan, USA.

Jeffrey, HJ (1990). Chaos game representation of gene structure. *Nucleic Acids Research*, 18(8):2163–2170.

Koelle, Katia. Private communications with Katia Koelle. University of Michigan, Center for the Study of Complex Systems.

McPhee, Nicholas Freitag and Hopper, Nicholas J. (1999). Analysis of genetic diversity through population history. In Banzhaf, Wolfgang, Daida, Jason, Eiben, Agoston E., Garzon, Max H., Honavar, Vasant, Jakiela, Mark, and Smith, Robert E., editors, *Proceedings of the Genetic and Evolutionary Com-*

putation Conference, volume 2, pages 1112–1120, Orlando, Florida, USA. Morgan Kaufmann.

Poli, Riccardo and McPhee, Nicholas Freitag (2001). Exact schema theory for GP and variable-length GAs with homologous crossover. In Spector, Lee, Goodman, Erik D., Wu, Annie, Langdon, W. B., Voigt, Hans-Michael, Gen, Mitsuo, Sen, Sandip, Dorigo, Marco, Pezeshk, Shahram, Garzon, Max H., and Burke, Edmund, editors, *Proceedings of the Genetic and Evolutionary Computation Conference (GECCO-2001)*, pages 104–111, San Francisco, California, USA. Morgan Kaufmann.

V. Solovyev, S. Korolev, H. Lim (1993). A new approach for the classification of functional regions of DNA sequences based on fractal representation. *Int. Journal of Genome Research*, 1(2):109–128.

Voolich, Johanna and Devaney, Robert L. (2005). The chaos game. http://math.bu.edu/DYSYS/applets/chaos-game.htm.

Chapter 13

GENETIC PROGRAMMING INSIDE A CELL

Gene Regulation and Self-Organization:
Inspirations from Genetic Programming in vivo

Christian Jacob[1,2] and Ian Burleigh[1]

[1]*Department of Computer Science, University of Calgary;*
[2]*Department of Biochemistry & Molecular Biology, University of Calgary*

Abstract   We present an agent-based, 3D model of the lactose (*lac*) operon, a gene regulatory system the bacterium *E. coli*. The *lac* operon is a prime example of a 'real
genetic programming' system, which has been studied extensively and lends itself
to rigorous mathematical analysis and computational simulations. We suggest
natural gene regulatory systems, as observed within *E. coli*, to serve as testbeds
for future *in silico* genetic programming systems.

Keywords: agent-based, biological modelling, gene regulatory system, lactose operon, bioinformatics, simulation, swarm intelligence, self-organization

1.   Introduction

The last decade has brought about a revolution in the understanding of
epigenesis—the still awe-inspiring processes of evolving a simple, undiffer-
entiated cell into a complex adult organism—and other natural development
processes. Genetic programming (GP) (Koza, 1992; Banzhaf et al., 1997), as
a relatively new research area, is now entering a stage of maturation, where we
strive to use evolutionary and developmental principles to automatically construct and 'grow' more and more complex systems, such as computer programs.
Interestingly enough, complex patterns and structures emerge within highly dynamic systems without any central control, which would globally regulate the
development of particular subsystems. emergence and self-organization principles play a major part in the decentralized construction of complex structural
computational entities or 'agents' (Kauffman, 1995; Holland, 1998).

Agent-based, massively parallel, decentralized approaches provide an appropriate level of abstraction, where local interaction rules determine agent behaviors, from which the overall 'collective system intelligence' emerges (Bonabeau et al., 1999; Kennedy and Eberhart, 2001). In conjunction with using GP to evolve agent-behavior programs, 'swarm intelligence' systems have the potential to inspire not only our understanding of developmental processes and their evolution, but to inspire current and future GP methodologies and applications from studying and modeling 'programming *in vivo*' (Jacob, 2000).

In this paper, we discuss one of the simplest gene regulatory systems—an example of 'real genetic programming'—with the objective of elucidating the underlying self-organization and swarm-interaction principles. We do this, first of all, to understand how to build agent-based models of biomolecular systems and, secondly, to derive abstractions for use in future genetic programming systems. We present a 3D-space, agent-based model of the lactose (*lac*) operon within the bacterium *Escherichia coli* (*E. coli*), which is one of the most basic and extensively investigated systems of gene regulation (Müller-Hill, 1996; Ptashne and Gann, 2002).

The observable dynamics of biomolecular systems, such as gene regulation within a cell, results from the interactions of a (usually large, but finite) number of 'bio-agents,' such as proteins, peptides, signaling or macro-molecules. Our agent-based models apply swarm intelligence algorithms in order to simulate bio-molecular systems, an approach which is gaining a much broader acceptance within the life sciences research community (Burleigh et al., 2003; Jacob and Burleigh, 2004), thus complementing most of the current, more abstract mathematical and computational models (Salzberg et al., 1998; Bower and Bolouri, 2001).[1]

The paper is organized as follows: In Section 2 we introduce operons as the basic modular units on bacterial genomes and describe the *lac* operon in detail. In Section 3, we present our model to explain how the on/off switching of genes results from the interactions among several bio-agents. Section 4 analyses typical simulation runs where the *E. coli* bacterium—*i.e.*, its genome—reacts to an influx of lactose. In Section 5, we offer an outlook of the future of GP, based on what we have learned from our *E. coli* model.

2. Operons as Self-Regulating Genetic Modules

An *operon* is a group of genes located on the DNA (Deoxyribose Nucleic Acid) of bacteria that are transcribed as a unit. The so-called *lac* operon, found

---

[1]Several alternative and complementary computer-based models of the *lac* operon exist, including simple grammar-based approaches (Collado-Vides, 1992), functional hybrid Petri net models (Matsuno et al., 2001), systems based on rewrite rules (Suen and Jacob, 2003), and systems based on large sets of differential equations (Tomita et al., 2000).

in the *E. coli* bacterium, is one of the best-studied gene regulatory systems, and is still used as a basis for investigating more complex genetic systems (Jacob and Monod, 1961; Beckwith and Zipser, 1970; Müller-Hill, 1996; Ptashne and Gann, 2002). *E. coli* is a prokaryotic organism without a nucleus that is normally found in a lactose-rich environment, such as the gut of humans. *E. coli* requires the energy source of glucose for much of its growth and has evolved a solution for obtaining glucose from its environment by converting lactose into glucose and galactose. This conversion is accomplished through the enzyme β-galactosidase, which is one of the products of the *lac* operon. In the presence of lactose, the *lac* operon is turned on and, hence, produces β-galactosidase. When lactose is no longer present, the *lac* operon turns itself off and, consequently, stops the production of β-galactosidase, thus conserving cellular resources. Gene-based self-regulation is an emergent property, mediated by the interactions of proteins, enzymes, molecules, and DNA. In order to understand how this 'emergence' can be accomplished through the interactions of 'swarms' of agents, we will describe the lactose operon in detail. The main components of the *lac* operon as a regulatory unit on the bacterial DNA consists of four genes: *lacZ*, *lacY*, *lacA*, and *lacI* (Figure 13-1).

Module One: *lacZ-Y-A*.   The *lacZ-Y-A* genes appear as a single module and are located adjacent to one another on the operon (Figure 13-1(a)). A control complex consisting of a *promoter* (P) and an *operator* (O) precedes the three genes. RNA polymerase reads the *lacZ-Y-A* sequence of genes, resulting in the production of their corresponding proteins Z, Y, and A through the processes of transcription and translation (explained in Section 3).

Module Two: *lacI*.   The *lacI* gene, the second key module, is located downstream of the main *lac* complex (Figure 13-1(a)). It likewise contains a promoter region, and produces proteins with the help of RNA polymerase. The *lacI* gene product is known as a *repressor*, which has a high affinity towards and binds to the operator region, thus preventing RNA polymerase from reading and expressing the *lacZ-Y-A* genes.

Flipping the Switch: On, Off, and In-between.   When lactose enters the cell, it binds to the repressors, forming a repressor-lactose complex (Figure 13-1(b)). Due to conformational changes, the repressor is no longer able to bind to the operator region of *lacZ-Y-A*. Consequently, RNA polymerase is now free to read *lacZ*, *lacY*, and *lacA* —producing β-galactosidase, lactose permease, and transacetylase, respectively. Among these three gene products, β-galactosidase is the enzyme that converts lactose into glucose and galactose.[2] β-galactosidase will then break down any lactose it encounters into glucose and galactose. Once lactose is removed from the system, the repressor is, again, free to bind to the operator region and terminate the production of β-galactosidase; hence, the *lac* operon is switched off. In this manner, the *lac* operon is able to regulate its own gene products, depending on the presence of lactose.

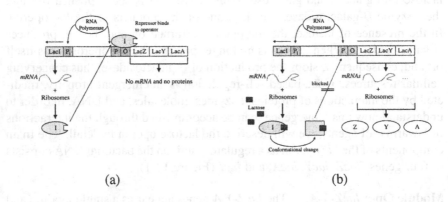

(a)   (b)

Figure 13-1. (a) After RNA polymerase docks onto P_i, the *LacI* promoter site, it transcribes the *LacI* gene into its *mRNA* representation, which is then translated by ribosomes into the repressor protein I. This repressor binds to the *LacZ-Y-A* operator site, which in turn blocks RNA p) and start scanning for promoter/operator sections. Once transcription is initiolymerase; hence, none of the three genes are expressed. (b) When lactose enters into the cell, it induces a shape change in the repressors that disables them from binding to the operator. Consequently, the *LacZ-Y-A* genes are accessible by the RNA polymerase and are expressed as proteins Z, Y, and A.

3.   The Emerging Switch

Our computer implementation of the lactose operon model and its visualization incorporates a swarm-based approach within a 3D visualization engine (Jacob and Burleigh, 2004; Burleigh et al., 2003). Each individual element in the simulation is treated as an independent agent governed by simple rules of interaction (Figure 13-2 and 13-3). Dynamic elements in the system move randomly in 3D space, executing specific actions when colliding with or getting close to other agents, which all operate within the boundaries of a spherical cell.

---

[2]Lactose permease enhances the movement of lactose from the outer environment into the cell, whereas transacetylase does not seem to play a role in this regulatory system (Ptashne and Gann, 2002; Alberts et al., 1998).

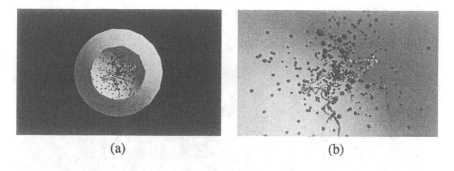

(a)   (b)

Figure 13-2. Zooming into a simulated *E. coli* cell. (a) All intra-cellular interactions are confined within a spherical cell. (b) Closeup of the circular DNA and a number of interacting 'bioswarm' agents.

From DNA to Proteins

We represent the actual encoding of the *lac* operon gene as a circular DNA double-helix[3] with its characteristic Watson-Crick complementarity pattern (Figure 13-3) (Watson and Crick, 1953). Groups of three nucleotide bases (Adenine, Cytosine, Guanine, and Thymine) form *codons*, which encode for specific amino acids, the basic building blocks of proteins. We chose to use codons for representing genetic sequences that make up the DNA strands.

There are two distinct gene regions in the *lac* operon: the *lacI* and the *lacZ-Y-A* region (see Section 2). For the purposes of this model, we only include the *lacI* and *lacZ* gene regions. The *lacY* and *lacA* genes do not greatly impact the function of the system and are therefore not included in our current model.[4]

Transcription.   The processes of transcription and translation serve as intermediary steps in order to produce proteins from a given gene. Once genes are 'switched on', *i.e.*, their operator region is not blocked by any repressor (Figure 13-1(b)), RNA polymerase has access to the encoding regions of the structural genes on the DNA. Transcription is the process of converting DNA into an intermediate molecule known as messenger Ribonucleic Acid (mRNA). The enzyme RNA polymerase is responsible for this particular conversion, which proceeds as follows: (1) RNA polymerase searches along the DNA structure

---

[3]The DNA is kept still within the cell. In this model, we do not consider any thermal fluctuation of DNA, such as translation, rotation, or chain flexibility.

[4]The codons around the two operator sites and the stop codons represent actual sequences from the *E. coli* genome. The rest of the circular DNA consists of random codons. Incorporation of the complete *lac* operon-related genome is possible in this model and will be a part of the next version of our biomolecular simulation system currently under construction.

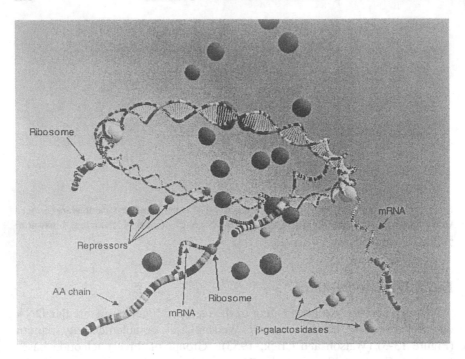

Figure 13-3. An annotated snapshop of our Lactose operon simulation: RNA polymerases (brown) attach to the DNA strands (turning pink) and start scanning for promoter/operator sections. Once transcription is initiated, RNA polymerases produce *mRNA* strands, undergoing translation by multiple ribosomes. The ribosomes construct the amino acid (AA) chains of unfolded proteins (repressors and β-galactosidases) based on the *mRNA* codon sequence. The snapshot also shows the key proteins involved in the switching behavior: β-galactosidases and repressors.

until it encounters an appropriate promoter region. (2) Starting at the promoter region, RNA polymerase begins to synthesize *mRNA* based on the genes found downstream from the promoter.[5] (3) Once transcription is complete, the *mRNA* strand is free to undergo a second conversion process (through translation), whereas RNA polymerase reiterates the process of transcription.

In our model, RNA polymerases, the initiators of transcription, are represented as dark (detached) or brighter (attached) large spheres (Figure 13-3). Once RNA polymerase attaches to a DNA region, it starts scanning along the chain of codons. Transcription occurs once RNA polymerase has encountered

---

[5]Here we make the simplifying assumption that *mRNA* copying begins right after the promoter region. In general, however, promoters can be quite distant from a coding region.

a viable promoter region. Genes adjacent to the promoter region are transcribed into *mRNA*, represented as a twisted single-stranded helix. As an example of the bio-agent rules that govern the overall simulation, Table 13-1 describes the simple programs for the polymerases.

Table 13-1. Rules governing the behavior of RNA polymerase as an example swarm agent.Pseudocode is presented with each state of RNA polymerase outlined. The corresponding biological actions are described in the right column.

Iterate Pseudo Code	Biological State and Action

`case state of`
 	
`  FLOATING: /* initial state */`
`    if near DNA:`
`      attach to nearest DNA codon`
`      state = DOCKED`
`    else:`
`      move randomly within the cell`
`  DOCKED:`
`    if promoter region is reached:`
`      state = READY_TO_TRANSCRIBE`
`    else:`
`      move along DNA to next codon`
 	
`  READY_TO_TRANSCRIBE:`
`    create an empty mRNA molecule`
`    state = TRANSCRIBING`
 	
`  TRANSCRIBING:`
`    if a stop codon is reached:`
`      release constructed mRNA`
`      state = DETACHED`
`    else if blocked by a repressor:`
`      destroy partial mRNA`
`      state = DETACHED`
`    else:`
`      move to the next codon`
`      append codon mRNA`
 	
`  DETACHED:`
`    detach self from DNA`
`    move randomly`
`    state = FLOATING`
 	
`end case`
	Floating:
	RNA polymerase is usually found near DNA and moves about the cell in a random manner. In this state, RNA polymerase will attempt to attach itself to the nearest free DNA strand.
	
	Docked:
	Once RNA polymerase has docked onto a free DNA strand, it will begin reading the DNA.
	
	Ready to Transcribe:
	When a promoter/operator sequence is found, the RNA polymerase will begin to initiate transcription.
	
	Transcribing: RNA polymerase will transcribe the DNA sequence into an mRNA molecule. RNA polymerase reads each codon sequentially, and appends a new base to the growing mRNA molecule. This process is completed once RNA polymerase encounters the appropriate stop codon. RNA polymerase will then detach itself from the DNA.
	
	Detached:
	Once RNA polymerase has detached from DNA, it will again resume its random movement within the cell.

Translation.   During translation a protein is synthesized from an *mRNA* strand. This *mRNA*-to-protein conversion is achieved through the action of ribosomes and transfer RNA (*tRNA*) as follows: (1) A ribosome locates and attaches to a free *mRNA* strand. (2) The ribosome begins to read the strand and synthesizes a chain of amino acids with the support of *tRNA*. (3) The chain then folds into a 3-dimensional protein structure. Once translation is complete, the ribosome detaches from the *mRNA* strand and releases the newly made protein.

The process of translation occurs once an *mRNA* strand has been synthesized. Ribosomes (Figure 13-3) attach to a free *mRNA* strand and begin to synthesize the associated amino acid (AA) chain, which is shown as a strand of disks. Multiple ribosomes can simultaneously read a single *mRNA* strand.[6] Once an AA chain is completely synthesized, it turns into its associated protein, such as a repressor or β-galactosidase.[7]

From Proteins to DNA

In the case of the *lac* operon, repressor proteins and β-galactosidase enzymes are synthesized through the processes of transcription and translation. Repressors have a natural affinity for the operator region of the *lac* operon. They attempt to bind to the operator region and physically block transcription of the *lacZ* gene, which turns the *lac* operon off. This sequence of events is illustrated in Figures 13-4(a–c) through snapshots taken during our simulation over 2000 iteration steps. In Figure 13-4(c) the operator site is surrounded by a number of repressors, which ensure that the operator is blocked (almost) all the time, so that no RNA polymerase can proceed past the operator site.

At this point it should be noted that the 'switch-off' state is a collective property, resulting from the interactions of multiple repressor proteins with the operator site, in the following sense. Any repressor that binds to an operator does in fact detach after a certain time period. Consequently, a single repressor will not be able to keep an operon section switched off continuously. However, a 'swarm' or group of repressors that tend to be around the operator site can cooperatively accomplish to block the operator for a much longer period. Once a repressor releases, another one will attach to the vacant operator. This aspect is reflected in our model and will be discussed in more detail in the following section. Hence, the expression of β-galactosidase is cooperatively suppressed as illustrated in Figure 13-4(c).

Once lactose is introduced into the cell (Figure 13-4(d)), repressor-lactose complexes are formed, which cause any bound repressor to be released from

---

[6]In the *E. coli* bacterium, ribosomes are abundant within the cell. For proper visualization, we assume that there is always a sufficient number of ribosomes, which we only make visible when they attach to an *mRNA*.
[7]In order to keep the model simple, we skip the complicated—and still largely unknown—processes of folding an AA chain into the specific 3-dimensional shape of a protein.

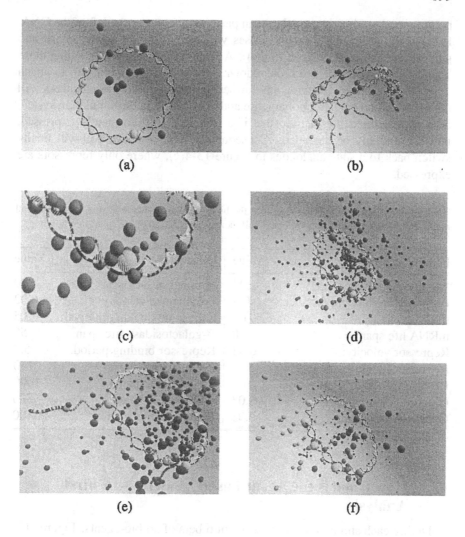

(a)   (b)

(c)   (d)

(e)   (f)

Figure 13-4. Different stages of the *lac* operon simulation. (a) RNA polymerases scan the DNA strands and search for promoter regions. (b) RNA polymerases synthesize *mRNA* molecules. Ribosomes synthesize proteins. (c) Repressors (center bottom) around the operator block RNA polymerase from transcribing the *LacZ* gene. (d) Lactose is introduced into the system. (e) Lactose binds to repressors preventing them from blocking RNA polymerase. One RNA polymerase (on the left) has just started to transcribe part of the *LacZ* gene. (f) Most of the lactose is split into glucose and galactose. A number of β-galactosidases are visible in the left half.

the operator site. This, in turn, enables RNA polymerases to pass beyond the operator and initiate expression of β-galactosidase. In Figure 13-4(e), one polymerase has already started to scan past the operator to the left of the DNA. Each of the produced β-galactosidases will start to break down lactose into glucose and galactose (Figure 13-4(f)). As soon as all lactoses, including those bound to any repressor, are broken down, repressors will again start to attach to the *lacZ* operator, blocking any further production of β-galactosidase. All the particles (except RNA polymerase and ribosomes) in the simulation system have a predefined lifespan, so that if a protein is not constantly expressed, it will eventually be degraded. Consequently, the simulated cell will finally switch back to a state analogous to Figure 13-4(c), where only repressors are expressed.

Table 13-2. Control parameter settings for the biomolecular agents in Figure 13-4. The cell radius defines the unit step size (velocity: cell radius / iteration step; life span: iteration step).

Parameter	Value	Parameter	Value
Number of polymerases:	24	Number of lactoses:	400
Polym-DNA docking distance:	0.3	Polymerase velocity:	0.02
mRNA velocity:	0.01	Ribosome docking interval:	3.5
mRNA life span:	18	β-galactosidase life span:	50
Repressor velocity:	0.03	Repressor binding period:	5.0
Repressor floating period:	20.0	Repressor life span:	140
Lactose velocity:	0.03	Lactose life span:	1000
Glucose velocity:	0.03	Glucose life span:	500
Galactose velocity:	0.03	Galactose life span:	500

4.   How Good is the Agent-based Model? — A First Analysis

During each simulation we track the numbers of all bio-agents. Figures 13-5(a) and (b) show concentration graphs of two typical runs over 5000 time steps, similar to the simulation illustrated in Figure 13-4. Initially, there are no repressors or β-galactosidases in the system. Although the number of repressors then starts to increase over the first 200 iterations, it cannot prevent the production of β-galactosidase enzymes. However, once the repressor concentration has reached its first peak level at around $t = 500$, it almost completely blocks the *lacZ* operator, which drastically reduces expression of β-galactosidase. At $t = 500$, lactose is introduced into the cell, which triggers the formation of repressor-lactose complexes, and the concentration of free repressors decreases rapidly. Now free repressors are too few to block the operator. After a short delay the number of β-galactosidases increases, resulting in a corresponding

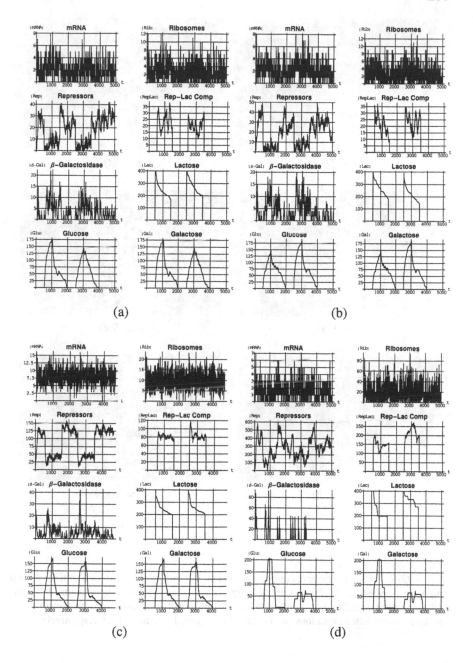

Figure 13-5. Evolution of the concentrations of biomolecular agents during four of our lactose simulations. (a) and (b) show two typical runs with the configuration parameters as described in Table 13-2. (c) Polymerase velocity is increased by a factor of 10: $v_{poly} = 0.2$. (d) 10-fold reduction of the time between ribosome docking: $t_{dock}(rib) = 0.35$.

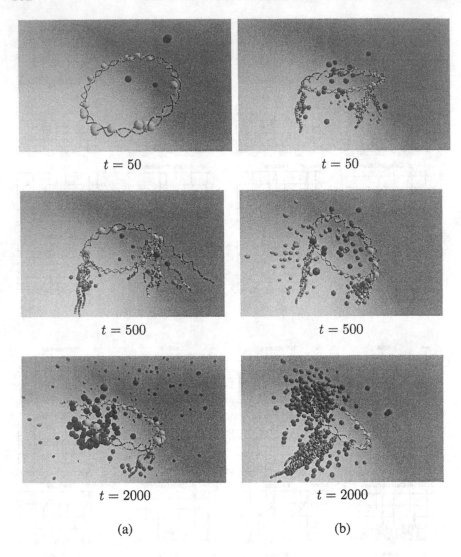

$t = 50$ $t = 50$

$t = 500$ $t = 500$

$t = 2000$ $t = 2000$

(a) (b)

Figure 13-6. Example snapshots during the evolution resulting from different settings of two bio-agent parameters. (a) *Polymerase velocity*, $v_{poly} = 0.2$: increased by a factor of 10. (b) *Ribosome docking delay*, $t_{dock}(rib) = 0.35$: 10-fold reduction of the time between ribosome docking. The detailed evolutions are illustrated in Figures 13-5c and 13-5d, respectively.

rise of both glucose and galactose. The lifetime of lactose within the cell was set to 1000 time steps, which reduces the lactose concentration to zero at around $t = 1500$. This causes the repressor concentration to build up again and resume the repression of β-galactosidase production, which brings the system back to its initial state with a relatively high number of repressors and a low base level of β-galactosidase. By reintroducing lactose at $t = 2500$ one can observe similar interaction dynamics. Figures 13-5(a) and 13-5(b) result from two runs with the same parameter settings (Table 13-2), which illustrate the inherent noise in the agent model. However, the switching behavior occurs consistently.

In order to find out how changes of some of the bio-agent control parameters would affect the overall evolution of the *lac* operon simulation, we show two more experiments, where we modified the velocity of RNA polymerases and the docking interval for ribosomes. The graphs in Figure 13-5(c) result from a 10-fold increase of RNA polymerase velocity to $vel_{poly} = 0.2$ units per time step. As in the previous two experiments, we introduced lactose at $t = 500$ and again at $t = 2500$. With the polymerases' faster speed, the different base levels for repressors, β-galactosidases and rep-lac complexes obviously become less noisy. Hence, transcription speed determines the level of noise suppression in the system. Snapshots of this experiment are illustrated in Figure 13-6(a). In another experiment (Figure 13-5(d)), we reduced the *mRNA* docking interval between ribosomes from originally $t_{doc}(rib) = 3.5$ to $t_{doc}(rib) = 0.3$ time steps. This results in a drastic increase of the number of repressors, which almost immediately reduce any increase in β-galactosidase to a very low base level. Interestingly, the *lac* operon switch is still functional. Snapshots of this experiment are illustrated in Figure 13-6(b).

5. Gene Regulation and Genetic Programming

Evolutionary optimization techniques can be used for bio-agents finding suitable or alternative settings for the bio-agent control parameters. This would allow a fine-tuning of the model with respect to measurements retrieved from *in vitro* and *in vivo* experiments.

A combination of both automatic and interactive fitness evaluation turns out to be quite useful for both parameter tuning and 'reverse engineering.' The automatic fitness function would take care of simulation aspects that can easily be compiled into a mathematical formula, such as keeping the average density of particles within a certain range, or checking whether the switch is turned on/off. These constraint criteria would act as filters for the simulations that are then shown to an interactive evaluator, *i.e.*, the model designer, who is usually an expert in the system under study. If we go back to the *lac* operon model discussed here, the microbiologist would observe a set of simulations on the computer screen. Looking at the interaction dynamics of the particles (*e.g.*, Figure 13-6) and at plots of system-related aspects of the tracked particles (*e.g.*, Figure 13-5), the expert is able to decide whether the parameter settings proposed by the evolutionary system make sense within the context under investigation or not. This interactive breeding of model parameters does not only provide a tool for optimization in the classical sense, but serves as a platform for exploratory investigations in general—an inspirational tool to think about emergent patterns in complex systems (Kwong and Jacob, 2003).

Within the same breeding scenario, GP can expand the scope of constructing, investigating, and analyzing agent-based models of bio-molecular systems or, in general, 'swarm' systems in the following ways:

We can use GP to evolve interaction rules between the bio-agents. A rule set would be shared by the same types of agents, such as repressors, β-galactosidases, RNA polymerases, or ribosomes. Such rules can become relatively complicated (see Table 13-1), but one can certainly identify elementary behavioral commands (random walking, attaching, detaching, *etc.*) which serve as suitable building blocks for the evolutionary construction of interaction programs. The evaluation criterion for this scenario could, first of all, be formulated as a regression problem, where measurements from wet lab experiments of the system under study determine the desired system output. Again, the expert's intervention through interactive fitness evaluation would complement the automatic rule-evolving GP system. However, approaching the evolution of interaction rules from a simplistic regression perspective is in many cases too naive, not realistic and not feasible. Most biological systems, for which computational and mathematical models would be highly desirable, are only partially understood. Consequently, there are usually not enough experimental data available to compare a fitness function to. In this case, GP provides a promising vehicle to evolve different agent types, in combination with their interaction rules. Hence, one can investigate different ways of generating some desired temporal and spatial dynamics that result in specific—partly observable or measurable—system outputs. Questions about a particular system could be asked, such as whether a different set of agent interaction rules leads to similar behavior (*e.g.*, in the case of the *lac* operon: is the switch still working?).

6.   Conclusion and Future Work

We have presented a 3D agent-based model of the *lac* operon gene regulatory system, including a fast visualization engine.[8] The model focuses on simulating important aspects of a biomolecular system including basic genetic processes such as transcription and translation. We believe that such simulations and visualizations will serve as powerful educational tools, and will support biologists in their understanding of complex gene regulatory systems, and decentralized, massively-parallel biological systems in general. Furthermore, such exam-

---

[8]Currently, we work with a Java3D version (used in a CAVE^{TM} Automated Virtual Environment) and a C++/OpenGL version of our simulations.

ples of (relatively simple) 'real genetic programming' systems should serve as an inspirational platform for future genetic programming systems *in silico*. Studying real genetic programming systems, such as the one within *E. coli*, gives us a much better understanding not only of the underlying mechanisms of gene regulation (with major consequences for gene therapy, drug design, *etc.*), but can also provide alternative ways of constructing computer programs with built-in self-regulation mechanisms. In addition to studying robustness properties within our *lac* operon model, we are currently working on a GP approach that incorporates aspects of gene regulation and Boolean networks (Kauffman, 1995).

One can find further information about our lactose operon model on our *Evolutionary & Swarm Design* web site (www.swarm-design.org), which is being expanded to incorporate other types of bio-molecular agents as well as several communicating cells, and other swarm-based models of biological systems, such as the λ-switch and an artificial immune system (Jacob et al., 2004).

References

Alberts, Bruce, Bray, Dennis, Johnson, Alexander, Lewis, Julian, Raff, Martin, Roberts, Keith, and Walter, Peter (1998). *Essential cell biology: an introduction to the molecular biology of the cell.* Garland, New York.

Banzhaf, Wolfgang, Nordin, Peter, Keller, Robert, and Francone, Frank D. (1997). *Genetic Programming: An Introduction.* Morgan Kaufmann, San Francisco, CA.

Beckwith, Jon R. and Zipser, David, editors (1970). *The Lactose Operon.* Cold Spring Harbor Laboratory Press, Cold Spring Harbor, NY.

Bonabeau, Eric, Dorigo, Marco, and Theraulaz, Guy (1999). *Swarm Intelligence: From Natural to Artificial Systems.* Santa Fe Insitute Studies in the Sciences of Complexity. Oxford University Press, New York.

Bower, James M. and Bolouri, Hamid, editors (2001). *Computational Modeling of Genetic and Biochemical Networks.* MIT Press, Cambridge, MA.

Burleigh, Ian, Suen, Garret, and Jacob, Christian (2003). Dna in action! a 3d swarm-based model of a gene regulatory system. In *First Australian Conference on Artificial Life*, Canberra, Australia.

Collado-Vides, J. (1992). Towards a grammatical paradigm for the study of the regulation of gene expression. In Goodwin, Brian and Saunders, Peter, editors, *Theoretical Biology. Epigenetic and Evolutionary Order from Complex Systems*, pages 211–224. Johns Hopkins University Press, Baltimore, ML.

Holland, John H. (1998). *Emergence: From Chaos to Order.* Addison-Wesley, Reading, MA.

Jacob, Christian (2000). The art of genetic programming. *IEEE Intelligent Systems*, 15(3):83–84.

Jacob, Christian and Burleigh, Ian (2004). Biomolecular swarms: An agent-based model of the lactose operon. *Natural Computing*, 3(4):361–376.

Jacob, Christian, Litorco, Julius, and Lee, Leo (2004). Immunity through swarms: Agent-based simulations of the human immune system. In *Artificial Immune Systems, ICARIS 2004, Third International Conference*, Catania, Italy. LNCS 3239, Springer.

Jacob, François and Monod, Jacques (1961). Genetic regulatory mechanisms in the synthesis of proteins. *Molecular Biology*, 3:318–356.

Kauffman, Stuart (1995). *At Home in the Universe: The Search for Laws of Self-Organization and Complexity*. Oxford University Press, Oxford.

Kennedy, James and Eberhart, Russel C. (2001). *Swarm Intelligence*. The Morgan Kaufmann Series in Evolutionary Computation. Morgan Kaufmann Publishers, San Francisco.

Koza, John R. (1992). *Genetic Programming: On the Programming of Computers by Means of Natural Selection*. MIT Press, Cambridge, MA, USA.

Kwong, Henry and Jacob, Christian (2003). Evolutionary exploration of dynamic swarm behaviour. In *Congress on Evolutionary Computation*, Canberra, Australia. IEEE Press. emergence.

Matsuno, H., Doi, A., Tanaka, A., Aoshima, H., Hirata, Y., and Miyano, S. (2001). Genomic object net: Basic architecture for representing and simulating biopathways. In *Ninth International Conference on Intelligent Systems for Molecular Biology*, Copenhagen, Denmark.

Müller-Hill, Benno (1996). *The lac Operon - A Short History of a Genetic Paradigm*. Walter de Gryter, Berlin.

Ptashne, Mark and Gann, Alexander (2002). *Genes & Signals*. Cold Spring Harbor Laboratory Press, Cold Spring Harbor, NY.

Salzberg, S.L., Searls, D.B., and Kasif, S., editors (1998). *Computational Methods in Molecular Biology*, volume 32 of *New Comprehensive Biochemistry*. Elsevier, Amsterdam.

Suen, Garret and Jacob, Christian (2003). A symbolic and graphical gene regulation model of the lac operon. In *Fifth International Mathematica Symposium*, pages 73–80, London, England. Imperial College Press.

Tomita, M., Hashimoto, K., Takahashi, K., Matsuzaki, Y., Matsushima, R., Saito, K., Yugi, K., Miyoshi, F., Nakano, H., Tanida, S., Saito, Y., Kawase, A., Watanabe, N., Shimizu, T., and Nakayama, Y. (2000). The e-cell project: Towards integrative simulation of cellular processes. *New Generation Computing*, 18(1):1–12.

Watson, James D. and Crick, Francis H. C. (1953). A structure for deoxyribose nucleic acid. *Nature*, 171:737–738.

Chapter 14

EVOLUTION ON NEUTRAL NETWORKS
IN GENETIC PROGRAMMING

Wolfgang Banzhaf[1] and Andre Leier[1]

[1]*Department of Computer Science, Memorial University of Newfoundland,
St. John's, NL, A1B 3X5, CANADA*

Abstract   We examine the behavior of an evolutionary search on neutral networks in a
simple linear genetic programming system of a Boolean function space problem.
To this end we draw parallels between notions in RNA-folding problems and in
Genetic Programming, observe parameters of neutral networks and discuss the
population dynamics via the occupation probability of network nodes in runs on
their way to the optimal solution.

Keywords: neutrality, linear GP, networks, population dynamics

1.   Introduction

For more than a decade now, neutrality has been observed to play an important
role in Genetic Programming (GP) runs. This was originally believed to be an
atypical phenomenon, perhaps related to the choice of representation (Koza,
1992; Altenberg, 1994a; Angeline, 1994). It was later realized that introns or
non-effective code, as it became to be called, constitute the bulk of material
generating neutrality in GP and that this type of code would appear in most
representations of GP systems (Nordin and Banzhaf, 1995). For a long time
the debate centered around questions of reasons for the emergence of this type
of code which certainly was unintended by the designers of GP systems, and
originally deemed disadvantageous (Soule et al., 1996; Langdon and Poli, 1998;
Soule and Heckendorn, 2002).

During the same time, it was proposed that the theory of neutral mutations as
put forward in the seventies and eighties for natural evolution (Kimura, 1983),
could be understood in terms of the existence of neutral networks (Schuster,

1995; Forst et al., 1995; Reidys et al., 1997). Subsequent to that proposal various natural evolutionary systems have been examined, and the existence of neutral networks has been confirmed (Huynen et al., 1996; Babajide et al., 1997). Its benefits for evolution were gradually revealed (Nimwegen et al., 1998; Schultes and Bartel, 2000), and thus it was natural to ask what neutral networks would have to offer for evolutionary search.

Barnett proposed to adopt a search paradigm different from a population-based Genetic Algorithm (GA) search in landscapes with considerable neutrality (Barnett, 2001). Smith et al (T. Smith and O'Shea, 2001) argue that, due to higher evolvability, GA systems with neutrality in search behave more aptly in difficult search landscapes.

Recently, the confluence of both lines of inquiry can be observed in GP as well. Early observations (Banzhaf, 1994) spoke to the advantage of using plenty of neutrality. In the context of circuit design using Cartesian GP Miller and coworkers argued for search efficiency as one characteristic of representations with neutrality (Vassilev and Miller, 2000b; Vassilev and Miller, 2000a; Vassilev et al., 2003). Ebner (Ebner et al., 2002) pointed out how neutral networks can influence evolvability and Yu (Yu and Miller, 2001) studied the interaction between neutral and adaptive mutations in the context of search in Boolean function landscapes.

In this contribution we shall discuss neutrality and the benefit of neutral networks in the context of a simple Boolean search problem using a linear GP representation, that consists of registers and logic operators. We shall show the relation between genotype and phenotype networks, discuss how the search benefits from neutrality as offered by non-effective code, and demonstrate the population dynamics of a search process. In the final section we shall put our eyes on robustness of the evolutionary solutions, and ask ourselves how evolvability of the search process can be improved if the observations put forward here can be generalized.

2.   Problem, GP representation and Search Operators

In order to be able to examine the effects we are interested in, we have chosen a small problem instance of a Boolean problem space. While it can be argued that this space is not suitable to solve real problems, the emphasis here is on trying to understand the influence of neutrality, notably its benefits.

The problem space under consideration is the NAND space where two binary inputs x_1 and x_2 are used and the output x_3 is studied under various NAND-combinations of inputs.

$$x_3 = f_{NAND}(x_1, x_2) \qquad (14.1)$$

This follows work done by (Langdon and Poli, 1999) where it was shown, for tree-based GP, that there is a complexity threshold above which all Boolean functions can be reached by a combination of Boolean operators on inputs.

We use a linear GP representation because it is much easier to analyse in terms of non-effective code (Banzhaf et al., 1998; Brameier and Banzhaf, 2001), and because it is easier to understand. The representation consists of a set of instructions in a register machine language, interpreted by the CPU as a program. As for the content of the registers, we allow only Boolean values "0" and "1" as the operators of these programs in the logical NAND operation.

Even with so small a set of elements, combinatorics is at play, forcing us to quickly relinquish the plan to depict everything exhaustively. One choice we have is whether we want to have only a single type of register (read-and-write) which can act both as source and destination register of the programs executed, or two types of registers (input and calculation) which differ in that input registers hold the input values constantly, *i.e.* are only acting as source registers, and calculation registers can act both as source and destination registers.

Table 14-1 shows the combinatorics in these two different systems, depending on the length of programs allowed. In the following, we shall concentrate on $C = I = 2$. The first calculation register also works as the output register.

Table 14-1. Comparison of the number of programs for different number of registers. C: Number of calculation registers; I: number of input registers; L: Length of programs in number of instructions. The number of programs is calculated by $(I + C)^{2L} C^L$.

C Registers	I Registers	$L = 2$	$L = 3$	$L = 4$	$L = 5$	...	$L = 10$
2	0	64	512	4.1×10^3	3.3×10^4		1.1×10^9
3	0	729	19,683	5.3×10^5	1.4×10^7		2.1×10^{14}
1	2	81	729	6.6×10^3	5.9×10^4	...	3.5×10^9
2	2	1,024	32,768	1.0×10^6	3.4×10^7		1.1×10^{15}
3	2	5,625	421,875	6.3×10^6	2.4×10^9		5.6×10^{18}

A typical program (for $R0$, $R1$ calculation registers and $R2$, $R3$ input registers, output in register $R0$) looks like this:

```
R0 = R1 NAND R2
R1 = R1 NAND R0
R0 = R3 NAND R1
R1 = R1 NAND R2 (*)
R1 = R1 NAND R0 (*)
R1 = R2 NAND R1 (*)
```

which we code as the following genotype:

```
012 110 031 112 110 121
```

This is different from the phenotype of that program which results after removing the introns[1] ((*)-marked code, above) to yield

```
R0 = R1 NAND R2
R1 = R1 NAND R0
R0 = R3 NAND R1
```

which we code as the following phenotype:

```
012 110 031
```

Figure 14-1 depicts which functions can be reached with programs of different length up to $L = 8$. As seen in the figure, there is a large discrepancy between the presence of different Boolean functions, with some like "Equivalance" being frequently found and thus being easy, and others like "Identity" being seldomly found and thus being difficult. Note the complexity threshold again: Below program length 5 there is no solution to the Equivalence function.

In the following, our GP system will be set up to find the most difficult function, the "Equivalence" function, and we shall study how the system achieves this solution and what can be said about the neutral networks it uses to find it.

After introducing the representation, we have to say a few words about the search operator(s) we shall employ in our GP runs. In this contribution we decided again for the operator mutation, which is the easiest to analyse. Whereas it can again be argued that this is not an efficient way to traverse the problem space at hand, we would counter, that at least we can understand what is going on in the system.

For illustration purposes, suppose a mutation would change a bit in the genotype mentioned below.

```
012 110 031 112 110 121 -> 012 110 031 012 110 121
```

This would mean, that the phenotype now changes, too:

```
012 110 031 -> 012 110 012
```

In other words, by switching one bit, one of the instructions has been rendered non-effective, whereas a previously non-effective one has become effective.

The evolutionary dynamics we have chosen is again a very simple one, we observe and examine runs with a population of $\mu(1 + \lambda)$ searchers, where the notation is borrowed from Evolutionary Strategies. There are μ independent searchers (providing for statistics), each one acting in an elitist way ($+$ strategy), and exploring the neighborhood with λ trials (in our case, $\lambda = 10$). If one of these neighbor states is equal or better in fitness, the searcher assumes the new state; if not, it remains where it was.

---

[1]The last three instructions only affect register $R1$ and not the output register $R0$.

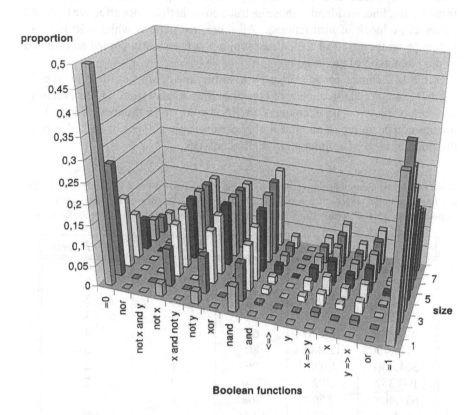

Figure 14-1. Boolean function space for various length of programs. For $L = 5$ "$\Leftrightarrow$" has a 0.00114 % share of the search space, in contrast to "$= 1$" with a share of 23.4 %. For $L < 5$ "$\Leftrightarrow$" is not present at all.

3. Non-effective Code, Neutral Networks, and the Genotype-Phenotype Map

As we have mentioned in the beginning, we expect that neutrality should play an important role in the search process in our Boolean function landscape. Neutrality is provided by non-effective code. This is unintentionally generated by a sequence of instructions if a later instruction simply overwrites what has been computed before. It might even happen that all instructions are non-effective. This is the case, if no data is written into the predetermined output register of the GP system. We refer to the corresponding phenotype as the "empty phenotype."

The Genotype-Phenotype-Mapping (GPM) function is provided through re-moving the non-effective code. This is analogous to the neutrality provided in

RNA folding (Gruener et al., 1996). By analysing a program's code, beginning from the last line, we identify those instructions which are not effective (it could be an entire block of instructions). All other instructions which will have an influence on the result of the calculation, are subsequently copied and treated as the phenotype of the program.

Table 14-2 shows, for an exhaustive examination of all possible genotypes in a small example, the frequency of corresponding phenotypes. This is precisely the sort of picture one encounters in RNA folding landscapes: Many very uncommon phenotypes, and few highly common phenotypes, if looked at from the point of view of enumeration of all genotypes.

Table 14-2. Redundancy of genotypes mapping into phenotypes for $C = 2; I = 2; L = 5$. The last line shows total number of genotypes and phenotypes. G: Number of genotypes; P: number of phenotypes; R=G/P: Redundancy. The fitness value relates to $\Leftrightarrow$ as the reference function.

G	P	R	Best Fitness	Worst Fitness
1,192,960	1,192,960	1	0	4
87,808	5,488	16	2	2
415,744	12,992	32	1	3
749,568	15,616	48	1	3
948,224	14,816	64	1	4
1,030,400	12,880	80	1	3
384,000	4,000	96	1	2
100,352	392	256	2	2
657,408	856	768	1	2
1,413,120	920	1,536	1	2
2,560,000	1,000	2,560	1	2
405,504	144	2,816	1	3
1,753,088	428	4,096	2	3
917,504	56	16,384	2	2
4,096,000	100	40,960	2	2
131,072	2	65,536	2	2
4,259,840	40	106,496	1	2
3,276,800	10	327,680	2	2
1,048,576	1	1,048,576	2	2
8,126,464	4	2,031,616	2	3
33,554,432	1,262,705			

Each genotype can be considered a node in a graph. A mutation would then provide a link between nodes in the graph, allowing evolution to move if this step is actually allowed by selection. Due to the genotype-phenotype mapping, however, there is also a graph of nodes constituting the network of phenotypes. Each of these nodes has a particular fitness depending on how the fitness function was defined for the problem. A movement on the genotype network driven by mutation now induces a corresponding movement on the phenotype network. Figure 14-2 shows the graph of phenotypes in a Boolean problem small enough that all phenotypes can be enumerated and drawn (length of programs: 2 instructions only).

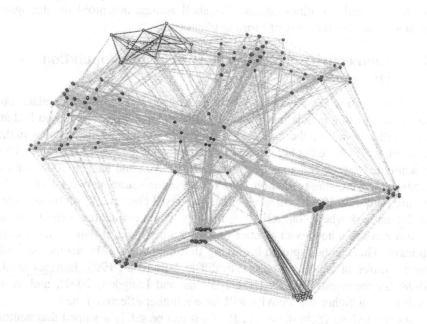

Figure 14-2. Phenotype network graph for a Boolean function problem with $C = 2; I = 2; L = 2$. Nodes have different colors, depending on the particular fitness they represent which is calculated as the difference to the AND function. Two neutral networks are shown with black edges. Self-connections of nodes are not shown.

The links between nodes correspond, as we said, to mutations, except that we have not shown self-connections which may still have a substantial impact on evolutionary search. These links are distributed unequally between nodes, induced by the GPM.

Neutral networks are constituted by those nodes in the network which have the same fitness and are connected by mutations. Note that there is a difference between this definition of neutrality and the definition used by *e.g.* (Ebner et al., 2002). Here we consider all phenotypes with the same fitness to be in the same neutral network, provided there is a mutational link. Ebner *et al.*

considers neutral networks only between the same phenotypes (which surely will have the same fitness). There are two disconnected components of the neutral network to the second-best fitness level.

Strictly speaking, the phenotype network has no *direct* meaning for the evolutionary search. Our GPM is a simple many-to-one projection and the connectivity of nodes on a path in the phenotype network is not necessarily related to the path in the genotype network. That is to say, some phenotype nodes are hiding the fact that the genotypes represented by them are actually not connected at all. Therefore, the connectivity distribution of the phenotype network seems to be only of minor interest. We shall address this problem later again by suggesting another way of forming phenotypes.

4.   Connectivity of Neutral Networks and Population Dynamics

It is interesting to study the connectivity of neutral networks, and relate it to the dynamics of a population of searchers on the network. The reason is that, as is well known from the study of random walks on graphs, those nodes in the network which have the highest connectivity tend to be visited the most. This is a simple Markov chain result (Lovacz, 1993; Noh and Rieger, 2004), and it leads to the following prediction: The search in the neutral network will not be a pure random drift. It will have a bias, and will concentrate on those nodes of the network where connectivity is highest. If in the mutation neighborhood of those nodes a node with a better fitness can be found, it will be discovered quickly. This can be captured by saying that the nodes of the neutral network have a different effective fitness (Nordin and Banzhaf, 1995; Banzhaf et al., 1998; Stephens and Vargas, 2000; Banzhaf and Langdon, 2002), and those nodes with a higher connectivity will have a higher effective fitness.

As pointed out (Schuster et al., 1994), it can be safely assumed that neutral networks for different levels of fitness are strongly intertwined. *I.e.* it will not be difficult to encounter transition nodes from one of these networks to another with a higher fitness. These so-called portal nodes (Nimwegen et al., 1998) are spread throughout the network and provide ample chance to jump off a neutral network onto one with better fitness. The only problem in our Boolean example is that in fact the problem is so easy (only 5 different fitness values) that it is difficult to observe all the phenomena. By looking at Figure 14-3 we can compare an exhaustive mapping of the search space in terms of connectivity characteristics with a mapping based on 100,000 GP runs. With this amount of sampling, the GP runs are already approaching full knowledge of the search space.

Connectivity characteristics lends itself as a new way of observing the system, and allows an alternative definition of phenotypes. The only condition of these

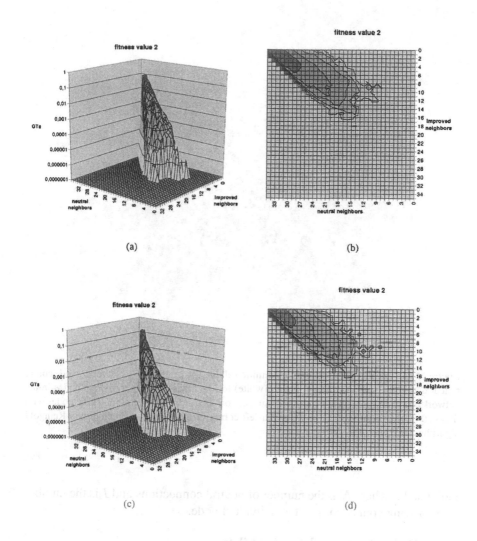

Figure 14-3. Distribution according to connectivity characteristics: A genotype's connectivity characteristics is given by a triplet of values (I, N, D) where I (D) is the number of neighbors with improved (deteriorated) fitness and N the number of neutral neighbors. Since the total number of neighbors is constant (35), two values (here: I and N) are sufficient for characterization. The 3D/2D plots show the proportions of connectivity for all genotypes of fitness 2 in the genotype network (Figures (a) and (b)) and for all visited nodes of fitness 2 within $100, 000$ GP runs (Figures (c) and (d)).

phenotypes will be that the fitness of an individual should be carried by the phenotype. So our alternative phenotypes look like this: $(fitness, N, I)_i$ for

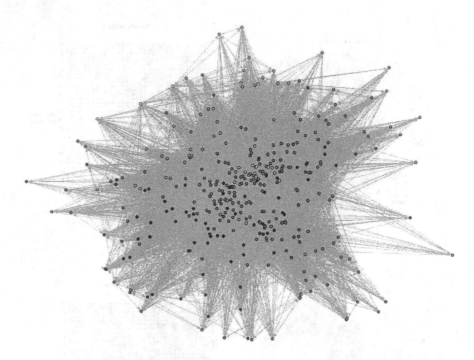

Figure 14-4. The alternative phenotype definition allows to visualize a PT network. Node colors reflect the fitness levels from high fitness (white) to low fitness (dark gray). Pale nodes in the network center correspond to nodes in the subnetwork depicted in next figure. Three nodes with fitness 0 (perfect solutions) lie in the upper left corner of the network. Fruchterman-Reingold algorithm (2D) was used to create graphs.

individual i, where N is the number of neutral connections and I is the number of improving connections of the individual node.

5.   Robustness and Evolvability

Two of the main functions of neutrality in biological systems are considered to be (i) robustness of phenotypes against mutation and (ii) evolvability. For (i) to work, a viable genotype would try to locate itself in the center of a neutral network such as to make sure that any mutation that might happen to it still allows it to stay on the neutral network. In the absence of neutrality, a viable genotype/phenotype pair might always stand a high probability to produce deleterious mutations.

The other function is to provide more potential for evolvability. Following Kirschner and Gerhardt (Kirschner and Gerhart, 1998) evolvability can be

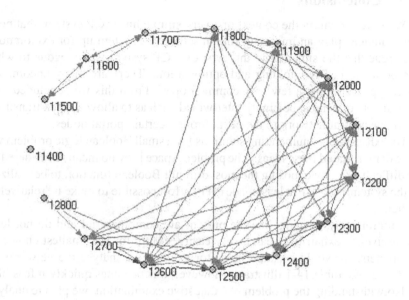

Figure 14-5. Neutral network of the most frequently visited nodes. More than 95% of all edges in the PT network passed during 1,000 GP runs belong to this subnetwork. Node labels specify fitness value (one digit), number of neutral neighbors (two digits) and number of improved neighbors (two digits). Self-connections are not shown, although they contribute over 50% .

defined as the capacity of an organism to generate heritable variation. It is interesting to note that modern metazoa seem to have developed in that direction.

In the context of evolutionary computation this would come about by allowing genotype/phenotype pairs to escape local optima through higher dimensional saddles, produced by neutral changes to the pair. Furthermore, if the network provides a clear guide via effective fitness, it could accelerate evolution even in the case of not being caught in a local minimum. Evolution would most probably be attracted to genotypes/phenotypes which are highly connected in the network, and thus have a better chance to be connected to higher-fitness states.

Another aspect of evolvability - not discussed here - is modularity (Altenberg, 1994b; Wagner and Altenberg, 1996). For this to work, a clearer picture of what building blocks are should be developed. We feel that more research needs to be done on the question of building blocks in GP before this question can be approached. For recent progress in this field, see (Langdon and Banzhaf, 2005).

6.   Suggestions for Future Work, Summary and Conclusions

We have shown, in the context of a very simple linear GP system, that neutral mutations play an important role in setting the system up for exploration. We argue that the situation in this type of a GP system is analogous to what can be found in RNA-folding and optimization: There are many uncommon phenotypes, and just a few very common ones. From this we concluded that neutral networks must be highly intertwined such as to allow a quick transition from one neutral network to the next, through certain portal nodes.

By exhaustively enumerating solutions for a small Boolean logic problem we have demonstrated these ideas. The problem space is by no means considered to be difficult. Yet, by choosing the most difficult Boolean function to be realized in the system, we have at least made every effort possible to make it "relatively" difficult.

Unfortunately, systems like the present are combinatorial and do not lend themselves to exhaustive search very easily, except for the smallest choice of parameters. It would be interesting, for example to analyse the networks of $C, I > 2$. As Table 14-1 illustrates, however, this becomes quickly infeasible.

Notwithstanding the problem of exhaustive examination, we plan to analyse networks locally, around local optima or best fitness phenotypes found so far. We also want to provide more thorough statistical measures of network characteristics, such as centrality of neutral networks *etc.* It would be most interesting to be able to pinpoint the nodes which most searchers have to pass through and to manipulate the search in order to either lead it towards these nodes or away from them.

Acknowledgements

The authors wish to thank NSERC for support under Discovery grant RGPIN 283304-04. Software used to visualize our networks: Pajek 1.0 by Vladimir Batgelj & Andrej Mrvar

http://vlado.fmf.uni-lj.si/pub/networks/pajek

References

Altenberg, Lee (1994a). Emergent phenomena in genetic programming. In Sebald, Anthony V. and Fogel, Lawrence J., editors, *Evolutionary Programming — Proceedings of the Third Annual Conference*, pages 233–241, San Diego, CA, USA. World Scientific Publishing.

Altenberg, Lee (1994b). The evolution of evolvability in genetic programming. In Kinnear, Jr., Kenneth E., editor, *Advances in Genetic Programming*, chapter 3, pages 47–74. MIT Press.

Angeline, Peter John (1994). Genetic programming and emergent intelligence. In Kinnear, Jr., Kenneth E., editor, *Advances in Genetic Programming*, chapter 4, pages 75–98. MIT Press.

Babajide, A., Hofacker, I.L., Sippl, M.J., and Stadler, P.F. (1997). Neutral networks in protein space. *Fold. Des.*, 2:261–269.

Banzhaf, W. and Langdon, W. B. (2002). Some considerations on the reason for bloat. *Genetic Programming and Evolvable Machines*, 3(1):81–91.

Banzhaf, W., Nordin, P., Keller, R., and Franconce, F. (1998). *Genetic Programming - An Introduction*. Morgan Kaufmann, San Francisco, CA.

Banzhaf, Wolfgang (1994). Genotype-phenotype-mapping and neutral variation – A case study in genetic programming. In Davidor, Yuval, Schwefel, Hans-Paul, and Männer, Reinhard, editors, *Parallel Problem Solving from Nature III*, volume 866 of *LNCS*, pages 322–332, Jerusalem. Springer-Verlag.

Barnett, Lionel (2001). Netcrawling-optimal evolutionary search with neutral networks. In *Proceedings of the 2001 Congress on Evolutionary Computation, 2001*, pages 30 – 37. IEEE Press.

Brameier, Markus and Banzhaf, Wolfgang (2001). A comparison of linear genetic programming and neural networks in medical data mining. *IEEE Transactions on Evolutionary Computation*, 5(1):17–26.

Ebner, M., Shackleton, M., and Shipman, R. (2002). How neutral networks influence evolvability. *Complexity*, 7:19—33.

Forst, C.V., Reidys, C., and Weber, J. (1995). Evolutionary dynamics and optimization: Neutral networks as model-landscapes for rna secondary-structure folding-landscapes. In *Advances in Artificial Life, Proc ECAL 1995*. Springer-Verlag, LNAI Vol 929.

Gruener, W., Giegerich, R., Strothmann, D., Reidys, C.M., Weber, J., Hofacker, I.L., Stadler, P.F., and Schuster, P. (1996). Analysis of dna sequence structure maps by exhaustive enumeration - part i: Neutral networks. *Monatsh. hemie*, 127:355 – 377.

Huynen, M., Stadler, P.F., and Fontana, W. (1996). Smoothness within ruggedness: The role of neutrality in adaptation. *Proc. Natl. Acad. Sci. USA*, 93:397—401.

Kimura, Motoo (1983). *The Neutral Theory of Molecular Evolution*. Cambridge University Press.

Kirschner, M. and Gerhart, J. (1998). Evolvability. *Proc. Natl. Acad. Science (USA)*, 95:8420—8427.

Koza, John R. (1992). *Genetic Programming: On the Programming of Computers by Means of Natural Selection*. MIT Press, Cambridge, MA, USA.

Langdon, W. B. and Poli, R. (1998). Fitness causes bloat: Mutation. In Banzhaf, Wolfgang, Poli, Riccardo, Schoenauer, Marc, and Fogarty, Terence C., editors, *Proceedings of the First European Workshop on Genetic Programming*, volume 1391 of *LNCS*, pages 37–48, Paris. Springer-Verlag.

Langdon, W. B. and Poli, R. (1999). Boolean functions fitness spaces. In Poli, Riccardo, Nordin, Peter, Langdon, William B., and Fogarty, Terence C., editors, *Genetic Programming, Proceedings of EuroGP'99*, volume 1598 of *LNCS*, pages 1–14, Goteborg, Sweden. Springer-Verlag.

Langdon, William B. and Banzhaf, Wolfgang (2005). Repeated sequences in linear genetic programming genomes. *Complex Systems*. in press.

Lovacz, L. (1993). Random walks on graphs: A survey. Technical report, Department of Computer Science, Yale University, CT, USA.

Nimwegen, E.v., Crutchfield, J.P., and Huynen, M. (1998). Neutral evolution of mutational robustness. *Proc. Natl. Acad. Sci. USA*, 96:9716—9720.

Noh, J.D. and Rieger, H. (2004). Random walks on complex networks. *Phys. Rev. Lett.*, 92:118701-1-3.

Nordin, Peter and Banzhaf, Wolfgang (1995). Complexity compression and evolution. In Eshelman, L., editor, *Genetic Algorithms: Proceedings of the Sixth International Conference (ICGA95)*, pages 310–317, Pittsburgh, PA, USA. Morgan Kaufmann.

Reidys, C.M., Stadler, P.F., and Schuster, P. (1997). Generic properties of combinatory maps-neutral networks of rna secondary structures. *Bull. Math. Biol*, 59:339—397.

Schultes, E.A. and Bartel, D.P. (2000). One sequence, two ribozymes: Implications for the emergence of new ribozyme folds. *Science*, 289:448—452.

Schuster, P., Fontana, W., Stadler, P.F., and Hofacker, I.L. (1994). From sequences to shapes and back: A case study in rna secondary structures. *Proc. Roy. Soc. Lond. B*, 255:279—284.

Schuster, Peter (1995). Extended molecular evolutionary biology: Articial life bridging the gap between chemistry and biology. In Langton, C.G., editor, *Artificial Life: An Overview*, pages 39 – 60. MIT Press, Cambridge, MA.

Soule, Terence, Foster, James A., and Dickinson, John (1996). Code growth in genetic programming. In Koza, John R., Goldberg, David E., Fogel, David B., and Riolo, Rick L., editors, *Genetic Programming 1996: Proceedings of the First Annual Conference*, pages 215–223, Stanford University, CA, USA. MIT Press.

Soule, Terence and Heckendorn, Robert B. (2002). An analysis of the causes of code growth in genetic programming. *Genetic Programming and Evolvable Machines*, 3(3):283–309.

Stephens, C. R. and Vargas, J. Mora (2000). Effective fitness as an alternative paradigm for evolutionary computation I: General formalism. *Genetic Programming and Evolvable Machines*, 1(4):363–378.

T. Smith, Ph. Husbands and O'Shea, M. (2001). Neutral networks in an evolutionary robotics search space. In *Proceedings of the 2001 Congress on Evolutionary Computation, 2001*, pages 136 – 145. IEEE Press.

Vassilev, Vesselin K., Fogarty, Terence C., and Miller, Julian F. (2003). Smoothness, ruggedness and neutrality of fitness landscapes: from theory to application. In Ghosh, Ashish and Tsutsui, Shigeyoshi, editors, *Advances in evolutionary computing: theory and applications*, pages 3–44. Springer-Verlag New York, Inc.

Vassilev, Vesselin K. and Miller, Julian F. (2000a). The advantages of landscape neutrality in digital circuit evolution. In *Proceedings of the Third International Conference on Evolvable Systems*, pages 252–263. Springer-Verlag.

Vassilev, Vesselin K. and Miller, Julian F. (2000b). Embedding landscape neutrality to build a bridge from the conventional to a more efficient three-bit multiplier circuit. In Whitley, Darrell, Goldberg, David, Cantu-Paz, Erick, Spector, Lee, Parmee, Ian, and Beyer, Hans-Georg, editors, *Proceedings of the Genetic and Evolutionary Computation Conference (GECCO-2000)*, page 539, Las Vegas, Nevada, USA. Morgan Kaufmann.

Wagner, G.P. and Altenberg, L. (1996). Complex adaptations and the evolution of evolvability. *Evolution*, 50:967—976.

Yu, Tina and Miller, Julian (2001). Neutrality and the evolvability of boolean function landscape. In Miller, Julian F., Tomassini, Marco, Lanzi, Pier Luca, Ryan, Conor, Tettamanzi, Andrea G. B., and Langdon, William B., editors, *Genetic Programming, Proceedings of EuroGP'2001*, volume 2038 of *LNCS*, pages 204–217, Lake Como, Italy. Springer-Verlag.

Chapter 15

THE EFFECTS OF SIZE AND DEPTH LIMITS ON TREE BASED GENETIC PROGRAMMING

Ellery Fussell Crane[1] and Nicholas Freitag McPhee[1]

[1] *University of Minnesota, Morris, Morris MN 56267, USA*

Abstract   Bloat is a common and well studied problem in genetic programming. Size and depth limits are often used to combat bloat, but to date there has been little detailed exploration of the effects and biases of such limits. In this paper we present empirical analysis of the effects of size and depth limits on binary tree genetic programs. We find that size limits control population average size in much the same way as depth limits do. Our data suggests, however that size limits provide finer and more reliable control than depth limits, which has less of an impact upon tree shapes.

Keywords: size limits, depth limits, genetic programming, population distributions, tree shape

1.   Introduction

The causes and effects of code growth in Genetic Programming (GP) have been extensively researched (Langdon and Poli, 2002). In order to avoid the negative repercussions of bloat, a variety of corrective measures are employed to keep program sizes in check (Poli, 2003; Silva and Almeida, 2003; Luke and Panait, 2002; Koza, 1992). One frequently used method is to employ a fixed limit on program size by restricting either the depth or the size of syntax trees.

While these limits have the desired effect of keeping the sizes down, little is known about what other impacts such limits might have on the dynamics of GP. Previous research has shown that decisions such as these can have significant effects on the behavior of runs (Gathercole and Ross, 1996) and on important structural features such as the size and shape distributions of populations (Poli and McPhee, 2003; McPhee and Poli, 2002). It would therefore be useful to better understand what structural effects size and depth limits might have, especially given their widespread use.

In (McPhee et al., 2004), we examined these issues using variable length linear structures. Here we extend that work to binary tree GPs. Several important differences exist between these two structures. In variable length linear structures, which are essentially unary trees, a size limit is exactly the same as a depth limit. This is not the case in binary trees, where it is possible to have a large depth and small size.

To evaluate the effects of depth and size limits, we performed a large number of empirical runs using various limits on a problem that induces bloat. In this chapter, we present and analyze data taken from these runs. The focus of this analysis is learning how depth and size limits affect the average size of individuals in a population and how they affect tree shape. From this analysis, we also draw conclusions about the differences between size and depth limits, and provide a tentative recommendation for the use of size limits.

Of special significance to this result is the fact that depth limits have been widely used to combat bloat in genetic programming. This is in part a result of the use of depth limits in John Koza's first two highly influential books (Koza, 1992; Koza, 1994). In explaining his use of depth limits, Koza noted

> ... that for the default value of 17 for the maximum permissible depth ... for a program created by crossover is not a significant or relevant constraint on program size. In fact, this choice permits potentially enormous programs. For example, the largest permissible ... program consisting of entirely two-argument functions would contain $2^{17} = 131,072$ functions and terminals. (Koza, 1994, p. 659)

This reasoning regarding depth limits certainly seems plausible, and depth limits have served the needed goal of reducing program size for over a decade. The results in this paper make it clear, though, that depth limits can *severely* constrain the space of trees that GP is likely to explore (supporting, *e.g.*, (Daida, 2003)). Using our definition of depth, a depth limit of 17 theoretically allows for a tree with 262,143 nodes. In doing this study we generated nearly 100 million individuals with depth limit 17 using a problem with a strong tendency to bloat. The largest individual we generated had a size of 341.

While many researchers (including Koza) have moved to using size limits, many continue to use depth limits. Such researchers may be under the mistaken belief that these limits aren't significantly affecting the dynamics of their systems. It is valuable, then, to better understand the impact of both of these widely used types of limits.

Surprisingly, our results show that, with appropriate values, both size and depth limits have nearly the same effects upon the average size of a population. The key difference between the two limits appears to be in how they affect the relationship between population average size and population average depth. Size limits do not seem to affect this relationship at all, while depth limits appear to bias the population towards slightly smaller average depths.

When comparing data from runs using a depth limit with that from runs using comparable size limits, we find that the distributions of sizes are extremely similar. The distribution of depths are also quite similar, but depth limits clearly restrict the depths much more than size limits restrict sizes. In both cases, the distributions are also very similar to the gamma-like distributions seen in earlier work on variable length linear structures.

In Section 2 we present background material necessary for understanding the rest of the chapter, including problem set up and definition of terms. In Section 3 we present and analyze data generated from runs using depth limits, and in Section 4 we do the same for runs using size limits. Based on questions arising from those two sections, we present an analysis of the impact of depth and size limits on tree shape in Section 5. After discussing future avenues of research on this topic in Section 6, we summarize our conclusions in Section 5.

2.   Background

In this section, we define several terms and concepts used in this chapter. We also define the test problem and parameters we use.

Convergent average size and the strength of limits

In (McPhee et al., 2004), we defined the notion of a population's *convergent average size* in populations where a strong size limit is in place. We now extend this definition to account for tree depth.

In the presence of bloat, the average size and average depth of individuals in any population increase rapidly during the early generations of a run. After this initial period of unchecked tree growth, the population "hits" the size or depth limit, and the population average size remains at a relatively constant value over time. We refer to this value as the run's *convergent average size*, and more precisely define it as the mean of the population's average size over all of the generations after a run has converged. Figure 15-1 in Section 3 provides several examples of the population average size "converging" after reaching a limit.

Closely related to convergent average size is the notion of size or depth limit strength. Though all of the runs using limits that we examined experienced the convergence described above, it is clear from both (McPhee et al., 2004) and the work presented later in this chapter that not all limits cause the same amount of deviation from the convergent average size. Some limits cause very small amounts of variation from the convergent average size, and we refer to them as *stronger* limits than those which cause larger amounts of variation. Once again, this is easy to observe in Figure 15-1, where the larger limits clearly have more variation around the convergent average size than do the smaller limits.

We therefore define a size or depth limit's strength as the standard deviation of population average size over all of the generations after a run has converged.

Binary Syntax Trees

In our previous work (McPhee et al., 2004) we studied the impact of size limits on variable length linear structures. Those structures were essentially trees with two different unary functions (labeled 0 and 1) and a single type of leaf (labeled 0).

In this chapter we extend our previous work to binary trees, which are more frequently used than linear structures. We will have two functions or internal nodes, again labeled 0 and 1, and a single type of leaf or terminal node, again labeled 0. Thus individuals will consist of binary trees where every internal node is labeled with a 0 or a 1, and every leaf is labeled with a 0.

We also define the *size* of a tree to be the number of nodes (both internal nodes and leaves) in the tree. The *depth* of a tree is the number of edges along the longest path from the root node to a leaf. Thus, for example, a tree consisting of just a single leaf node has depth 0 and size one, while a full tree of depth 2 has size 7. More generally, the size of a full tree of depth d is $2^{d+1} - 1$.

Crossover Operator

Because our primary interest is the effect of size limits on code growth due to crossover, we focus exclusively on the standard subtree-swapping GP crossover operator. Thus there will be no use of mutation or any other genetic operators in this study.

The crossover operator acts by removing a non-empty subtree of an individual and replacing it with a subtree taken from another individual. In the work reported here, the subtrees are chosen uniformly from the set of all a tree's (non-empty) subtrees, including the entire tree itself. Note that we are *not* using any sort of bias. This includes, for example, the common bias of choosing 90% of the crossover nodes as internal nodes.

The One-Then-Zeros Problem

We have used the *one-then-zeros* problem in a number of previous studies of the effect of bloat and genetic operators on variable length linear structures (McPhee et al., 2004; Rowe and McPhee, 2001). This problem has the advantage of being simple to explain and amenable to schema theory analysis. It also has a natural tendency to bloat, *i.e.*, the average size of individuals tends to increase over time in a manner that is not directly dependent on their fitness.

One limitation of this previous work has been the restriction to variable length linear structures, while a large proportion of the GP community uses (non-unary) tree structures to represent expressions and programs. In this study we extend our earlier work to examine binary trees, and as a result need to generalize the one-then-zeros problem to the case of binary trees.

We thus introduce the *degree-N one-then-zeros problem*. In this problem the trees will consist of N-ary internal nodes, all labeled either 0 or 1, and leaf nodes, all labeled 0. Regardless of the degree, the fitness function is the same. The fitness of a tree (or string in the unary case) is 1 if the root node is labeled 1, and *all* other nodes (internal and leaf) are labeled 0; the fitness is 0 otherwise. Thus the only fit trees are those that follow the pattern, and those trees are all equally fit. Given this, our earlier work used the degree-1 one-then-zeros problem, and the work presented here uses the degree-2 one-then-zeros problem.[1]

Another important property of this problem is that it has no direct structural bias in the sense that (with two exceptions discussed below) the fitness function doesn't favor any particular sizes or shapes. Thus most of the data on sizes, depths, and tree shapes presented in this paper are being driven by the underlying dynamics of GP and standard subtree crossover, and not by particular properties of this problem. The two exceptions are (a) trees with a single (leaf) node are guaranteed to be unfit (since the only leaf label is 0), so there is a bias away from that particular tree shape and (b) this problem induces bloat, so there is a general pressure towards larger sizes and depths. If, as seems likely, the bloat is being driven in large part by the benefits of accurate replication (McPhee and Miller, 1995), then this can be obtained using any large tree, regardless of its shape and depth.

Experimental Setup

All the runs presented in this paper use the same parameters with the exception of the size or limit.

Number of generations All runs were for 3,000 generations.

Control strategy We use a non-elitist generational control strategy.

Initialization The populations were initialized entirely with fit individuals consisting of full trees of depth 2.

Size and depth limits These were implemented such that an otherwise fit individual received a fitness of 0 if its size was *strictly greater* than the size limit, or if its depth was *strictly greater* than the depth limit.

Selection mechanism We used fitness proportionate selection in these experiments. Since all individuals have either fitness 0 or 1, this reduces to uniform selection from the set of individuals with fitness 1.

---

[1]This could obviously be generalized further to account for trees with a mixture of node arities, but that would add complexity that would only complicate the current presentation.

Operators We used crossover exclusively in these experiments, so every in-
    dividual was constructed by choosing two fit parents and performing
    subtree crossover as described above. There was no mutation or copying
    of individuals from one generation to the next.

In each run the convergent average size of the population was calculated by
taking the mean value of the population averages in the final 1000 generations of
the run. This region was selected because in all cases studied here the population
had always converged by generation 2000.

We did a series of about 30 runs each for a variety of size and depth limits in
order to better understand the larger trends. In particular, we looked at a series
of depth limits ranging from 5 to 50. We chose a set of 10 values following a
geometric (exponential) series, yielding the set of values {5, 6, 8, 10, 13, 17,
23, 29, 38, 50}. We chose the geometric series in an effort to broadly sample
this range while still focusing more on the smaller values where (as was seen
in (McPhee et al., 2004)) small differences were likely to be more significant.
We then used a similar set of size limits ranging from 50 to 5,000, yielding the
values {50, 83, 139, 232, 387, 645, 1077, 1796, 2997, 5000}. To better see
the impact of some even larger size limits, we also did runs with size limits
of 10,000, 12,000, and 15,000. Due to space limitations, only a representative
sample of these runs are discussed in this paper, but the trends we present here
hold for the entire data set.

3.   Depth Limit Analysis

Figure 15-1 presents data about population average size over time for runs
using a number of different depth limits. Each point in this graph represents
the average size of the individuals in the population at a specific generation
for one run. This provides excellent visual evidence that depth limits have an
impact upon population size that is extremely similar to that of the size limits
examined in (McPhee et al., 2004). In each case, we see the average size of
the population increase rapidly in the early generations due to bloat and then
quickly reach a convergent average size.

Similar to (McPhee et al., 2004), the strength of the limit being used seems
to control how much variation there is once the convergent average size has
been reached. In the case of the depth limit 8 data, for instance, this variance is
very small- no more than about 3. The depth limit 50 data, however, varies by
as much as two hundred. Clearly, the stronger depth limit of 8 provides much
tighter bounds on the convergent average size than does the weaker limit of 50.
This observation has led us to the more precise definition of size limit strength
given in Section 2.

A key feature of Figure 15-1 is that the population average sizes of runs
using depth limits are very small relative to the maximum size allowable by the

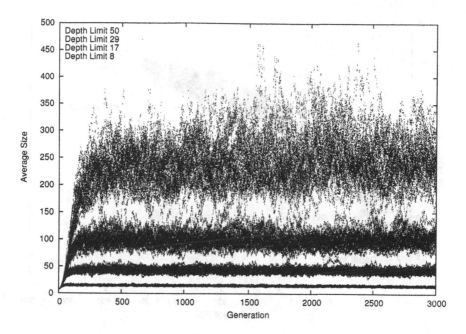

Figure 15-1. Population average size over time for a large number of runs using various depth limits. The "bands" of data correspond, from top to bottom, to runs using depth limits of 50, 29, 17, and 8.

depth limit. Depth limit 17, for instance, would allow for a maximum tree size of $2^{18} - 1$, or 262,143. The convergent average size of the runs using depth 17, however, is approximately 42. This is clearly very much smaller than the possible program sizes allowable by the limit, and it is not *a priori* obvious that this would be the case. As mentioned in Section 1, literature suggests that using a depth limit like 17 allows for the exploration of the space of very large trees. As we shall examine in Section 5, program sizes within a population appear to have a left skewed gamma distribution. This indicates that very little exploration of large sizes is in fact occurring. This is an important result, and suggests that existing assumptions about the behavior of depth limits are incorrect.

Interestingly, the average depth of the population appears very correlated with the population's average size. In other words, there seems to be very little variation in average size for a given average depth. Figure 15-2 illustrates this phenomenon by presenting the average sizes that were contained in Figure 15-1 and their corresponding average depths without accounting for time. Though there seems to be a general relationship between average size and average depth, it is also clear that each depth limit behaves slightly differently. There seems to be a "natural" relationship between average size and average depth

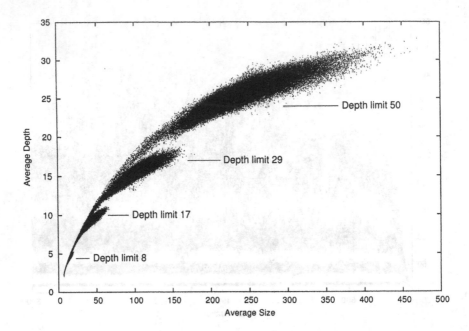

Figure 15-2. Population average size versus population average depth for runs using a variety of depth limits. The labeled clusters represent the space of convergent values for runs using different depth limits.

that populations would follow in the absence of any size or depth limits. (See Figure 15-4 for an additional example, and Section 6 for additional discussion.) Indeed, it appears that for all of the depth limits we examined, runs follow this "natural" relationship until they reach convergence, where they cluster slightly below the "natural" curve. As the corresponding depths for thee average sizes are lower than those in the natural relationship, this suggests that depth limits cause trees to become slightly more bushy once the population has reached convergence. We examine this idea further in Section 5.

An Exceptional Case

We performed hundreds of runs to generate the data presented in this study. As we have shown, the behavior exhibited by runs using certain depth limits is remarkably consistent. In Section 4, we show this to be true for size limits as well. There was one run out of the hundreds, however, which displayed startlingly different behavior.

This run, which used a depth limit of 23, had a convergent average size of about 50,000. Every other run using depth limit 23 had a convergent average size of approximately 70. Further, there were individuals in the exceptional case which reached sizes of upwards of 3.7 million nodes. These observations made us conclude, initially, that some form of programming or software error was responsible for the deviant behavior of the run. Further investigation revealed the truth: the run, though definitely abnormal, was valid.

Examination of the run's early generations suggested that, through a series of stochastic events, the population grew to consist of large, bushy trees, rather than the usual "stringy" trees which seem to be common in the other runs (see Section 5) and which are predicted by (Daida, 2003). This initial behavior likely produced a positive feedback loop which led to a continued increase in tree size. This resulted in the enormous average size observed after the population had reached convergence.

This exceptional run, therefore, provides us with an example of the kind of behavior implied by the quote in Section 1. Though we are in no position to claim just how frequently this actually occurs, the fact that it happened only once in the hundreds of runs we performed suggests it is very rare. It also suggests disturbing implications about the reliability of depth limits. Though this errant run may be the exception (and our data certainly supports that idea), the fact that it is possible to unpredictably have program sizes balloon vastly beyond normal ranges makes the choice of using depth limits questionable. Size limits, for instance, would not have allowed the behavior described above, as they explicitly limit program size.

There are at least two specific concerns about the possibility of this sort of aberrant run. The first is the obvious implications for computing resources. Using our hardware, for instance, a typical run using a depth limit of 23 took approximately five minutes to complete. The exceptional run took about 8 hours to complete. Though the times are, of course, specific to both our problem and hardware, it seems reasonable to assume a proportionate amount of resources would be required for a similar run using other problems and hardware. Second, and perhaps more important, is the problems of doing statistical analysis on a set of runs containing such outlier results.

4.   Size Limit Analysis

Figure 15-3 presents data in much the same fashion as Figure 15-1, though for runs using a variety of size limits rather than depth limits. Like the runs using depth limits, discussed in Section 3, we see a distinct convergence in both size and depth after a very small number of generations, again mirroring the the findings of (McPhee et al., 2004). Figure 15-3 and 15-1 are in fact extremely similar. The scales of the two graphs differ, but this is simply due to the disparate strengths of the limits being shown. From a comparison of the

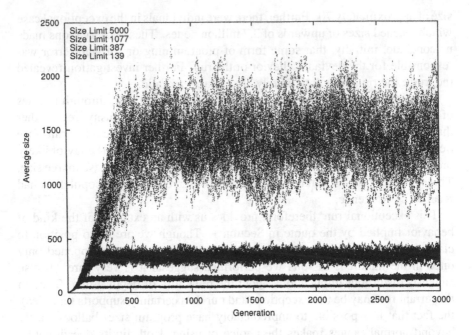

Figure 15-3. Population average size over time for a large number of runs using various size limits. The "bands" of data correspond, from top to bottom, to runs using size limits of 5000, 1077, 387, and 139.

two figures, it appears that size and depth limits have almost the same, if not identical, effects upon population average size.

This is an important observation, as it is not conceptually obvious that size and depth limits would restrict population sizes in a similar way. Indeed, the fact that depth limits, which could conceivably allow an enormous range of sizes, behave in the same way as size limits, which explicitly limit tree size, is quite remarkable.

Figure 15-4 shows the relationship between population average size and population average depth, as we did in in Figure 15-2 in Section 3. Unlike the depth limits analyzed in Section 3, the size limits used here do not display any marked deviance from the "natural" relationship between average size and average depth discussed earlier. This is so much the case, in fact, that it becomes hard to discern which data corresponds to which size limit.

By comparing Figures 15-2 and 15-4, several inferences can be made. The "natural" relationship between average size and average depth for this problem appears the same whether depth or size limits are used. Size limits seem to have no impact upon this relationship. Depth limits, however, evidently bias this relationship to some extent by lowering the depth slightly. Whether this bias

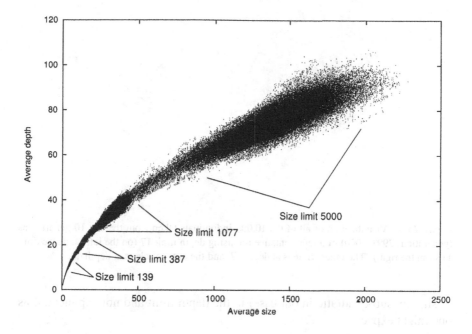

Figure 15-4. Population average size versus population average depth for a number of size limits. The labeled clusters represent the space of convergent values for runs using different depth limits.

has a positive or negative impact upon a given run is almost certainly problem dependent, and there is no evidence to suggest what the extent of the bias might be for problems with fitness functions that alter tree shape.

Sub-Quadratic Relationship Between Size and Depth Limits

Given the close relationship between size and depth limits, an obvious question is, for a given depth limit, what size limit is roughly equivalent in the sense that it yields a similar convergent average size? An initial analysis of our data suggests that, at least for this problem, the relationship can be roughly approximated by $S \approx 0.410063 * D^{1.92}$, where S is the size limit and D is the depth limit. The details of the constants aren't important except to note that the exponent is slightly less than two. Thus the "equivalent" size limit grows roughly with the square (or less) of the depth limit instead of the exponential relationship one might expect.

From a practitioner's standpoint, this reinforces the idea that one can use size limits to achieve a qualitatively similar results to those obtained with depth limits. It also suggests that "equivalent" size limits are polynomial (quadratic

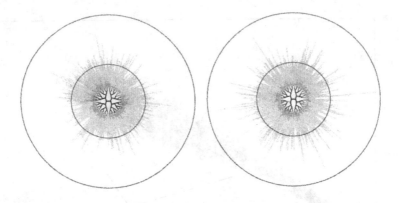

Figure 15-5. Visualization of all of the 10,000 individuals taken from the last 10 generations (generations 2991-3000) of a representative run using depth limit 17 (on the left) and size limit 118 (on the right). The inner circle is at depth 17, and the outer circle is at depth 40.

or slightly sub-quadratic in our case) in the depth limit and not exponential as one might expect.

5.   Impact of Limits on Tree Shapes

In the previous section we found that there are depth and size limits that lead to similar convergent average sizes. We saw earlier, however, that depth limits tend to push the tree shapes off the "natural" shape and size limits don't (see, *e.g.*, Figs 15-2 and 15-4). This then raises the question of whether the shapes of the trees using "equivalent" size and depth limits are in fact different. To see this we used the visualization techniques of (Daida et al., 2005) to visualize the entire population of a single run for two pairs of limits (depth limit 17 and size limit 118, and depth limit 50 and size limit 600) that are roughly equivalent. By equivalent, we mean that in each pair the size and depth limits produced similar convergent average sizes.

Fig 15-5 shows a visualization of every individual present in each of the last 10 generations (*i.e.*, generations 2991 to 3000)[2] of a representative run using depth limit 17 (on the left) and size limit 118 (on the right). The inner circle is at depth 17, so the size limit case has more trees that exceed that depth, and they exceed it by considerably more. Thus while the *average* sizes and depths of these two runs are extremely close, their distributions seem to be somewhat different.

---

[2]Note, then, that each graph is displaying an aggregate view of 10,000 individuals.

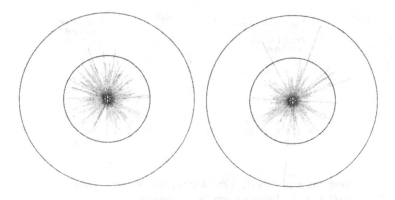

Figure 15-6. Visualization of the entire population of 1000 individuals in the final generation (generation 3000) of a representative run using depth limit 50 (on the left) and size limit 600 (on the right). The inner circle is at depth 50, and the outer circle is at depth 100.

Figure 15-6 shows a visualization of all the individuals present in the last generation (*i.e.*, generation 3000) of a representative run using depth limit 50 (on the left) and size limit 600 (on the right). The inner circle is at depth 50, and again the size limit case has more trees that exceed that depth, and they exceed it by considerably more.

One of the key features of the visualizations in (Daida et al., 2005; Daida, 2003) was the lack of variety of tree shapes, with the majority of the trees sharing a significant amount of structure. In our visualizations, however, there is a *much* wider variety of sizes and shapes. In Figure 15-5, for example, there are at least a few trees containing branches in almost every part of the space up to depth 17, whereas the population visualizations in (Daida et al., 2005; Daida, 2003) cover only a tiny fraction of the space.

It seems likely that this is a result of structural differences between the degree-2 one-then-zeros problem used here, and the regression problems used in (Daida et al., 2005; Daida, 2003). In the one-then-zeros problem, all that matters is the simple pattern of having a one at the root and zeros elsewhere (which is largely independent of tree size and shape) and avoiding size or depth limits as appropriate. This implies that the "meaning" of subtrees is largely independent of context in the one-then-zeros problem, so a subtree can be moved, via crossover, to an entirely different location in the tree without (in many cases) changing the fitness. This is in strong contrast to most GP problems (like regression), where context is crucial to the "meaning" of a subtree, and moving a subtree to a different location often has a large, and typically detrimental, effect on the fitness. This context dependence presumably plays a large role in the uniformity of shapes seen in (Daida et al., 2005; Daida, 2003), just as the lack

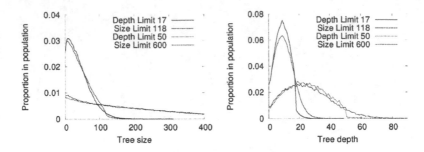

Figure 15-7. Distribution of sizes (left) and depths (right) for depth limits 17 and 50 and size limits 118 and 600. Note the different scales for proportions.

of this sort of dependence presumably plays a large role in the dispersion of shapes in our examples.

Figures 15-5 and 15-6 speak volumes about the distribution of tree *shapes*, but leave open the question of how the sizes and depths are distributed. Previous work on variable length linear structures (Poli and McPhee, 2003; McPhee et al., 2004) has shown a strong tendency for the size distribution of populations to be similar to a gamma distribution, with a very large proportion of short strings balancing out a small number of much longer strings. An open question has been whether these results would generalize to N-ary trees, and the distributions in Figure 15-7 suggest that they do.

The graphs in Figure 15-7 show the distribution of sizes depths for the same two pairs of depth and size limits used in Figures 15-5 and 15-6. In all cases the distributions are again very similar within each pair, lending weight to the idea that corresponding size and depth limits can have very similar impacts on population structure. Note, for example, the size distributions for depth limit 50 and size limit 600, which are nearly indistinguishable over the bulk of their range.

We also find in all cases that the distributions are similar to the gamma-like distributions found in earlier work on variable length linear structures. Thus we find here that the distributions of both sizes and depths are skewed significantly to the left, with a large number of small sizes/depths being balanced by a much smaller number of large sizes/depths.

These graphs also point out the specific impacts of size and depth limits on particular distributions. In the size distribution graph we see a sharp dip in the size limit 118 distribution right around size 118. There is a similar, but smaller, dip in the size limit 600 distribution that is off the right hand side of the graph. There are also similar, but more pronounced, dips in the depth distributions for the runs using depth limits, which again suggests that depth limits are having a stronger (perhaps undesirable) impact on our population distributions.

It's worth noting that in each case where a limit creates a dip in the corresponding distribution, there is perforce an increase in some other part of the distribution to compensate. In the depth limit 17 depth distribution, for example, this is seen quite clearly as a significant increase in the proportions of depths around 10, indicating that a size limit of 118 allows for a slightly broader exploration of a range of depths than does the otherwise similar depth limit of 17. Similarly, in the size limit 600 size distribution the small dip (not visible in this graph) leads to a small rise in the proportions of very small trees when compared to the depth limit 50 distribution. These dips and compensations are consistent with predictions from the "theory of holes" (Poli and McPhee, 2003; McPhee et al., 2004), where schema theory analysis shows that limits like these (in the case of variable length linear structures) lead to the sort of shifts in distributions seen in this work.

6.   Future Work

This study directly addresses one of the major questions from (McPhee et al., 2004), namely how well the distribution results from variable length linear structures generalize to N-ary trees. Two other questions from that earlier paper remain open, however. First, prior results on different mutation operators (Rowe and McPhee, 2001) and combinations of genetic operators (McPhee and Poli, 2002) suggest that these can themselves act to limit size and depth, so studying their interaction with explicit limits might be fruitful. Second, preliminary data suggests that population size plays a significant role in determining the strength of limits and the convergent average sizes and depths. The specifics of this relationship are unclear at the moment and warrant further investigation.

Additionally, this work on binary trees raises questions about the "natural" relationship between size and depth (see Figures 15-2 and 15-4). This seems likely to be related to both the the Flajolet line (Langdon and Poli, 2002, Chapter 11) and Region I of (Daida and Hilss, 2003). Exploring the details of these relationships is beyond the scope of this paper, but such an exploration would likely be fruitful.

The work presented here is all for a single "toy" problem, and a key question is obviously how well the results generalize to other problems. Since our results on the relationship between size and shape look quite similar to results obtained by other researchers with a broader range of problems (Langdon and Poli, 2002; Daida and Hilss, 2003, Chapter 11), we can hope that other results will generalize (at least qualitatively) as well. As seen in Section 5, however, there is at least one important structural difference between the degree-2 one-then-zeros problem and the regression problems studied in (Daida et al., 2005). Thus some additional work is clearly necessary to better understand which results will generalize to other problems, and to what degree.

The exceptional case discussed in Section 3 appears to be reasonably rare (we only saw such a thing once in over 300 runs), but we currently lack sufficient data to estimate how often it is likely to occur. Given how profoundly different the performance and results of such a run are going to be, knowing more about their frequency would be helpful.

We've seen (*e.g.*, Section 5) that there are size and depths limits that lead to similar outcomes. It would be useful to know more about the nature of that relationship, with the ultimate goal being the development of a model with predictive power that would allow us to map from size limits to roughly equivalent depth limits and vice versa.

7.   Conclusion

Throughout this chapter, we have examined the behavior of depth limits and size limits on binary tree genetic programs. The results of this investigation have yielded several major findings.

In Section 3 we show that depth limits, contrary to GP folklore, do not typically allow for large ranges of tree size. Instead, we observe that they produce tree sizes that are nearly the same as those produced by size limits with maximum sizes that are orders of magnitude below the maximum size possible using the depth limit. In only one case out of the hundreds of runs generated for this study did we observe tree sizes that were anywhere near the maximum possible using depth limits. This leads us to conclude that although in the vast majority of cases depth limits seem to control code growth very similarly to size limits, their consistency is questionable. Furthermore, since the one case where this inconsistency manifested took vastly more computational resources than the normal cases and led to results that were wildly different from the other cases, the unreliability of depth limits is worrying.

In both Sections 3 and 4 we show that there is a well defined relationship between population average size and population average depth which is visible using either size limits or depth limits. Size limits did not appear to affect this relationship in any meaningful way, though depth limits appeared to add a small yet significant bias towards smaller depths. Though it is unclear how strong this bias actually is, lack of understanding regarding it supports the idea that using depth limits holds a great deal of uncertainty.

Visualization of our populations suggests that runs with size limits are able to explore more of the tree space than those with depth limits. We also showed that both types of limits induce gamma-like distributions of both sizes and depths, similar to those seen in earlier work with variable length linear structures (Poli and McPhee, 2003; McPhee et al., 2004).

Another finding of this study has been that our observations of how size limits affect population average size were almost identical to those made in our earlier work using variable length linear structures (McPhee et al., 2004). This has important implications about the generalizability of research using linear structures. Use of analytical tools such as schema theory on N-ary syntax trees is exceedingly difficult, which makes the use of linear structures to simplify analysis desirable. A question that has always arisen from such analysis is whether the results can be generalized to N-ary trees. We show in this study that, in at least the context we use here, many of them do.

It's important to remember that all these results are in the context laid out in Section 2, including the use of the degree-2 one-then-zeros problem, so care must be taken to not over generalize. We do believe however, that many of these results will generalize, at least qualitatively, to a variety of other problems.

Acknowledgments

We wish to thank Wolfgang Banzhaf and Jason Daida for their helpful reviews of this chapter. We would also like to thank all of the participants in the GPTP workshop for their insightful comments and suggestions.

The population visualizations in Section 5 were generated using Daida, *et al*'s Mathematica notebook; we are very grateful for their willingness to share these resources. The remainder of our graphs were generated with gnuplot, and we greatly appreciate the work of all the authors of gnuplot and the many other open source tools that were used in generating and analyzing our data, and presenting our results.

References

Daida, Jason M. (2003). What makes a problem GP-hard? A look at how structure affects content. In Riolo, Rick L. and Worzel, Bill, editors, *Genetic Programming Theory and Practice*, chapter 7, pages 99–118. Kluwer.

Daida, Jason M. and Hilss, Adam M. (2003). Identifying structural mechanisms in standard genetic programming. In Cantú-Paz, E. et al., editors, *Genetic and Evolutionary Computation – GECCO-2003*, volume 2724 of *LNCS*, pages 1639–1651, Chicago. Springer-Verlag.

Daida, Jason M., Hilss, Adam M., Ward, David J., and Long, Stephen L. (2005). Visualizing tree structures in genetic programming. *Genetic Programming and Evolvable Machines*, 6. Prepublication Date: 6 August 2004.

Gathercole, Chris and Ross, Peter (1996). An adverse interaction between crossover and restricted tree depth in genetic programming. In Koza, John R., Goldberg, David E., Fogel, David B., and Riolo, Rick L., editors, *Genetic Programming 1996: Proceedings of the First Annual Conference*, pages 291–296, Stanford University, CA, USA. MIT Press.

Koza, John R. (1992). *Genetic Programming: On the Programming of Computers by Means of Natural Selection*. MIT Press, Cambridge, MA, USA.

Koza, John R. (1994). *Genetic Programming II: Automatic Discovery of Reusable Programs*. MIT Press, Cambridge Massachusetts.

Langdon, W. B. and Poli, Riccardo (2002). *Foundations of Genetic Programming*. Springer-Verlag.

Luke, Sean and Panait, Liviu (2002). Lexicographic parsimony pressure. In Langdon, W. B. et al., editors, *GECCO 2002: Proceedings of the Genetic and Evolutionary Computation Conference*, pages 829–836, New York. Morgan Kaufmann Publishers.

McPhee, Nicholas Freitag, Jarvis, Alex, and Crane, Ellery Fussell (2004). On the strength of size limits in linear genetic programming. In Deb, Kalyanmoy et al., editors, *Genetic and Evolutionary Computation – GECCO-2004, Part II*, volume 3103 of *Lecture Notes in Computer Science*, pages 593–604, Seattle, WA, USA. Springer-Verlag.

McPhee, Nicholas Freitag and Miller, Justin Darwin (1995). Accurate replication in genetic programming. In Eshelman, L., editor, *Genetic Algorithms: Proceedings of the Sixth International Conference (ICGA95)*, pages 303–309, Pittsburgh, PA, USA. Morgan Kaufmann.

McPhee, Nicholas Freitag and Poli, Riccardo (2002). Using schema theory to explore interactions of multiple operators. In Langdon, W. B. et al., editors, *GECCO 2002: Proceedings of the Genetic and Evolutionary Computation Conference*, pages 853–860, New York. Morgan Kaufmann Publishers.

Poli, Riccardo (2003). A simple but theoretically-motivated method to control bloatin genetic programming. In Ryan, C. and *et al*, editors, *Proceedings of the Sixth European Conference on Genetic Programming (EuroGP-2003)*, volume 2610 of *LNCS*, pages 204–217, Essex, UK. Springer Verlag.

Poli, Riccardo and McPhee, Nicholas Freitag (2003). General schema theory for genetic programming with subtree-sw apping crossover: Part II. *Evolutionary Computation*, 11(2).

Rowe, Jon E. and McPhee, Nicholas F. (2001). The effects of crossover and mutation operators on variable length linear structures. In *Proceedings of the Genetic and Evolutionary Computation Conference (GECCO-2001)*, San Francisco, California, USA. Morgan Kaufmann.

Silva, Sara and Almeida, Jonas (2003). Dynamic maximum tree depth. In Cantú-Paz, E. et al., editors, *Genetic and Evolutionary Computation – GECCO-2003*, volume 2724 of *LNCS*, pages 1776–1787, Chicago. Springer-Verlag.

Chapter 16

APPLICATION ISSUES OF GENETIC PROGRAMMING IN INDUSTRY

Arthur Kordon[1], Flor Castillo[1], Guido Smits[2] and Mark Kotanchek[3]
[1]*The Dow Chemical Company*, Freeport, TX; [2]*Dow Benelux*, Terneuzen, The Netherlands; [3]*Evolved Analytics*, Midland, MI

Abstract   This chapter gives a systematic view, based on the experience from The Dow Chemical Company, of the key issues for applying symbolic regression with Genetic Programming (GP) in industrial problems. The competitive advantages of GP are defined and several industrial problems appropriate for GP are recommended and referenced with specific applications in the chemical industry. A systematic method for selecting the key GP parameters, based on statistical design of experiments, is proposed. The most significant technical and non-technical issues for delivering a successful GP industrial application are discussed briefly.

Keywords: Genetic programming, symbolic regression, industrial applications, design of experiments, real world problems, parameter selection

1.   Introduction

Recently, Genetic Programming (GP) has demonstrated its growing potential to resolve various industrial problems in modeling, process monitoring and optimization, and new product development (Kotanchek *et al*, 2003). In parallel to the theoretical development in the area of GP, much effort has been spent in developing a robust methodology for practical implementation that is applicable for a broad range of solutions. Unfortunately, the industrial application efforts are not so well published as the theoretical development and are virtually unknown to the research community. The objective of this chapter is to present a systematic view of the key results from exploiting GP in a large global company, such as The Dow Chemical Company.

The chapter is organized in the following manner. Some guidance on finding practical problems which are appropriate to be resolved by GP is given in Section 2. A methodology for selecting robust key GP parameters, based on Design Of Experiments (DOE), is described in Section 3. The key technical and non-technical issues to be resolved for successful GP applications in industry are presented in Section 4.

2.   When is Genetic Programming an Appropriate Industrial Solution?

One of the significant factors for success in the current industrial R&D environment is the speed of introducing an emergent technology into practice. Usually a new technology is introduced in two phases: (1) capability exploration and (2) proof-of-concept application. In the first phase, the features of the technology are assessed and matched with the existing specific needs of each industry. An important component is the estimate of the potential effort for adopting the new technology into the existing work processes in research and manufacturing. Critical for business acceptance, however, is the second phase, which includes a convincing demonstration of the benefits in a well-selected case study. Usually it is based on real data and very often illustrates a novel solution to a difficult industrial problem.

The first question that needs to be addressed in any new technology introduction is a clear definition of its competitive advantages relative to other, similar approaches.

Competitive Advantages of Genetic Programming

Computational intelligence is a research area that includes many competitive approaches with different technical nature (fuzzy logic, evolutionary computation, neural networks, swarm intelligence, etc.) for solving complex practical problems. On the one hand, this opens new opportunities and broadens the scope of potential applications. On the other hand, however, it requires additional efforts from industrial practitioners to understand the technical features of very diverse technologies and to estimate their potential value. The comparative analysis is not trivial and has to take into account not only the relative technical advantages but also the total cost-of-ownership (potential internal research, software development and maintenance, training, implementation efforts, etc.).

From our experience, one generic area where GP has demonstrated a clear competitive advantage is the development of simple empirical models. The specific approach within GP is symbolic regression (Koza, 1992). We have shown in several cases that the models generated by symbolic regression are a low-cost alternative to both high fidelity models (Kordon *et al*, 2003a) and expensive hardware analyzers (Kordon *et al*, 2003b). The specific competitive advantages of symbolic regression generated by GP and related to the generic area of empirical modeling are defined as follows:

- **No *a priori* modeling assumptions** – GP model development does not require assumption space limited by physical considerations (as is in case of first-principle modeling) or by statistical considerations, such as variable independence, multivariate normal distribution and independent errors with zero mean and constant variance.

- **Empirical models with improved robustness** – Using Pareto front GP (Smits and Kotanchek, 2004) allows the simulated evolution and model selection to be directed toward solutions based on an optimal balance between accuracy and expression complexity. The derived symbolic regression models have improved robustness during process changes relative to both conventional GP and neural-network-based models.

- **Easy integration into existing work processes** – Since the derived final solutions, generated by GP are symbolic expressions there is no need for specialized software environment for their run-time implementation. This feature allows for a relatively easy integration of the GP technology into most of the existing model development and deployment work processes.

- **Minimal training of the final user** – The symbolic regression nature of the final solutions generated by GP is universally acceptable by any user with mathematical background at the high school level. This is not the case either with the first-principle models (where specific physical knowledge is required) or with the black-box models (where some training on neural networks is a must). In addition, a very important factor in favor of GP is that process engineers prefer mathematical expressions and very often can find an appropriate physical interpretation. They usually don't hide their distaste toward black boxes.

- **Low total cost of development, deployment, and maintenance** – Contrary to the common opinion, the key disadvantage of GP – the computationally intensive and time-consuming model generation-- does not add significantly to the development cost because it does not occupy the model developer's time. What is required from the model developer is to set the parameters at the beginning of the simulation and to assess the selected models at the end. With the Pareto front GP method, the derived models have minimal total cost. They are derived and automatically selected at the optimum performance-- complexity Pareto front and as such, have better robustness (*i.e.*, reduced need for model re-tuning during process changes and maintenance cost), are parsimonious (even with potential interpretation by the experts), and with minimal implementation requirements and cost. The alternative approaches require specialized software, expertise on the specific technology, training on the approach and the related software, and significant model validation and support expenses.

The major disadvantages of GP relative to other techniques are (1) the absence of commercial software infrastructure, (2) the computational effort typically required for the model building, and (3) typically lower absolute model accuracy relative to techniques such as neural networks.

Recommendations for Industrial Problems Appropriate for Genetic Programming

With this impressive list of competitive advantages over first-principle, statistical and neural network frameworks for modeling, GP has very broad application potential in industry. Since the mid-90s we've explored the capabilities of GP, developed our internal software toolboxes on MATLAB and *Mathematica*, and gradually introduced the technology to the businesses. Critical for the sustainability of the support of this R&D effort was the continuous series of successful applications that demonstrated the value from our GP development agenda.

Our experience in applying GP to real industrial problems in the chemical industry suggests these suitable targets::

- **Fast development of nonlinear empirical models** – Symbolic-regression problems are very suitable for industrial applications, and are often optimal in terms of both development and maintenance costs. One area with tremendous potential is inferential or soft sensors, *i.e.* empirical models that infer difficult-to-measure process parameters, such as NOx emissions, melt index, interface level, *etc.*, from easy-to-measure process variables such as temperatures, pressures, flows, *etc.* (Kordon *et al*, 2003b). The current solutions in the market, which are based on neural networks, require frequent re-training and specialized run-time software.

  An example of an inferential sensor for propylene prediction based on an ensemble of four different models derived by Genetic

Programming is given in (Jordaan *et al*, 2004). The models were developed from an initial large manufacturing data set of 23 potential input variables and 6900 data points. The size of the data set was reduced by variable selection to 7 significant inputs and the models were generated by five independent GP runs. As a result of the model selection, a list of 12 models on the Pareto front was proposed for further evaluation to process engineers. All selected models have high performance (R^2 of 0.97 – 0.98) and low complexity. After evaluating their extrapolation capabilities with "What-If" scenarios, the diversity of model inputs, and physical considerations, an ensemble of four models was selected for on-line implementation. Two of the models are shown below:

$$GP\_Model1 = A + B \left| \frac{Tray64\_T^4 * Vapor^3}{Rflx\_flow^2} \right|$$

$$GP\_Model2 = C + D \left| \frac{Feed^3 \sqrt{Tray46\_T - Tray56\_T}}{Vapor^2 * Rflx\_flow^4} \right|$$

where A, B, C, and D are fitting parameters, and all model inputs in the equations are continuous process measurements.

These models are simple and interpretable by process engineers. The difference in model inputs increases the robustness of the estimation scheme in case of possible input sensor failure. The inferential sensor is in operation since May 2004.

• **Emulation of complex first-principle models** – Symbolic regression models can substitute parts of fundamental models for on-line monitoring and optimization. The execution speed of most complex first-principle models is too slow for real-time operation. One effective solution is to replace a portion of the fundamental model with a simpler symbolic regression called an emulator, which is based only on a subset of variables. The data for the emulator are generated by design of experiments from the first-principle model. Usually the fundamental model is represented with several simple emulators, which are implemented on-line. One interesting benefit of emulators is that they can be used to validate fundamental models as well. The validation of a complex model in conditions where the process is chanting continuously requires tremendous efforts in data collection and numerous model parameter fittings. It is much easier to validate the simple emulators and to infer the state of the complex model on the basis of the high correlation between them. An example of such an application for optimal handling of by-products is given in (Kordon *et al*, 2003a). The mechanistic model is very complex, and includes over 1500 chemical reactions with more than 200 species. Ten input variables and 12 output variables were suggested by domain experts. A data set based on a four levels design of experiments was generated and used for model development and validation. For 7 of the outputs a linear emulator gave acceptable performance. For the remaining 5 emulators, a nonlinear model was derived by GP. An example of a nonlinear emulator selected by the experts is given below:

$$Y_5 = \frac{6x_3 + x_4 + x_5 + 2x_6 + x_2x_9 - \dfrac{x_2 - 3x_3\sqrt{x_6}}{(x_2{}^2 + x_7x_1{}^3)}}{\ln(\sqrt{x_9x_{10}{}^2})}$$

where Y is the predicted output (used for process optimization), and the x variables are measured process parameters. The emulators have been used for by-product optimization between two chemical plants in The Dow Chemical Company since March 2003.

- **Accelerated first-principle model building** – Beginning first-principle modeling not from scratch but from symbolic regression models and building blocks (transforms) can significantly reduce the hypothesis search space for potential physical/chemical mechanisms. New product development effort can be considerably reduced by eliminating unimportant variables, enabling rapid testing of new physical mechanisms and reducing the number of experiments for model validation. The large potential of this type of application was demonstrated in a case study for structure-property relationships (Kordon *et al*, 2002). The GP-augmented solution was similar to the fundamental model and was delivered with significantly less human effort (10 hours vs. 3 months).

- **Linearized transforms for Design Of Experiments** – GP-generated transforms of the input variables can eliminate significant lack of fit in linear regression models without the need to add expensive experiments to the original design, which can be time-consuming, costly, or maybe technically infeasible because of extreme experimental conditions. An example of such type of application for a chemical process is given in (Castillo *et al*, 2002).

A selected set of GP applications from the above-mentioned industrial problems is given in Table 16-1. For each application the following information is given: initial size of the data set (including all potential inputs and data points), reduced size of the data set (after variable selection and data condensation), model structure (number of inputs used in the selected final models and the number of models; some of them are used in an ensemble), and a corresponding reference which contains a detailed description of the application, including the GP parameters used. In all the cases the final solutions obtained with the help of GP were parsimonious models with a significantly reduced number of inputs.

Table 16-1. Selected GP applications in Dow chemical

Application	Initial data size	Reduced data size	Model structure	Reference
Inferential sensors				
Interface level prediction	(25 inputs x 6500 data pts)	(2 inputs x 2000 data pts)	3 models 2 inputs	Kordon and Smits, 2001
Interface level prediction	(28 inputs x 2850 data pts)	(5 inputs x 2850 data pts)	One model 3 inputs	Kalos *et al*, 2003
Emissions prediction	(8 inputs x 251 data pts)	(4 inputs x 34 data pts)	Two models 4 inputs	Kordon *et al*, 2003b
Biomass prediction	(10 inputs x 705 data pts)	(10 inputs x 705 data pts)	9 models ens 2-3 inputs	Jordaan *et al*, 2004
Propylene prediction	(23 inputs x 6900 data pts)	(7 inputs x 6900 data pts)	4 models ens 2-3 inputs	Jordaan *et al*, 2004
Emulators				
Chemical reactor	(10 inputs x 320 data pts)	(10 inputs x 320 data pts)	5 models 8 inputs	Kordon *et al*, 2003a
Accelerated modeling				
Structure-property	(5 inputs x 32 data pts)	(5 inputs x 32 data pts)	One model 4 inputs	Kordon *et al*, 2002
Structure-property	(9 inputs x 24 data pts)	(9 inputs x 24 data pts)	7 models 3 -5 inputs	Kordon and Lue, 2004
Linearized transforms				
Chemical reactor model	(4 inputs x 19 data pts)	(4 inputs x 19 data pts)	3 transforms	Castillo *et al*, 2002

3.   How to Select the Genetic Programming Parameters

Another important issue in industrial applications of GP is the GP algorithm parameter selection. As a first step, the parameters can be selected according to the rule-of-thumb recommendations of Koza (Koza, 1992). However, a more systematic statistical approach is recommended since the numerous parameters and settings used by GP introduce uncertainty about the way they affect the search algorithm and therefore the solution found. This has significant theoretical implications. Among them is the amount of information the parameters provide and the possible restrictions in the set of right solutions. It is therefore important to understand the effect of the parameters, the effect of the various combinations of them, and how robust they are to different data sets. This is of special importance given that the GP algorithm is used with a variety of data sets with different degrees of complexity.

The optimum set of GP parameters can be determined through statistical experimental design techniques, such as design of experiments (DOE). This section explains how to use an appropriate DOE and the appropriate set of replications to understand the effect of GP parameters.

Statistical Experimental Design: Design of Experiments

Design of Experiments is a statistical approach that provides enhanced knowledge of a system by quantifying the effect of a set of inputs (factors) on an output (response). This is accomplished by systematically running experiments at different combinations of the factor settings (Box et al, 1978).

A classical DOE is the 2^k design, in which all factors are investigated at an upper and lower level of a range, resulting in 2^k experiments where k is the number of factors. This design has the advantage that the effects of the individual factors (main effects), as well as all possible interactions (combination of factors), can be estimated. However, the number of experimental runs increases rapidly as the number of factors increases. If the number of experiments is impractical, fractional factorial design can be used. In this case, only a fraction of the full 2^k design is run by assuming that some interactions among factors are not significant. However, this assumption can sometimes confound the main effects and interactions, so they therefore cannot be estimated separately.

Depending on the type of fractional factorial, main effects may be confounded with second-, third-, or fourth-order interactions. The level of confounding is dictated by the design resolution. The higher the design resolution, the less confounding occurs among factors. For example, a resolution III design confounds main effects with second-order interactions; a resolution IV design confounds second-order interaction with other second-order interactions; and a resolution V design confounds second-order interactions with third-order interactions. Felt and Nordin (2000) investigated the effect of 17 GP parameters on three binary classification problems using highly fractionated designs assuming, in some cases, that even second- and third-order interaction are not significant, *i.e.,* the combined effect of two factors and three factors has no effect on the response. However, these assumptions have not been verified.

Given that the study of GP parameters involves computing experiments as opposed to pilot plant or laboratory experiments, it is desirable to run a full factorial when possible, so that any second and third order interaction which may have statistically significant effects on the response can be quantified.

Pareto Front Genetic Programming DOE

The GP experimental design we would like to describe differs from that of Felt and Nording in three aspects. First, it allows the estimation of interactions. Second, it uses the convergence to the Pareto front as the response variable. Third, the robustness of GP parameters to the different data sets is investigated with industrial data sets with different degrees of complexity based on dimension of input matrix and degree of input correlation.

The need for a more systematic DOE approach is also driven by the significant benefits of the Pareto front-based GP, demonstrated in several industrial applications (Smits and Kotanchek, 2004). In this approach, the optimal models fall on the curve of the non-dominated solutions, called Pareto front, *i.e.*, no other solution is better than the solutions on the Pareto front in both complexity and performance. As discussed above in Section 2.2, parsimonious models with high performance are the greatest importance in industry. These occupy the lower left corner of the Pareto front indicated in the diagram in Figure 16-2. In that context, the goal is to select GP parameters that consistently drive simulated evolution toward the lower left of this diagram. The Pareto front GP parameters (factors) and their ranges are presented in the following table:

Table 16-2. Factors for the Pareto Front GP Doe

Factor	Low level (-1)	High Level (+1)
x1 - Number of cascades	10	50
x2 - Number of generations	10	50
x3 - Population size	100	500
x4 - Probability of function selection	0.4	0.7
x5 - Size of archive	100	500

The response variable proposed is the convergence to the Pareto front (Smits and Kotanchek (2004) which includes the prediction error $(1-R^2)$ as the performance measure and the sum of the number of nodes of all sub-equations as the value of complexity. The factor x1, number of cascades, is the number of independent runs with a freshly generated starting population. The ranges of the factors have been selected based on the experience from various types of practical problems, related to symbolic regression. Since the objective is a consistent Pareto front GP, they differ from the recommendations for the original GP.

Once the factors and ranges are selected the necessary number of replications must be determined. This is of key importance because in the case of GP parameters we do not know for sure if the variability of the response is the same for the different combination of factors. The following figure illustrates this situation for three factors.

To estimate the number of required replications, an initial set of n replications can be run, from which the standard deviation of the response is calculated. In our case, the response is the convergence to the Pareto Front. In this case a fixed level of complexity for the number of nodes is selected.

For this level the corresponding number of models is observed and the standard deviation of the response between these models can be estimated. Figure 16-2 illustrates the concept.

Once the standard deviation is calculated the number of replications can be found applying the half width (HW) confidence interval method (Montgomery, 1999)[1]. The half width can be use to represent the percent error in the point estimate of the mean response. The half width (HW) is defined as:

$$HW = t_{n-1,\,a/2} \frac{S}{\sqrt{n}}$$

---

[1] $100(1-a)\%$ *confidence interval* is a range of values in which the true answer is believed to lie with 1- a probability. Usually a is set at 0.05 so that 95% confidence interval is calculated. Half width, sometimes called accuracy of the confidence interval, is the distance between the estimated mean and the upper or lower range of the confidence interval.

Where $t_{n-1,a/2}$ is the upper $a/2$ percentage point of the t distribution with $n-1$ degrees of freedom, S is the standard deviation and n is the number of runs.

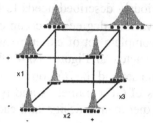

Figure 16-1. Combination of factors in a 2^3 design showing different variances for the different factor combinations.

A plot of the $100(1-a)\%$ HW confidence interval reveals the number of replications above which little improvement in HW is obtained. This is illustrated in Fig. 3.3 with an example with 95% confidence interval in which $S=0.08$. The graph shows that beyond 10 replications there is little to be gained in terms of half width.

The same procedure can be applied for the different combinations of factors, and the desirable half width can be fixed so that the experimental design can be completed with the required number of replications for the required accuracy. If we knew for certain that the variability of the response is about the same for the different combination of factors (experimental runs), we could find the confidence interval of the *difference in mean response* for any two combinations of factors, and find the number of replications required[2] which in this case will be the same for all combinations of factors. (see, for example, Montgomery, 1999).

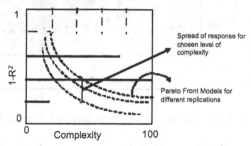

Figure 16-2. Spread of response for a chosen level of complexity.

---

[2] In this case the HW confidence interval is t $_{an-a,a/2}$ $\{2S^2/n\}^{1/2}$. Where a is the number of combination of factors (experimental runs), S is the standard deviation and n is the number of replications

Robustness of Pareto Front GP Parameters to Different Data Sets.

To address the issue of the robustness of GP parameters to the data set, the experimental design previously described needs to be executed for different industrial data sets with various degrees of complexity—for example, low, medium, and high. The complete set of experiments follows an orthogonal array design which is depicted in Figure 16-4 where y_{ij} is the response associated with the *ith* data set and the *jth* combination of GP parameters. If there are n_1 combinations of GP parameters and n_2 data sets, then we need $n_1 * n_2$ runs for the total experimental design and each run of the design will have the required number of replications as indicated by the desired half width. For simplicity, Figure 16-2 only shows one replication per experimental run. The $n'_1\ n_2$ experimental design is an orthogonal design composed of an inner array (GP parameter combinations) and an outer array (the data sets). This type of design allows quantifying the interactions (combined effect of two and three factors). It also reveals information on the combinations of GP parameters that result in a reasonable response even when different data sets are used (combinations of GP parameters that produce correct responses with minimum variation between data sets). Of particular importance in this case are the interactions between the GP parameters and the data sets since these interactions determine the sensitivity of the GP parameters to the type of data set. This is illustrated in the following diagram, Figure 16-5.

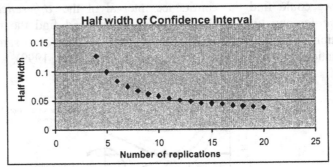

Figure 16-3. 95% Half width confidence interval versus number of replications.

In this case the diagram of the interaction shows a response that is not sensitive to the type of data set if the upper level (+) of parameter x_i is used. Determination of these types of interactions is fundamental to understand the robustness of Pareto front GP parameter combinations.

A proper statistical analysis of the orthogonal design can be valuable; it can provide information on how the response is affected by the Pareto front GP parameter, and how the choice of data can modify that effect. This can be used to determine the best set of parameters for different applications of GP symbolic regression in the chemical industry (and elsewhere).

GP Parameter Variables					Different Types of Data Sets			
					Data 1	Data 2	Data 3	......
X1	X2	X3	X4	X5				
-1	-1	-1	-1	-1	$y11$	$y21$	$y31$	
-1	-1	-1	1	-1	$y12$	$y22$	$y32$	
1	1	1	-1	-1	$y13$	$y23$	$y33$	
-1	1	-1	1	-1	$y14$	$y24$	$y34$	
-1	1	-1	1	-1	$y15$	$y25$	$y35$	
1	1	1	1	1	$y16$	$y26$	$y36$	
1	-1	1	1	1	$y17$	$y27$	$y37$	
1	-1	1	1	-1	$y18$	$y28$	$y38$	
1	-1	1	1	1	$y19$	$y29$	$y39$	
1	-1	-1	1	-1	$y110$	$y210$	$y310$	
1	1	1	1	-1	$y111$	$y211$	$y311$	
-1	1	-1	-1	-1	$y112$	$y212$	$y312$	
1	1	-1	-1	1	$y113$	$y213$	$y313$	
1	-1	-1	-1	1	$y114$	$y214$	$y314$	
1	-1	-1	-1	1	$y115$	$y215$	$y315$	
1	1	1	-1	-1	$y116$	$y216$	$y316$	
1	-1	1	-1	-1	$y117$	$y217$	$y317$	
-1	1	1	-1	1	$y118$	$y218$	$y318$	
-1	-1	1	-1	1	$y119$	$y219$	$y319$	
1	1	-1	1	1	$y120$	$y220$	$y320$	
-1	-1	1	-1	-1	$y121$	$y221$	$y321$	
-1	-1	-1	1	1	$y122$	$y222$	$y322$	
-1	1	1	-1	-1	$y123$	$y223$	$y323$	
1	1	-1	-1	-1	$y124$	$y224$	$y324$	
-1	1	1	1	1	$y125$	$y225$	$y325$	
-1	-1	1	1	-1	$y126$	$y226$	$y326$	
-1	1	-1	-1	1	$y127$	$y227$	$y327$	
-1	1	-1	1	1	$y128$	$y228$	$y328$	
1	-1	-1	1	-1	$y129$	$y229$	$y329$	
-1	-1	1	-1	1	$y130$	$y230$	$y330$	
1	1	-1	-1	1	$y131$	$y231$	$y331$	
-1	-1	-1	-1	1	$y132$	$y232$	$y332$	

Figure 16-4. Orthogonal design with 32 runs in three data sets

4. Issues with Genetic Programming Applications

Applying a new technology, such as GP, in industry requires resolving not only many technical issues, but also systematically and patiently handling problems of a non-technical nature. A short overview of the key technical and non-technical issues is given below.

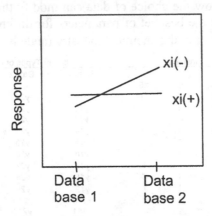

Figure 16-5. Diagram of the interaction of the *ith* GP parameter with the data set type.

Technical Shortcomings

- **Available computer infrastructure** – Even with the help of Moore's Law, GP model development requires significant computational efforts. It is recommended to allocate a proper infrastructure, such as a computer cluster, to accelerate this process. The growing capability of grid computing to handle computationally intensive tasks is another option to improve the GP performance, especially in a big global corporation with thousand of computers. However, development of parallel GP algorithms in user-friendly software is needed.
- **Professional GP software** – The current software options for GP implementation, either external or internally developed, are still used for algorithm development and research purposes. One of the obstacles to mass scale applications of GP is the lack of professional-seeming and user friendly software packages, from well-established vendors, that would also handle continuous product development and product support. Without such a product, the implementation effort is very high and it will be very difficult to convince people to use for GP industrial applications purposes.
- **Symbolic regression is still not accepted as a modeling standard** – One of the difficulties in developing professional GP software is that symbolic regression   via   GP is still not

included in the recently developed Predictive Model Markup Language (PMML, 2004). Most of the other modeling methods— linear regression, neural networks, rule-based models, support vector machines, *etc.*, are techniques supported by this standard and included in the professional software of well-known empirical modeling vendors like the SAS Institute, SPSS, and StatSoft. The best-case scenario for more widespread industrial applications of symbolic regression with GP is to bundle the technology in the existing popular statistical and data mining tools, such as JMP, STATISTICA, Enterprise Miner, or some other package. If that were done, GP would be introduced to the modeling and statistical communities in a natural way and could be used in combination with the other well-known methods.

- **Special attention to data preparation** – Another requirement of using symbolic regression in an integrated statistical software environment is the need for careful data preparation, including outlier removal, data pre-processing, scaling, normalization, *etc.*, before beginning the simulated evolution. Existing GP software tools do not have built-in capabilities for data preparation. The hidden assumption is that the available data is of high quality, which for industrial data sets is often not the case.

- **Technical limitations of GP** – In spite of the fast theoretical development since the early 90's, and increasing computational speed, GP still has several well-known limitations. Generating solutions in a high-dimensional search space takes significant time. Model selection is not trivial and is still more of an art than a science. Integrating heuristics and prior knowledge is not yet a straightforward process for practical applications. Generating complex dynamic systems by GP is still in its infancy.

Non-technical Issues

- **Critical mass of developers** – It is very important at this early phase of industrial applications of GP to coordinate development efforts. The probability for success based only on individual attempts is very low. The best-case scenario would be the creation of a virtual group that includes not only specialists directly involved in GP development and implementation, but also specialists with similar areas of expertise like machine learning, expert systems, and statistics.

- **GP marketing to business and research communities** – Since GP is virtually unknown not only to business-related users but also to other research communities as well, it is necessary to promote the approach by significant marketing efforts. Usually an approach to marketing research-grade includes a series of promotion meetings based on two different presentations. One of these presentations is directed toward the research communities focuses on the "technology kitchen," which gives enough technical details to describe GP, demonstrates the differences from other known methods, and clearly illustrates the competitive advantages of GP. The second presentation, for the business-related audience focuses on the "technology dishes," *i.e.*, it demonstrates with specific industrial examples the types of applications that are appropriate for GP, describes the work process to develop, deploy, and support a GP application, and illustrates the potential financial benefits of applying GP.

- **Management support** – Consistent management support for at least several years is critical for introducing any emerging technology, including GP. The best way to win this support is to define the expected research efforts and assess the potential benefits from specific application areas. Of decisive importance, however, is the demonstration of value creation by resolving practical problems as soon as possible.

- **Lack of initial credibility** – As a new and virtually unknown approach, GP has almost no application history for convincing a potential user. Any GP application requires a risk-seeking culture and significant communication efforts. The successful application discussed in this chapter are a good start to gain credibility and increase the potential GP customer base.

5.   Summary

Among the emerging technologies in the area of computational intelligence, GP has clear competitive advantages and potential for solving a broad range of industrial problems. Several application areas in the chemical industry—for example, inferential sensors, emulators of complex first-principle models, accelerated development of fundamental models, and generation of linearized transforms for design-of-experiments-model-building—already have demonstrated the power of GP and created value. However, a number of technical and non-technical issues, such as well-defined data preparation, development of well-supported professional software packages, GP marketing to business and research communities, consistent management support, *etc.*, have to be resolved before we can expect mass-scale applications of GP in industry.

References

Box, G., Hunter, W., and Hunter, J. (1978). *Statistics for Experiments: An Introduction to Design, Data Analysis, and Model Building*, New York, NY: Wiley.

Castillo, F., Marshall, K, Greens, J. and Kordon, A. (2002). Symbolic Regression in Design of Experiments: A Case Study with Linearizing Transformations, In *Proceedings of the Genetic and Evolutionary Computing Conference (GECCO'2002)*, W. Langdon, *et al* (Eds), pp. 1043-1048. New York, NY: Morgan Kaufmann.

Feldt R. and Nordin P. (2000). Using Factorial Experiments to Evaluate the Effects of Genetic Programming parameters. In *Proceedings of EuroGP'2000*, pp. 271-282, Edinburgh, UK

Kalos A., Kordon, A, Smits, G., and Werkmeister, S. (2003) Hybrid Model Development Methodology for Industrial Soft Sensors, *In Proceedings of the American Control Conference (ACC'2003)*, pp. 5417-5422, Denver. CO.

Kordon A. and Smits, G. (2001) Soft Sensor Development Using Genetic Programming, In *Proceedings of the Genetic and Evolutionary Computing Conference (GECCO'2001)*, L. Spector, *et al* (Eds), pp. 1346 – 1351, San Francisco, Morgan Kaufmann.

Kordon A., H. Pham, C. Bosnyak, M. Kotanchek, and G. Smits, (2002). Accelerating Industrial Fundamental Model Building with Symbolic Regression: A Case Study with Structure – Property Relationships, In *Proceedings of the Genetic and Evolutionary Computing Conference (GECCO'2002)*, D. Davis and R. Roy (Eds), Volume Evolutionary Computation in Industry, pp. 111-116. New York, NY: Morgan Kaufmann.

Kordon A., Kalos, A. and Adams, B. (2003a), Empirical Emulators for Process Monitoring and Optimization, *In Proceedings of the IEEE 11th Conference on Control and Automation MED'2003*, pp.111, Rhodes, Greece.

Kordon, A., Smits, G., Kalos, A., and Jordaan, E.(2003b). Robust Soft Sensor Development Using Genetic Programming, In *Nature-Inspired Methods in Chemometrics*, (R. Leardi-Editor), Amsterdam: Elsevier

Kordon A. and Lue, C. (2004) Symbolic Regression Modeling of Blown Film Process Effects, In *Proceedings of the Congress of Evolutionary Computation CEC'2004*, pp. 561-568, Portland, OR.

Kotanchek, M, Smits, G. and Kordon, A. (2003). Industrial Strength Genetic Programming, In *Genetic Programming Theory and Practice, pp 239-258,* R. Riolo and B. Worzel (Eds), Boston, MA:Kluwer.

Koza, J. (1992). *Genetic Programming: On the Programming of Computers by Means of Natural Selection,* Cambridge, MA: MIT Press.

Jordaan, E., Kordon, A., Smits, G., and Chiang, L. (2004), Robust Inferential Sensors based on Ensemble of predictors generated by Genetic Programming, *In Proceedings of PPSN 2004*, pp. 522-531, Birmingham, UK.

Montgomery, D. (1999) *Design and Analysis of Experiments,* New York, NY: Wiley.

Predictive Modeling Markup Language (PMML V 3.0) Specification, (2004) Data Mining Group, http://www.dmg.org/pmml-v3-0.

Smits, G. and Kotanchek, M. (2004), Pareto -Front Exploitation in Symbolic Regression, *Genetic Programming Theory and Practice, pp 283-300,* U.M. O'Reilly, T. Yu, R. Riolo and B. Worzel (Eds), Boston, MA:Springer.

Chapter 17

CHALLENGES IN OPEN-ENDED PROBLEM SOLVING WITH GENETIC PROGRAMMING

Jason M. Daida[1]

[1]*The University of Michigan, Center for the Study of Complex Systems and Space Physics Research Laboratory, 2455 Hayward Avenue, Ann Arbor, Michigan USA   48109-2143, daida@umich.edu*

Abstract: This chapter describes how genetic programming might be integrated as a tool into the human context of discovery. To accomplish this, a comparison is made between GP and a well-regarded strategy in open-ended problem solving. The comparison indicates which tasks and skills are likely to be complemented by GP. Furthermore, the comparison also indicates directions in research that may need to be taken for GP to be further leveraged as a tool that assists discovery.

Key words: genetic programming (GP), open-ended problem solving, McMaster Problem Solving

1.   Introduction

On July 25, 2002, Raymond Orbach testified before members of the United States Congress about the Office of Science, a government agency that funds basic research in the physical sciences. As director of the agency that has initiated high profile investigations like the Human Genome Project, Orbach spoke about, among other things, how the Japanese scientists were able to gain leadership over the United States in global climate change research. He stated that they were able to do so because they adapted the architecture of their computer to the problem rather than the reverse. In so doing, "they have realized effective performance on global climate change models an order of magnitude greater than we can achieve" (Orbach 2002).

Although Orbach was alluding to the use of hybrid vector processing[1], his comment would apply to those of us in the genetic programming (GP) community. There is something to be said about adapting machines to the needs of our problems.

In this, GP is perhaps, uniquely situated. Although pitched as a technology that can compete against human experts, in actuality the technology has gained favor with practitioners for its ability to complement and partner with experts. For example, unlike other heuristic methods that produce "black box" solutions, GP can and has produced expert-level solutions that come in the form of computer code that human experts can later examine. It is not unusual to hear stories that such examinations yielded insight, which have in turn lead to discovery and innovation.[2]

Unfortunately, our understanding of how GP is used as a tool within the larger discovery process is largely anecdotal and is focused more on the technology than on the people and organizations who would use this technology. This chapter, then, takes a small step in trying to understand GP in the context of this human activity. However, instead of conducting a fieldwork study—which should eventually be done—our group has asked the following question: "How does GP compare with what is known about how people learn and do open-ended problem solving?"

We contend that by comparing GP with one of the well-regarded strategies of open-ended problem solving, a person can

- Identify where in the problem-solving process GP is most compatible
- Indicate areas of investigation that could further leverage GP in discovery and innovation

Consequently, this chapter is organized as follows: Section 2 describes GP as an invention machine and offers this chapter's motivation for comparing GP with the way humans do problem solving. Section 3 provides background to MPS, a well-regarded learner's strategy that describes what needs to occur in basic open-ended problem solving. Section 4 compares GP with MPS and indicates where is GP most compatible in this problem solving process. Section 5 describes areas of investigation that could further leverage GP in discovery and innovation. Section 6 concludes.

---

[1] Hybrid vector processing represents an architecture that is not common in US supercomputers, but was used specifically for building Japan's Earth Simulator. Climate models that run on the Simulator do rely heavily on mathematical operations that take advantage of vector processing. See (Triendl 2002).

[2] Anecdotal evidence of this has often come up during the U-M Center for the Study of Complex Systems Workshop on Genetic Programming Theory and Practice. For example, see (Caplan and Beker 2004; Castillo, Kordon, *et al.* 2004; MacLean and Wollesen, *et al.* 2004).

2. GP as an Invention Machine

Koza states, "Genetic programming is an automated method for solving problems," which "can be used as an automated invention machine" (Koza, Jones *et al.* 2004). Koza and his colleagues have actively promoted this view of GP in a number of prior works (Koza, Bennett III *et al.* 1999; Koza, Keane *et al.* 2000; Koza, Keane *et al.* 2003). By 2003, there were at least 32 instances of solutions by GP that met criteria that humans would otherwise need meet, if such solutions were to be deemed as innovative (*e.g.*, peer-review or patent law). As of the first quarter of 2005, one of these 32 was sufficiently innovative to receive a patent (Keane, Koza *et al.* 2002). Koza and his colleagues reasonably contend that someday GP would routinely make discoveries and inventions (Koza, Keane *et al.* 2003).

However reasonable such claims are today, they would have been dismissed in the late 80s and early 90s. Back then, Koza had just introduced GP, which garnered attention in part because it was an automated method for producing computer code. Although there were antecedents in automatic code production, Koza's was the first to make a compelling, broad-based case. See (Koza 1992). At the time, it was considered novel that computers could program themselves at all.

The change in perception between then and now is partly because of the maturation of the field of GP. It is also partly because GP is easily scaleable. In particular, Koza (Koza, Keane *et al.* 2003; Koza, Jones *et al.* 2004) has argued that one of the primary reasons for GP's current ability to produce human-competitive results is because GP can take advantage of the exponential gains in computational processing power. In other words, GP had to wait until computer technology could match what GP needed for producing such results. If the current number of human-competitive results is any indication, the wait is over.

So we are now at a stage where GP can solve for difficult, real-world problems, which are generally characterized as open-ended and that require solutions that are inventive. A manager who does not know about how GP works, but would like to use it to solve real-world problems, can reasonably ask what kind of problems it can solve.

The following is a short, informal list of sample problems that GP can or cannot solve given the current state-of-the-art:

- Design a patentable analog circuit that meets a given set of specifications See (Keane, Koza *et al.* 2002; Koza, Jones *et al.* 2004)
- Identify a statistical model that can be used for a given Design of Experiments application in an

industrial chemical process See (Castillo, Kordon *et al.* 2004)
- Design a word processor that is comparable in function to Microsoft Word version 1.0. (Unlikely)
- Answer the question: Why are the tops and bottoms of beer cans tapered? (Unlikely)

In some senses, what GP can and has solved is reversed from the human experience. For example, GP performs at an expert level: the first two questions represent contemporary problems that have required expert answers. However, GP stumbles on expert level programming: the third question represents a programming problem for an application that is decades old. Furthermore, GP stumbles on problems that could be used in the hiring of an expert: the fourth question represents a classic interview question for many competitive companies in technology (Poundstone 2003).[3]

Insight as to why some questions are potentially harder or easier for GP to solve might be gleaned if we examine what goes into the way humans approach problem solving. The next section introduces research on problem solving from a field that has not previously received much attention from the GP community.

3.   What Is Open-Ended Problem Solving?

The idea of comparing and contrasting what genetic and evolutionary computation do to what people do for open-ended problem solving is not new. In (Goldberg 2002), Goldberg articulates the beginning of a computational theory of innovation based on his work with competent genetic algorithms (GA). His work not only seeks to inform how to design competent GAs for innovation using theory to inform practice, but also to inform what competent GAs say about the design process for innovation.

My research group's approach to this comparison, at least for GP, has taken a different route for two reasons: our long-term research interest in problems that are difficult for GP to solve and our experience in education in open-ended problem solving. Our long-term research interest has been described in previous works, including (Daida 2004; Daida 2005). As for education, I've been developing and teaching an engineering course involving design and open-ended problem solving for several years.

In science and technology education in general, there has been keen interest in teaching students how to do open-ended problem solving. In particular, engineering education in the United States has institutionalized

---

[3]   Using genetic and evolutionary programming to solve brain teasers and other puzzles is considered in (Michalewicz and Fogel 2000).

this interest as part of the accreditation standards for engineering schools and colleges. There have also been a number of studies that not only recommend how to teach open-ended problem solving (as in curricula developed for project-based learning), but also those that analyze open-ended problem solving as a complex task that involves a variety of skills, states, and goals. It is out of engineering education research concerning analyses of problem solving by learners that we introduce MPS.

MPS is an evidence-based strategy for problem solving that has been articulated for the engineering education community by Donald Woods at McMaster University *e.g.*, see (Woods, Hrymak *et al.* 1997; Woods 2000). In some ways, it is a consequence of directed observation, cognitive psychology, and a study of over 150 basic strategies to solve problems in a number of fields, including business, science, mathematics, engineering, art, and psychology. See the references in (Woods 2000). In other ways, it also represents an explicit strategy that has been tested and validated through extensive observational and field research. The McMaster Problem Solving Program is highly regarded in engineering education research to the degree that many colleges have incorporated it into either their first-year curricula or assessment programs.

MPS consists of six stages that subdivide 37 general problem-solving skills (both cognitive and attitudinal). Woods depicts MPS as a circular set of "rooms" with a center "hallway," as shown in Figure 17-1. The process of problem solving that Wood is trying to convey is that a learner starts with "Engage," then enters the "hallway" to go to any of the five other stages. The learner can visit the stages in any order: what matters is that eventually all stages are visited. An implication of this work is that missing any of the stages results in an approach to problem solving that is prone to failure. Another implication is that if any of the cognitive or attitudinal skills are missing or underdeveloped in any *one* of the stages, that open-ended problem solving may also be prone to failure. At least from an educational standpoint, the idea is to develop each of the attitudinal and cognitive skills needed for each stage to become a doable proposition with associated

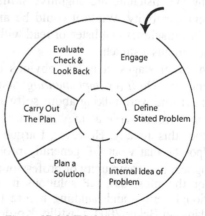

Figure 17-1. MPS 6-stage strategy. Redrawn and used with permission from Woods (Woods 1994).

exercises and concrete outcomes. MPS can apply to a broad cross-section of learners—from elementary school students to professionals.

If GP is to be used in the discovery process, it also implies GP would apply to somewhere in MPS. In the next section, we subsequently examine how each of these stages and associated skills compares to GP.

4.   Comparing GP with MPS

Tables 17-1 and 17-2 compare MPS with GP. Each table lists the six stages of MPS and is based on (Woods 2000). Depending on which table is discussed, each stage is expanded (or collapsed) to show (or to hide) the cognitive/meta-cognitive skills and the attitudinal skills that are needed for that stage. The comparisons are informal and speculative: there is no attempt to rigorously measure the degree to which a match or mismatch occurs. Even at this level, however, the comparison does illuminate some of the reasons why some problems can be solved by GP while others can't, why people have used GP as a tool to assist in discovery, and where potential research areas are for GP investigators to leverage.

In particular, Table 17-1 indicates the MPS stages where GP does not seem to complement. Those stages are expanded to show the skills that are needed for them. The collapsed, highlighted stages correspond to those that do seem to complement GP.

For some stages, it is obvious that GP is not a close match for that stage. For example, the *Engage* stage is something that pertains to people and that reading and listening are cognitive skills to which GP does not have any inherent capability. While it could be argued that one day, perhaps, there would be machines that listen or read with understanding *and* be crafted with GP, it remains a stretch.

For other stages, it is less obvious that GP is not a close match. For example, the *Do It* (or *Implementing*) stage calls for a solution to be put into action. If one were talking about software, it would refer to the writing of code that would serve as the "software" solution. Again, it is arguable that GP does this already. However, I argue from a professional programmer's standpoint—that what GP generally produces isn't code that would pass a Turing test in a community of professional programmers.

For the most part, GP solutions in the real world do seem to require additional vetting and handling before they are adopted into practice *e.g.*, (Caplan and Beker 2004; Castillo, Kordon *et al.* 2004; MacLean, Wollesen *et al.* 2004). The challenges of implementing a GP solution do increase if the form of a solution differs greatly from the representational

Table 17-1. Comparison of MPS with GP where stages do *not* correspond well. Expanded stages from (Woods 2000) elaborate what is included in those stages that do not compare well with GP. (The grayed stages, those which GP does compare favorably, are collapsed and are elaborated upon in Table 2).

Task	Cognitive	Attitudinal
Engage: I Want To & I Can • Read the problem • Listen to someone describing a task to be done • Observe a situation and identify the opportunity • Manage distress • Be motivated • Continue to work on the problem	• Read • Listen	• Courage and drive to attack the problem • Distress management skills • Motivated, patient, active • Willing to cope with ambiguity and to risk • Monitor
Define the Stated Problem • Classify given information into: goal constraints, inferred constraints, criteria, inferred criteria, description of system	• Identify main items • Use definitions to identify parts • Analyze / classify	• Patient, attentive, systematic, tolerant, active, underline key ideas • Monitor
Explore: Create Internal Idea of Problem **Plan a Solution**		
Do It: Carry Out the Plan	• Analyze • Manage resources • Judge critically	• Concern for accuracy • Active, systematic, careful, attentive to detail • Monitor
Evaluate, Check, & Look Back	• Reflect • Elaborate • Analyze • Communicate • Judge critically • Select "cues" • Generalize, evaluate, create	• Stress management • Motivated, persistent • Monitor

forms used during problem solving. For example, the problem-solving forms for Koza's analog circuits consist of mathematical and computational representations that can be manipulated and tested on a computer. Although however complete the representation, the working form of a solution ultimately resides in a physical instance of the actual circuit. Consequently, the stage

Table 17-2. Comparison of MPS with GP where stages do correspond well. Gray stages are those in which GP does compare favorably. They are expanded and detailed [from (Woods 2000)] to show where in these stages might GP compare well. The other, remaining stages are collapsed.

Task	Cognitive	Attitudinal
Engage: I Want To & I Can		
Define the Stated Problem		
Explore: Create Internal Idea of Problem	• *Apply heuristics*	• *Able to learn*
• *See the situation from a wide variety of viewpoints*	• *Simplify, make*	*from mistakes*
• *Ask "What if?" often and do simple estimations to*	*assumptions*	• *Monitor*
predict the results	• *Generalize*	• *Flexible*
• *Translate the situation to a preferred style*	• *Identify "cues"*	• *Willing to take*
• *Estimate values for answer*	• *Apply criteria*	*risk, to make*
• *From experience knowledge estimate values for the*	• *Translate*	*assumptions*
different parameters that affect the answer	• *Exploit personal*	*and to postpone*
• *Make simplifying assumptions and solve the simple*	*preference*	*judgment*
problem to begin to get a sense of what the problem		• *Persistent*
is about and what are the dominant factors or issues	• Access	
• *Repeat making a variety of simplifying assumptions*	knowledge	• Distress
• *Divide the problem into workable subproblems*	• Access past	management
	problems that	when stuck
• Identify the key content-knowledge (e.g., "This is	were solved	• Focus on each
about forces"; "That's Physics"; "The major laws	successfully	sub-problem
that might relate are...")	• Analyze	separately
• Use pattern recognition skill to identify whether this	• Create	• Organized
is an exercise or a problem	• Reason	• Stress
• Try to clarify your internal image by writing out	• Judge critically	management
what you see as being the problem		
• Write down a "good" goal statement		
• Check the reliability of data		
Plan a Solution	• *Analyze, manage*	• Systematic,
	resources, decide,	organized
	identify sequences	persistent,
	and consequences	tenacious, careful
	• *Apply heuristics*	• Monitor
	• Judge critically	
Do It: Carry Out the Plan		
Evaluate, Check, & Look Back		

Implementing would include the actual building of that circuit.[4] It is rare that GP actually controls and builds physical artifacts that result from its

---

[4]   Another example would include (Lohn, Hornby, *et al.* 2004). At the workshop talk associated with this chapter, Lohn described the special challenges that arose when having to fashion the antennas from wire stock.

code solution; typically some other technologies or humans would do it, instead.

Table 17-2 indicates the MPS stages where GP does seem to complement. As in the previous table, the highlighted stages correspond to those that do seem to complement GP. However, unlike the previous table, the highlighted stages are expanded to show the skills that are needed for them.

Most of what GP does well matches with the stage entitled *Explore: Create Internal Idea of a Problem.* Unlike some of the other stages, which are described by self-explanatory descriptors, *Explore* does bear some explanation, since as Woods describes, "[It] is probably the most underrated, most challenging and least understood stage of all the stages" (Woods 2000 p. 449).

Open-ended problem solving presumes that the method and information that is ultimately used by the method are not known ahead of time. At some point during problem-solving then, there would need to be time set aside to explore. Metaphorically speaking, *Explore* is the stage where one tries to glean a path in the uncharted landscape of a problem: the process is not straightforward, the way is not clear, and time is spent trying to put together a variety of guesses that might hopefully illuminate where to go next. According to (Woods 2000), this stage requires one to "explore the situation from many conflicting points-of-view," to "connect the goal and the given data," and to "guesstimate an answer."

It is not surprising then, that, practitioners have used GP in the discovery process and that GP's use would likely fall in *Explore*. True, the current level of programming skill that GP offers in its solutions isn't yet laudable. However, what GP brings to the table does complement the skills that humans *need* during *Explore*. Humans need to learn from mistakes, to take risks, to persist in spite of failures, and to do distress management when stuck. These attitudinal skills during *Explore* are crucial, since attitudes help to shape our assumptions of what a solution should be. If there were a way to vet out unnecessary assumptions, it would be welcome. Unnecessary assumptions have a way of handicapping our ability to solve problems.

At least in GP, there is a way to assemble and to sift through potential guesses in a systematic manner, without burdening assumptions brought upon by one's attitudes. Since insight is a way of seeing beyond assumption, GP can and has helped in providing insight as to how a problem can be solved, if only because the technology provides a way to circumvent potential assumptions brought about by attitudes, which are themselves shaped by particular points-of-view. And of those attitudes, some of the most pervasive are those concerning failure—either real or imagined. In that area, GP shines. In the process of deriving a solution (or, in Woods's terms, a *guesstimate* since a final solution is often not GP code), GP assembles and sifts through a multitude of failures as an inherent part of identifying success. Its search in combinatorial space is littered with dead ends. There are so many negative outcomes during a GP search that were a human to replicate what GP does, that human would likely be regarded as equally heroic and stupid. Of course, what matters is insight and if GP provides that, better it than a human.

Given this comparison of GP with MPS in Tables 17-1 and 17-2, one should note that GP is not a technology that leverages equally well in all stages of open-ended problem solving. There are some stages that it applies to better than others and so it is limited in what it can and cannot provide to the discovery process. Consequently, the next section explores what these limitations mean for the GP community.

5.   Implications for GP

A useful and perhaps obvious observation about MPS is that the process of open-ended problem solving consists of a variety of different skills that need to be applied to perform distinct tasks within a particular stage. That observation has consequences for GP because the observation suggests that the technology *needs* other types of functionality for it to be leveraged in the discovery process. In other words, the bottleneck in the adoption of GP in the discovery process in general may not necessarily lie in advancing the technology itself. Rather, the bottleneck may lie not in having the appropriate tools that are ancillary to GP, per se, but that are integral to using GP in the context of discovery. Specifically, there is a lack of tools that support GP and that match well to the other stages in MPS.

An Illustration

Koza has argued that the exponential increase in computational horsepower should be harnessed so that GP can start solving difficult, real-world problems. An obvious place to do this is to have GP work with large populations of hundreds of thousands to millions of individuals, instead of the populations of several hundred to a few thousand individuals that researchers study. Reasonable investigations, then, would include research in distributed architectures amenable to GP, research in operators that could leverage such distributed architectures for GP, and research in GP phenomena that occur at those scales.

Having a better GP that is capable of assembling millions of guesses can lead to a kind of dysfunction, however, if one considers the entirety of open-ended problem solving. If GP were a human doing open-ended problem solving with the kinds of capabilities that it currently has, it would be one that suffers from *racing*. Racing refers to a mental condition where a stream, arguably a torrent, of free-associative thought happens unchecked. Unfortunately, the ability to turn those thoughts into a reality, however brilliant, is crippled because of an inability to plan, implement, and evaluate consequences at the rate at which those thoughts occur. In other words, ability to crunch through millions of guesses is not really helpful unless there is a way to sustain its throughput throughout the entire process of open-ended problem solving.

There are at least two key stages in MPS that currently receive scant attention in the GP community, if only because it would seem that these research developments should happen somewhere else in some other field: *i.e.*, *Evaluating* and *Implementing*. My list is by no means exhaustive and in this chapter only illustrates how MPS can serve as a way to enhance the use of GP in the context of open-ended problem solving. As others have pointed out in this year's workshop, there are *many* other ways of applying MPS to GP. In any case, the following sections offer examples of extending GP in *Evaluating* and *Implementing*.

Evaluating (Understanding)

Perhaps the greatest bottleneck to using GP in the context of human discovery lies in our ability to understand its results and to subsequently isolate valuable insights, innovations, and discoveries. Certainly, GP outputs code that is eminently more readable and more transparent than black-box heuristics like neural nets. That being said, anyone who has tried to analyze GP code would conclude that the production of readable code isn't one of GP's strong points. Not many people can "read" GP-produced code fluently, *and* have expertise in the domain of a problem, to be able to evaluate whether such code contains anything worthwhile. Even for those who can "read" GP-code, the process tends to be slow and manpower intensive.

Root-Bernstein wrote the following when he was discussing tools used by scientists in the discovery process:

> Tools of thought, in and of themselves, are useless to a scientist until linked by 'transformational thinking'—that is, the ability to translate a problem expressed in one form (such as numbers) into another form more amenable to problem solving (words, perhaps, or mental images); to mentally manipulate these words, images, or models to solve the problem; and then to translate this solution into yet another form (such as an equation or diagram or experimental protocol) that can be communicated to other scientists. (Root-Bernstein 1989), p. 313.

It might be that the tools—like GP—have progressed to the point where another intermediate form may be needed, one that focuses on a rapid evaluation of results in the broader context of determining what is creative to an expert or to a field. Such a form might correspond to something that currently exists as forms that are used to communicate results to other people. It might be, though, that such forms could also be chosen to suit the needs of a semi-automated means for doing such an evaluation.

Again going back to Koza's analog circuits, Koza and his colleagues have sidestepped the issue of being able to read GP-produced code by focusing on the artifacts produced as an outcome of executing GP code— *i.e.*, circuit schematics—as opposed to just the code itself. The selection of this form happens to be one that is understandable to analog circuit experts, but also one that is amenable to rapid, automated analysis. While current automated analysis methods fall short of being able to determine whether an analog circuit is creative to an expert or to a field, they do allow for a rapid evaluation of GP-produced results without the need for understanding computer code.

Even though the notion of extending circuit diagrams to solve other problems is not an option for many other fields, the notion of identifying artifacts that could be used for rapid evaluation might be. For example, in our own work, those artifacts have turned out to be forms for visualizing quantitative results *e.g.*, (Daida, Hilss et al. 2005). Our ability to see and to evaluate statistical phenomena with these new visualization methods have afforded studies that were not previously possible by either archetypes or two-variable statistics that have been common in our field *e.g.*, (Daida 2005). Although researchers have long understood that genetic and evolutionary computation could benefit from visualization, not many papers have been published in this area, particularly for GP.

Implementing

Analogous to the MPS stage *Do It*, implementing a GP solution is more than simply turning code into a physical or logical artifact that people would then use. Perhaps the next biggest drawback to using GP in the context of human discovery lies in implementing GP-produced findings into the workflow of the people who would stand to benefit from these findings. Protocols for incorporating GP-produced findings for one's workflow are either nonexistent, nontrivial, or both.

That there needs to be any special handling for GP-findings requires some explanation. There is the matter of perception because many humans rightfully distrust solutions that are either not understandable or not conventional. There is also the matter of hidden consequences, because GP

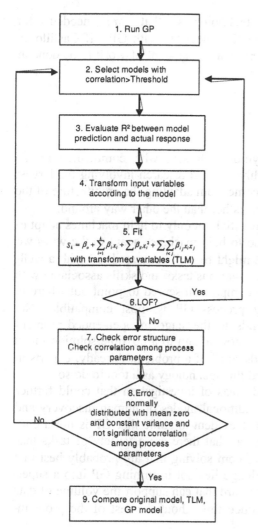

1. Run GP

2. Select models with correlation>Threshold

3. Evaluate R^2 between model prediction and actual response

4. Transform input variables according to the model

5. Fit
$$S_k = \beta_o + \sum_{i=1}^{k} \beta_i x_i + \sum \beta_{ii} x_i^2 + \sum_{i<j} \sum \beta_{ij} x_i x_j$$
with transformed variables (TLM)

6. LOF? — Yes

No

7. Check error structure Check correlation among process parameters

8. Error normally distributed with mean zero and constant variance and not significant correlation among process parameters — No

Yes

9. Compare original model, TLM, GP model

Figure 17-2. Example of methodology that implements GP-derived solution [from (Castillo, Kordon et al. 2004)]. Only the first, topmost box, is where most published research stops. Used with permission.

can take shortcuts that may not be obvious to humans. Of these, the latter may, in the long run, be more worrying since hidden consequences sometimes have a way of turning catastrophic.

The identification of protocols, such as those indicated in (Caplan and Beker 2004; Castillo, Kordon *et al.* 2004; MacLean, Wollesen *et al.* 2004) represent a promising start. Although there are not yet enough examples from which to draw general conclusions about the kinds of protocols that work best, such work already alludes to the kinds of organizational structures and methodologies that may need to happen to accommodate GP into the discovery process. For example, Figure 17-2 depicts the protocol from (Castillo, Kordon *et al.* 2004), which describes a means of using GP to identify transforms that eliminate lack-of-fit in a Box-Behnkin design. In Castillo *et al.*'s case, the technology of GP provides only a portion—albeit a pivotal portion—of the total overall solution that is needed to implement GP into this industrial setting. In particular, nearly all of the technology that directly involves GP is confined to the work represented by the first, topmost box of Figure 17-2. The rest of the Castillo *et al.*'s methodology is what was needed to make the GP-derived solutions to be useful. Of course, implicit in the rest of their methodology are the personnel, organization, and technologies that are needed for implementation, which are not directly associated with GP. If Castillo *et al.*'s protocol is any indication, there is a fair amount of work to be done in *Implementing*.

6.   Conclusions

This chapter began with Raymond Orbach, who commented on an approach to some of the most highly profiled research involving the largest of supercomputers. Effectiveness came from adapting the architecture of the computer to the needs of a problem, rather than the other way around.

As a technology, GP has the potential not only to help machines adapt to the needs of our problems, but also to help machines adapt to the ways we solve them. To highlight how this might be so, I compared GP with a well-regarded strategy that articulates the various tasks and skills associated with open-ended problem solving. The comparison served to point out where in the open-ended problem solving process GP is most compatible. Not surprisingly, this match corresponds to the stage in open-ended problem solving where one needs to explore how a path to a possible solution might come about in the uncharted "landscape" of a problem. Already, experts in various problem domains have used this technology as a tool to do so.

The comparison also indicated areas of investigation that could further leverage GP into the process of traditional modes of human discovery and innovation. Although it may be self-evident to some that GP is not a one-stop tool, the comparison made clear that there are a variety of tasks that need to be done in open-ended problem solving that are probably best met with other technologies. The challenge lies not in turning GP into a super-tool, but in developing an infrastructure that can support the volume of data and information that GP can produce throughout the rest of the problem-solving process.

To show how this might be done, I highlighted two MPS stages— *Evaluating* and *Implementing*—that point to the kinds of infrastructural development needed to support GP. For example, there are bottlenecks in *Evaluating* GP-derived solutions in trying to determine whether they are, in fact, discoveries or innovations. There are also many unknown consequences and issues in *Implementing* GP-derived solutions in an industrial workflow. Either of these issues currently receives scant emphasis within the GP research community, if only because these have been considered ancillary to the study of the technology.

In conclusion, if we were to address the broader challenges of using GP as a tool for discovery and innovation, these "ancillary" areas really should *not* be left to the province of a discovery's research community (*e.g.*, like the analog-circuit design community). Given the overall context of problem solving, the "ancillary" is actually essential to GP. After all, adapting GP to meet the needs of the problem instead of the other way around gets to the heart of Orbach's observation. GP needs these other technologies. Consequently, if GP is to be such a tool that helps us to chart a path into the unknown, it is in our field's best interests to make it so—it is not someone else's "problem."

Acknowledgments

A chapter like this is an outcome of many conversations with many people. I thank the following individuals from my research group UMACERS: R. Tang, M. Samples, M. Byom, M. Pizzimenti, F. Tsa, M. Rio, C. Kureka, B. McNally, X. Loy, T. Weltzer, and K. McNamara. Foundation Coalition member J. Froyd introduced me to MPS, while G. Herrin provided me the latitude in integrating MPS in my classes. The long conversations with Dow researchers A. Kordon, M. Kotanchek, G. Smits, and F. Castillo were enlightening. Reviews from U. M. O'Reilly, T. McConaghy, and A. Kordon were appreciated and helpful. Gratitude is extended to the workshop organizers R. Riolo, W. Worzel, and T. Yu. As ever, I extend my appreciation to S. Daida and I. Kristo.

References

Caplan, M. and Y. Beker (2004). Lessons Learned Using Genetic Programming in a Stock Picking Context: A Story of Willful Optimism and Eventual Success. *Genetic Programming Theory and Practice II*. U.-M. O'Reilly, T. Yu, R. L. Riolo and W. Worzel. Boston, Kluwer Academic Publishers: 31–48.

Castillo, F., A. Kordon, *et al.* (2004). Using Genetic Programming in Industrial Statistical Model Building. *Genetic Programming Theory and Practice II*. U.-M. O'Reilly, T. Yu, R. L. Riolo, and W. Worzel. Boston, Kluwer Academic Publishers: 31–48.

Daida, J. M. (2004). What Makes a Problem GP-Hard? A Look at How Structure Affects Content. *Genetic Programming Theory and Practice*. R. L. Riolo and W. Worzel. New York, Springer: 99–118.

Daida, J. M. (2005). Considering the Roles of Structure in Problem-Solving by Computer. *Genetic Programming Theory and Practice II*. U.-M. O'Reilly, T. Yu, R. L. Riolo and W. Worzel. New York, Springer: 67–86.

Daida, J. M. (2005). Towards Identifying Populations that Increase the Likelihood of Success in Genetic Programming. *GECCO 2005*. In print.

Daida, J. M., A. M. Hilss, *et al.* (2005). "Visualizing Tree Structures in Genetic Programming." *Genetic Programming and Evolvable Machines* **6**: 79–110.

Goldberg, D. (2002). *The Design of Innovation: Lessons from and for Competent Genetic Algorithms.* Boston, Kluwer Academic Publishers.

Keane, M. A., J. R. Koza, *et al.* (2002). General-Purpose Controllers. Patent #6,847,851. Issued 25 January 2005. U. S. Patent Office. United States. Assignee: Koza, J.R.

Koza, J. R. (1992). *Genetic Programming: On the Programming of Computers by Means of Natural Selection.* Cambridge, The MIT Press.

Koza, J. R., F. H. Bennett III, et *al.* (1999). *Genetic Programming III: Darwinian Invention and Problem Solving.* San Francisco, Morgan Kaufmann Publishers.

Koza, J. R., L. W. Jones, *et al.* (2004). Toward Automated Design of Industrial-Strength Analog Circuits by Means of Genetic Programming. *Genetic Programming Theory and Practice II.* U.-M. O'Reilly, T. Yu, R. L. Riolo, and W. Worzel. Boston, Kluwer Academic Publishers: 121–142.

Koza, J. R., M. A. Keane, *et al.* (2003). *Genetic Programming IV: Routine Human-Competitive Machine Intelligence.* Norwell, Kluwer Academic Publishers.

Koza, J. R., M. A. Keane, *et al.* (2000). "Automatic Creation of Human-Competitive Programs and Controllers by Means of Genetic Programming." *Genetic Programming and Evolvable Machines* 1(1/2): 121–164.

Lipson, H. and J. B. Pollack (2000). "Automatic Design and Manufacture of Robotic Lifeforms." *Nature* 406(31 August 2000): 974–978.

Lohn, J. D., G. S. Hornby, *et al.* (2004). An Evolved Antenna for Deployment on NASA's Space Technology 5 Mission. *Genetic Programming Theory and Practice II.* U.-M. O'Reilly, T. Yu, R. L. Riolo, and W. Worzel. Boston, Kluwer Academic Publishers: 301–313.

MacLean, D., E. A. Wollesen, *et al.* (2004). Listening to Data: Tuning a Genetic Programming System. *Genetic Programming Theory and Practice II.* U.-M. O'Reilly, T. Yu, R. L. Riolo, and W. Worzel. Boston, Kluwer Academic Publishers: 245–262.

Michalewicz, Z. and D. B. Fogel (2000). *How to Solve It: Modern Heuristics.* Berlin, Springer-Verlag.

Orbach, R. L. (2002). Testimony of Dr. Raymond L. Orbach, Director, Office of Science, Before the House Science Committee Subcommittee on Energy. Washington, D.C.

Poundstone, W. (2003). *How Would You Move Mount Fuji? Microsoft's Cult of the Puzzle: How the World's Smartest Companies Select the Most Creative Thinkers.* Boston, Little, Brown and Company.

Root-Bernstein, R. S. (1989). *Discovering: Inventing and Solving Problems at the Frontiers of Scientific Knowledge.* Cambridge, Harvard University Press.

Triendl, R. (2002). "Our Virtual Planet." *Nature* 416(11 April 2002): 579–580.

Woods, D. R. (1994). *Problem-Based Learning: How to Gain the Most from PBL.* Waterdown, ON, Woods Publishing.

Woods, D. R. (2000). "An Evidence-Based Strategy for Problem Solving." *Journal of Engineering Education*: 443–459.

Woods, D. R., A. Hrymak, et al. (1997). "Developing Problem Solving Skills: The McMaster Problem Solving Program." Journal of Engineering Education: 75–91.

Chapter 18

DOMAIN SPECIFICITY OF GENETIC PROGRAMMING BASED AUTOMATED SYNTHESIS: A CASE STUDY WITH SYNTHESIS OF MECHANICAL VIBRATION ABSORBERS

Jianjun Hu[1], Ronald C. Rosenberg[2] and Erik D. Goodman[3]

[1] *Department of Computer Science, Purdue University, West Lafayette, IN, 47906;*
[2] *Department of Mechanical Engineering, Michigan State University, East Lansing, MI, 48824;*
[3] *Department of Electrical and Computer Engineering, Michigan State University, East Lansing, MI, 48824.*

Abstract   Genetic programming has proved its potential for automated synthesis of a variety of engineering systems such as electrical, control, and mechanical systems. Given any of these application domains, a set of generic GP functions can be developed for its synthesis. In this chapter, however, we illustrate that while a generic GP system can often be used to prove a concept, realistic or industrial automated synthesis often requires domain-specific GP configuration, especially of the GP function sets. As a case study, it is shown how the open-ended topology search capability of GP readily exploits "loopholes" in a generic bond-graph-based GP function set and evolves high-performance but unrealistic mechanical vibration absorbers, even though the bond graphs would be readily implementable in, for example, the electrical domain. The preliminary attempt to constrain evolved topologies to only those that would be readily implementable in the mechanical domain was not sufficiently restrictive.

Keywords: automated synthesis, genetic programming, passive vibration absorber, bond graphs, mechatronic systems, domain knowledge

1. Introduction

Since 1997, it has been demonstrated that genetic programming can generate human-competitive designs in a variety of domains, including analog circuits

(Koza et al., 2003), antennas, and mechanical linkage mechanisms (Lipson, 2004). Each of these domains is defined by a set of realizable building blocks to be assembled into a system. However, the building blocks of the modeling tools, such as analog circuits or bond graphs, are composed of primitive components, some of which do not have directly corresponding physical entities. One question is how it is possible to evolve physically realizable systems using primitive building blocks and how domain knowledge should be incorporated into the GP system to evolve practical solutions. This chapter describes a preliminary foray into this question, and illustrates that the question is non-trivial, even for the domain of passive linear mechanical dynamic systems.

We are interested in evolving human-competitive results in a classical mechanical engineering domain, the design of vibration absorbers, which are widely used, for example, in machine tools. The widespread and critical application of vibration absorbers in structural control (Soong, 1990; JR et al., 1997), space structures (Bruner, 1992), vehicle suspension (Hirata et al., 1995), and helicopter vibration make it an important domain in which to develop automated approaches to facilitate creation of innovative solutions. Although the first vibration absorber technology was invented a century ago (Frahm, 1911), research in this field is still far from complete, and innovations continue to arise frequently (Filipovic and Schroder, 1998).

In this chapter, we report lessons and failures to date involved in an effort to evolve human-competitive vibration absorbers using the primitive building blocks of bond graphs – a generic modeling tool for dynamic systems (Karnopp et al., 2000). In our previous work, a generic synthesis framework based on genetic programming and bond graphs (GPBG) was used to successfully evolve a variety of mechatronic systems (Fan et al., 2001; Seo et al., 2002). Here, we want to demonstrate that the GPBG system has the potential to duplicate significant innovations in passive vibration absorber design in terms of fitness function values. Unfortunately, most of the solutions evolved to date are not practical for physical realization. We show that to prepare the GP/bond graph paradigm for wide industrial adoption, it is necessary to re-configure the generic GP system to accommodate domain-specific physical implementation constraints.

The remainder of this paper is organized as follows: Section 2 reviews some representative vibration absorber designs as well as previous work on automated synthesis of electrical circuits, mechatronic systems, and mechanisms. Section 3 defines the vibration absorber design problem and presents our GPBG framework for their automated synthesis. The experiments and an analysis of results are then introduced in Section 4. Finally, Section 5 concludes this chapter with a discussion of planned future work.

2.   Related Work

The idea of exploiting domain knowledge in configuring GP systems is well known. In the very beginning, one has to consider the types of system components and possible meaningful topological operations to design the GP function set. However, most of the previous work of using GP for hard problems belongs to domains where physical implementation is not a serious problem. Examples include the analog circuit synthesis (Koza et al., 1999), control systems (Koza et al., 2000), or computer programs. All of these systems allow very flexible implementation. The physical constraints on the topologies of the designs are not a big issue. Despite this, Koza (Koza et al., 2004a) suggested that exploiting domain, or problem-specific knowledge, may be helpful to improve efficiency. McConaghy and Gielen (McConaghy and Gielen, 2005) discussed the issue of how to evolve industrially useful analog circuits, including use of specialized GP for real-world problems, which is a similar thrust to ours. In our previous work, we tried to evolve MEMS systems which can only be implemented using a certain types of physical building blocks, which puts constraints on the GP function set design (Fan et al., 2003). However, in that work, the realization constraints were so strong that the set of available components and connection topologies was strongly restricted, so the GP results were realizable.

The invention history of vibration absorbers has spanned almost a century. The first patented vibration absorber was invented by H. Frahm (Frahm, 1911). As shown in Figure 18-1, his passive vibration absorber attaches a mass to a primary vibrating system through a damper and spring. By tuning the damping coefficient and the spring's stiffness, one can dramatically reduce the magnitude of vibration in response to a specified frequency of vibration. The limitation of these passive vibration absorbers is that they work well only at that specified frequency. If the frequency of the excitatory vibration changes, the vibration absorber will become ineffective or even become harmful due to the "de-tuning" phenomenon. A natural solution is to add an active controller to the whole system, as shown in Figure 18-1(b). The benefits of active vibration absorbers are that they can track a change in frequency of the excitation source and that they work for a wide frequency band. They are especially useful for vibration sources of unknown characteristics. The shortcoming of active controllers is that the combined system could suffer from control-induced instability and from large control effort requirements, making them inapplicable in many industrial applications (Jalili, 2002). The third type of vibration absorber, as shown in Figure 18-1(c), combines the advantages of passive and active absorbers by integrating a tuning control mechanism with tunable passive devices, such as variable rate damping and stiffness (Franchek et al., 1995; Nemir et al., 1994). These adaptive passive vibration absorbers are welcomed by industry due to their low energy requirements and low cost. There are several reviews available for further details (Karnopp, 1995; Jalili, 2002).

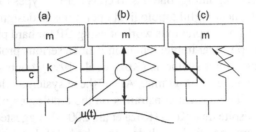

Figure 18-1. A typical primary structure equipped with three versions of vibration control systems (absorbers): (a) passive, (b) active, and (c) semi-active configuration

Vibration absorbers are a class of dynamic systems which can be modeled as analog circuits, block diagrams, bond graphs, etc. A special characteristic of these particular dynamic systems is that the building blocks usually have a fixed number of interface ports and may not be connected arbitrarily. Automated synthesis of dynamic systems has been investigated intensively in the past ten years (Koza et al., 1999; Koza et al., 2003; Koza et al., 1997; Koza et al., 2000; Lohn and Colombano, 1999). Instead of using electrical circuits and block diagrams, we developed a GP-based framework for automated synthesis of mechatronic systems using bond graphs as the modeling scheme. The so-called GPBG approach has been applied to automated synthesis of analog filters (Fan et al., 2001), redesign of an old-fashioned mechanical printer (Seo et al., 2002) and pump (Seo et al., 2003), automated synthesis of MEMS systems (Fan et al., 2004), and synthesis of robust analog filter circuits (Hu et al., 2005). Figure 18-2 illustrates a very simple bond graph, marked up to show sites at which topological modifications are allowed in the GPBG system, and a corresponding electrical circuit. In previous work with the GPBG system, no attempt has been made to duplicate or compare its designs with those invented by experts.

3.   Mechanical Vibration Absorber Synthesis Using Bond Graphs and Genetic Programming

In this section, we define the vibration absorber synthesis problem and present an improved methodology for open-ended computational synthesis of multi-domain dynamic systems based on Genetic Programming and Bond Graphs (Karnopp et al., 2000)–the GPBG approach. Compared to the basic GPBG approach introduced in (Seo et al., 2003), methodological improvements have been made in several aspects to be discussed next.

Problem Definition: Synthesis of Passive Vibration Absorbers

In this work, we are mainly interested in synthesizing passive vibration absorbers to reduce the vibration response of primary systems of various configurations. Figure 18-3 shows a primary system and its corresponding bond graph model. The design task is to attach some new components to the primary system such that the frequency response at the excitation frequency ω be minimized. Figure 18-4 shows the first vibration absorber, invented by H. Frahm in 1911, and its bond graph model. The frequency response of the stand-alone primary system and the primary system with vibration absorber is shown in Figure 18-5. It can be seen that the vibration absorber can significantly quench the response of the primary system at the excitation frequency. An advanced version of the vibration absorber synthesis problem is to minimize the sum of the frequency responses at two excitation frequencies (dual-frequency vibration absorber) or across a frequency band in which response is to be minimized, corresponding to the band-vibration absorber (Filipovic and Schroder, 1998).

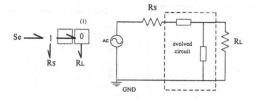

Figure 18-2. A bond graph and its equivalent electrical circuit. The dotted boxes in the left graph indicate modifiable sites at which further topological manipulations can be applied.

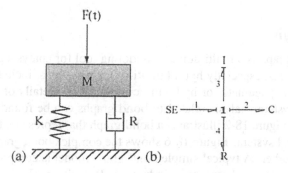

Figure 18-3. Schematic of the primary system and its bond graph model (a) The primary system under perturbation of excitation force F(t); (b)The bond graph model of the embryo system.

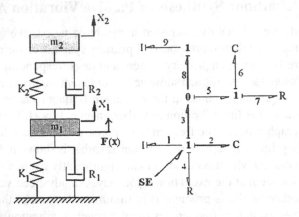

Figure 18-4. Schematic of the first patented vibration absorber and its bond graph model.

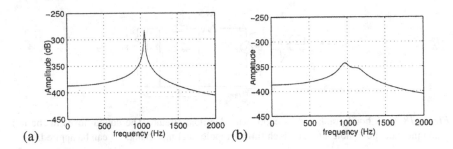

(a)

(b)

Figure 18-5. Frequency responses of the primary system under perturbation of excitation force F(t): (a) without vibration absorber; (b) with a vibration absorber.

Bond Graphs

The bond graph is a multi-domain modeling tool for analysis and design of dynamic systems, especially hybrid multi-domain systems, including mechanical, electrical, pneumatic or hydraulic components. Details of notation and methods of system analysis related to bond graphs can be found in (Karnopp et al., 2000). Figure 18-2 illustrates a bond graph that represents the accompanying electrical system. Figure 18-6 shows the complex bond graph model of a vibration absorber. A typical simple bond graph model is composed of (using notation from electrical systems): inductors (I), resistors (R), capacitors (C), transformers (TF), gyrators (GY), 0-Junctions (J0), 1-junctions (J1), sources of effort (SE), and sources of flow (SF). In this paper, we are only concerned with linear dynamic systems represented as bond graphs, which are composed of inductors (I), resistors (R), capacitors (C), sources of effort (SE) (as input signals), and sources of flow (SF) as output signal access points.

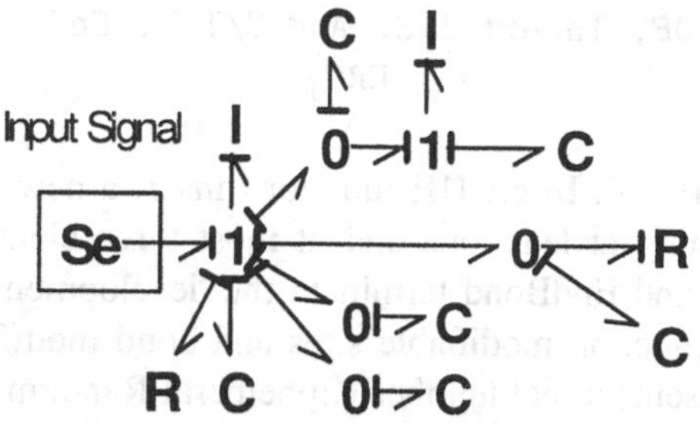

Figure 18-6. The bond graph structure of a vibration absorber with 7 components exclusive of the embryo components. (Component sizing values are omitted in the figure for simplicity.)

Evolving Dynamic Systems Using Bond Graphs and Genetic Programming: the GPBG framework

The problem of automated synthesis of bond graphs involves two basic searches: the search for a good topology and the search for good parameters for each topology, in order to be able to evaluate its performance. We developed a developmental GP system for synthesizing mechatronic systems represented as bond graphs (Seo et al., 2003). It includes the following major components: 1) an embryo bond graph with modifiable sites at which further topological operations can be applied to grow the embryo into a functional system, 2) a GP function set, composed of a set of topology manipulation and other primitive instructions which will be assembled into a GP tree by the evolutionary process (execution of this GP program leads to topological and parametric manipulation of the developing embryo bond graph), and 3) a fitness function to evaluate the performance of candidate solutions.

Choosing a good function set for bond graph synthesis is not easy. In our earliest work (Fan et al., 2001), a basic GP function set was used for evolutionary synthesis of analog filters. In that approach, the GP functions for topological operation included {Insert_J0/J1, Add_C/I/R, and Replace_C/I/R}, which allowed evolution of a large variety of bond graph topologies. The shortcoming of this approach is that it tended to evolve redundant and sometimes causally ill-posed bond graphs. Later, we used a causally well-posed modular GP function set to evolve more concise bond graphs with much less redundancy (Hu et al., 2004). However, that encoding had a strong bias toward a chain-type topology and thus may have limited the scope of topology search. In this paper, we have improved the basic function set in (Fan et al., 2001) and developed the

following hybrid function set approach to reduce redundancy while enjoying
the flexibility of topological exploration:

$$F=\{ \texttt{Insert\_J0E, Insert\_J1E, Add\_C/I/R, EndNode, EndBond,}$$
$$\texttt{ERC}\}$$

where the Insert_J0E, Insert_J1E functions insert a new 0/1-junction into a
bond while attaching at least one and at most three elements (from among
C/I/R). EndNode and EndBond terminate the development (further topology
manipulation) at junction modifiable sites and bond modifiable sites, respectively; ERC represents a real number (Ephemeral Random Constant) that can
be changed by Gaussian mutation. In addition, the number and type of elements attached to the inserted junctions are controlled by three "flag" bits. A
flag mutation operator is used to evolve these flag bits, each representing the
presence or absence of the corresponding C/I/R component. Compared with
the basic set approach, this hybrid approach can effectively avoid adding many
bare (and redundant) junctions. At the same time, Add_C/I/R still provides
the flexibility needed for broad topology search. For any of the three C/I/R
components attached to each junction, there is a corresponding parameter to
represent the component's value, which is evolved by a Gaussian mutation operator in the modified genetic programming system used here. This is different
from our previous work in which the "classical" numeric subtree approach was
used to evolve parameters of components. Our comparison experiments (to be
published elsewhere) showed that this function set was more effective on both
an eigenvalue and an analog filter test problem, so this new function set was
used in this paper.

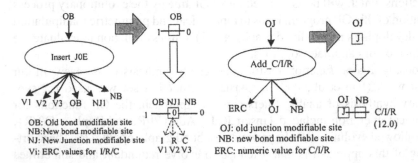

Figure 18-7. Left: the Insert_J0E GP function inserts a new junction into a bond along with
a certain number of attached components. Insert_J1E works in a similar way. Right: The
Add_C/I/R GP function adds a C/I/R component to a junction.

Evolving Vibration Absorbers

In this work, we are interested in evolving three types of vibration absorbers. The vibration absorbers of each type are evolved with several different configurations, such as different maximum numbers of masses to be used, the starting embryo and its modifiable site(s), and the maximum number of components. The synthesis problems include the following.

Single frequency vibration absorber In this problem, we want to see first whether the GPBG system can reinvent the first patented vibration absorber, shown in Figure 18-4. The design problem is extracted from (Jalili, 2002). The parameters of the primary system are as follows:

m_p = 5.77 kg; k_p=251.132 *1e6 N/m; c_p= 192.92 kg/s

The parameters of the standard passive absorber solution are the following:

m_a = 0.227 kg; k_a=9.81e6 N/m; c_a= 355.6 kg/s

We used the bond graph embryos in Figure 18-3 for this problem. The modifiable site is the 1-junction. We could also have different function sets for this GP-based synthesis. Since it is not physically realistic to have many masses attached to the primary structures, we limit the maximum number of masses to 2 in all the experiments.

In this problem, the synthesis objective is to synthesize a vibration absorber such that the frequency response

$$f_{raw} = |TF(j\omega)|_{\omega=\omega_0} \tag{18.1}$$

of the primary system mass (displacement) at the frequency ω of excitation force $f = f_0 * sin\omega t$ is minimized. The normalized fitness is defined as:

$$f_{norm} = \frac{NORM}{NORM + f_{raw}} \tag{18.2}$$

where NORM is a normalization term aimed at adjusting the f_{norm} into the range of [0,1]. This process transforms the minimization of deviation from target frequency response into a maximization of fitness process as used in our GP system. Since tournament selection is used as the selection operator, the normalization term can be an arbitrary positive number. Here, NORM is set to 10, which gives a fitness range within [0, 1].

According to Equ.18.1, we need to calculate the frequency response as the ratio $\frac{X_1(s)}{F(s)}$ where X_1 is the displacement of the primary mass. However, we can only extract from a bond graph the source effort signal $X(s)$. We use the following procedure to get the f_{raw}:

- calculate A, B, C, D matrices from a given bond graph;
- convert A, B, C, D into transfer function TF_{raw};

- $TF_{norm} = TF_{raw} * 1/s$ is equal to $\frac{X_1(s)}{F(s)}$;

- convert TF_{norm} back to A', B', C', D' matrices and simulate its frequency response with Matlab.

Dual frequency vibration absorber This problem is borrowed from Olgac *et al.* (Olgac et al., 1996)'s patented vibration absorber. In this problem, the primary system parameters and corresponding standard passive absorber parameters used in (Olgac et al., 1996) are as follows:

$$m_p = 7.756 \text{ kg}; \ k_p\text{=62,000 N/m}; \ c_p\text{= 2,500 kg/s}.$$
$$m_a = 4 \text{ kg}; \ k_a\text{=722,470 N/m}; \ c_a\text{= 1513.2 kg/s}$$

The excitation force is

$$f = f_1 * sin\omega_1 t + f_2 sin\omega_2 t$$

where $\omega_1 = 25Hz$ and $\omega_2 = 70Hz$.

The raw fitness in this case is defined as:

$$f_{raw} = |TF(j\omega)|_{\omega=\omega_1} + |TF(j\omega)|_{\omega=\omega_2}$$

and the normalized fitness is defined in Equation 18.2. Since, in this paper, only passive vibration absorbers are evolved, we are not aiming at outperforming the dual frequency absorber invented by Olgac *et al.* (Olgac et al., 1996), but at determining how well a passive absorber can approximate the performance of the active absorbers for this problem.

Bandpass frequency vibration absorber This problem is taken from the vibration absorber invented by Filipovic and Schroder, reported as patent pending (Filipovic and Schroder, 1998). Their active absorber with a local feedback force has the capability to absorb all disturbance in a given frequency band, rather than only at discrete frequencies as do most other vibration absorbers. In this problem, we are interested in testing how closely the evolved passive absorbers can approximate the performance of the invention.

The parameters of the primary system are the following:

$$m_p = 20,000 \text{ kg}; \ k_p\text{=25,300,000 N/m}; \ c_p\text{= 39,700 kg/s}$$

The natural frequency is thus $\omega_n = 35.7$ rad/s. Filipovic and Schroder (Filipovic and Schroder, 1998)'s absorber sets the following parameters for the corresponding passive absorber:

$$m_a = 5,00 \text{ kg}; \ k_a\text{=632,500 N/m}; \ c_a\text{= 4,900 kg/s}$$

with the natural frequency $\omega_a = \omega_n$. The excitation force frequency bandwidth is $bw = 10 rad/s$ and the center frequency is $wo = 35 rad/s$.

To evolve a bandpass vibration absorber, we sum the frequency responses at 12 logarithmically distributed sampling frequencies in the frequency band.

Modified Developmental Genetic Programming

Compared to the GP systems used in (Koza et al., 1999) for analog circuit synthesis, our GP system made the following modifications. First, a flag bit mutation operator is introduced to evolve the configuration of C/I/R elements attached to a junction. Second, a subtree-swapping operator is used to exchange non-overlapping subtrees of the same individual (GP tree). In such operations, two type-compatible nodes are randomly selected such that the two subtrees do not overlap, and then a normal crossover operation is applied. This operator does not add or remove components, but reconfiguring the connections among existing components or subcomponents was found to enable better topology search in our experiments. Next, an ERC mutation operator is developed to evolve the parameter values for all C/I/R components. We found that our parameter search method had the benefit of reducing the sizes of high-performance GP trees as one single parameter node replaces a numeric subtree of standard GP. Finally, single individual elitism is used throughout the evolution process. The running parameters are specified in Section 4.

4.   Experiments and Results

Experimental Settings

Compared to the evolutionary synthesis of electrical circuits, a mechanical vibration absorber usually has a much smaller number of components. So the topological and parameter search space is thus greatly decreased. Most of the experiments are finished in less than an hour. Some of them require only a few minutes. Here we set the maximum number of components to be 7. Other standard GP parameters are summarized in Table 18-1.

Table 18-1. Experimental parameters for vibration absorber synthesis

Parameter	Value	Parameter	Value
No. of subpopulations	5	Tournament Selection Size	7
Sub population size	400	pCrossover	0.4
Maximum evaluation	100000	pMutationStandard	0.05
Migration Interval	5 gen	MutateMaxDepth	3
Migration Size	40	pMutationParameter	0.3
Init.MaxDepth	3	pSwitchBit	0.2
Init.MinDepth	2	pSwapSubtree	0.05
StronglyTyped	True	TreeMaxDepth	7

Results

Single-frequency vibration absorber.   Figure 18-8 shows an evolved single frequency vibration absorber and its frequency response compared to the responses of the primary structure without any absorber and with the standard passive absorber invented in 1912. It is very interesting that the frequency response of the evolved vibration absorber has a very deep spike at the excitation frequency to minimize the frequency response at that single frequency. If the excitation frequency is relatively constant with little shifting, our evolved absorber will achieve better performance at that specific frequency. Another observation of the evolved design is that it does not contain any damper but a single mass and four springs which can be reduced to 3 springs (C in the figure). In practice, it is possible to implement such mechanical vibration absorbers. However, implementing an all-spring suspension of the absorber mass has serious consequences outside the notch frequency as there is no dampers to consume the energy.

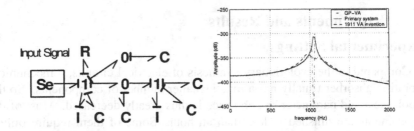

Figure 18-8. The evolved single-frequency vibration absorber and its performance compared to standard vibration absorber.

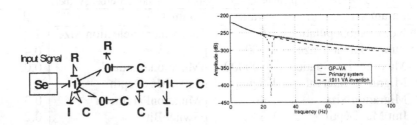

Figure 18-9. The evolved dual-frequency vibration absorber and its performance compared to standard vibration absorber.

Dual-frequency vibration absorber.   In this problem, the two excitation frequencies are 25Hz and 75Hz, respectively. Very interestingly, the GP system again evolved an absorber at 25Hz with greatly reduced response while the frequency response at 75Hz is worse than the standard passive absorber (Figure 18-9). In contrast to the solution in the previous problem, GPBG selected a damper for inclusion in this dual-frequency vibration absorber. We also checked the parameter values of the evolved solution. The mass value is 3.93 kg, the damper ratio is 1499.58, and both are in a very reasonable range. The sizing values of the other three springs are also easy to realize. However, the shortcoming of our evolved VA is that the frequency response at 75Hz is not damped well, probably because of our (in hindsight, inadequate) definition of the fitness function, which simply minimizes the average the frequency responses at these two frequencies. In this respect, our vibration absorber is worse than the standard one.

Bandpass vibration absorber.   Figures 18-6 and 18-10 show the evolved bandpass vibration absorber. It consists of one damper, one mass and five springs. The parameters of this VA are relatively easy to realize, although we did not impose restrictive parameter constraints during the evolution. The mass of the PVA is 10 kg, the damper ratio is 5994.39 kg/s. The spring parameters are all within realizable range. In this problem, the target frequency band is from 4.77Hz to 6.37Hz. As we can see from the figure, the evolved VA has much lower frequency responses across the chosen band. Compared to the standard passive absorber, our solution is significantly better, while also using only passive components. However, we also find that this solution is not as good as the active bandpass absorber proposed by Filipovic and Schroder (Filipovic and Schroder, 1998). Their active VA is able to almost completely damp any frequency response within the target band area. This discrepancy suggests the necessity and promise of introducing synthesis of both controllers and passive vibration absorbers simultaneously.

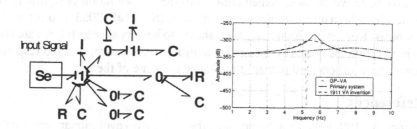

Figure 18-10. The performance of the evolved bandpass vibration absorber compared to the standard vibration absorber.

5.   Discussion and Conclusions

In this chapter, we present a GP-based method being developed for automated synthesis of passive mechanical vibration absorbers. With three vibration absorber problems, we showed that GP can easily find designs with competitive performance in terms of the fitness function. However, we find that many of these evolved solutions are not practically useful, or are extremely difficult to implement. It is found that genetic programming is able to exploit the loopholes in the GP function set: it evolves a solution with springs attached in parallel to a mass, which is not realizable by mechanical means. GP can also cheat the fitness function by evolving a high value only at the sampling frequency (problem 1), while introducing a worse response at a nearby frequency. We also showed that seeking to introducing a more robust type of fitness function (problem 3) can be healthy for evolving better results, as also suggested by McConaghy and Gielen (McConaghy and Gielen, 2005).

As shown by many researchers (Yu and Bentley, 1998), domain-specific knowledge can be incorporated in various GP components such as the fitness function or the genetic operators. Penalty terms can be added to fitness functions to bias the population toward legal phenotypes. However, our lesson is that it may be more effective to constrain search within physically legal solutions by incorporating domain-constraints within GP operators rather than adding penalties in fitness functions as an a posteriori approach. This suggests that exploiting domain- or problem-specific knowledge is strongly desirable for successful GP applications to real-world problems, through which we may significantly reduce the search space and avoid the evolution process being misled by individuals without reasonable ways of physical implementation.

Currently, we are working to implement a physically realizable vibration-absorber-specific GP function set. Human competitiveness is achieved only when the evolved solutions can be implemented to solve real problems. Another kind of work that we plan to do is to evolve active or semi-active vibration absorbers, in which most contemporary progress in vibration design is being made. Since both mechatronic system synthesis (Seo et al., 2003) and controller synthesis (Koza et al., 2000) have been shown to be very successful, we are now trying to combine these two system capabilities to rediscover delayed response vibration absorbers, and perhaps to advance the state of the art.

References

Bruner, A. (1992). Active vibration absorber for the csi evolutionary model: design and experimental results. *Journal of Guidance, Control and Dynamics*, 15:1253–1257.

Fan, Zhun, Hu, Jianjun, Seo, Kisung, Goodman, Erik D., Rosenberg, Ronald C., and Zhang, Baihai (2001). Bond graph representation and GP for automated analog filter design. In Goodman, Erik D., editor, *2001 Genetic and Evolutionary Computation Conference Late Breaking Papers*, pages 81–86, San Francisco, California, USA.

Fan, Zhun, Seo, Kisung, Hu, Jianjun, Goodman, Erik D., and Rosenberg, Ronald C. (2004). A novel evolutionary engineering design approach for mixed-domain systems. *Journal of Engineering Optimization*, 36(2):127–147.

Fan, Zhun, Seo, Kisung, Hu, Jianjun, Rosenberg, Ronald C., and Goodman, Erik D. (2003). System-level synthesis of MEMS via genetic programming and bond graphs. In Cantú-Paz, E., editor, *Genetic and Evolutionary Computation – GECCO-2003*, volume 2724 of *LNCS*, pages 2058–2071, Chicago. Springer-Verlag.

Filipovic, D. and Schroder, D. (1998). Bandpass vibration absorber. *Journal of Sound and Vibration*, 214(3):553–566.

Frahm, H. (1911). Device for damping vibrations of bodies. us patent 989 958.

Franchek, M. A., Ryan, W., M., and Bernhard, R. J. (1995). Adaptive-passive vibration control. *J. Sound Vib.,*, 189(5):565–585.

Hirata, T., Koizumi, S., and Takahashi., R. (1995). H control of railroad vehicle active suspension. *Automatica*, 31:13–24.

Hu, J., Goodman, E., and Rosenberg., R. (2004). Topological search in automated mechatronic system synthesis using bond graphs and genetic programming. In *Proc. of American Control Conference ACC 2004*, Boston.

Hu, Jianjun, Goodman, Erik, and Rosenberg, Ronald (2005). Topologically open-ended synthesis of dynamic systems with high robustness using genetic programming: a case study of analog filter synthesis. *IEEE Transactions on Evolutionary Computation (forthcoming)*.

Jalili, Nader (2002). A comparative study and analysis of semi-active vibration control systems. *Journal of Vibration and Acoustics*, 124(4):593–605.

JR, B.F. Spencer, s.J.Dyke, and Deoskar, H.S. (1997). Benchmark problems in structural control-part i: active mass driver. In *Proceedings of the ASCE Structures Congress, Portland, OR*.

Karnopp, D (1995). Active and semi-active vibration isolation. *ASME J. Manuf. Sci. Eng.*, 117:177–185.

Karnopp, D.C., Margolis, D. L., and Rosenberg., R. C. (2000). *System Dynamics: Modeling and Simulation of Mechatronic Systems.Third Edition*. John Wiley & Sons, Inc., New York.

Koza, John R., Andre, David, Bennett III, Forrest H, and Keane, Martin (1999). *Genetic Programming 3: Darwinian Invention and Problem Solving*. Morgan Kaufman.

Koza, John R., Bennett III, Forrest H, Andre, David, Keane, Martin A., and Dunlap, Frank (1997). Automated synthesis of analog electrical circuits by means of genetic programming. *IEEE Transactions on Evolutionary Computation*, 1(2):109–128.

Koza, John R., Jones, Lee W., Keane, Martin A., and Streeter, Matthew J. (2004). Towards industrial strength automated design of analog electrical circuits by means of genetic programming. In O'Reilly, Una-May, Yu, Tina, Riolo, Rick L., and Worzel, Bill, editors, *Genetic Programming Theory and Practice II*, chapter 8. Kluwer, Ann Arbor.

Koza, John R., Keane, Martin A., Streeter, Matthew J., Mydlowec, William, Yu, Jessen, and Lanza, Guido (2003). *Genetic Programming IV: Routine Human-Competitive Machine Intelligence*. Kluwer Academic Publishers.

Koza, John R., Keane, Martin A., Yu, Jessen, Bennett III, Forrest H, and Mydlowec, William (2000). Automatic creation of human-competitive programs and controllers by means of genetic programming. *Genetic Programming and Evolvable Machines*, 1(1/2):121–164.

Lipson, Hod (2004). How to draw a straight line using a GP: Benchmarking evolutionary design against 19th century kinematic synthesis. In Keijzer, Maarten, editor, *Late Breaking Papers at the 2004 Genetic and Evolutionary Computation Conference*, Seattle, Washington, USA.

Lohn, J.D. and Colombano, S.P. (1999). A circuit representation technique for automated circuit design. *IEEE Transactions on Evolutionary Computation*, 3(3):205–219.

McConaghy, Trent and Gielen, Georges (2005). Analog structural synthesis challenges from an industrial cad perspective. In Riolo, Rick L. and Worzel, Bill, editors, *Genetic Programming Theory and Practice*. Kluwer.

Nemir, D., Y., Lin, and Y., Lin (1994). Semi-active motion control using variable stiffness. *J. Struct. Div. ASCE*, 120(4):1291–1306.

Olgac, N., Elmali, H., and S.Vijayan (1996). Introduction to the dual frequency fixed delayed resonator. *Journal of Sound and Vibration*, 189(3):355–367.

Seo, Kisung, Fan, Zhun, Hu, Jianjun, Goodman, Erik D., and Rosenberg, Ronald C. (2003). Toward an automated design method for multi-domain dynamic systems using bond graphs and genetic programming. *Mechatronics*, 13(8-9):851–885.

Seo, Kisung, Hu, Jianjun, Fan, Zhun, Goodman, Erik D., and Rosenberg, Ronald C. (2002). Automated design approaches for multi-domain dynamic systems using bond graphs and genetic programming. *The International Journal of Computers, Systems and Signals*, 3(1):55–70.

Soong, T.T. (1990). *Active Structural Control Theory and Practice*. John Wiley, New York.

Yu, Tina and Bentley, Peter (1998). Methods to evolve legal phenotypes. In Eiben, Agoston E., Back, Thomas, Schoenauer, Marc, and Schwefel, Hans-Paul, editors, *Fifth International Conference on Parallel Problem Solving from Nature*, volume 1498 of *LNCS*, pages 280–291, Amsterdam. Springer-Verlag.

Chapter 19

GENETIC PROGRAMMING IN INDUSTRIAL ANALOG CAD: APPLICATIONS AND CHALLENGES

Trent McConaghy[1] and Georges Gielen[1]

[1]*Katholieke Universiteit Leuven, Leuven, Belgium*

Abstract   This paper investigates the application of genetic programming to problems in industrial analog computer-aided design (CAD). One CAD subdomain, analog structural synthesis, is an often-cited success within the genetic programming (GP) literature, yet industrial use remains elusive. We examine why this is, by drawing upon our own experiences in bringing analog CAD tools into industrial use. In sum, GP-synthesized designs need to be more robust in very specific ways. When robustness is considered, a GP methodology of today on a reasonable circuit problem would take 150 years on a 1,000-node 1-GHz cluster. Moore's Law cannot help either, because the problem itself is 'Anti-Mooreware' – it becomes more difficult as Moore's Law progresses. However, we believe the problem is still approachable with GP; it will just take a significant amount of 'algorithm engineering.' We go on to describe the recent application of GP to two other analog CAD subdomains: symbolic modeling and behavioral modeling. In contrast to structural synthesis, they are easier from a GP perspective, but are already at a level such that they can be exploited in industry. Not only is GP the only approach that gives interpretable SPICE-accurate nonlinear models, it turns out to outperform nine other popular blackbox approaches in a set of six circuit modeling problems.

Keywords: analog, CAD, synthesis, industrial, genetic programming, robust, yield

1.   Introduction

One of the flagship problems in Genetic Programming is that of analog structural synthesis, where the aim is to automatically determine the circuit components, interconnections, and suggested component dimensions to meet a set of circuit design goals. This is an industrially relevant problem and a challenge to automated design techniques.

In this domain, GP has evolved several patent-quality circuits (Koza et al., 2003), which is a remarkable success by almost any measure. It is an especially notable accomplishment from an artificial intelligence perspective because "patent-worthiness" is a good measure of success for testing techniques in automated "creative" design.

Given such impressive results, a GP researcher might have expected GP to be barnstorming the field of analog design. However, this is not the case; GP is actually not in use *at all* for topology design in industry. In fact, industrial analog engineers and CAD developers would be very surprised to hear that analog synthesis is considered a success within the field of GP. In effect, the bar of "GP success," even success on industrially relevant problems, is different than the bar of "usefulness to industry." How can GP make the transition? In this paper, we draw upon our experiences in industrial analog CAD, with the aim to identify what would make GP useful to that field.

This chapter is organized as follows. We first describe analog CAD's context, then how GP-based synthesis would fit in. We highlight industrial robustness issues and tactics, which we use to reframe the problem of GP-based synthesis. Then, we show two other analog CAD applications where GP is making inroads: symbolic modeling and behavioral modeling.

2.   The Problem Domain: Analog CAD

Context.   Electronic Design Automation (EDA) is the field devoted to building computer-aided design (CAD) tools for electrical engineers. Because of the massive size of the semiconductor industry and the constant changes in design constraints due to Moore's Law, EDA is an active industry, with billions in revenue every year. Analog CAD (Gielen and Rutenbar, 2002) is a subfield devoted to tools for analog circuit designers.

Design "Implementation".   When researchers in GP read about GP for analog synthesis, they're used to reading about "front-end design," in which the problem input is circuit specifications (*e.g.* get power consumption < 10mW), and the target output is a "netlist," which describes the synthesized circuit in terms of components, interconnections, and component dimensions.

That's actually just one step in a much broader flow. Somehow, that netlist has to get into the real world, *i.e.* as part of a discrete circuit, or as a "chip" (VLSI circuit). The industrial value is in chips. The back-end flow is as follows: Once the netlist is determined, it is converted into a "layout," which is essentially a set of overlapping polygons, where specific shapes represent specific types of components and interconnects. The layout is integrated into an overall system layout, which is sent to a billion-dollar fabrication facility. The system layout is used for creation of process masks, which are a sort of physical filter on whether to dope / etch / *etc.* different parts of a silicon wafer. Process mask generation can cost hundreds of thousands of dollars or more. Using the masks, many chips at once are fabricated on a wafer. The chips are sliced apart from each other, then packaged, and finally tested.

If a problem is detected after a step, then the process backtracks to the previous step. The most expensive step is creation of the process masks, so this is where it is most important to avoid backtracking. In a worst case, which still often happens in practice, a fabricated chip does not work at all, and to make it work one needs to go back to front-end design. This is known as a "respin." Obviously, respins are to be avoided because of mask costs, but even more importantly, loss of profitability in time-to-market.

A new analog topology significantly raises the chance of a respin due to lack of experience with that topology; this makes adoption of an analog structural synthesis tool a risky proposition (and costly to try). But, ultimately, GP would need to demonstrate working chips.

3. GP Application: Analog Structural Synthesis, Part I Designer Perspective

Since the late 1980's, analog designers have been presented with impressive-sounding claims about "analog synthesis." Researchers have labeled "analog synthesis" to mean many things, including global parameter optimization, automated conversion from netlist to layout, and automated topology design (the version that GP targets). For a survey, see (Gielen and Rutenbar, 2002).

Our focus here is automated topology design. Most analog designers would acknowledge that if such a technology actually worked, it would drastically change the field. Their counterparts in digital design have already experienced such a revolution: the mid 1980's introduction of digital circuit logic synthesis.

Unlike digital synthesis, few claims of analog synthesis have held true. The analog synthesis techniques were typically too unscalable or brittle to be useful in industry. Of the dozens of various types of analog synthesis technologies reported over the last twenty years, just a few have found their way into industrial use, and that was only recently (Synopsys, 2005; Cadence, 2005b; Cadence, 2005a). None of these do automated topology design. Thus, when designers hear about a new structural synthesis technology, from GP or elsewhere, they immediately question them, and to a much stronger degree than automation-friendly digital designers.

How do the claims of GP look, from a designer's perspective?

For starters, they're not shocked, even when they see the patent results. With every other structural synthesis technology reported until now, something was missing, something that limited its widespread industrial use. Despite their limited understanding of GP, designers have no real reason to treat GP specially. They simply believe that something's missing for GP too.

They're right. When an analog designer digs more deeply into the GP methodology for automated topology design, he/she finds problems. Some are obvious (to an electrical engineer), and some are subtle. But, whereas prior analog structural synthesis approaches had showstopping problems of brittleness and scalability, we believe that GP has no such problems. Instead, GP faces "engineering-style" challenges in problem setup, and especially in improving GP's speed.

Current Industrial Practice

It is fruitful to look at what flow and automation tools that industry uses which are closest to the analog structural synthesis problem.

Figure 19-1 illustrates the overall flow of front-end design for cell-level circuits.

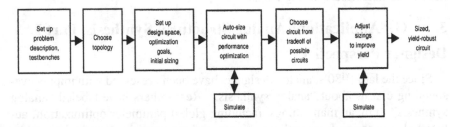

Figure 19-1. State of the Art Industrial Front End Analog Design Flow

The automation happening at the front end is in local / global optimization tools (Synopsys, 2005; Cadence, 2005b), which take in a fixed topology, and automatically determine the component values in order to best meet the design specifications. This step is often referred to as circuit sizing or circuit optimization, rather than synthesis. The topology has been manually designed beforehand. Yield improvement is typically manual, though there is a shift to automation there too.

These tools need to make chips that meet certain performance measures once they've been manufactured. Thus, the tools need a means for estimating performance and taking robustness into account.

Performance Estimation and Robustness

In analog synthesis, robustness is strongly related to performance estimation. A performance estimator takes in a candidate design (*i.e.* a topology and component values in our case), and estimates the performances of the circuit.

To achieve a robust design, one has to estimate performance as accurately as possible.

The ideal performance estimator would predict with 100% accuracy how a design performs after layout, manufacturing, and testing without actually fabricating it. It would run quickly enough to be invoked thousands or millions of times throughout optimization, to allow automated exploration of designs. SPICE is the most accurate and general estimator, but there are also faster, less general, less accurate ones.

Layout issues. "Layout parasitics" are effects that were not accounted for prior to layout. An example layout parasitic is when the material between two wires acts like a circuit component (*e.g.* a capacitor) which is supposed to be an open circuit.

Environmental conditions. The manufactured chip will need to work at the desired performance level, even as temperatures change, power supply changes, and load changes. These are conditions of the circuit's operating environment.

Manufacturing variations. When manufacturing a VLSI circuit, random variations get introduced into the implementation of the designs as an inherent effect of the fabrication process. The automated tool must model this and handle it.

The simplest model is so-called "Fast/Slow corners," which in effect try to capture the 3-sigma extremes in each type of transistor's operating speed due to manufacturing variations. This approach is popular for its simplicity and availability. However, corners do not model the problem well because they do not bracket the variations in analog design goals (they are really only suitable for digital design).

Some approaches build empirically-based statistical models to estimate a probability density function, such as (Power et al., 1994). These models almost always make assumptions that render them inaccurate, for example, assuming that certain random variables are independent when they are not, or ignoring local statistical variations as in (Alpaydin et al., 2003).

One approach (Drennan and McAndrew, 2003) uses a more physical basis for randomness modeling and is quite accurate, though an implication is that for every transistor, 8 random variables are introduced; thus, a medium sized circuit could have hundreds of random variables.

Analog Structural Synthesis Problem

The problem of analog structural synthesis is the same as the sizing problem, except the design space is broadened drastically, to include choice of the topology (devices and connections among devices, in addition to device sizes).

Synthesis cannot make assumptions about the topology; this has big implications, which we will discuss later.

Current Industrial Practice: Details

We are now ready to ask how the industrial tools account for robustness.

For environmental variations, they use a set of user-defined "corners," with each corner specifying a temperature, power supply, *etc.* SPICE is used to estimate performance for each corner, and the worst-case value is taken.

For layout, they can ignore it for a first-pass design. Then, after layout has been done, if layout parasitics degrade the performance too much, the most important parasitics can be inserted into the design and a local optimization performed.

For manufacturing variations, they (Synopsys, 2005; Cadence, 2005b) use model corners, which as mentioned, is less accurate. There are many other approaches in the literature (Phelps et al., 2000; Schenkel et al., 2001; Smedt and Gielen, 2003), but each is forced to trade off accuracy for feasible runtime, or pessimistic design. GP tactics such as (Teller and Andre, 1997; Hu and Goodman, 2004b) are too expensive for refining designs.

4.   Analog Design for Robustness (on a Fixed Topology)

This section highlights how a fixed topology implicitly brings robustness, or conversely, what other robustness issues must be considered when evolving a topology.

Robustness in Manual Topology Design

By definition, optimization approaches operate on manually designed topologies. For VLSI circuits, and perhaps as a surprise to GPers, *manually-designed topologies are almost always designed with robustness in mind.*

We now examine what analog designers do to make topologies more robust. We will refer to a well-known circuit shown in Figure 19-2.

Topologies Are Designed For Process Variations.   The effect of "local" or "mismatch" variations within a chip ("mismatch") has always been smaller than "global" variations which are between chips and between runs (1-2% vs. 10-20%).

The main tactic to deal with global variations is to design structures in which performance is a function of *ratios of sizings*, rather than absolute values. For example, in common-source gain stages, a load resistor would have variation of 10-20%. So, designers use a PMOS load instead, matched up to an NMOS gain transistor, and gain is dependent on the ratios (*e.g.* in Figure 19-2, M5a is a resistive load for M3a).

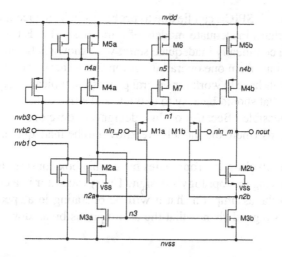

Figure 19-2. "High-speed operational transconductance amplifier (OTA)" analog circuit

Differential design is another tactic to move away from "absolute" values. Here, "mirrors of structures" are created, and the circuit operates on a difference between two voltages, rather than one voltage and ground. The Figure 19-2 OTA is symmetrical about a vertical axis centered on M5 and M7; the output is a function of the difference between the positive and negative inputs, nin_p and nin_n.

A precise current is expensive to generate; it's a much better idea to generate one or a few reference currents and copy them throughout the circuit with "current mirrors." The OTA does this: the three transistors on the left are the "biasing" circuitry to generate currents, which are then copied throughout the circuit. Sometimes a single current can be shared, rather than trying to match two separate currents. The OTA's differential pair (M1a and M1b) does this: instead of having different "tail" currents, they share the same current which goes through M6 and M7.

Negative feedback is a well-known general engineering technique for compromising some performance in the interest of precision. Analog circuits often do this too, such as for improving common-mode rejection ratio of a differential amplifier or for reducing variation of an amplifier's gain (Razavi, 2000).

Trust and Re-Use.   The topology is trusted because it has been created and characterized by expert analog designer(s), and has been fabricated and tested in many process generations. Topology re-use is widespread because past success means more confidence that the topology will work. A new topology is typically a derivative of an existing topology, because similarity maintains trust.

SPICE can lie. SPICE can lie due to problems in its device models, convergence, and perhaps inadequate models of parasitics. SPICE transistor models seem to be in a continually inadequate state, with known deficiencies (*e.g.* nonsmooth transitions from one operating region to another). Part of the difficulty is that the models have to work for several processes, typically require hundreds of parameters that should be easy to extract, and strive to have as good a physical basis as possible. Because of this, designers consciously avoid transistor operating regions where the models are known to be inadequate.

Whitebox Constraints. Topologies have whitebox constraints based on the strategy underlying the topology's design. Every transistor in a circuit has been designed with the assumption that it will be operating in a specific operating region; there is a good chance that the assumptions break down outside those constraints.

Clear Path To Layout. The designer knows that, for manually-designed topologies, there is a clear path to layout; to a large extent, the designer has already anticipated the parasitics. Layout designers also have tactics to improve robustness, such as: folding transistors, guard rings, and careful routing to avoid cross-coupling between sensitive wires (Hastings, 2000; Lampaert et al., 1999). Analog *layout* synthesis is another analog CAD subproblem (Rutenbar and Cohn, 2000); it is difficult to model and solve well, as illustrated by continued research activity. When layout parasitics are more pronounced, such as in RF design, there are ways to tighten the coupling between sizing and layout design (DeSmedt and Gielen, 2003; Zhang et al., 2004; Bhattacharya et al., 2004).

To properly account for layout effects in synthesis, one possibility is to unite the front-end design space (topology and circuit sizes) with the back- end space (layout), and approach the whole problem at once, as in Section 5.2 of (Koza et al., 2003). Unfortunately, runtime was 1.5 orders of magnitude slower, and that work drastically simplified the layout synthesis problem – it didn't even extract the parasitics from the layout before simulating the netlist.

Synthesis Exaggerates "Cheating" of Search Algorithms. We say a "cheat" occurs when design has good measured performances, but which upon inspection is useless (*e.g.* not physically realizable). An example is too many long, narrow transistors; the solution is to add more constraints on width/length ratios. Each added constraint takes time to detect, correct, and re-run. There is more opportunity for structural synthesis to cheat compared to optimization, because synthesis design space is drastically larger, and SPICE can cheat more readily. Evolvable hardware research is filled with examples of odd designs; however, in non-reprogrammable analog VLSI, one cannot embrace odd designs because of the high cost of fabrication.

5.   GP Application: Analog Structural Synthesis, Part II

An Updated Model of the Analog Synthesis Problem

Most earlier GP structural synthesis work such as (Koza et al., 1999; Lohn and Colombano, 1998; Zebulum et al., 2002; Sripramong and C.Toumazou, 2002; Koza et al., 2003) did not have a very thorough model of the problem compared to analog CAD optimization, but is has been getting better recently. In (Koza et al., 2004a), corners have been added to account for environmental and (very roughly) manufacturing variations. And, they employ testbenches directly from an industrial CAD vendor (Synopsys, 2005). Though some recent research has not yet acknowledged the need for more robustness (Dastidar et al., 2005).

GP does not have whitebox constraints, because it does not make assumptions about what region each transistor will operate in. GP actually has stronger performance measures in one regard: it also tries to match waveforms of behavior.

Compared to analog CAD optimization work, GP's biggest deficiency in problem modeling is its lack of a good model of manufacturing variations. The closest, robust HFC (Hu and Goodman, 2004a), did have Monte Carlo sampling, but the randomness model is not suitable for VLSI circuits.

Beyond analog CAD optimization, GP-evolved circuits must somehow get the same advantages as a manually-designed topology. Such circuits must get designer trust, including an explanation and formulae for behavior; ultimately, successful fabrication and testing. On the way, there are the hurdles of SPICE (mis)behavior, layout parasitics, search space cheats, and extra challenges from first-order process variations.

New Computational Challenges

Ultimately, the only way to accurately model manufacturing variations is via *simulation* on *good statistical models*. Let us examine the runtime of a typical structural synthesis run that uses brute force Monte Carlo sampling. Except for layout, we will temporarily ignore all the extra challenges wrought by a non-fixed topology.

Let us say: 8 corners (for environmental variations), 10 Monte Carlo samples (for manufacturing variations, 10 is optimistic), and simulation time of 1 minute for a circuit at one corner and one sample on all testbenches on a 1 GHz machine. Parasitic-extracted layouts might mean 10x longer. Larger designs and/or longer-than-transient analyses could easily take 6x, 60x, or even 600x longer to simulate.

It is typical for a GP run to explore 100 million designs for more challenging problems. 1 billion or even 10 billion would not be unreasonable (Koza et al., 2003). But let us have 1,000 1-Ghz machines in parallel.

Then, total run time = 152 years! And it's even longer for tougher problems, where simulation time is 6x-600x longer and number of individuals is 10x-100x more. One might ask if Moore's Law can ease this challenge.

The Impact of Moore's Law

Mooreware vs. Anti-Mooreware.   GP is considered an example of "Mooreware" (Koza et al., 1999), where an algorithm becomes more effective with more computational power, and therefore with the march of Moore's Law over time.

However, Moore's Law, when attacking VLSI design problems, is a double-edged sword. Each new technology generation also requires more modeling effort, and therefore more compute time! For example, the need for substrate noise modeling is growing; to model this takes 30 minutes on four modern processors (Soens et al., 2005), *i.e.* 120x more computational effort.

Thus, analog synthesis is an "Anti-Mooreware" problem: it gets more difficult as Moore's Law progresses. So, we cannot rely on the "Mooreware" aspect of GP to eventually be fast enough.

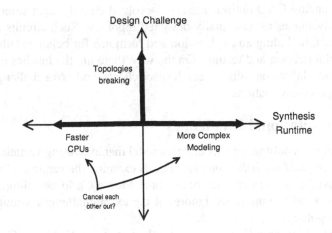

Figure 19-3. Effects of Moore's Law on Analog Structural Synthesis

Moore's Law Breaks Topologies.   Topologies are getting constrained in new ways due to Moore' Law. Here is an example. Supply voltages and threshold voltages are steadily decreasing, but threshold voltages cannot scale as quickly because of fundamental physical constants. At some point, "cascode" configurations, which stack two transistors on top of each other, are unusable

Table 19-1. GP-generated symbolic circuit models with < 10% train and test error.

Perf. Char.	Expression
ALF	-10.3 + 7.08e-5 / id1 + 1.87 * ln(-1.95e+9 + 1.00e+10 / (vsg1*vsg3) + 1.42e+9 *(vds2*vsd5) / (vsg1*vgs2*vsg5*id2))
fu	10(5.68 - 0.03 * vsg1 / vds2 - 55.43 * id1+ 5.63e-6 / id1)
PM	90.5 + 190.6 * id1 / vsg1 + 22.2 * id2 / vds2
voffset	- 2.00e-3
SRp	2.36e+7 + 1.95e+4 * id2 / id1 - 104.69 / id2 + 2.15e+9 * id2 + 4.63e+8 * id1
SRn	- 5.72e+7 - 2.50e+11 * (id1*id2) / vgs2 + 5.53e+6 * vds2 / vgs2 + 109.72 / id1

(*e.g.* M4b and M5b in figure 19-2 are in cascode). The alternatives are less ideal: folded cascodes mean larger power consumption, and extra stages mean slower speed and instability risk. Figure 19-3 summarizes.

The Road Ahead for GP and Structural Synthesis

GP has come a long way along the road of analog structural synthesis and the milestones have been remarkable, but a full industrial-strength version is orders of magnitude away.

Speeding up GP sufficiently may actually be possible because there are so many facets to the problem and the algorithms. It comes down to an "algorithm engineering" problem. There are possible speedups at (1) the general EA level, for example in population management, handling modularity / hierarchy, exploiting advances in theory, reuse of run information, in representation and operators, parallelism; (2) at the robustness level, for example exploiting the transparency in manufacturing variations, environmental variations, and simulation analyses; and (3) at the domain-specific level of cell-level analog circuits, for example to guide design of representation, operators and building blocks, special constraints, faster performance estimators. Koza has elaborated on some possibilities (Koza et al., 2004b).

6.   GP Application: Symbolic Modeling

Given the overall goal of finding ways to aid analog engineers in the design process, we can ask ourselves what other problems GP might help in. That's a question that we asked in the last year, and so far we've demonstrated two other industrially-relevant applications. Let's examine each, starting with symbolic modeling.

In all designs that an engineer does, the more he or she understands a circuit, the more he will be able to improve it (in terms of performance and yield), and the more productive he or she will be. This is independent of whether the tools are automated or manual. Equations are a very useful tool for helping designers improve understanding, *e.g.* equations that map design variables (*e.g.* component values) to circuit performances (*e.g.* power consumption). Such equations have traditionally been created by hand, but they are so useful that since the early 90s, there has been considerable research effort to devise algorithms to automate this (Gielen, 2002). This subfield of of analog CAD is called "symbolic analysis" when the equations are directly extracted from the topology, or "symbolic modeling" when the equations come from SPICE simulations. The ideal approach would produce SPICE-accurate, interpretable equations of arbitrary nonlinear circuits. So far, no approach could do all those things at once.

Interestingly (and almost surprisingly), no one had yet used GP in symbolic regression mode on SPICE-generated training data. So, we applied it, with a few modifications to GP to keep the expressions readily interpetable (McConaghy et al., 2005). Table 19-1 gives models for each of six different performance expressions, for the circuit previously examined (Figure 19-2).

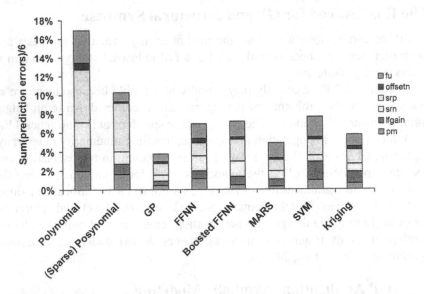

Figure 19-4. Comparison of prediction error for several state-of-the-art modeling approaches.

GP turned out to predict remarkably well. In a separate study on six circuit datasets (McConaghy and Gielen, 2005a), we found that GP could generate nonlinear expressions that outperformed several state-of-the-art approaches, as shown in Figure 19-4.

Table 19-2. GP-generated behavioral models for a latch circuit.

Train error	Expression
15.11%	dx1/dt = nBit dx2/dt = Bit * x1
6.25%	dx1/dt = - 21.3 - 9.28e-03 * bufclk * x1 + 1.0e+04 * nBit * bufclk
3.32%	dx1/dt = 2.21e-02 - 3.72e-02 * x1 - 21.8 * Bit*nBit * bufclk dx2/dt = nBit * bufclk * x1 dx6/dt = x1

7. GP Application: Behavioral Modeling

Another challenge in circuit design is how to manage system-level design. One of its sub-problems is how to simulate a whole system in a feasible time, ideally fast enough to optimize with. A good approach is behavioral models, which approximate the dynamic behavior of each of the system's sub-blocks. Automatically devising behavioral models is very difficult: it's common for a student to spend his whole Ph.D on (manually) designing a good behavioral model for one building block! There's a long history of attempts to automated approaches as well, starting from linear, progressing to weakly nonlinear, and finally recent successes in strongly nonlinear behavioral models. But those approaches are, once again, black box. With behavioral modeling, even more than symbolic analysis, trustworthiness of a model is very important, and black-box models compromise that because there is no guarantee how the model will perform under other input stimuli.

Once again, we saw opportunity. We adapted our GP system to build dynamic models, and tested it on a strongly nonlinear circuit (McConaghy and Gielen, 2005b). It successfully built interpretable behavioral models with good prediction ability. Table 19-2 gives some of the behavioral models generated, at different levels of complexity and accuracy.

8. Conclusions

While GPers have considered analog synthesis a success story for GP, and with good reason from an AI perspective, it still remains for GP to be put into industrial analog design practice.

To understand why, we examined the problem context and the details of how a design is implemented. It comes down to achieving more robust designs, with the main aim of reducing risk of costly manufacturing respins. Furthermore, it needs to be trusted by the designer. To address this, the GP computational effort goes up drastically, and Moore's Law cannot be relied upon to help because the problem is "Anti-Mooreware." Thus, we have a grand "algorithm engineering" challenge for clever GP researchers.

Structural synthesis is not the only opportunity for GP in analog CAD. We demonstrated GP as applied to two other applications, symbolic modeling and behavioral modeling, where the barrier to entry was far lower, and the industrial payoff much sooner.

GP is not barnstorming the field of analog design... yet. But it is slowly gaining ground in multiple aspects of analog CAD.

9.   Acknowledgements

The first author would like to thank John Koza, Matthew Streeter, Sameer Al-Sakran, Lee Jones, and Martin Keane for the invigorating discussions which motivated the writing of this paper.

References

Alpaydin, G., Balkir, S., and Dundar, G. (2003). An evolutionary approach to automatic synthesis of high-performance analog integrated circuits. *IEEE Transactions on Evolutionary Computation*, 7(3):240–252.

Bhattacharya, Sambuddha, Jangkrajarng, Nuttorn, Hartono, Roy, and Shi, Richard (2004). Correct-by-construction layout-centric retargeting of large analog designs. In *Proceedings of the Design Automation Conference*.

Cadence (2005a). Neocell product. *Website of Cadence Design Systems Inc.*

Cadence (2005b). Neocircuit product. *Website of Cadence Design Systems Inc.*

Dastidar, T.R., Chakrabarti, P.P., and Ray, P. (2005). A synthesis system for analog circuits based on evolutionary search and topological reuse. *IEEE Transactions on Evolutionary Computation*, 9(2):211–224.

DeSmedt, B. and Gielen, Georges G.E. (2003). Watson : Design space boundary exploration and model generation for analog and rf ic design. *IEEE Transactions on Computer-Aided Design*, 22(2):213–223.

Drennan, P.C. and McAndrew, C.C. (2003). Understanding mosfet mismatch for analog design. *IEEE Journal of Solid State Circuits*, 38(3):450–456.

Gielen, G.E. (2002). Techniques and applications of symbolic analysis for analog integrated circuits: A tutorial overview. In Rutenbar, R.A., Gielen, G.E., , and Antao, B.A., editors, *Computer Aided Design of Analog Integrated Circuits and Systems*, pages 245–261. IEEE Press, Piscataway, NJ.

Gielen, G.E. and Rutenbar, R.A. (2002). Computer-aided design of analog and mixed-signal integrated circuits. In Rutenbar, R.A., Gielen, G.E., , and Antao, B.A., editors, *Computer Aided Design of Analog Integrated Circuits and Systems*, chapter 1, pages 3–30. IEEE Press, Piscataway, NJ.

Hastings, Alan (2000). *The Art of Analog Layout*. Prentice-Hall.

Hu, J. and Goodman, E. (2004a). Robust and efficient genetic algorithms with hierarchical niching and sustainable evolutionary computation model. In *Proceedings of the Genetic and Evolutionary Computing Conference.*

Hu, Jianjun and Goodman, Erik (2004b). Topological synthesis of robust dynamic systems by sustainable genetic programming. In O'Reilly, Una-May, Yu, Tina, Riolo, Rick L., and Worzel, Bill, editors, *Genetic Programming Theory and Practice II*, chapter 9. Kluwer, Ann Arbor.

Koza, John R., Andre, David, Bennett III, Forrest H, and Keane, Martin (1999). *Genetic Programming 3: Darwinian Invention and Problem Solving.* Morgan Kaufman.

Koza, John R., Jones, Lee W., Keane, Martin A., and Streeter, Matthew J. (2004a). Towards industrial strength automated design of analog electrical circuits by means of genetic programming. In O'Reilly, Una-May, Yu, Tina, Riolo, Rick L., and Worzel, Bill, editors, *Genetic Programming Theory and Practice II*, chapter 8. Kluwer, Ann Arbor.

Koza, John R., Keane, Martin A., and Streeter, Matthew J. (2004b). Routine high-return human-competitive evolvable hardware. In Zebulum, Ricardo S., Gwaltney, David, Horbny, Gregory, Keymeulen, Didier, Lohn, Jason, and Stoica, Adrian, editors, *Proceedings of the 2004 NASA/DoD Conference on Evolvable Hardware*, pages 3–17, Seattle. IEEE Press.

Koza, John R., Keane, Martin A., Streeter, Matthew J., Mydlowec, William, Yu, Jessen, and Lanza, Guido (2003). *Genetic Programming IV: Routine Human-Competitive Machine Intelligence.* Kluwer Academic Publishers.

Lampaert, Koen, Gielen, Georges G.E., and Sansen, Willy (1999). *Analog Layout Generation for Performance and Manufacturability.* Kluwer Academic Publishers.

Lohn, J.D. and Colombano, S.P. (1998). Automated analog circuit synthesis using a linear representation. In *Proceedings of the Second International Conference on Evolvable Systems: From Biology To Hardware*, pages 125–133. Springer-Verlag.

McConaghy, Trent, Eeckelaert, Tom, and Gielen, Georges G. E. (2005). Caffeine: Template-free symbolic model generation of analog circuits via canonical form functions and genetic programming. In *Proceedings of the Design Automation and Test Europe Conference.*

McConaghy, Trent and Gielen, Georges G. E. (2005a). Analysis of simulation-driven numerical performance modeling techniques for application to analog circuit optimization. In *Proceedings of the International Symposium on Circuits and Systems.*

McConaghy, Trent and Gielen, Georges G. E. (2005b). Ibmg: Interpretable behavioral model generator for nonlinear analog circuits via canonical form functions and genetic programming. In *Proceedings of the International Symposium on Circuits and Systems.*

Phelps, R., Krasnicki, M., Rutenbar, R.A., Carley, R., and Hellums, J.R. (2000). Anaconda: Simulation-based synthesis of analog circuits via stochastic pattern search. *IEEE Transactions on Computer Aided Design.*

Power, J.A., Donellan, B., Mathewson, A., and Lane, W.A. (1994). Relating statistical mosfet model parameters to ic manufacturing process fluctuations enabling realistic worst-case design. *IEEE Transactions on Semiconductor Manufacturing*, 7:306–318.

Razavi, Behzad (2000). *Design of Analog CMOS Integrated Circuits.* McGraw-Hill.

Rutenbar, Rob A. and Cohn, John M. (2000). Layout tools for analog ics and mixed-signal socs: A survey. In *Proceedings of the ACM International Symposium on Physical Design*, pages 76–83.

Schenkel, F., Pronath, M., Zizala, S., Schwencker, R., Graeb, H., and Antreich, K. (2001). Mismatch analysis and direct yield optimization by spec-wise linearization and feasibility-guided search. In *Proceedings of the Design Automation Conference.*

Smedt, B. De and Gielen, Georges G.E. (2003). Holmes: Capturing the yield-optimized design space boundaries of analog and rf integrated circuits. In *Proceedings of the Design Automation and Test Europe Conference*, page 10256.

Soens, C., Wambacq, P., Plas, G. Van Der, and Donnay, S. (2005). Simulation methodology for analysis of substrate noise impact on analog / rf circuits including interconnect resistance. In *Proceedings of the Design Automation and Test Europe Conference.*

Sripramong, T. and C.Toumazou (2002). The invention of cmos amplifiers using genetic programming and current-flow analysis. *IEEE Transaction on Computer-Aided Design of Integrated Circuits and Systems.*

Synopsys (2005). Circuit explorer product. *Website of Synopsys Inc.*

Teller, Astro and Andre, David (1997). Automatically choosing the number of fitness cases: The rational allocation of trials. In Koza, John R., Deb, Kalyanmoy, Dorigo, Marco, Fogel, David B., Garzon, Max, Iba, Hitoshi, and Riolo, Rick L., editors, *Genetic Programming 1997: Proceedings of the Second Annual Conference*, pages 321–328, Stanford University, CA, USA. Morgan Kaufmann.

Zebulum, R., Pacheco, M., and Vellasco, M. (2002). *Evolutionary Electronics: Automatic Design of Electronic Circuits and Systems by Genetic Algorithms.* CRC Press.

Zhang, Gang, Dengi, E. Aykut, Rohrer, Ronald A., Rutenbar, Rob A., and Carley, L. Richard (2004). A synthesis flow toward fast parasitic closure for radio-frequency integrated circuits. In *Proceedings of the Design Automation Conference*, pages 155–158.

Index